ROADSIDE HISTORY OF

NEBRASKA

Candy Moulton

1997
Mountain Press Publishing Company
Missoula, Montana

© 1997 Candy Moulton

Photographs not otherwise credited are by the author

Maps by Jennifer Hamelman

Cover art: *Approaching Chimney Rock,*
by William Henry Jackson courtesy of Scotts Bluff
National Monument, National Park Service

Library of Congress Cataloging-in-Publication Data

Moulton, Candy Vyvey, 1955–
  Roadside history of Nebraska / Candy Moulton.
    p.   cm.
  Includes bibliographical references and index.
  ISBN 0-87842-347-8 (alk. paper).–ISBN 0-87842-348-6 (alk. paper)
  1. Nebraska–Guidebooks. 2. Nebraska–history, Local. 3. Automobile
  travel–Nebraska–Guidebooks. I. Title.
  F664.3.M68 1997   97-22949
  917.8204'33–dc21   CIP

PRINTED IN THE UNITED STATES OF AMERICA
Mountain Press Publishing Company
P.O. Box 2399 · Missoula, MT 59806
(406) 728-1900

CONTENTS

ACKNOWLEDGMENTS

R ESEARCHING THIS BOOK has been a delight. I have explored the state I always thought was simply the place to where Wyoming snow blew after a winter storm. I quickly found that Nebraska has its own winter storms, and the snow blows in not only from Wyoming but also from South Dakota, Colorado, and Kansas, depending on which way the wind shifts.

I would never have even thought to begin this book if it weren't for two of the Dans in my life: Dan Greer, my editor at Mountain Press; and Dan Neal, my editor at the Casper *Star-Tribune*, who supported my desire to follow the Oregon Trail and write about it for the paper.

Mary Ethel Emanuel of the Nebraska Division of Travel and Tourism took me on my first tour of the Nebraska section of the Oregon Trail in 1992. As I wrote my Oregon Trail articles and, later, as I researched and wrote this book, she provided much valuable assistance, found and supplied me with reference materials, and pointed me toward antiquarian bookstores. The superintendents and managers of Nebraska's varied historic sites and attractions also provided invaluable assistance by opening their doors, often during nonworking hours and usually at no charge, and by directing me to research materials. My sincere thanks to all of them.

Researching and writing any book is a challenge, but preparing a roadside guide involves the additional challenge of travel. That is also the great pleasure in such a work. I am grateful to the Nebraskans who left the latchstring out, allowing me to ride the grubline: Mark and Ila Tiensvold of Rushville, Chic and Jeanne Margritz of Red Cloud, Otto and Jean Berthoud of Nebraska City, and Nancy and Bill Pitre of Omaha. I am particularly indebted to Nancy for chauffeur services in both the Omaha and Lincoln areas and for her help with research, and to Bill for research suggestions.

My cousins Philip Pitre, Michael and Sandy Pitre, and particularly Randy and Peggy Reavis provided much insight into Nebraska sports, activities, places, and lifestyle. Thank you all so much.

For research assistance I am grateful to the staff of the Nebraska State Historical Society and Historic Preservation Office, particularly John Carter, Sharon McDonald, and Ame McBride. For other research assistance I want to thank Bobbi and Gary O'Mara, Gege Herring, Sierra Adare, Kathleen O'Neal Gear, Gene Gressley, Lenessa Herring, Arthur C. Johnson, and D. L. Birchfield. Thanks also to the staff at the Wyoming State Museum, particularly Jean Brainard, Ann Nelson, Lavaughn Breshnahan, and Roger Joyce, and to Rick Ewig at the American Heritage Center, University of Wyoming.

For manuscript suggestions I thank Sierra Adare and most particularly R. Eli Paul, senior research historian at the Nebraska State Historical Society, who made critical comments about this work. I value his insights, research suggestions, and advice. I also must thank Linda Woodward, who pointed me toward Eli in the first place.

While I often traveled alone, on some research trips I had the company and research assistance of Betty Vyvey and Bob and Bobbie Herring. On my first trip along the Oregon Trail in Nebraska, my companions included Chuck Coon of the Wyoming Division of Tourism and Kit Miniclier of the *Denver Post*, two fine friends with whom I drank my first (and last) prairie fire in North Platte.

I could not have done the research, nor written the book, without the support of my family, Steve, Shawn, and Erin Marie. They not only put up with my absences, long hours at the computer, and voluminous piles of research books and papers; they also trudged through the predawn rain to see sandhill cranes, fought blizzard conditions and nearly impassable roads in the Sandhills, and were drenched in a summer storm that flooded our campsite.

We had a great time exploring Nebraska. I sincerely hope you enjoy the tales we uncovered along the way.

NEBRASKA CHRONOLOGY

1500–1650 Lower Loup people live near Loup River southwest of Genoa.

1675   French traders see Pawnee villages along Republican River.

1720   French traders and Pawnee allies attack Pedro de Villasur and troops near Columbus.

1730   Kiowas migrate into northwestern Nebraska, become friends of the Gatakas, and eventually become the Kiowa Apaches.

1785   Ponca Indians have a village and fort near Verdel.

1795   James Mackay opens first fur trading post in Nebraska near Bellevue.

1800   Omaha Chief Blackbird dies of smallpox that ravages his tribe.

1802   Cruzette opens fur trading post.

1803   Sioux move into northwestern Nebraska, forcing the Kiowa Apaches, Crows, and Cheyennes out of the region. The Cheyennes form alliances with the Sioux, however, and remain in the Black Hills and farther west, eventually living near the Sioux.

1803   (April 30) United States acquires Nebraska Territory through the Louisiana Purchase.

1804   Meriwether Lewis and William Clark explore the Louisiana Territory; they return to Nebraska in 1806 on their way back to St. Louis.

1806   Zebulon Pike crosses through southeast Nebraska en route to Santa Fe, meeting with the Pawnees near Guide Rock.

1810   Wilson Price Hunt party of Astorians heads west to Pacific Coast.

1812   Robert Stuart and companions camp near Scottsbluff en route from Fort Astoria to St. Louis; they are the first white men in the region.

1812   Manuel Lisa opens a fur trading post at Bellevue, known as Fort Lisa.

1815   Omaha tribe negotiates first treaty with U.S. government at Portage des Sioux.

1816   Skidis capture an Ietan girl, intending to sacrifice her to Morning Star in the spring of 1817; Pitalesharo rescues her in 1817.

1819   Military establishes Cantonment Missouri (later Fort Atkinson) as first western outpost.

1819	Yellowstone Expedition arrives in Nebraska; Col. Henry Atkinson commands.
1819–20	Maj. Stephen Long launches his exploration of the western country and uses the first steamboat to reach Nebraska, the *Western Engineer*. He calls the area "The Great American Desert."
1820–24	Joshua Pilcher operates a fur post at former Lisa site.
1822–23	Cabanne operates a fur trading post at site of Omaha.
1825	Mexican treaty talks (to end Pawnee attacks on Mexico) take place at Fort Atkinson.
1827	(March) U.S. Army abandons Fort Atkinson.
1828	Hiram Scott dies near the bluff that now bears his name.
1830	Prairie du Chien treaty goes into effect and establishes "Half-Breed Tract" in southeastern Nebraska.
1833	Pawnees enter their first treaty with the U.S. government.
1833	Baptist missionary Moses Merrill and his wife open a mission for Otoe Indians at Bellevue, the first mission west of the Missouri.
1837	Alfred Jacob Miller sketches Chimney Rock, probably the first artist to do so.
1841	Chartran's trading post opens to trade with Brulé Sioux on Chadron Creek. It remains open for about three years.
1841	Bidwell-Bartleson wagon train crosses the plains, the first emigrants on the Oregon Trail.
1841	Congress approves Pre-emption Law giving settlers the right to claim land and purchase it at a cost of $1.25 per acre.
1841–72	James Bordeaux operates a trading post on Chadron Creek.
1842	John C. Frémont explores the West.
1842	Congress approves Donation Acts, encouraging settlers to claim land in areas such as Oregon and New Mexico.
1843	Oregon migration begins; during the next thirty years more than 350,000 emigrants cross Nebraska en route to Oregon and California.
1846	U.S. Army builds the first Fort Kearny at Nebraska City (originally called Camp Kearny).
1846	Brigham Young and the first of the Mormons cross the Missouri and establish Winter Quarters at Florence.
1847	Mormon migration to Utah begins.
1847	Fort Kearny relocates from Nebraska City to a site farther west.
1849	Thousands of gold seekers follow the California Trail.

1849	American Fur Company sells Fort John (near Fort Laramie) and relocates to temporary quarters at Robidoux Pass, southwest of Scotts Bluff; in 1850 the company relocates to Helvas Canyon and opens a new trading post, again called Fort John.
1851	Painter Rudolph Kurz visits Papillion village of Omaha Indians.
1851	(September 8) Plains Indians begin negotiations for their first treaty with the U. S. government at Horse Creek (near Mitchell), signing the treaty September 17.
1854	(March 15–16) In exchange for two reservations, the Otoe, Missouria, and Omaha Indians cede lands west of the Missouri River, opening most of eastern Nebraska to white settlement.
1854	(May 30) Congress approves the Kansas-Nebraska Act, establishing Nebraska Territory. The Kansas-Nebraska Act repeals the 1820 Missouri Compromise.
1854	(August 1) John Calhoun is appointed surveyor general of Nebraska and Kansas.
1854	(August) Richard Brown crosses the Missouri and starts the town of Brownville; Bellevue and Omaha are already founded.
1854	(August) Lt. William Grattan and twenty-eight men are killed near Fort Laramie, precipitating hostilities along the Oregon Trail.
1854	(October 16) Territorial Governor Francis Burt takes office in Bellevue.
1854	(October 18) Territorial Governor Francis Burt dies.
1855	(January 16) The first territorial legislature convenes in Omaha, the new territorial capital.
1855	(September 3) Gen. William S. Harney and U.S. troops attack Sioux under Little Thunder at Blue Water Creek, avenging the Grattan deaths of the previous year. The battle is variously referred to as the Bloody Blue Water, the Battle of Blue Water, or the Harney Massacre.
1855	William Russell, Alexander Majors, and William Waddell start freighting from Nebraska City; their freighters subsequently forge the Ox-Bow Trail from Nebraska City to Fort Kearny.
1856	(December 1) A tremendous snowstorm buries eastern Nebraska Territory.
1857	(September 24) Pawnees sign away the last of their land in Nebraska in the Table Rock Treaty at Nebraska City; they move to a reservation at Genoa.
1857	A financial panic hits Nebraska as wildcat banks, which had issued money with no security, fail.
1858	First Territorial Convention convenes in Plattsmouth.

1859	(October 16) Henry Kagi of Nebraska City participates in the raid at Harper's Ferry, Virginia, with John Brown. Kagi dies in the raid; Brown hangs for treason.
1860	Congress approves a subsidy for development of a telegraph line from western Missouri to San Francisco.
1860–61	William Russell, Alexander Majors, and William Waddell of Nebraska City start the Pony Express.
1861	The Civil War starts.
1861	(May 9) Governor Algernon S. Paddock calls for volunteers to serve the Union in the 2nd Nebraska Cavalry.
1862	President Abraham Lincoln signs the Pacific Railway Act.
1862	Congress approves the Homestead Act.
1862	First troops stationed at Fort Omaha, Military District of Nebraska.
1863	(January 1) The Homestead Act goes into effect. Daniel Freeman files the first claim in the country under its provisions on Cub Creek, a tributary of the Blue River.
1864	(November 29) Sand Creek Massacre of Cheyenne and Arapaho Indians occurs in Colorado.
1864	Military establishes Fort Mitchell on the site of earlier establishments known as Camp Shuman and Camp Mitchell.
1865	(April 1) The steamboat *Bertrand* sinks off De Soto Bend.
1865	Bloody Year on the Plains.
1865	Union Pacific Railroad construction starts from Omaha.
1865	The U. S. Army organizes the Pawnee Scouts under Capt. Frank North.
1866	William Henry Jackson crosses the plains, sketching and painting.
1867	The military establishes Sidney Barracks as a temporary camp. (It later became Fort Sidney.)
1867	(March 1) Nebraska becomes a state; Lincoln becomes the permanent capital of Nebraska.
1868	Omaha establishes a horsecar line.
1868	Sioux agree to a treaty at Fort Laramie that leads to establishment of agencies where they receive annuities along the North Platte River; later they receive goods along the White River.
1869	Fremont, Elkhorn & Missouri Valley Railroad construction begins.
1869	First Texas cattle ship to market on Union Pacific from Schuyler.
1869	President Andrew Johnson establishes Santee Sioux Reservation near Niobrara.

1869	The University of Nebraska gets its charter. It opens in Lincoln in 1871.
1872	The first Grange in Nebraska organizes in Orleans; the Nebraska State Grange organizes as well.
1872	Nebraska State Department of Agriculture approves Arbor Day as a holiday.
1873	(April 13; Easter Sunday) A tornado tears through Omaha, destroying some 2,000 homes.
1873	(Summer) Grasshoppers ravage crops throughout Nebraska. (They return in 1875.)
1873	John Neligh opens a flour mill in Neligh.
1873	The government establishes the Red Cloud and Spotted Tail Indian Agencies on the White River to distribute annuities to the Sioux and Cheyenne Indians.
1873	Congress approves the Timber Culture Act, which makes it possible to make a homestead claim based upon the planting of trees. The legislation sponsor is Nebraska Sen. Phineas W. Hitchcock.
1874	(February) Military establishes a tent camp on the White River in northwestern Nebraska, initially called Camp Robinson (later, after December 1878, called Fort Robinson, named for Lt. Levi Robinson).
1874	Luther North accompanies Lt. Col. George A. Custer in exploration of the Black Hills, confirming the existence gold in the region.
1874	(September 5) The Army establishes Fort Hartsuff.
1874	Irishman John O'Neill establishes O'Neill, encouraging settlers from his homeland to settle the area.
1875	(May) Sioux chiefs reject a $6 million government offer for the Black Hills.
1875	(September) Thousands of members of the Sioux Nation watch as the Allison Commission fails to purchase the Black Hills.
1876	(Spring) Henry T. Clarke builds a toll bridge across the North Platte River to serve traffic on the Sidney-to-Deadwood Trail; the government establishes Camp Clark to protect the bridge.
1876	(April) Troops from Fort Hartsuff have a skirmish with the Sioux in the Battle of the Blowout.
1876	(June 26) Lt. George A. Custer dies in the Battle of the Little Bighorn, Montana Territory.
1876	(July 17) William F. Cody kills Yellow Hair (Yellow Hand), claiming the "first scalp for Custer" in a skirmish on Warbonnet Creek.
1876	(October) Red Cloud is brought in to Fort Robinson.

1876	(November 26) Pawnee Scouts participate in Dull Knife Battle, Wyoming Territory.
1876	D. C. "Doc" Middleton kills his first man in a bar incident in Sidney; he goes on to become a notorious horse thief, serves time in prison, and eventually becomes a deputy sheriff in Gordon.
1877	Frank and Luther North, along with William F. "Buffalo Bill" Cody, start ranching on the Dismal River.
1877	(September 5) A sentry at Fort Robinson stabs and kills Lakota Chief Crazy Horse.
1877	(September 18) Sam Bass and five companions rob a Union Pacific express train near Big Springs.
1878	Creighton University and the University of Nebraska at Omaha open.
1878	(November 27) Homesteaders Ami Ketchum and Luther Mitchell shoot and kill cattleman Bob Olive in the first deadly encounter between homesteaders and cattlemen in Nebraska. Olive's brother Print leads a vigilante group that hangs Mitchell and Ketchum. Eventually someone burns the homesteaders' bodies, and Nebraska becomes the "Man Burner State."
1879	Federal courts affirm that Indians are "people" in *Standing Bear v. Crook*.
1879	(January 9) Dull Knife's Cheyenne warriors break away from Fort Robinson. They are located at a hideout January 22 and eventually surrender after battles that leave sixty-four Cheyennes and eleven U.S. soldiers dead.
1879	(June 23) Congress appropriates $50,000 to establish Fort Niobrara.
1880	The Farmer's Alliance organizes near Filley; within two years 65,000 members belong to 2,000 alliances.
1880	Plattsmouth has its first railroad bridge built across the Missouri. (It is replaced in 1903.)
1880s	Omaha becomes a livestock shipping and processing center.
1880s	Electric streetcars replace horsecar line in Omaha.
1881	Ice dams Missouri River, flooding Omaha.
1881	William F. Cody organizes his first Wild West Show.
1881	(May 11) A wayward soldier kills 2nd Lt. Samuel A. Cherry, whose name is now associated with Cherry County (the largest of Nebraska's counties).
1885	(April 22) This day becomes Arbor Day as the holiday spreads nationwide.

1886	Susan LaFlesche earns her medical degree and returns to the Omaha reservation to serve her people as a doctor.
1886	(August 15) James Coffee ships the first load of cattle from Coffee Siding (near Harrison) to Chicago on the Fremont, Elkhorn & Missouri Valley Railroad (later the Chicago & Northwestern).
1888	(January 12) The Schoolchildren's Blizzard sweeps the plains, killing hundreds of people.
1888	(August 23) A pontoon bridge over the Missouri River at Nebraska City opens; it washes out the following spring, and operators don't replace it.
1893	Drought results in financial panic; grasshoppers eat the few crops that do grow.
1894	Fort Sidney closes.
1895	Ak-Sar-Ben organizes as a charity to promote Nebraska.
1896	Military abandons Fort Omaha (operations relocate to Fort Crook).
1896	Carl Swanson emigrates to Omaha from Sweden.
1896	William Jennings Bryan of Lincoln, "The Great Commoner," is the Democratic candidate for U.S. president.
1897	Union Pacific Railroad Company organizes as a group of investors led by Edward H. Harriman purchases the railroad when the line goes bankrupt.
1897	(June) Three companies of black soldiers cross the Sandhills on bicycles en route from Montana to St. Louis.
1898	(June 1–October 31) Omaha hosts Trans-Mississippi and International Exhibition.
1898	Spanish-American War breaks out; Nebraska sends troops.
1900	(December) Some individuals kidnap Edward Cudahy, the son of a livestock packing magnate. Pat Crowe is subsequently charged with the crime but found innocent.
1900	Jerpe Commission Company (forerunner to Swanson Foods) begins operations in Omaha.
1902	Omaha Street Car Services consolidates and forms Omaha & Council Bluff Street Railway Company.
1902	President Theodore Roosevelt creates the Nebraska National Forest, a completely man-made preserve.
1904	(April 28) Congress approves the Kinkaid Homestead Act, sponsored by Rep. Moses Kinkaid of O'Neill, enlarging the size of homesteads and opening a huge area of northwestern Nebraska to settlement.
1906	Chicago, Quincy & Burlington Railroad reaches Fremont.

1906	(October 22) The government abandons Fort Niobrara, retaining a 16,000-acre tract that becomes Fort Niobrara National Wildlife Refuge.
1908	A group of teenage girls spearheads the construction of a church in Keystone that serves Protestants and Catholics, with an altar at each end of the building (and the door on the side).
1909	Fort Omaha Signal Corps adds a balloon school.
1909	Anti-Greek riots occur in Omaha.
1911	The first wooden automobile bridge across the Missouri at Plattsmouth opens.
1913	A powerful storm sweeps across the heartland, and a tornado destroys some 2,000 homes in Omaha.
1917	Father Edward Flanagan starts Boys Town near Omaha.
1918	Potash production peaks at Antioch, and the population swells to some 5,000 people.
1924	Flying Field at Fort Crook becomes Offutt Field.
1924	Meridian Bridge provides access between Nebraska and South Dakota, replacing ferry service.
1927	Residents in Arthur build a church of baled rye straw.
1928	Jerpe Commission Company becomes Swanson Foods.
1928	Construction starts on Omaha's Joslyn Art Museum.
1929	State legislator Arthur Bowring introduces legislation creating the first Nebraska driver's license.
1931	Sioux holy man Black Elk shares his vision with John Neihardt, who writes the classic *Black Elk Speaks*.
1932	(May) The Farmer's Holiday Association organizes in Des Moines, Iowa, and in August leads a protest in Sioux City, Iowa. A week later the Nebraska Farmer's Holiday Association organizes in Dakota City, and members close roads leading into Sioux City from the west before participating in protests in Omaha.
1933	Farmers march on Lincoln to prohibit foreclosures of their property. They block roads leading into Omaha, halt a train headed to Sioux City, Iowa, and burn bridges providing access to that city.
1934	Nebraska adopts a unicameral, nonpartisan legislature.
1934	Boys Town becomes a municipality.
1934	Civilian Conservation Corps workers build a camp and start making improvements to Ponca State Park.
1935	The worst year of dust storms in a decade-long drought.
1935	The U.S. Olympic equestrian team trains for the games at Fort Robinson.

1937	The unicameral form of government goes into effect.
1938	Vic and Maude Thompson establish what is believed to be the first roadside rest area in Nebraska on their ranch near Newport. In 1966 they dedicate the area as a Centennial Memorial Forest and proclaim their ranch a wildlife refuge.
1942	(March 20) Construction begins on the Sioux Ordnance Depot in Sidney.
1942	Fort Robinson becomes a K-9 training center for World War II (it also serves as a remount station).
1945	Japanese balloon bomb explodes in Omaha.
1945	The U.S. Supreme Court approves a water distribution plan involving the Platte River and affecting the states of Nebraska, Colorado, and Wyoming.
1946	The Strategic Air Command, the U.S. Air Force's long-range bombing and missile striking force, makes its headquarters at Offutt Field.
1948	(January 3) Offutt Field transfers to U.S. Air Force.
1948	(May 28) Offutt becomes base headquarters for the Strategic Air Command.
1949	(January 2) A snowstorm sweeps across the plains, closing roads and stranding people for weeks.
1949	(January 24) President Harry Truman obtains $500,000 from Congress to launch "Operation Snowbound" in an effort to save millions of head of cattle and sheep from starvation.
1949	(March 1) Maj. Gen. Lewis A. Pick declares "Operation Snowbound" complete. Officials estimate seventy-six deaths and losses totaling $190 million.
1949	(August 9) The first oil well in Nebraska comes in south of Gurley.
1950	Swanson Foods develops chicken pot pie.
1953	(December) Swanson Foods begins production of TV dinners.
1955	Omaha replaces Chicago as the nation's chief livestock center, with more than 6 million head of livestock received.
1962	Cabelas opens for business in the Chappell home of owners Dick and Mary Cabela; it becomes a leading sporting goods store, headquartered in Sidney.
1968–69	Swift & Armour meatpacking plants close.
1969	Gov. Norbert Tiemann proclaims O'Neill the "Irish Capital of Nebraska." Governor James Exon dedicated a marker to that effect in 1972, and the legislature approved a resolution to the same end in 1977.

1970	Interstate 80 construction is complete across Nebraska.
1974	Cooper Nuclear Station opens in Brownville, the largest of its kind between the Mississippi River and the Pacific Ocean.
1976	Federal Land Policy & Management Act replaces Homestead Act.
1980s	Iowa Beef Packers, headquartered at Dakota City, pays $5.7 million in fines for meatpacking violations.
1982	A new law regulates groundwater irrigation pumping.
1982	Residents approve a resolution limiting further corporate farming except by family members.
1986	Kay Orr becomes Nebraska's first woman governor.
1986	Congress establishes the Soldier Creek Wilderness of the Nebraska National Forest. Between July 8 and 14, 1989, 48,000 acres burn in a forest fire.
1989	Union Pacific Railroad refurbishes the Cowshed into the Harriman Dispatch Center in Omaha.
1993	(May) Governor Ben Nelson and representatives from Wyoming, South Dakota, and Colorado dedicate historic markers to recognize the 1851 treaty between Plains Indians and the government.
1993	Hundreds of people follow Nebraska's Oregon Trail in wagons and on horseback in a commemoration of the trail's sesquicentennial.
1995	(New Year's Day) Nebraska Huskers become National Football League champions.
1995	South Sioux City advertises for people to "Return to Sioux Land" in order to have adequate workers for an expanding labor market.
1996	(New Year's Day) Nebraska Huskers repeat as National Football League champions.

NEBRASKA FACTS

Territory: May 30, 1854

Statehood: March 1, 1867

Nickname: Cornhusker State

Motto: Equality Before the Law

Bird: Western Meadowlark

Flower: Late Goldenrod

Tree: Cottonwood (replaced the American Elm in 1972)

Grass: Little Bluestem

Flag: Adopted March 28, 1925, the state flag has a state seal in gold and silver against a field of blue.

State Seal: Adopted May 31, 1867, the great seal contains many symbols of the state. A riverboat represents commerce, the hammer and anvil stand for mechanical art, and wheat and corn stand for agriculture.

Animal: White-tailed deer

Gem: Blue Agate

Song: "Beautiful Nebraska"

Population: 1,578,385 (1990 census)

Area: 77,355 square miles

NEBRASKA FIRSTS

- In the fall of 1795, a Spanish party led by James Mackay built the first European settlement—a fur trading post—in Nebraska, at a site in the vicinity of Bellevue.
- In 1837 Alfred Jacob Miller sketched Chimney Rock, probably the first artist to do so.
- The first Nebraska territorial governor, Francis Burt, took office at Bellevue, but he died two days later, initiating a sectional fight for the capital.
- The first official survey west of the Mississippi River was authorized November 2, 1854, to include land extending 108 miles from the Missouri River west, along the 40th parallel to the 6th Principal Meridian.
- The *Nebraska Palladium*, at Bellevue, was the first newspaper in the region. It later combined with the *Nebraska City News*.
- Daniel Freeman filed on the first homestead near Beatrice on January 1, 1863, under provisions of the 1862 Homestead Act.
- Farmers in Orleans, Nebraska, organized the first Nebraska Grange in 1872; within two years the state had 596 Granges.
- In 1881 Buffalo Bill Cody held his first Wild West Show at Columbus, Nebraska.
- The first Farmer's Alliance started in southeastern Nebraska, near Filley, but within two years the movement spread and at least 2,000 alliances with about 65,000 members existed throughout the state.
- In 1929 Arthur Bowring introduced legislation creating the first Nebraska driver's license.
- Vic and Maude Thompson in 1938 established Spring Valley Park, the first roadside rest area in Nebraska.
- The first oil well in western Nebraska came in three miles south of Gurley on August 9, 1949.
- Swanson Foods created the first chicken pot pie in 1950; later Swanson developed TV dinners and trademarked the name.

PREFACE

BEFORE YOU DIP INTO THE PAGES of this book, I'd like to make a few comments about the work and about Nebraska.

As with any book that attempts to cover the history of a large region, some items are necessarily abbreviated or even omitted, not because they aren't important or interesting but simply because of the constraints of space. A history of every town in Nebraska and every important happening in the state could not be included within these covers. That is not the goal of a roadside history guide such as this.

I did not set out to overlook the residents of places not included; rather, I set out to tell some of the stories that form the fabric of Nebraska's past. I selected some because they seemed particularly necessary, others because they aren't as well known, and a few simply because I liked them.

My initial interest in writing about Nebraska goes back to my newspaper reporting on interstate water issues involving Wyoming and Nebraska. My interest grew when I first followed the ruts of the Oregon Trail by automobile as a guest of the Nebraska Division of Tourism in 1992 and became more pronounced as I traveled that pioneer route by wagon train in 1993. Since that time I have traveled most of Nebraska's roads and put many thousands of miles on my car in search of information, photographs, and a sense of Nebraska's spirit.

My travels in Nebraska became somewhat of a joke to my family and writer friends. Initially I thought I would avoid bad roads and do most of my traveling in the spring, summer, and fall. I believed such a schedule would give me the best roads and the best conditions. What actually happened is that I experienced Nebraska in all its nuances.

On one trip in early June I shivered and shook and wished I'd put my down-filled jacket into my bag when I left home. On another trip I drove through dust clouds that swirled high into the air, reminiscent of the Dust Bowl days of the 1930s. A herd of tumbleweeds raced over the western prairie near Ogallala, and one hit my windshield so hard it left a permanent chip.

My family and I had to evacuate our campsite in Neligh before dawn one August morning (at a police officer's request) when six inches of rain fell on our tent in the most horrendous thunderstorm I've ever experienced. I watched the sky in Nebraska City when the emergency sirens sounded a tornado warning. (I probably should have sought shelter, but I'm a mountain gal and have only seen one tornado.) Some places I couldn't get to at all in the spring and summer of 1995, as flooding closed the roads.

On my first journey through the Sandhills a raging late-March blizzard kept me from seeing the countryside; it was all I could do to see the road. My family and I stopped in Thedford and asked a snow-plow driver about the roads toward the west. He advised us not to continue if it wasn't absolutely necessary, but we bucked his advice and the drifts as we slowly made our way to Scottsbluff, where we gladly vacated the car for a motel room. The roads closed behind us, and some Sandhills ranchers didn't get to town for days following that storm.

By the way, I have consistently used the spelling *Sandhills* in this book, although some authors prefer *Sand Hills* or *sandhills*. Similarly, I chose to use *Sauk* rather than *Sac*, and *Otoe* instead of *Oto*, for two of the state's Indian tribes. While conducting research I found those names spelled myriad ways, so I relied on the advice of my friend Don Birchfield, who recently edited a ten-volume encyclopedia about Native Americans. And I use both *Sioux* and *Lakota* interchangably for that tribe.

In organizing this book, I considered comments and suggestions from several people, and in the end I decided to follow the pattern of European settlement as much as possible. Bear in mind that, for the most part, the Native Americans who settled this region also came from the east (although the Pawnees came from the south). Therefore, the work begins in the northeast, where the first fur traders established posts and where Nebraska's first military post was established. I follow the Missouri River south, where communities quickly boomed follow-ing approval of the Kansas-Nebraska Act in 1854. The region along the Oregon Trail falls in the center of the book, as it is in the center of the state. Although many people traveled that trail in the 1840s and early 1850s, before any towns existed in southeastern Nebraska Ter-ritory, permanent settlement didn't occur in that region until several years after the river towns developed. I conclude the book with the Sandhills and Panhandle regions. This organization is not perfectly chronological, but it is logical to me.

I have fond memories of people and places in Nebraska, particu-larly the people who opened their homes to me and showed me the human side of the modern state. I want to spend more time along the Missouri River, at Indian Cave State Park, in the Sandhills, and at the prehistoric Agate and Ashfall fossil beds. My family used to ship cattle to the Omaha Livestock Market, and I spent a glorious morning there taking pictures and imagining my grandfather walking the catwalk above the corrals. In Ponca, my mother and I strolled among the gravestones at the cemetery, looking for those of our ancestors.

I've been fortunate to receive advice from other writers and researchers in putting this book onto paper. Even with all their suggestions, I don't claim to know everything about Nebraska, although I have worked hard to find the latest information and to record all the stories as accurately as possible. If I have fallen short in my delivery, I hope you will overlook my unintentional errors.

Some people may believe Nebraska is all cows and corn and long, flat highways. Let me assure you there is much more to this state. It has a diverse Indian history, beautiful rolling prairies, varied river habitats, a marvelous array of wildlife, and some of the nicest people you'll meet anywhere. In Nebraska you can still buy a hamburger deluxe for $2, although it might be served on a napkin rather than a plate; if fried chicken suits you, it can be served family style at the local restaurant.

Most Nebraska residents can spot a tourist (or a writer) a mile away. Some may cast sideways glances, but more likely they are like the elderly man my mother and I met in a restaurant in Neligh on my first visit there. "Are you the folks in that Wyoming car?" he asked me. I told him we were, and he proceeded first to ask my business and then to tell me a part of his story. Such is life in the Heartland.

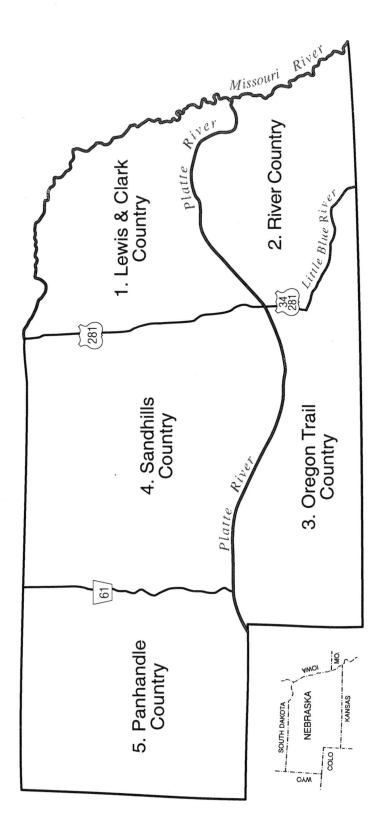

1. Lewis & Clark Country

2. River Country

4. Sandhills Country

3. Oregon Trail Country

5. Panhandle Country

Missouri River

Platte River

Little Blue River

Platte River

281

34
281

61

SOUTH DAKOTA

NEBRASKA

IOWA

MO.

KANSAS

COLO

WYO

WHERE THE HEARTLAND
BECOMES THE WEST

D RIVING ACROSS NEBRASKA NOW, it is difficult to picture the land as the earliest explorers saw it. Corn, sunflowers, soybeans, alfalfa, and wheat create a mosaic of colors. Once the region had tall and short grasses, but most early explorers considered it unproductive, a vast desert of use only to nomadic people. Even today many dismiss Nebraska as a place with nothing to offer except an outstanding college football team. Although more than 350,000 emigrants heading to California and Oregon crossed Nebraska after 1843 and the routes of the first transcontinental railroad (the Union Pacific), the first transcontinental highway (US 30, the Lincoln Highway), and a primary modern highway (Interstate 80) stretch the length of the state, all too often people fail to look beyond the view out their car window. Nobody can appreciate the nuances of Nebraska when driving 65 miles per hour or faster over pavement.

The wooded hillsides of eastern Nebraska along the Missouri River give way to the grass-covered plains stretching westward. This country became part of a high-stakes political battle that forged the United States in a manner never envisioned by the country's forefathers. The last major Indian-against-Indian battle occurred along the Republican River in 1873, when the Sioux annihilated a Pawnee hunting party. This is a state that wanted trees so badly it planted a forest, giving rise to the Timber Culture Act provisions of homestead law and a national holiday: Arbor Day.

Early Exploration and Settlement

The people who settled Nebraska had tenacity. They lived in houses dug out of the earth or made from pieces of prairie sod piled one on top of the other, which they called Nebraska marble. They heated those same homes by burning buffalo manure or corncobs. They endured heat, drought, tornadoes, blizzards, floods, and grasshoppers, all the while turning Nebraska from prairie to pantry.

Lewis and Clark skirted the northeastern edge of Nebraska, following the Missouri and seeing only a few wooded areas of the present-day state, but after crossing the Dakota plains they said the region "offered no hope of settlement by white man." The expedition of Stephen Long in 1820 endorsed that view, labeling the central plains the "Great American Desert." For years, that was the image most people had of Nebraska. The pioneers who headed toward Oregon and California saw it only as a gently rolling, never-ending sea of grass. They followed the rivers, drank foul water, died of cholera, and cursed the plains. They had no intention of stopping, even if the Native Americans had given them permission to settle upon their lands. In a speech to the Senate in 1843, George McDuffie of South Carolina said: "The whole region beyond the Rocky Mountains, and a vast tract between that chain and the Mississippi, is a desert without value for agricultural purposes and which no American citizen should be compelled to inhabit unless as a punishment for crime. . . . I wish to God we did not own it."

Spaniards and Frenchmen first saw Nebraska in the 1700s. Various Native American tribes had made their homes in the region, hunting buffalo on the plains for generations. Paleo-Indians killed buffalo in western sections of the state more than 10,000 years ago, and tribes such as the Pawnee had raised corn and lived in permanent villages in present-day Nebraska since the 1600s. Francisco Vasquez de Coronado, in his fabled explorations for Quivara in 1540–41, did not reach Nebraska, journeying only as far onto the Great Plains as central Kansas. In 1601 Juan de Oñate marched with an army and a train of supply carts into Kansas, bringing the first wheeled vehicles onto the plains, but he, too, failed to make it to Nebraska. By about 1700, trade routes from Santa Fe and Taos had penetrated the area near Fort Laramie, then turned northeast toward Nebraska's White River before continuing to the Arikara villages on the Missouri River in present-day South Dakota.

The French started trading with Nebraska's native people in 1703, and in 1714 the French explorer Etienne de Bourgmont reached the confluence of the Platte and Missouri Rivers. He called the Platte "Nebraskier River," which is likely the first reference to the state's name. Most called the river the Platte, French for "flat." Spanish explorations continued between 1714 and 1720, when Don Pedro de Villasur led a series of journeys to Nebraska. For the 1720 expedition, Villasur probably followed an Indian trail to the Platte near Grand Island. There he and his forty-five men crossed the Platte and then the Loup River. After some unsuccessful attempts to negotiate with Otoe and Pawnee

Native American grass dancers. —Nebraska State Historical Society

Indians, Villasur and his troops camped in the tall grasses just south of present-day Columbus, where at dawn on August 14, 1720, a party of Indians, perhaps supported by French traders, attacked, killing thirty-five Spaniards. The short but deadly battle was a huge defeat for the Spanish and set back their efforts to trade with the tribes in Nebraska, although by 1753 Santa Fe traders had resumed their work with the Pawnees on the Loup River.

The most widely known early exploration of Nebraska was made by Canadian brothers Paul and Pierre Mallet. Born in Montreal, the Mallets came to the area near present Detroit, Michigan, in 1706. In 1739 they and seven companions set out to find a route to Santa Fe. The Mallets ascended the Missouri to the Niobrara, then realized they were headed northwest rather than southwest. They left the Niobrara and headed overland, this time traveling in the proper direction, until they found another river, which they called the Platte. James C. Olson, in *History of Nebraska*, says they probably reached the Platte at a site between South Bend and Fremont.

The Mallet party was the first known to have referred to the river as the Platte, and they followed it perhaps to a point west of its confluence with the Loup River, where they abandoned the Platte and continued traveling southwest, likely crossing the Republican River between Superior and Red Cloud in extreme southern Nebraska. They eventually reached Santa Fe, but they had lost their trade goods on the trek. Spanish authorities in Sante Fe notified the viceroy in Mexico City of their arrival, and he ordered the Frenchmen to leave Spanish territory and not to return without prior permission.

The Mallet brothers eventually made their way to New Orleans. Paul ultimately took up farming in Arkansas; Pierre launched another expedition to Santa Fe. The second attempt failed, but Pierre made a third effort in 1750, heading from New Orleans across eastern Texas to the Pecos River, where he was arrested. Spanish authorities sent Pierre to El Paso, then to Chihuahua and to Mexico City before they deported him to Spain, where he is believed to have died in prison.

The Mallet brothers had succeeded in finding a route to Santa Fe, opening the Southwest to French trading ventures. The French also initiated trade with Indians living along the Missouri, vying with the Spanish for control of the region until the late 1750s. The 1763 Treaty of Paris ceded all the land west of the Missouri River to Spain. That didn't end the French influence in the region, although the Spaniards hoped it would. Spanish traders extended their reach to the Upper Missouri in 1793 under the leadership of James Clamorgan. He employed such men as Bentura Collell, Joseph Robidoux, Gregoire Sarpy, and Antoine Roy, all of whom were led into that country by Jean Baptiste Truteau.

The Truteau party ventured to the Mandan villages and spent the winter near the future site of Fort Randall, conducting limited trade with the Sioux, Omaha, and Ponca tribes. The Spanish government authorized subsequent expeditions, led by James Mackay, in 1795–96. Mackay established the first European settlement in present-day Nebraska, a trading post that served the Otoe Indians at a site a mile above the Platte's mouth. Mackay also started construction of Fort Carlos IV in November 1795 near the Omaha Indian village headed by Chief Blackbird. Also called Fort Charles, the stockaded post consisted of a storehouse, trade room, and living quarters. It was located near the present community of Homer. In 1797 Mackay opened another a trading post about eight miles south of the mouth of the Platte, but it operated only that year and was then abandoned. Mackay didn't leave Nebraska, however; he remained at Fort Carlos IV and made an exploratory trip to the west, crossing through the Sandhills. He was probably the first white man to see that region, describing it as a "Great Desert of moving sand where there is neither wood nor soil nor stone nor water."

Given time, the Spanish traders may have continued pushing toward the northwest, but under the Treaty of San Ildefonso, signed

October 1, 1800, the Spanish government returned the country to France. Just three years later, the United States made its Louisiana Purchase, doubling the size of the country and starting its expansion to the Pacific.

The first Americans to reach Nebraska were William Clark and Meriwether Lewis, who began their now-famous expedition in 1804. Spanish records show a smallpox epidemic swept through the region in 1800–1801, and Lewis and Clark noted in their journals the burned remnants of the large Omaha village, which had been near Mackay's trading post at Homer. They reported about 300 earth lodges had been in the village and that some 400 men, women, and children had died of smallpox.

Americans also set out for Santa Fe not long after the Louisiana Purchase became final. The Spaniards already had established trails from Santa Fe north through Wyoming to the Montana country and to the Arikara villages on the Missouri. Many early traders followed a different trail across Nebraska that had been used for years by Pawnee Indians.

In 1806 Lt. Zebulon Pike ventured into the region along the Republican River. He met with the Pawnees at a site in south-central Nebraska near Guide Rock, where he found many Spanish items, including a Spanish flag. Pike convinced the Pawnees to replace it with a U.S. banner, then continued west into Colorado. Unprepared for harsh winter conditions there, the Pike party struggled to survive. The Ute Indians reported their whereabouts to Spanish officials in New Mexico, and they arrested the Americans (perhaps saving them from a miserable death).

James Clamorgan followed the route across Nebraska to Santa Fe in 1807–8, and several expeditions to Santa Fe started from Fort Atkinson, which the military established as its westernmost outpost in 1820. (The fort was preceded in 1819 by Cantonment Missouri.) After restrictions on trade with Mexico were lifted in 1821, William Becknell made his pioneering trip across present-day Kansas to Santa Fe, which established the route to the southern capital. Even after traders knew that the shortest route to Santa Fe lay across Kansas, many trading parties continued to depart from Fort Atkinson until the military abandoned it in 1827. Then travelers joined the Santa Fe Trail at Fort Leavenworth, Kansas.

The earliest white visitors to Nebraska found many Native American tribes living in the region, including the Omaha, Osage, Ponca, Otoe, Missouria, Pawnee, Sauk, Fox, and Kansas. Those tribes generally held lands on both sides of the Missouri River (Pawnee territory

5

Native Americans, part of the Hagatha. —Nebraska State Historical Society

extended into central Nebraska) and were never at war with white settlers. Native American tribes farther west, including the Arapaho, Cheyenne, Comanche, Kiowa, and Sioux, all conflicted with whites, particularly the military.

Through treaties in 1825, the Kansas and Osage tribes relinquished most of their land in Nebraska, and by 1846 the Kansas tribe had been completely dispossessed. The Omahas, Otoes, Missourias, and Pawnees negotiated several treaties and had relinquished most of their lands by 1854, when Congress created Nebraska Territory. The Omahas still have a reservation within Nebraska, but the Otoes gave up their lands in 1881, and the Pawnees turned over their last lands in 1875 and moved to Oklahoma. The Sauk and Fox tribes, latecomers to Nebraska, continue to have a small reservation in the extreme southeastern part of the state. The Sioux relinquished their lands in treaties negotiated in 1868, 1875, and 1876, while the Northern Cheyennes and Arapahos signed treaties in 1876 that dispossessed them of most of their ancestral lands and all of their Nebraska lands.

Although the Platte River flows the entire length of Nebraska, early attempts to navigate it were largely unsuccessful; the river spreads itself too wide and shallow to float vessels of any size. Some fur trappers attempted to float their pelts in bullboats from Fort Laramie to the Missouri River, but they abandoned their efforts after being plagued by sandbars and deep holes. Washington Irving called the Platte "the most magnificent and most useless of rivers." In 1866, when

Steam ferry, the Belle of Brownville, *about 1881.*—Nebraska State Historical Society

Gen. William T. Sherman visited Fort Kearny, he noted, "We had to cross the Platte, as mean a river as exists on earth, with its moving, shifting sand."

In January 1860 the 6th Territorial Legislature, in an attempt to convince Congress that the Platte could be navigated, approved a 20,000-acre land grant for John A. Latta to begin operation of a steamboat between Kearney and Plattsmouth. The proposal said the steamboat could be a means of freight delivery between the two communities and could act as a dredge for the river. The operation failed to get to first base, however, as opponents quickly pointed out there wasn't adequate water in the Platte to float a steamboat, even during flood stage in the spring.

Still, the Platte played a central role in the development of the West. It became the route taken across the plains by most of the early travelers to California and Oregon. The first wagons on what eventually became the well-traveled Oregon-California Trail went through Nebraska in 1830, when a party of fur traders led by William Sublette took ten wagons across South Pass to participate in rendezvous.

In 1841 the Bidwell-Bartleson emigrant party crossed the plains, and large-scale emigration began in 1843. In the ensuing decades, hundreds of thousands of emigrants walked beside oxen and wagons

Once wider and deeper, the Platte River bisects Nebraska and has had a major role in the state's development. This wagon bridge crossed the river near Lexington in 1905. —Wyoming State Museum, Stimson Collection

or rode horses and mules across Nebraska. The Oregon-California Trail followed the Little Blue River, crossed a dry stretch to reach the Platte River, then followed the Platte to Wyoming. The route in Nebraska was known as the Great Platte River Road, and during a thirty-year period at least 350,000 travelers followed it to Oregon, California, and Washington. They all crossed Nebraska and Wyoming, but few stayed; the vast majority went on to the fertile regions of the West Coast.

Travelers followed many roads across eastern Nebraska. Although most entered the state along the Little Blue River near Rock Creek Station at Fairbury, a significant number started their journey west from other points, such as Nebraska City, where the Ox-Bow Trail first started angling northwest toward the Platte and then followed it west. Later, a more direct western route—the Nebraska City to Fort Kearny road— saw heavy traffic from both emigrants and freighters. The various strands of the Oregon and California Trails in eastern Nebraska converged at Fort Kearny. From that point on, all travelers followed the Platte River Road. At times the route spread up to fifteen miles wide so travelers could find adequate grazing for their livestock.

During the period of overland migration, the Platte was much wider than it is today, sometimes nearly a mile across. Then as now, it had many branches or braids separated by islands. Heavy spring runoff scoured the Platte each year, depositing large amounts of sand and silt and making the river treacherous to cross. The changes in that scouring action have created significant impacts for wildlife and waterfowl; the habitat they prefer is no longer as prevalent along the Platte as it used to be.

In 1846 Brigham Young, leader of the Church of Jesus Christ of Latter-day Saints (the Mormon Church), brought the first of his people across the Missouri River to set up the settlement of Winter Quarters at the present site of Florence. An advance party intent on finding a new home farther west made it to the area near Columbus but couldn't cross the plains before winter. The scouts turned north upon the urging of the Ponca Indians and wintered with them in the Niobrara River region. Meanwhile, the bitter cold and harsh conditions at the main party's winter camp took a severe toll, and many Mormons died.

In the spring of 1847, the survivors started west, seeking a place where they could live and worship as they pleased. The Mormons forged their own trail on the north side of the Platte River, establishing way stations along the route. The earliest travelers planted crops that were tended and harvested by later travelers, making trail life an easier proposition. Wagon trains were used in the initial years of the Mormon migration; handcarts became common from 1856–60.

The Platte starts its course toward the Atlantic Ocean high in the mountains of Colorado and Wyoming. The North Platte has its headwaters in North Park, which straddles Colorado and south-central Wyoming; a secondary stream, the South Platte, rises in Colorado's South Park, about a hundred air miles from the headwaters of the North Platte. Those two forks join at North Platte, Nebraska, becoming the Platte, often described as "a mile wide, an inch deep, and uphill all the way."

The Platte River valley formed eons ago. During the Mesozoic Era some 60 million years ago, the land of Nebraska emerged as an ocean receded. Then the Rocky Mountains jutted from the earth, and the land tilted upward from east to west. Some 2 million years ago, in the Pleistocene epoch (the Ice Age), massive ice sheets crept into eastern and northern Nebraska, sending great amounts of water to swell rivers and add to the growing plains. The Platte as we know it started forming some 50,000 to 100,000 years ago.

Nebraska's many rivers—the Niobrara, Dismal, Frenchman, Calamus, Snake, Cedar, Republican, Elkhorn, Loup, Big Blue, Little Blue, Nemaha, and, of course, the Missouri and Platte—provide habitat for a plethora of wildlife, particularly waterfowl. The greatest gathering of waterbirds happens every spring, when some 350,000 red-headed, gray-bodied sandhill cranes stop and spend almost two months along the Platte between Grand Island and Kearney. A significant number of waterfowl also spend time along the Missouri.

All of Nebraska's rivers played a role in settlement of the state, as homesteaders claimed land along their banks, spreading from larger to smaller streams. They continue to provide water for agriculture and recreation. Long's characterization of the region as a desert is hardly accurate, given that Nebraska sits atop the huge Ogallala Aquifer and has 23,686 miles of streams, rivers, and canals, ranking it tenth in the nation. Although the Missouri and the Platte get the most attention, the Niobrara has more mileage within Nebraska's borders than any other river, running 486 miles from the Wyoming line to the Missouri River. The Niobrara, known as the Running Water, is likely also the youngest of the major rivers in Nebraska. It waters the northern portion of the state and provides wonderful opportunities for floating by canoe or inner tube on hot summer days.

Territorial Government

By 1854 people had begun to eye the land west of the Missouri River, and the Kansas-Nebraska Act proposed that year forced pro- and anti-slavery factions to take a look at the region. The law, according to Senator Charles Sumner, put "freedom and slavery face to face and bids them grapple." It provided for the repeal of the restrictions in the 1820 Missouri Compromise, which limited slavery to areas south of 36 degrees 30 minutes. In effect, the act opened both Kansas and Nebraska to slavery, which fanned the flames of sectional discord. The territories were allowed to determine for themselves whether they would enter the nation as slave or free states. That theory of popular sovereignty came in part to ensure southern support for the bill, sponsored by Senator Stephen A. Douglas.

The issue revolved around westward expansion more than around slavery, but in order to get the support he needed for the bill, Douglas had to introduce the slave clause. Douglas wanted to see an east-west railroad, as did many other leaders from both the North and the South. Some, like Douglas, preferred a northern route commencing, perhaps, from Chicago. Others favored a southern route. Douglas, in proposing the bill to establish Nebraska and Kansas Territories, sought approval for the northern railroad route.

When the issue also became embroiled in the controversy over slavery, Douglas quickly found his efforts would cost him dearly. The Kansas-Nebraska Act further divided the country's thinking about slavery issues and led to the downfall of the Whig Party. Southern members voted as a bloc and supported the Douglas bill, while northern Whigs voted against the measure and the likelihood of expansion of slavery. It cost Douglas much of his political power and set up the outcome of the 1860 presidential election, in which Douglas lost to Abraham Lincoln.

As the northern Whigs abandoned their party, they held a number of meetings to denounce the proposed Kansas-Nebraska Act. Those meetings most often were characterized as anti-Nebraska gatherings. The opposition came largely to Nebraska's potentially becoming a slave state because it was much larger than the proposed Kansas Territory. (At that time Nebraska Territory also included most of today's Dakotas and eastern Wyoming.)

Upon the bill's approval by Congress, Byron Reed, a correspondent for the *New York Tribune*, went to Kansas and found the area reeling. He wrote of the bloody battles in Kansas, and proponents of slavery not only denounced the *Tribune* but threatened vengeance on correspondents such as Reed. Fearing for his safety, Reed fled north to Nebraska Territory, where he found a haven in Omaha.

The United States struggled bitterly over the development of Nebraska Territory; the fight was one of the most divisive with which Congress had to deal in the nineteenth century. The confrontation involved slavery, Indians, expansionist views, and industrial development. It pitted governmental leaders against each other and threatened the very integrity of the country. Debate, argument, and eventually compromise resolved the issues and led to the establishment of Nebraska Territory, which encompassed more than 351,000 square miles—an area larger than France and the British Isles combined—extending from the Missouri to the Rockies and from Kansas to Canada.

Given the conflict surrounding its establishment, it might not be surprising that Nebraskans had a difficult time determining where to place their seat of government. The contest pitted people living in the Omaha area, north of the Platte River—who became known as the "North Platters"—against those living in the Lincoln region, south of the Platte River—the "South Platters."

The earliest territorial census ordered by Territorial Secretary of State and Acting Governor Thomas B. Cuming in 1854 indicated 1,818 people living south of the river and 914 residing to the north. Nevertheless, Cuming and his cronies located the territorial capital in Omaha, after first considering alternative sites in Plattsmouth, Florence, and Nebraska City. Surprisingly, they ignored Bellevue, which had enjoyed a long, relatively stable existence and had been the site of the swearing-in of the territory's first governor (who died two days later).

Once the territorial capitol, this ornate building still serves as an Omaha high school, April 1995.

Omaha's Capitol High School, 1906. —Wyoming State Museum, Stimson Collection

Railroad graders west of Sargent, Nebraska, 1886. –Nebraska State Historical Society, Solomon D. Butcher Collection

The designation of Omaha as the capital infuriated the South Platters, who immediately began campaigning for change. They explored the possibility of levying bribery charges against Cuming. They considered seceding and becoming part of Kansas Territory. They held their own independent legislative sessions in Florence. After thirteen years, the South Platters succeeded in relocating the capital to Lincoln, where it remains. Nebraska was admitted to the Union on March 1, 1867.

While these events were transpiring, other developments had profound impacts upon the future state. Two of the most significant events occurred in 1862, when Congress passed the Homestead Act and the Pacific Railway Act, opening Nebraska's central and western lands to settlement. The first homestead claimed in the nation, a property just west of present-day Beatrice settled by Daniel Freeman in 1863, is now a part of Homestead National Monument. In subsequent years all of central Nebraska fell under Homestead Act provisions as settlers poured in. They came not only from the eastern United States but also from Sweden, Germany, England, Ireland, and the Bohemian countries. The development of railroads spurred settlement; the various lines promoted the country because they wanted settlers who would ship crops on freight lines and because they wanted to sell

Bird's-eye view of Lexington, Nebraska, rail yards, 1905. —Wyoming State Museum, Stimson Collection

the lands granted to them by the government in exchange for developing their lines.

The Pacific Railway Act of 1862 further set the stage for Nebraska's future when congressional leaders determined that the eastern terminus of the great line linking east and the west would be Omaha. The Union Pacific Railroad Company started construction in 1865, laying rails along the Great Platte River Road. The Union Pacific promoted settlement by selling its land grant properties in the fertile Platte River valley, and as other railroads pushed into outlying areas of the state, the "Great American Desert" turned into a part of the nation's breadbasket.

However, the limited rainfall on the plains, particularly west of the 100th Meridian, continued to impede settlement. Even as late as 1867 most of western Nebraska remained unlikely to support towns and people. That year John Pope, commander of the Department of the Missouri, said the vast prairies "must always remain a great uninhabited desert . . . utterly unproductive and uninhabitable by civilized man."

Pope failed to consider the efforts already being made to the west, near Fort McPherson, where M. W. Hinman in March 1863 constructed a canal from the south bank of the Platte River to divert water onto

A photo of young boys gathering cow chips that's become widely recognized in rural America. The two boys photographed in the late 1890s are the sons of Mr. and Mrs. George Dew of the Wood Lake and Brownlee area of Cherry County, Nebraska. —Nebraska State Historical Society

the land. A year later John Burke constructed a new canal out of the South Platte. The ditches quickly showed the land's richness and potential productivity, but Indian uprisings in 1864 and 1865 curtailed those efforts.

In fact, there was opposition to irrigation project development until at least 1894. The efforts by some individuals to use irrigation to support crops such as corn and wheat threatened the promotional campaigns of railroad developers, who didn't want prospective settlers to think of the region as some desert land in need of irrigation. Most interesting of all, the opposition to irrigation came from western Nebraska newspapers more often than from the eastern Nebraska press. On January 1, 1895, the *Omaha Herald* reported: "The false pride that has held in check a concerted public action to place our State under the most rapid system of irrigation improvement is responsible for much of the suffering and poverty that exists from crop failures today." Those comments came in the wake of one of Nebraska's periodic "great droughts," when the soil curls and dries before blowing high into the

Cauliflower field at the State Industrial School, Kearney, Nebraska. —Nebraska State Historical Society, Solomon D. Butcher Collection

sky. There'd been a drought in 1873 and another in 1893. The worst, of course, came with the Great Depression of the 1930s, when the parched soil swirled into the air, darkening day into night and collecting in drifts against fences and homes.

Early observers recognized the potential for settlement along the rivers, particularly in the east, but development of western Nebraska appeared more tenuous. In *The Great Plains*, Walter Prescott Webb suggested agricultural production west of the 98th Meridian (roughly defined by US 81) had little hope for success; others placed the boundary at the 100th Meridian (some thirty miles west of US 183). As plains farmers started turning the sod, they employed many methods to ensure a good crop. One fundamental principle preached during the nineteenth century was that "rain follows the plow." Some claimed if farmers from Texas to Canada would just plow the sparse buffalo grass under, the moisture trapped beneath the hard soil would rise into the atmosphere; when temperatures were just right, that moisture would become rain and return to the earth. The more active the plowing operations, the more it would rain.

Weather conditions have exerted significant influence on Nebraska's history. The winter of 1856–57 caused untold hardship for new settlers as fierce storms pounded the region. Winter storms paralyzed the entire Great Plains region in 1888, killing thousands of head of livestock; another deadly blizzard pounded the land in 1949. Typically, during

Deep snow in Syracuse, Nebraska. —Nebraska State Historical Society

early spring and summer the nearly flat country of the Great Plains experiences some of the most violent weather anywhere in the United States. Nebraska residents have to contend with tornadoes, thunderstorms, and floods as warm, moist air from the Gulf Coast sweeps upward and crashes into cold air rolling down from the Northwest and Canada. The Republican River flooded in the mid-1930s, killing more than 100 people and pushing houses and barns from their foundations. In spite of it all, the people rebound, rebuild, and hope the next weather system skirts around them. By the late 1890s settlers had sunk their roots so deeply into the soil that almost nothing would dislodge them.

Farmers who once relied on rain turned to irrigation as they expanded their operations and made Nebraska the Cornhusker State. Irrigation along the Platte River has changed that great waterway more than any other event in recent history. The diversion of water from the river caused its width to shrink from a mile or more to less than a quarter of a mile in most areas. The water diversion, dams, and reservoirs along the Platte reduced springtime flows that used to scour riverbanks and islands. That scouring process historically helped create habitat for many waterbirds, so the elimination of that natural process has affected numerous species.

Elsewhere in Nebraska, diversion and dams have changed the rivers' natural courses and helped to shape the state. The Frenchman River in southwest Nebraska, for example, has so much irrigation diversion

Picking peaches, Watson Ranch, Kearney, Nebraska. —Nebraska State Historical Society, Solomon D. Butcher Collection

and so many underground wells drilled near it that the stream's headwaters, which once rose in eastern Colorado, now rise in Nebraska. To answer some of the concerns raised about proliferation of wells and irrigation, in 1982 the legislature approved a measure regulating groundwater pumping and a year later imposed user fees for groundwater extraction.

Twentieth-Century Changes

In 1934 Nebraska adopted a unicameral form of government, making it the only state in the nation with a one-house, nonpartisan legislature. That governmental body saves taxpayers' money, and proponents say it provides more representative government than in other states. The unicameral legislature passed overwhelmingly, although some claim that's because of two other important issues on the ballot in 1934: repeal of prohibition and provision for pari-mutuel betting.

During World War II, the state and its residents made primary contributions to the war effort. The greatest contribution was in crop and animal production to feed not only Americans and U.S. soldiers but also the Allies. The Cornhusker Ordnance plant at Grand Island, the Sioux Ordnance Depot at Sidney, and the Naval Ammunition Depot at Hastings prepared and stored military ammunition. Airfields dotted

A McCormick Deering corn picker, harvesting one of the staple crops of Nebraska. —Nebraska State Historical Society

the state's landscape at Scottsbluff, Alliance, Ainsworth, McCook, Kearney, Harvard, Grand Island, Bruning, Lincoln, and Scribner. Lt. Howard J. Otis, public information officer for the 2nd Air Force, wrote in July 1943: "It is truly an amazing sight to see these Army air bases suddenly rise into view from farms, cattle ranges, or hayflats. As one drives across the state, there first appears an orange and black checkerboard water tank rising above the horizon. Then the blue-green glass windows of a control tower came into sight. Hangars housing big, war birds, were seen."

In addition to providing land for military forces, training, and ammunition, Nebraska housed 12,000 prisoners of war. In all, Nebraska had twenty-three POW camps, including base camps at Scottsbluff, Fort Robinson, and Atlanta. The Union Pacific and other railroad lines provided transportation for U.S. soldiers en route to the war front, and many communities opened canteens along the route to provide aid and comfort. The most well known of the canteens, at North Platte, was perhaps the most famous in North America. It opened Christmas Day 1941, with aid provided by people from 125 communities in Nebraska.

Present-day Offutt Air Force Base, home of the former Strategic Air Command (SAC) in Bellevue, housed the Martin Bomber Plant during World War II. The plant churned out a variety of aircraft,

Nebraska atomic energy plant at Hallam, one of the modern industries in the state. —Nebraska State Historical Society

including two of the most famous B-29s of all time: the *Enola Gay*, used to drop the atomic bomb on Hiroshima, August 6, 1945, and the *Bocks Car*, which dropped the atomic bomb on Nagasaki three days later. SAC served a critical role during the Cold War as a high-level security base to monitor potential attacks upon the United States.

Though the state's economy has traditionally had an agricultural base, by 1995 only about 9 percent of all Nebraskans worked in agricultural jobs. In an effort to keep the land in the hands of families, in 1982 residents approved a constitutional amendment banning further corporate farming, except by family members.

By far the majority of the state's 1.6 million people live in the eastern third of the state. Omaha is a telecommunications industry center, Lincoln an educational mecca. The state's unemployment rate was the lowest in the nation—3.1 percent or lower annually—from 1989 to 1995. By 1995 the state struggled not to provide enough jobs but to provide enough workers for the available positions.

Nebraska has been fighting a "brain drain"; young, educated individuals are leaving the region, particularly the rural areas. Nebraska economic development officials have worked to address this problem by accomplishing a fourfold objective: keep people in the state, attract new employees, entice large companies, and assist small but growing businesses. The Federal Reserve Bank branch in Kansas City estimated that the brain drain cost Nebraska about $246 million each year in personal income between 1985 and 1990.

For rural areas the situation is more personal at times. Take for example Allen Adair, who in 1988 was thirty years old, single, and wanting a wife. He lived in Amelia, population four—as Adair put it, "just me and Aggie and Vida and Vida's son, Bob." The younger of the two women, Aggie, was eighty; the nearest community where Adair might find companionship was O'Neill, forty miles away, where the ratio of single men to single women was ten to one.

The population declined in 77 percent of Nebraska towns from 1980 to 1992. In fact, the frontier in Nebraska now is nearly as large as it was in 1890. Then Nebraska had nearly 41,000 square miles of frontier (land with fewer than six residents per square mile); now it has just over 36,000 square miles, according to a study by Rutgers University professor Frank Popper and his wife, Deborah. The Poppers proposed the radical idea that the people living in the frontier regions of the Great Plains be relocated so the area could be turned into a preserve called Buffalo Commons. That plan went over in the West like a lead balloon, as people who have worked the land for generations vigorously voiced their disgust with what they consider a ridiculous notion.

The Omaha Smelting Works in 1906, located on the bank of the Missouri River. The company remains in business in the 1990s. —Wyoming State Museum, Stimson Collection

Although the loss of young people hasn't slowed significantly, some areas of the state are starting to see slight growth, as city dwellers concerned about high crime move to smaller communities. In the central Nebraska town of Anselmo, the *Washington Post* and the *Sunday (Portland) Oregonian* reported in November 1995, the only crime in three years occurred when three dogs killed a poodle.

For our purposes, Nebraska has been divided into five regions: Lewis and Clark Country, River Country, Oregon Trail Country, Sandhills Country, and Panhandle Country.

Lewis and Clark Country

The Omaha and Ponca Indians occupied this land when the first Spanish and French explorers traveled up the Missouri River. Characterized by large, wooded hillsides near the Missouri River, the terrain flattens as it extends to the west. The region is bounded on the north and east by the Missouri River, on the south by the Platte River, and on the west by US 281.

This region has by far the largest number of residents. It is dominated by Omaha, headquarters of the Union Pacific Railroad. That community's early history was tied to agriculture through the Union Stockyards, once the nation's busiest livestock auction, and a plethora of packing plants and food industry businesses. Now it is a telecommunications center, hosts major cultural and sporting events, and remains the center of operations for the Union Pacific.

The Winnebago, Omaha, Ponca, and Santee Sioux tribes live on reservations in this section of Nebraska. Most of the land outside the Omaha metropolitan area is used for farming and ranching.

River Country

Southeastern Nebraska is River Country, bounded on the east by the Missouri, the north by the Platte, the west and southwest by US 34 and the Little Blue River, and the south by Kansas. The Omaha and Otoe Indians claimed this land historically. The Sauk and Fox tribes moved in later and remain on a tiny reservation near Preston. The Iowa tribe also has a reservation in the southeast fingertip of the region, near Rulo.

This region settled early. As soon after 1854 as allowed by the Kansas-Nebraska Act, town boomers started building communities along the Missouri. Both Nebraska City and Brownville played pivotal and important roles in the development of Nebraska. Lincoln, the state capital, is not near any river but lies in the vicinity of an early-day salt deposit that developers thought might spawn an important industry. Lincoln is the state's second-largest city (behind Omaha), and on days when the University of Nebraska Huskers play football, the stadium itself (capacity: 72,700) becomes the state's third-largest city.

There is great diversity among the people in River Country, from the farmers along the Platte to the professors in Lincoln. It is and always has been a virtual melting pot. Located just a river away from slaveholding Missouri during its formative years, this region had both pro- and anti-slavery settlers. Czechs, Germans, Poles, and immigrants from many other countries claimed homesteads after 1862. The region has a variety of physical attributes, too, including the flat fertile bottomlands along the Platte, the wooded hills near the Missouri, and the gently rolling acres along the Nemaha and Blue Rivers.

Oregon Trail Country

Besides the Native Americans and a limited number of explorers, fur trappers, and traders, few people saw any of Nebraska until 1843, when the great overland migration toward Oregon began. That year marked the start of the mass movement west as travelers left Independence, Missouri, headed toward Oregon. They entered present-day Nebraska along the Little Blue River, which they followed to a point south of present-day Hastings; then they continued northwest until they struck the Platte River, which they followed the remainder of their time in Nebraska.

Oregon Trail Country is bounded on the south by Kansas, on the west by Colorado, on the north by the Platte River, and on the east by US 34 and the Little Blue River. The general route of the Oregon Trail was also used by the Pony Express during its short run in 1860–61 and later by the Creighton Transcontinental Telegraph. Along the north side of the Platte River ran the Mormon Trail pioneered by Brigham Young and his followers in 1847 as they headed toward their Zion in Utah.

Some of the greatest herds of buffalo roamed in Oregon Trail Country, and thousands died at the hands of buffalo hunters like Texas Jack Omohundro, Doc Carver, and the greatest buffalo hunter of them all (at least in *his* eyes), William F. "Buffalo Bill" Cody. Those men nearly exterminated the species; later they helped to perpetuate the myth of the West in Buffalo Bill's Wild West Show and Congress of Rough Riders, which started in 1881 in North Platte.

The Texas Cattle Trail left its mark through this country as cowboys moved hundreds of thousands of head north to the railhead at Ogallala and beyond to pastures in Nebraska, Montana, and Wyoming.

Sandhills Country

The largest territory described in this book, the Sandhills cover some 18,000 square miles of rolling hill country. The stabilized dunes are held in place by a natural grass. Thousands of buffalo once roamed here, and both the Pawnee and the Sioux tribes lived here for generations. The Sioux traveled along the rivers that roll through the Sandhills to reach and plunder the villages of the Pawnees, who lived in permanent villages and tended cornfields long before the Sioux moved into the region. The two tribes quickly became bitter enemies. When the U.S. Army moved into Nebraska, the Pawnees formed an alliance with it to get protection from the hostile Sioux; the Pawnee Scouts, part of a regiment commanded by Capt. Frank North, became the first Native Americans to scout for the army.

The Sandhills were among the last portions of Nebraska to settle. Initially, homesteaders thought that sandy, grass-covered region had little value. But after cattle started moving north on the Texas Trail, cattlemen put their animals on those rolling hills, whose rich grasses had nurtured buffalo for centuries. The most infamous event in Nebraska's history played out in the Sandhills as powerful free-range cattlemen fought smaller homesteaders. After cattleman Print Olive led a lynch party that hanged Ami Ketchum and Luther Mitchell, someone set the bodies on fire, making Nebraska notorious as the "Man-Burner State."

The region is still primarily ranching country, with isolated homes and few towns. The military had stations along the Loup River at Fort Hartsuff and near the Niobrara River at Fort Niobrara, but only one engagement of any consequence between Native Americans and the military occurred in the region: the Battle of the Blowout, north of Fort Hartsuff. The fort primarily existed to protect homesteaders and settlers.

This section of the state is bordered on the south by the Platte River, on the east by US 281, on the north by South Dakota, and on the west by Nebraska 61. It is the region that has been least affected by development from white settlers. Although ranchers have built their homes and run cattle on the ground, in most cases they have caused little change to the natural environment.

Panhandle Country

Native Americans lived in Nebraska's panhandle for centuries before any European explorers saw the region. They butchered buffalo at a site in the extreme northwest corner of the state some 10,000 years ago, and more recently they lived along the White River. Fur traders, particularly those who dealt in buffalo hides rather then beaver pelts, did a brisk business from the 1840s until the 1870s. During the same period, the overland emigrants crossed through this area. They called it the "Valley of Monuments" for its unusual landforms, which they named Courthouse Rock, Jail Rock, and Chimney Rock.

Some of the final dramas in the Plains Indian wars occurred in this region. The Sioux received their first treaty annuities at agencies along the North Platte River, had other agencies along the White River, and negotiated the sale of their lands in the Black Hills here. One of the main routes to the Black Hills goldfields crossed these western lands, and Cheyenne Indians made their final bid for freedom in an 1879 outbreak from Fort Robinson.

Panhandle Country is bounded by Colorado on the south, Wyoming on the west, South Dakota on the north, and Nebraska 61 on the east. It is the most rugged of all Nebraska land, with the Wildcat Hills south of Scottsbluff and the beginnings of Pine Ridge in the northwest.

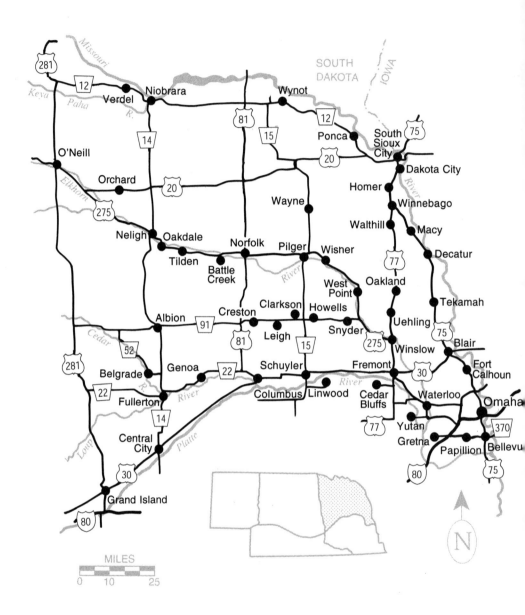

MILES

0   10   25

N

PART 1

LEWIS AND CLARK COUNTRY

THE ROLLING HILL COUNTRY along the Missouri River and the fertile farmland along the North Platte and Elkhorn Rivers are a microcosm of Nebraska. The state's largest metropolitan area dominates the region and always has, its industrial development progressing from fur trading posts, livestock markets, and packing plants to contemporary businesses such as insurance and telemarketing. The region along the Missouri River served the Spanish, French, and Americans who sought fur farther west and traded it at posts strategically placed along the western bank of the Missouri.

Meriwether Lewis and William Clark explored the region for the United States in 1804, meeting with native tribesmen in a council several miles north of the future site of Omaha. The state's northeastern boundary from Kansas to South Dakota is a part of the Lewis and Clark Trail. For this reason, I have designated northeastern Nebraska Lewis and Clark Country. Its northern, eastern, and southern borders are marked by the Missouri and the Platte, and the western boundary is formed by US 281, which extends from Grand Island due north to Spencer.

Long before the trappers and traders came to the region, it provided sustenance for indigenous people. The Pawnees lived along the Platte River, arriving by about 1500 and establishing villages where they could raise crops and, later, race their horses. The Omaha Indians claimed the use of land all along the Missouri. The Ponca tribe eventually ranged in extreme northeastern Nebraska as well. In later times, the Woodlands tribes (the Santee Sioux and Winnebagos) were forced from their native lands and received reservation territory in Nebraska's northeast corner. The Pawnees eventually dominated the western part of the region.

The earliest fur trade in the West centered on the rivers. French, Spanish, and American trappers went up the Missouri in boats or on foot to the western fur country. The Spanish traders also traveled overland to meet with Native Americans at locations within present-day Nebraska. They shipped their take downstream to markets in St. Louis and points east. Early-day entrepreneurs established a number of trading posts at strategic locations in the 1800s. The earliest operations in Lewis and Clark Country included James Mackay's post near the mouth of the Platte River, which he opened in 1795, and his subsequent Fort Carlos IV, near present-day Homer. Manuel Lisa started a post in 1813, and Cabanne's Post began operations in 1822. As the fur trade escalated, it became clear that conflicts could occur, and the U.S. War Department established its first western outpost at Cantonment Missouri in 1819. That site became Fort Atkinson a year later.

Two decades later the western fur trade was in decline, but settlers' interest in the western country was just beginning. Although most emigrants who headed toward Oregon and California after 1843 followed trails through southern Nebraska, some pioneers after 1855 followed the Platte, known as the Moonshell by the western Lakota and Brulé Sioux, on a route that became known as the Ox-Bow Trail.

In 1846 Brigham Young, leader of the Church of Jesus Christ of Latter-day Saints (the Mormon Church), led his people west from Nauvoo, Illinois, to escape persecution. Upon reaching the area of present-day Council Bluffs, Iowa, Young established a town known as Kanesville and negotiated with the Omaha Indians, who controlled the country to the west of the Missouri. Upon reaching an agreement with the Omaha tribe, Young and his followers crossed the river to establish Winter Quarters (a settlement now known as Florence). Some 600 people died during the late summer and harsh winter, and the rest were told they couldn't remain on Omaha Indian lands, so the Mormons retraced their steps to the eastern bank of the Missouri. In 1847 Young led his people along the north bank of the Platte River, on a route roughly followed by today's US 30, establishing communities at various sites and planting crops that would be harvested by other Mormons following the trail later in the year.

In 1854 Congress authorized the creation of Nebraska Territory. Settlement followed the rivers. By then, the eastern Nebraska Indians had relinquished most of their lands, retreating to reservations that included only a small fraction of the area they once claimed. The Pawnees were confined on land near Genoa on the Loup River. By 1865 the Omaha and Winnebago tribes shared land bordering the Missouri in the northeastern part of the state. The Santee Sioux, meanwhile, had been expelled from Minnesota after an uprising in

1862 and, after a series of temporary relocations, wound up in northern Nebraska, where they remain on a small reservation at Niobrara.

We will begin our exploration of Lewis and Clark Country in the south, at Omaha, then travel west and north.

Omaha Metropolitan Area

OMAHA

Nebraska's largest city owes its existence to fur traders who established posts at sites within today's metropolitan area. It is a blue-collar town, a city of the heartland dominated by livestock interests—the ranchers who shipped their cattle, hogs, and sheep to Omaha and the food producers who slaughtered that same stock and processed it at some of the nation's biggest packing companies. Early in Omaha's history the livestock giants included Swift, Armour, and Cudahy; today the industry is dominated by such companies as ConAgra, headquartered near the old stockyard, with its still-weekly sales, and the now-abandoned buildings and plants of predecessors and competitors.

Perhaps the most revolutionary food item to come out of Omaha started in the 1950s when Swanson Foods began packaging its trademark TV dinners. That industry grew rapidly, as viewers across the country settled in to watch *Bonanza, Gunsmoke,* or *To Tell the Truth* while dining on Swanson delicacies. Other companies soon saw the potential and began making their own version of convenience dinners.

But back to Omaha's beginnings.

The city takes its name from the Indian tribe that lived here when Lewis and Clark passed through at the beginning of their expedition in 1804. They reported seeing a hill with the remains of two hundred Indian houses on it. Some historians suggest those houses stood on the bluffs of present-day Omaha. The Omahas saw many visitors from France and Spain as those nations attempted to establish trade along the Missouri River in the eighteenth century. Lewis and Clark were among the first Americans in the region. They were followed in 1810 by the overland Astorians, who visited the area en route to the Pacific Coast in an effort to become a competitive force in the western fur trade. The river served as the primary means of travel in those days. Fur trappers and traders followed it to the western beaver country and used it to transport furs back from the mountains. Several fur trading posts operated in this region.

In 1819 Maj. Stephen Long led an expedition across the Great Plains to the foot of the Rocky Mountains. He convinced governmental leaders to authorize construction of a steamboat, the *Western Engineer,* to aid in the explorations. Constructed in Pittsburgh and brought down the Ohio and up the Mississippi and Missouri Rivers, the *Western Engineer* may have been the first of its kind to reach Nebraska. Its carved bow resembled a dragon, and a short smokestack belched black smoke from the dragon's mouth. That image frightened the Omaha Indians, who reportedly believed that "the White man is a bad man, he keeps the spirit of fire chained and forces the spirit to paddle his boats."

Long's party of painters, biologists, and geologists had a military escort as they traveled the Missouri to the Council Bluffs (not to be confused with Council Bluffs, Iowa), which they reached on September 17, 1819. They established a winter camp in the vicinity of Omaha and in the spring of 1820 abandoned the steamboat, traveling overland to find the sources of both the Platte and Red Rivers. Not long after Long's explorations concluded, the U.S. fur trade escalated; in the 1820s fur traders developed additional posts along the Missouri near present-day Omaha. The lands on which they did business belonged to the Native Americans.

The Omaha tribe negotiated its first treaty with the United States at Portage des Sioux in July 1815, allowing the government to have a say in tribal affairs. Ten years later the Omahas signed another treaty at Council Bluffs in which U.S. officials guaranteed them protection from more aggressive Indian tribes to the west. In that document the Omahas agreed not to sell any ammunition to "hostile" tribes, and they authorized the government to prosecute tribal members for any criminal offenses. In 1830 the Prairie du Chien treaty went into effect, under which the entire Omaha, Sauk, and Fox tribes, and certain bands of the Otoe, Missouria, Sioux, and Iowa tribes, ceded their territorial claims east of the Missouri River in what is now Iowa. Prairie du Chien established a reservation in southeastern Nebraska for mixed-blood members of those tribes.

Native Americans lived in several types of housing, as this camp of Big Bear shows. —Nebraska State Historical Society

Railroad tracks extended along the riverfront in Omaha, providing access to a variety of industries. —Wyoming State Museum, Stimson Collection

By 1852 land speculators gathered on the east bank of the Missouri River at Council Bluffs and supported efforts to negotiate a treaty with the tribes of the soon-to-be Nebraska Territory so they could cross the river and begin settlement. Those speculators cooled their heels for a full two years before the Omahas relinquished all their land except a 300,000-acre tract along the Missouri River. The treaty authorized the government to begin surveying a portion of the reservation for distribution to individuals. By 1854 the Indians had sold their land, Congress had approved the Kansas-Nebraska Act, and Nebraska Territory and the city of Omaha were officially on the map.

But that wasn't the end of the issue for the Omahas. In 1865 the tribe sold the northern portion of its reservation to the government, which in turn gave it to the Winnebagos, and in 1872 the Omahas sold another 50,000 acres on the western part of their reservation. As members of the eastern Woodlands culture, the Omahas in Nebraska found themselves caught between white settlers and the more aggressive, often hostile Plains Indians. Although they attempted to adopt the social customs of the white people, the Omahas faced great hardship because they didn't always receive the government annuities promised to them, and the ever-increasing numbers of white settlers significantly affected the amount of wild game available for hunting.

Construction of a ninety-five-foot fill across Papio Valley on the Union Pacific Railroad near Omaha, 1906. —Wyoming State Museum, Stimson Collection

Union Pacific Railroad

It is fair to say that Omaha is what it is today because President Abraham Lincoln signed the Pacific Railway Act in 1862. Although early speculation raced wildly about the route of the transcontinental railroad authorized by that act, by December 2, 1863, it was fairly clear that the Union Pacific's starting point would be on the east bank of the Missouri at Council Bluffs. But a bridge across the river at Omaha ensured the city's status and future growth. The bands of steel eventually marked a course along the Platte River across Nebraska, and the Union Pacific established Omaha as its headquarters. That placed the city at the forefront in railroad expansion and made it a transportation hub. Omaha already had steamboat, freight, and ferry services on the Missouri, and the Union Pacific provided a method to move people and products overland.

Joseph Barker Jr., an immigrant from England, wrote his mother on July 27, 1866, "For myself, my faith in the future of Omaha and the permanence of the railroad here grows. . . . I went over the town and railway improvements last week and this, and I found very large and important improvements going on at the Railway." The Union Pacific provided industrial jobs and transportation opportunities. The

Homestead Act had been approved in 1862 as well, and after construction of the railroad in 1865 many people rode the trains west in search of land. Furthermore, the line meant farmers and ranchers had a way to ship their produce and livestock to market. After the Civil War, cattlemen drove hundreds of thousands of head of livestock north from Texas to Kansas, Nebraska, Colorado, Wyoming, and Montana. They also pushed the cattle to the railroad terminal points in both Kansas and Nebraska. At western sites such as Ogallala, cowboys loaded their herds onto trains bound for eastern cities and the Omaha Livestock Market, one of the biggest enterprises of its kind in the United States.

In 1881 the Union Pacific built a steel-framed freight house not far from the Missouri to serve the growing industrial city. The rail company shipped coal over the line from mines in the west, particularly Wyoming, and enjoyed tremendous success. By 1890, however, the tide had turned. Mining operations slowed, and the Union Pacific faced tremendous financial difficulties. UP officials under the leadership of Sidney Dillon struggled to place the line on solid footing by cutting costs drastically. The line ceased construction and development. It laid off employees and sought an infusion of new money. But even those efforts couldn't turn the tide. The line survived by shipping the products of farmers and ranchers and by selling its land grant holdings; by the early 1890s it had disposed of some eight million of the eleven million acres it once held.

In May 1891 UP president Dillon rode the rails himself to view the country and see what the future might hold. Springtime in Nebraska is green, a period of growth and revitalization of the land, and Dillon felt encouraged as he telegraphed UP cohort Jay Gould: "The corn is up and is being cultivated, and the barley is at least knee high. Country never looked finer at this time of year than it does today. . . . This means more business for the Union Pacific than it can do when the crop is harvested." Farther west he sent a similar report to Gould: "Country looking fine and well filled with cattle. . . . Every indication that we shall have good business."

What Dillon failed to recognize, or chose to ignore, was the depression creeping into the economy and the effect it would have upon agriculture and mining. Drought conditions in the middle part of the decade and the Panic of 1893 further affected agricultural production, and shipments of those commodities quickly started declining. By 1897 the handwriting was clearly on the wall, and on July 1, 1897, a syndicate led by Edward H. Harriman purchased the Union Pacific line between Omaha and Ogden, Utah. The purchase took place at a receivership auction in Omaha in the old freight building, which had been the earliest Union Pacific Depot, known as The Cowshed. The freight house remained in use until 1977, when it became a storage area and a practice location for a drum and bugle corps. In 1989 the Union Pacific modernized its entire system and refurbished The Cowshed into the multimillion-dollar Harriman Dispatch Center. The renovation cost $50 million, nearly as much as Harriman and his partners paid for the entire Union Pacific line at its bankruptcy auction in 1897—just over $58 million.

By 1995 the Union Pacific had 20,000 employees and an annual payroll of more than $100 million. The Harriman Dispatch Center features high technology. The computerized dispatching center is located within an eighteen-inch concrete bunker, making it virtually invulnerable to tornadoes and floods. It has its own emergency electrical system and diesel generators for additional backup to operate the communications fiber-optic systems. Even so, when the great flood of 1993 placed railroads traveling through Kansas City, Missouri, in jeopardy, the Harriman Center faced a crisis of its own. The flooding along the Missouri and Mississippi Rivers didn't threaten the Harriman facility itself, but the volume of crisis calls taxed the center to its limit. The Union Pacific set up a command dispatch post in the conference room above the concrete bunker. There groups of UP officers working twelve-hour shifts oversaw rail routing.

In more routine situations Harriman Center dispatchers sit at computer consoles and watch train and weather movements throughout the UP system. The center has 20,000 miles of railroad lines—nearly the entire central and western United States—graphically displayed in one room. Green lines mark moving trains, red lines depict halted trains, and blue lights indicate track repairs. Omaha dispatchers signal trains whether to stop or go and monitor traffic at North Platte, Nebraska, the world's largest "hump station," or freight corridor. Like air traffic controllers, train dispatchers have at their fingertips the most sophisticated equipment. However, rail dispatchers can't change the altitude of the individual trains, making split-second timing a critical element of their job; one error could cause significant, even deadly, disturbance to rail traffic.

Among the items in the Union Pacific museum in downtown Omaha is the Lincoln Car, used in 1865 as part of the funeral train for President Lincoln. It is furnished with the original oak desk, bookcase, and reading chair that were in it at the time of Lincoln's assassination. It is significant that the UP museum has the Lincoln Car, since the nation's sixteenth president made the railroad possible when he signed the Railway Act in 1862.

Union Station, Omaha, in 1906. —Wyoming State Museum, Stimson Collection

Stately old Union Station now houses the Western Heritage Museum. Inside the white marble building, weathered wood benches sit upon a checkerboard simulated-marble floor. The walls of simulated travertine stone are trimmed in painted silver leaf and imitation patent leather, and murals painted in 1930 by Los Angeles artist Joseph W. Keller depict various stages of the development of transportation.

Across the tracks from Union Station is the equally impressive Burlington Station, no longer in use but grand nevertheless. Thomas R. Kimball, one of Nebraska's most well-known architects, designed Burlington Station in the Greek Revival style. Completed in 1898, Burlington Station underwent extensive remodeling in 1930. Nearby, dwarfed by the historic structures, is the modern Amtrak station, a nondescript building. The contrast between Union and Burlington Stations and the Amtrak station clearly shows the decline of rail travel in the United States.

Fort Omaha

The first troops stationed in the Military District of Nebraska in 1862 lived in rented quarters, but by October 1864 the availability of such housing was so limited that the army authorized a company-sized post at Omaha, with the first wood buildings constructed and ready for use by November. When the Civil War ended, the military once again used rented facilities for housing and in 1865 sold the post

Union Station, Omaha, April 1995, is now home of the Western Heritage Museum.

quarters. The use of rented buildings continued until 1868, when Gen. William T. Sherman authorized construction of "cheap barracks for one regiment" on a parallelogram-shaped eighty-acre parcel of land. Construction was completed by November 1868, and the facility took the name Sherman Barracks, which was soon changed to Omaha Barracks.

The frame buildings all faced inward upon a rectangular parade ground, with the post headquarters, guardhouse, bakery, storehouses, and sutler's store on the east side. The post had ten company-sized barracks, a hospital, icehouse, quarters for laundresses, and housing for the married enlisted men. In 1878 the post gained three new brick buildings for officers' housing. The first structure completed was the commanding general's home, first occupied by Gen. George Crook and still known as Crook House. It now operates as a tourist attraction. General Crook served at Fort Omaha as commander of the Department of the Platte from 1875 to 1882 and again from 1886 to 1888.

The post's name changed again in December 1878, this time to Fort Omaha, and by 1886 it had thirty-eight buildings. The "cheap barracks" held up until 1896, when the army abandoned the fort, saying it was inadequate for present needs. The only post occupation between 1896 and 1905 occurred during the Spanish-American War of 1898, when the 2nd Nebraska Regiment used the area as a staging location for troops. From 1909 until the end of World War II, Fort Omaha once again housed troops, and the war department replaced the "cheap barracks" with brick structures.

Fort Omaha's soldiers patrolled the streets of early-day Omaha and helped keep the peace during the infamous trial of Print Olive and Fred Fisher for their part in the hanging and burning of homesteaders Ami Ketcham and Luther Mitchell (see page 273). The troops also helped squelch a prison riot in Lincoln, the 1919 courthouse riot in Omaha, and the Pullman strike of 1894.

Standing Bear v. Crook

Perhaps the most important event associated with Fort Omaha is the 1879 trial of Ponca chief Standing Bear, in which a court ruled that an Indian is a "person" in the eyes of the law and thus is protected by constitutional guarantees of personal liberty. (Indians didn't earn citizenship rights until after World War I.)

In 1858 the Ponca Indians entered a treaty, which the U.S. government termed "a very beneficial treaty with the Ponca tribe." The pact may have benefited the United States, but it certainly had lasting repercussions on the Poncas, forcing them to struggle for their food and their very survival.

In 1876 the government ordered the Poncas under Standing Bear and other chiefs to Indian territory (Oklahoma). "We got ready and started, wishing first to visit the Omaha reserve, but this was not allowed us," the Ponca chiefs said in a statement published in a Sioux City, Iowa, newspaper. "After some days we reached the country of the Osages, and looked over the country and found it stony and broken, and not a country we thought we could make a living in. We saw the Osages there, and they were without shirts, their skin burned, and their hair stood up as if it had not been combed since they were little children. We did not wish to sink so low as they seemed to be."

After the inspection trip the Ponca chiefs did not want to move to Oklahoma. They had to make their own way home to Nebraska, where they intended to remain, but the following year the government ordered a forced relocation to Oklahoma, where many of the Poncas died. Unable to bear the hardships forced upon his tribe, in early 1879 Standing Bear broke away from the reservation in Oklahoma to return to Nebraska, where his people sought refuge with their friends and relatives, the Omahas.

At Fort Omaha, General Crook immediately received orders to take the Poncas into custody and return them to Oklahoma. As Crook's men prepared to arrest the Indians, *Omaha World-Herald* editor Thomas Tibbles, a former abolitionist crusader in Kansas, heard of the plan and vowed to fight "for exactly the same principals [sic] for which he [had] fought twenty-four years ago, *the equality of all men before the law,*"

Kay Graber wrote in her introduction to *The Ponca Chiefs: An Account of the Trial of Standing Bear.*

Tibbles—perhaps with the behind-the-scenes support of General Crook—organized the fight for Standing Bear, arranging for attorneys to file a writ of habeas corpus on behalf of the Ponca chief against General Crook. The writ centered on the issue of whether Indian people had the same basic civil liberties as all other Americans. Attorneys John L. Webster and A. J. Poppleton represented Standing Bear (Ma-chu-nah-zah).

As the Poncas languished in the Omaha Barracks, prisoners of Crook's military, the Omaha tribe came to their aid, offering to share their reservation and to support the Poncas until they could provide for themselves. A letter signed by twenty members of the Omaha tribe dated April 21, 1879, spelled out the Omahas' concern for the Poncas: "They are our brothers and our sisters, our uncles and our cousins, and although we are called savages we feel that sympathy for our persecuted brethren that should characterize Christians, we are willing to share what we possess with them if they can only be allowed to return and labor, improve and provide for themselves where they may live in peace, enjoy good health, and the opportunity of educating their children up to a higher state of civilization."

After hearing the testimony on both sides of the case, U.S. District Judge Elmer S. Dundy on May 12, 1879, filed his opinion in the matter, writing:

> The reasoning advanced in support of my views, leads me to conclude:
> First. That an *Indian* is a PERSON within the meaning of the laws of the United States. . . .
> Second. That General George Crook . . . has the custody of the realtors under color of the authority of the United States, and in violation of the laws thereof.
> Third. That no rightful authority exists for removing by force any of the realtors to the Indian Territory. . . .
> Fourth. That the Indians possess the inherent right of expatriation as well as the more fortunate white race, and have the inalienable right to "*life, liberty* and the pursuit of happiness," so long as they obey the laws and do not trespass on forbidden ground. And
> Fifth. Being restrained of liberty under color of authority of the United States, and in violation of the laws thereof, the realtors must be discharged from custody, and it is so ordered.

Fort Omaha Balloon School

In 1909 the signal corps at Fort Omaha added a balloon school and balloon plant to their facilities at the post, with the first balloon flight in 1909. During World War I, 16,000 men learned balloon operations at Fort Omaha–Florence Field, with training underway in Florence and the region between Florence and Fort Calhoun to the north. The balloons used highly flammable hydrogen gas, and accidents were common. One incident injured twenty-two men. Earle Reynolds of Florence related this story in the 1988 Florence historical souvenir newspaper: "There was a red-headed kid who was bedding down one of the balloons one night and he was putting sand bags on the ropes holding the balloon. He somehow rubbed his head in the ropes, causing sparks which ignited the balloon, killing the young soldier as well as four or five others."

During World War II, the Japanese released incendiary devices—balloon bombs—intended to travel eastward on air currents and land on the United States mainland. The Japanese launched 9,000 balloon bombs, each some thirty-three feet in diameter and carrying an anti-personnel bomb suspended in a ballast-and-ordnance-dropping mechanism. The devices did reach the mainland, landing in Nebraska and other western and midwestern states, but the news media cooperated in maintaining silence about them, denying the Japanese any information that the balloons had reached the United States. The media reported about the bombs only after a woman and five children in Oregon were killed by one.

One Japanese balloon bomb exploded in Omaha April 18, 1945, at a location near Fiftieth Street and Underwood Avenue. Although the *World-Herald* didn't report any information until August 15, 1945, people of the region knew about the balloon bombs; the word spread via the grapevine and through church groups and service organizations.

By 1947 the army had declared Fort Omaha surplus property, and the navy took it over for use as a reserve training center. In 1973 the defense department again declared it excess to their needs. The site is now the home of Metro-Tech College, which uses several of the fort's earliest buildings.

Racial Conflict

By 1880, fully one-third of Omaha's population came from other countries. Germans, Swedes, Danes, Czechs, Irish, British, Scottish, Welsh, Canadians, Russian Jews, Poles, Australians, Italians, and Norwegians called the community home. That large number of ethnic groups gave the city great diversity, which can be an asset but sometimes leads to conflict. In 1891 blacks were the targets in many areas of Nebraska, while anti-Greek riots occurred in 1909. During World War I, Councils of Defense pressured German-Americans because of the perception they may have been sympathetic to their former homeland.

After World War I many black people settled in Omaha, and during the summer of 1919, as in 1891, race riots broke out. The worst conflagration occurred on September 28, 1919, when a crowd of thousands gathered in front of the courthouse and demanded the release of a black man, Will Brown, accused of attacking a white couple two days earlier. The mob harassed black people and set fire to the courthouse; at least two people were shot and killed, including one sixteen-year-old mob leader, Louis Young. When Mayor Ed Smith interceded, rioters attempted to lynch him. Supporters immediately rescued him, cutting him from the telegraph pole he'd been hanged from and taking him to a hospital. Eventually, as the courthouse burned, Will Brown fell into the hands of the rioting mob, and he was lynched; then his body was burned, tied behind an automobile, and dragged through the streets of Omaha. The riot lasted nine hours, and 1,800 federal and state troops had to be called in to enforce a martial-law decree.

The *Omaha World-Herald* won a Pulitzer Prize for its "Law and the Jungle" editorial after the riot, which drew attention to the city's misfortune and humiliation and the effects of inefficient government.

Weather Stories

Every Nebraska community has its tales of natural disaster, and Omaha is no exception. One of the earliest documented weather legends occurred in April 1881 when an ice dam on the Missouri River in South Dakota broke, sending a wall of water rushing downstream. At Omaha the muddy Missouri was five miles wide and twenty-four feet above low water, establishing a record that stood until 1952, when the river crested more than thirty feet above the usual low-water mark. For that flood, Omaha residents raised more than thirteen miles of levees in six days, while Nebraska Civil Defense director Sam W. Reynolds invoked martial law and commandeered supplies. In all, 1,500 army specialists directed the work of private citizens and troops until the water crested at 4 A.M. on Friday, April 18.

On Easter Sunday in 1913 a powerful storm system swept across the heartland. Milton Tabor, editor of the *Topeka Daily Capital,* was on a picnic when a tornado descended upon him. "It was an enormous hollow cylinder, bright inside with lightning flashes, but black as blackest night all around. The noise was like 10 million bees, plus a roar that beggars description," he wrote. That tornado system wasn't spent when it left the Topeka area. A twister touched down in Omaha later in the

ACTUAL TORNADO CLOUD OMAHA
MARCH 23rd 1913
MEGEATH STATIONERY CO. OMAHA

One of the most destructive tornadoes ever to hit Omaha struck on March 23, 1913. The powerful storm caused significant damage and killed or injured many people. —Nebraska State Historical Society

day, cutting a path seven miles long and 1,000 feet wide, destroying some 2,000 homes, and leaving at least 140 people dead.

Two major calamities occurred in 1975. One, a snowstorm, dumped eleven inches of snow and had fifty- to sixty-mile-per-hour winds, creating drifts up to twenty feet high. Fourteen people in Nebraska died. The second, a tornado, destroyed 2,459 buildings, making it the worst disaster since 1913. Because of early warning systems only 3 people died, although at least 135 were injured.

Omaha patrolman David Campbell had one of the wildest rides of the storm, driving down 72nd Street with the tornado right beside him. The *World-Herald* reported on Campbell's experience: "It was awful at Pacific (Street). The air was filled, cars were sailing about, the (electrical) lines were flying. I thought I was going to be electrocuted. Everything lit up blue for a hundred feet around."

The Cudahy Kidnapping

Pat Crowe was only seventeen when he started working as a butcher in Omaha, but he and his partner didn't tend to the business end of the operation, often letting their customers fall behind in payments. Eventually they couldn't meet their own financial obligations and closed the operation. Crowe blamed much of his financial hardship on competition from Edward A. Cudahy, a meatpacking magnate who had a nearby retail store. At age twenty, Crowe started working for Cudahy, but his employment ended when company officials determined he'd been dipping into the till.

Crowe then went on a crime spree. Reports came from Denver and Kansas City about his activities, including one incident where he took diamonds worth $6,000. But Crowe never forgot about the butcher shop he lost as a result of competition from Cudahy, and he vowed to get his revenge one day.

A week before Christmas 1900, Crowe allegedly launched his plan. That night fifteen-year-old Edward Cudahy Jr. delivered some books to Mrs. C. B. Rustin at her home three blocks from his own. He failed to return home as expected, although his dog made the trek without a problem, and by midnight his father had become so worried that he contacted the police. The following morning Cudahy coachman Andrew Gray found a ransom note in the front yard of the family home. A later telephone call confirmed the situation.

News of the kidnapping quickly dominated Omaha, particularly after the local newspapers reported on the note: "Your son is safe. We have him and will take good care of him, and will return him to you in consideration of the payment of $25,000. We mean business."

The kidnappers posed as sheriffs, grabbing Eddie (as the boy was known) as he returned from delivering the books. They took him to a location in South Omaha, where they chained him with leg irons and fed him coffee and crackers. Meanwhile, his father put the ransom money inside a white wheat sack and dropped it five miles out of town on West Center Road near a lantern tied with black and white ribbons. By early the morning of December 20, with the ransom successfully delivered, young Eddie Cudahy was back at his home.

Reporters found it first, but authorities quickly identified the house where Eddie had been held. Strewn about inside were cigar stubs and burned matches. In checking out the house, police found it had been rented for $5 a month by the James Schneiderwinds to a man using the alias James L. Conner—which happened to be the name of Crowe's brother-in-law. Crowe quickly became the prime suspect. He was variously reported to be in Chicago, in Rhode Island, in Missouri, on an ocean liner, and at Nantucket Beach. Cudahy offered a reward for the arrest and conviction of the person or persons responsible. If it involved only one man, Cudahy would pay $5,000, but the reward increased to $15,000 for two convictions and to $25,000 if three people were involved.

The reward offer, combined with flamboyant newspaper reports by the *Omaha Evening World-Herald*, the *Omaha Daily Bee*, and the *Omaha Daily News*, resulted in a flurry of tips for the police. Then the Cudahys received another threatening note, reported by the *Bee* December 30 and 31: "Cudhy: If you value the boy's life at the price of a bulet you will withdraw the reward at once and let well enough alone. If you don't do this we will finish the job with a bulet. If any man whether guilty or inocent is ever arrested a bulet will close the boy's mouth. You will think of this warning when it is to late." Though he no doubt gave the note careful consideration, Cudahy didn't withdraw his reward offer, and he soon had support from the Omaha city council, which offered an even larger reward of $8,000 for one conviction.

Although by early 1901 the case centered on Crowe, the police didn't stop their investigation with him. In February they arrested James Callahan, a former Cudahy employee, whom Eddie Cudahy identified as one of his guards during the kidnapping. Even with Cudahy's identification, the jury returned a verdict of not guilty. The judge himself disagreed with that verdict, saying he could not "conceive of twelve intelligent men. . . [returning] a verdict of this kind."

It took authorities years to nab Crowe. He slipped into Omaha in the spring of 1905, gave an exclusive interview to a *World-Herald* reporter, then left before a capture could occur. The Nebraska city continued to draw him, however, and on September 6, 1905, he was involved in a gunfight on South 16th Street, wounding a policeman outside a saloon. Crowe escaped, but his luck ran out a month later when detectives arrested him in Butte, Montana, and returned with him to Omaha to face kidnapping charges in the five-year-old Cudahy case.

Crowe first faced charges for shooting police officer A. H. Jackson, but he won acquittal when it couldn't be determined who had fired the first shot. Then the Cudahy trial started. Those on the jury were primarily working men, which may have affected the outcome of the case; at the same time, Edward Cudahy and other meat packers were involved in a Chicago trial on a charge of restraint of trade, which affected blue-collar workers. Other factors played a part in the trial as well. The thin boy who had been kidnapped five years earlier had matured; by 1905 he stood more than six feet tall and had a deep voice and a commanding presence. Among the evidence presented was a letter written by Crowe to his family priest, Father Murphy of Vail, Iowa, in 1904. In that letter, according to a version published in the *Omaha World-Herald*, February 14, 1906, Crowe said, "I am guilty of the Cudahy affair. I am to blame for the whole crime. After it was over

I regretted my act and offered to return $21,000 to Mr. Cudahy, but he refused to take it."

In spite of the confession, the jury acquitted Crowe—an act that caused spectators in the courtroom of Judge A. L. Sutton to cheer. "Many believed the jury voted against Cudahy because of the feelings against the beef trust in the ongoing Chicago trial. The *World-Herald* commented that the jury saw Crowe as a 'modern Robin Hood' with Cudahy in the role of a modern baron," Garneth Oldenkamp Peterson wrote in "A Really Spectacular and Truly Named Desperado; Pat Crowe and the Cudahy Kidnapping Case," published in *Nebraska History*.

Omaha Stockyards

Most of the Omaha livestock yards are gone now, bulldozed under and turned into a shopping mall. The stately red-brick Livestock Exchange building has little traffic, although it houses a variety of offices; there's been discussion that it ought to be torn down. It has seen better days; upstairs offices are overheated during springtime, and the plaster on bathroom walls has fallen to the floor.

Outside, trucks back to chutes and disgorge their cargo of cattle, sheep, and hogs for weekly sales. Down under the sales pavilion, the darkened cattle pens contain isolated groups of animals. Herefords and Holsteins low over the weathered boards as Angus and crossbred cattle

View of South Omaha stockyards, 1906. —Wyoming State Museum, Stimson Collection

45

A yardman moves steers through the lot at the Omaha stockyards, April 1995.

Livestock Exchange Building, Union Stockyards, Omaha, April 1995.

mill in tiny lot sections. The sparrows fly under the concrete ceiling and around the dark gray concrete pillars that hold it in place.

To understand how the changes in custom and culture have affected the Omaha stockyards, it is necessary to realize what the area once was—site of the leading livestock auction in the nation.

The Union Stockyards Company started in 1876 under the management of John Smiley but failed two years later. Then W. A. Paxton formed two companies, Union Stockyards and Omaha Stockyards, which he operated in South Omaha until 1879, when he relocated to Council Bluffs, Iowa. The Omaha stockyards resurfaced in 1883 when Alexander Swan of Wyoming's Swan Land and Cattle Company organized the South Omaha Land Syndicate and the Union Stockyards Company. Swan persuaded Paxton to return to Omaha. The company supported development of slaughterhouses and packing plants, an industry that started in Omaha in 1871 when the Gresselman & Potter firm opened a pork-packing business. In 1885 Charles Kaufmann launched a packing plant, which he had managed by the George Hammond & Company. The industry quickly spawned other companies, including Fowler Brothers, Armour-Cudahy, Thomas J. Lipton, and Swift and Company.

The Omaha stockyards handled millions of head of stock annually, and by the 1950s two of every three dollars generated in Omaha came from agriculture, primarily from selling and packing meat. Union Stockyards once had 160 acres of buildings, paved pens, and alleys, with trade valued at more than $1 million a day. Livestock men from throughout Nebraska and many other western states shipped cattle to Omaha via the rails of the Union Pacific.

But ranchers who traditionally shipped to Omaha from distant places such as Idaho and Wyoming found after the 1970s that they could make a better profit by selling their stock closer to home. Rail shipments slowed and then ceased, and the railroads started hauling coal instead of cattle.

As the rail lines cut back on hauling livestock and in many cases abandoned spur routes that provided access for ranchers, livestock producers changed their business practices. They sold animals in video auctions, in which a video of their stock showed at a sale barn in some remote location. Or they hired trucks to ship animals to auctions located closer to home than Omaha.

The decline in business led to a subsequent reduction in Union Stockyards operations. By 1995 pen sales occurred on Mondays and Tuesdays only, with ring sales on Wednesdays. Much of the historic yard area is replaced by a shopping mall, and the rest appears only as a reminder of the heyday of Omaha's livestock industry.

The Swanson Foods Story

Seventeen-year-old Carl Swanson immigrated from Sweden in 1896. Upon arrival at Ellis Island, New York, he placed a sign about his neck: "Carl Swanson, Swedish. Send me to Omaha. I speak no English." The young man had $68, a small bundle of clothes, and plans to join his two sisters, Hanna and Cora, in Nebraska. Upon his arrival in Omaha, Carl first worked on a farm. He studied English, shorthand, typing, and bookkeeping at the YMCA and eventually attended Nebraska Business College.

Swanson subsequently had various jobs. He worked at a South Omaha grocery, at the Merchants Restaurant, and as a bookkeeper for Hanson & Company, where he came into contact with John P. Hjerpe. The two pooled their resources, took in Frank Ellison as a third partner, and started the Jerpe Commission Company. The company was intended to be named for Hjerpe, but the sign painter made a mistake, and the partners had little extra cash for a new sign, so they let it ride. That was 1900 and the beginning of a company that became an American food icon.

The three partners started their operation with one horse, one wagon, and a delivery boy. They had $456 in working capital. In 1905 the company incorporated. It remained dedicated to consignment of food products. The owners promised farmers the best available price and kept a percentage of the receipts as their share of the sale.

In 1918 Ellison died of influenza, and his one-third share reverted to the two other partners. By that time Swanson's dominant personality had begun to impact the business. Younger than Hjerpe by eighteen years, Swanson was more willing to take risks than the conservative elder partner. After World War I the company started full-scale food processing and began competing with the giants in the food industry.

In the meantime, Swanson married Caroline Rosine Gerock of Council Bluffs, Iowa, and they started their family, with sons Gilbert and Clarke and daughter Gretchen. As business expanded, it quickly became clear the heart of it lay with chickens, turkeys, and eggs. Swanson himself worked hard, and he expected the same from his employees. A sign in his office said, "Anybody Who Enjoys Working Hard Can Have a Hell of a Good Time in this Company."

Swanson appreciated a good day's labor and recognized employees who showed their dedication. When temporary employee Gladys Goodwin opened the switchboard fifteen minutes early during the Thanksgiving and Christmas rush period (known in the company as "turkey time"), Swanson noticed and hired her full-time. She remained with the company for thirty years.

In 1921 Swanson entered the butter business, purchasing a nine-story Omaha building and converting it into a creamery. The next year the company expanded its food processing program when it purchased the first of ten plants to pack poultry. Eventually the Swanson company had food-handling operations in twenty locations from coast to coast, including plants in Nebraska at Omaha, Oxford, Seward, Tecumseh, Fairbury, and Fremont. Other plants operated in Minnesota, Iowa, Colorado, Missouri, Arkansas, and California. By 1941 Swanson was known as the "butter king."

In 1928, Swanson bought out the interests of John Hjerpe, and the Jerpe Company became Swanson's. The depression challenged Swanson perhaps more than any other event in his business life, but he managed to weather the storm. As Omaha banker W. Dale Clark put it in Robert G. Phipps's book *The Swanson Story: When the Chicken Flew the Coop*:

> If people want to pay their debts they find a way to do it. They don't take the easy way and run.
> Some took bankruptcy or did not work as hard as they should have. Carl Swanson just worked harder. Things have not always been easy for the Swansons. Hard times brought out their strengths. I'm sure there were times when their credit was strained but nobody called their line. Everybody felt they were doing the best they could, and that inspired confidence.

Carl Swanson's sons followed him in the business, learning from the ground up. They started at the Omaha plant, scraping chicken manure from trays under the live animals and cleaning the pens. They checked the quality of eggs by inspecting them with a candle, one of the most boring occupations in which a person can engage. Eggs held up to a light—historically a candle—that show a cloudy look between the white and the yolk are of inferior quality. Candling also helps identify those that are partially incubated, because the inspector can see the beginnings of a chick.

Eventually Clarke and Gilbert attended college, then returned to the family business. By the time Gilbert attended a three-month course at Iowa State College in Ames (now Iowa State University) to learn more about butter making, sanitation, and bacterial control, the family firm was processing more butter in one location than any other producer in the world. Gilbert cut his management teeth in the Fayetteville, Arkansas, chicken operation. Most of the chickens he found upon arrival were scrawny, so Gilbert worked with the University of Arkansas College of Agriculture and Home Economics to help develop better animal husbandry practices and to teach chicken producers better ways to raise their stock.

Although the size of the chickens gradually improved, getting to that point was a painful process for Gilbert, who once wrote a letter of resignation to his father. However, his mother intercepted the letter and sent Clarke to Arkansas for moral support. Gilbert agreed to remain on the job, and by 1934 the Fayetteville plant became the country's number-one supplier of broilers. Another decade later the Arkansas operation became the most profitable branch in the company chain.

Clarke, meanwhile, started his management career at age twenty, taking over operations at the creamery in 1928. It wasn't a pleasant place to work. "The place absconded [*sic*] in noise and clatter and wet floors, and the heat was escalated by escaping steam. In addition the odor was overwhelmingly unpleasant," Phipps wrote. Chickens used to head to market as live cargo, hauled in crates in the back of uncovered wagons. Eventually they were transported to processing plants by the trainload in cars called "poultry Pullmans." By 1934 Carl Swanson believed the future of poultry operations involved eviscerating—or cleaning the entrails from—the birds before quick-freezing them.

The change in processing tactics meant the company had to employ new methods. Carl Swanson looked at Omaha's meatpacking industry for ideas. They sometimes claimed they used "everything from the hog except the squeal," and Swanson decided to follow suit. According to Phipps, the company sold chicken heads and feet to fish hatcheries and entrails to fertilizer plants. Mattress factories used feathers, and companies developing medicinal products utilized the oil sacs in the birds' tails.

In developing its reputation, Swanson had relied heavily upon eggs. Various plants graded, stored, shipped, and sold eggs. Later the company opened an egg-cracking plant, where the yolks and whites of each egg were separated. The yolks sold to companies for "sunshine cookies," and the whites went into mixes for angel food cake. Swanson started drying eggs, and during World War II about 15 percent of the company's egg production went into military rations. It's pretty clear how the men in the field felt about the eggs, Phipps reports:

> One soldier wrote: "I wish you would take some of your dried eggs, compare them with the dirty water from the Missouri River, and tell me which is which." Another comment was addressed simply to Mr. "Powdered Eggs" Swanson, Omaha, Nebraska, and it was equally blunt: "We would come over and get you now but Hitler is closer."

Swanson built much of his empire on turkeys, and by 1944 company plants processed 250,000 of the birds daily, dominating the turkey industry. That year the company changed its name to C. A. Swanson

& Sons. On October 9, 1949, Carl Swanson died, and the company management rested solely on the shoulders of his sons. They met their responsibility with confidence. The company built on chickens, turkeys, butter, and eggs took a step forward in the 1950s when the Swansons started to utilize the quick-freeze methods developed by Clarence Birdseye in the 1920s.

No single company can be credited with the development of convenience food, but Swanson Foods definitely played a major role. The initial success came with the company's development of chicken pot pie in 1950, followed by turkey pot pie and heat-and-serve meals. With great foresight, Clarke and Gilbert coined—and trademarked—the term "TV dinners." They even packaged their meals in trays resembling the front of a television set. The products hit the market in December 1953.

The first TV meal included a slice of turkey, cornbread dressing, thick gravy, fresh peas topped with butter, and whipped sweet potatoes. It sold for 98 cents and made life much easier for the many women who had remained in the workplace following World War II. When the turkey dinner became a resounding success, the Swansons launched their fried chicken dinner, and a food empire already on solid ground had an even more secure base.

Besides giving Americans dinners to eat in front of the television, the Swanson empire made other contributions to the nation, and specifically to Omaha. Carl Swanson helped fund a new building for the YMCA, and the Immanuel Medical Center in Omaha benefited from a Swanson contribution in 1956. More recently the Gretchen Swanson Family Foundation and the Gilbert C. Swanson Family Foundation have helped meet needs in Omaha. The Swanson Center for Nutrition went into operation in 1974, the first of its kind in the United States. Affiliated with the University of Nebraska and Creighton University medical schools, the center conducts research in nutrition, particularly that of young children and people at poverty level. The Swanson family pledged $1 million for the facility.

Other Faces of Omaha

Through the decades a number of events and personalities affected the Omaha story. In 1895 Ak-Sar-Ben formed as a charity to promote the best of the state with its own name taken from a backward spelling of Nebraska. The Ak-Sar-Ben remained a vital operation in Omaha a century later when discussion centered on whether to allow gambling at the facility.

The city hosted the Trans-Mississippi and International Exhibition from June 1 to October 31, 1898. It opened amid concern that the

United States' involvement in the Spanish-American War (which started on April 11, 1898, when America declared war on Spain) would significantly affect the number of people who would attend the exhibition. Organizers particularly worried that war news would limit any opportunities they had for free publicity about fair events. While that may have been true to an extent, an incident at the exhibition grounds just prior to the opening day actually led to publicity. On May 23, 1898, two women officers with the local Salvation Army, who were offended by nude statues at the exhibition grounds, took an ax and disfigured one statue, then started to do the same to another when they were arrested. The women faced charges of malicious destruction of the property and the case got newspaper attention.

The Trans-Mississippi Exhibition opened with speeches, music, and parades. Twenty-eight states and numerous foreign countries participated, including Denmark, Austria, France, Canada, Russia, England, China, Germany, Switzerland, and Mexico. Some 450 Native Americans from twenty-three different tribes participated in events at the Indian Congress on July 4, and President William McKinley visited October 12, with 98,845 people in attendance that day. The exposition cost $82.5 million and hosted about 2.6 million people, each of whom paid for admission—50 cents for adults, 25 cents for children.

At about the same time, Anna Wilson made her living, and her fortune, in a house of ill repute. When the "Omaha Madam," as she became known, died in 1911, her estate of about $1 million went to charities. For years on Memorial Day, admirers gathered at her grave. That tradition faded through the decades, but in the 1970s the Prospect Hill Brass Band revived the practice of honoring the Omaha Madam. The same year of Wilson's death, workers built the first north-south highway connecting Omaha and Kansas City and it quickly became known as the "King of the Trails."

Like other American communities that developed in the nineteenth century, Omaha's existence emerged without any organized plan, but the City Beautiful movement urged Omahans to take a look at their town and improved its image by developing new parks linked with winding, scenic boulevards originally designed for carriages and later renovated to automobile traffic. The city featured a public horsecar line as early as 1868, which was replaced with an electric streetcar system by the 1880s. By 1902 the Omaha streetcar services consolidated to form the Omaha & Council Bluffs Street Railway Company.

Today Omaha is a multicultural city with such world-class attractions as the Joslyn Art Museum, the Henry Doorly Zoo, and Rosenblatt Stadium. All three facilities draw visitors from throughout the nation.

George Joslyn, president of the Western Newspaper Union, amassed a huge fortune. Upon his death, his wife, Sarah, decided to build a memorial in his honor. She commissioned prominent Omaha architect John McDonald and his son Alan to design the Joslyn Memorial. Construction started in 1928 on the pink marble building that resembles an Egyptian temple. Later enlarged, the facility now houses the Joslyn Art Museum.

Henry Doorly Zoo already enjoyed a wide reputation for its exotic animals and Lied Jungle by 1995, when the zoo added a new major attraction—Kingdoms of the Seas—a 71,000-square-foot facility with climate-controlled settings that represent saltwater oceans, freshwater beaches, jungle habitats, and even the polar regions. The $16 million facility features a seventy-foot-long tunnel, which Omaha zoo officials say is North America's longest underwater walk-through tunnel. Among the fish living in the aquarium are a number of sharks that swim within a few feet of visitors as they pass through the tunnel. The aquarium area housing the penguins can produce up to twenty tons of snow daily. The electric bill for the facility ranges as high as $250,000 per year and it uses 600,000 pounds of table salt, which is mixed with twenty other salts to create man-made saltwater for the exhibits. Two million gallons of water recycle through the exhibit areas every day.

In 1993, when the Lied Jungle opened, zoo attendance soared to more than 1.3 million, about double the previous year's record. Henry Doorly Zoo was one of the first places to house captive-bred, rare black-footed ferrets in the mid-1980s when Wyoming Game & Fish Department officials decided to divide the only known population of the endangered animals. A rancher near Meeteetse, Wyoming, found the last known colony of wild ferrets on his land in 1981. After an outbreak of canine distemper threatened the species' existence, game officials captured the wild animals and started a captive breeding operation in Wyoming. As it became clear how vulnerable the species was to an incident of disease, fire, or other disaster, the game managers decided to send some of the captive-bred ferrets to other locations, including Henry Doorly Zoo.

Rosenblatt Stadium is home to the Omaha Royals. Since the 1950s it has hosted the College World Series, which pits the top collegiate baseball teams in the nation against each other. Two hundred eighty teams play annually, trying to earn a berth to the College World Series, which is held every June. Only the top eight teams make it to Rosenblatt.

Although much of Omaha's early development relates to the Union Pacific and various agricultural businesses, the city has long been a center for the insurance industry. The Woodmen of the World building and Mutual of Omaha dome are long-standing landmarks. In more recent years, the city has become a telemarketing center.

Both the University of Nebraska at Omaha and Creighton University, founded in 1878, offer educational opportunities in the region. Creighton's medical school attracts students from throughout the plains and Rocky Mountain region. The Omaha metropolitan region includes several other communities, including Papillion and Bellevue to the south, Boys Town to the west, and Florence in the north.

PAPILLION

About three and a half miles east of Papillion is the site of an Omaha village visited by Swiss artist Rudolph F. Kurz in May 1851. The Omahas lived in skin tents and earth lodges and built scaffolds on which they cured meat. The Indians had a high enclosure in which they confined horses for safety, and one side of the village had a trench around it, perhaps as a defense mechanism. A 1970 excavation of the site, sometimes referred to as the Kurz Village, yielded fragments of glass, ironstone, gun flints, iron, and brass, with earth stains indicative of circular lodge sites. Archaeologists found pottery that was between 600 and 900 years old, indicating early use of the location. Most evidence suggests the Omaha Indians used the site until 1855, when they were relocated to reservations in present-day Thurston County. The site near Papillion is believed to have been the last occupied Omaha village of the pre-reservation era.

BELLEVUE

Spanish and French fur trappers were the first to venture into the area that is now Nebraska. By 1703 the French had established regular trade with Native Americans of the region. Spanish traders and explorers developed routes through western Nebraska on the Old Spanish Trail linking Santa Fe with the Mandan villages on the Missouri River in South Dakota. The Spanish also ventured onto the plains, and in 1714 Gen. Pedro de Villasur started making overland trips into central Nebraska, likely following Indian trails. In 1720 a group of French traders and their Pawnee allies attacked a Spanish party led by Villasur at a location near Columbus, driving the Spanish from the region.

The French maintained control of the plains fur trade for almost sixty years. By the last two decades of the eighteenth century, Spanish explorers once again had started trading furs, sending several expeditions along the Missouri River as far north as present-day South Dakota. In the fall of 1795, a Spanish party led by James Mackay built the first European settlement—a fur trading post—in Nebraska, at a site in the vicinity of Bellevue, and probably near Papillion Creek. The post only stood for one year before Mackay and the Spaniards abandoned it; they also built a trading post farther upriver in 1795 (Fort Carlos IV near Homer). In 1797 the Spaniards reestablished a trading post near Bellevue, this one located some eight miles north of the earliest post.

St. Louis businessman Manuel Lisa was among the first to take an active approach to development along the Missouri. He journeyed north in the summer of 1807 with a party of about fifty men; his wife was the first white woman to live in Nebraska. Lisa had met Lewis and Clark in St. Louis as they returned from their survey of the Louisiana Purchase lands, and he enticed John Colter, a member of that party, to return west with him. Lisa intended to open a trading post along the Missouri River at the mouth of the Bighorn. Colter accompanied him to the western lands and went on a solo exploratory journey that took him through much of present-day northwestern Wyoming and into the lands of Yellowstone National Park.

Lisa quickly became a major player in the western fur trade. In addition to his post farther west, Lisa opened a trading post in the vicinity of today's Bellevue in 1812–13. The post remained in operation until 1823, and Lisa remained a leader in the fur trade until his death in St. Louis on August 12, 1820, according to Richard Edward Oglesby in *Manuel Lisa and the Opening of the Missouri Fur Trade.* His death was a serious blow to the Missouri Fur Company, but the remain-

The first permanent mission in Nebraska was organized in Bellevue in 1846, with the mission building completed two years later. The Presbyterian Church organized at the site in 1850 and completed a church building in 1856.
—Nebraska State Historical Society

A painting by Shimonsky depicts the Sarpy Trading Post of 1854 in Bellevue. —Nebraska State Historical Society

ing partners carried on with Thomas Hempstead as business manager in St. Louis and Joshua Pilcher working as field representative in charge of the company's trading posts and traders.

On October 19, 1822, the *Missouri Intelligencer* in Franklin, Missouri, reported that a Missouri Fur Company boat had arrived with "furs & peltries worth $14,000, from the Rocky Mountains. Another parcel belonging to the same company, worth $10,000 is on the river, and expected to arrive in the week coming." The company sought to control the fur trade by developing a series of trading posts along the Missouri, including Fort Vanderburgh near the Mandan villages in central North Dakota, Fort Recovery in central South Dakota, and a post at Bellevue in central Nebraska. From 1820 to 1824, Pilcher operated out of a post once used by Lisa at a site probably about five miles southeast of Fort Calhoun. John P. Cabanne operated a post near there for the rival American Fur Company. Not long before the Missouri Fur Company abandoned Lisa's post, it built a new one at Bellevue. The timing of the construction is not certain, although most sources place it at about 1823. Some suggest there may have been a Missouri Fur Company post near Bellevue as early as 1819 or 1820, but it is difficult to pinpoint the location. Certainly a post had been opened there by the summer of 1823, when naturalist Paul Wilhelm traveled up the Missouri. He wrote:

> As far as the shallow little Butterfly Creek (Riviere au Papillion), the banks are covered with timber, later no more with trees but only meadow growth. On the sandbanks close to the water were low willows, whose seed easily takes root. . . . Then a stretch of prairie comes

close to the bank, extending as far as a row of hills called Coates a Kennel, on the slope of which the American Company at that time had a factory.

We reached this settlement by sundown after traveling along a meadow overgrown with tall nettles and flax-like weeds. The little Mosquito Creek flows into the stream from the left between willows. I set out from the boat in order to deliver my letters to the overseers of the American Fur Company and stayed overnight.

Lucien Fontenelle, the son of wealthy New Orleans parents, left home at age sixteen in 1816, and by 1819 he had become involved with the fur trade in Kansas. A year later he worked for the Missouri Fur Company at the Omaha villages in northeastern Nebraska, and by 1824 he was in charge of the company post at Bellevue. Fontenelle married an Omaha woman, Me-um-ba-ne, or Bright Son, and in 1825 he formed a partnership with Andrew Drips, Charles Bent, and William Vanderburgh. They trapped in the Rocky Mountains in 1827 and 1828, when they disbanded the partnership at rendezvous along the Green River in western Wyoming. Fontenelle returned to Bellevue and operated the Missouri Fur Company trading post. By the late 1820s, however, farming had already started in the area around Bellevue, at least in part to supply goods to fur trappers heading up the Missouri and Platte Rivers. Bellevue was the last outfitting post on the route until the westbound parties reached the buffalo range, nearly two weeks' travel beyond Bellevue. There they could do reasonably well by living off the land.

Fontenelle undertook some trapping expeditions of his own in the West, and he maintained the post at Bellevue until the spring of 1832, when he sold it to the Office of Indian Affairs. He then moved downriver a mile and opened a new trading post. He operated that post and trapped for the American Fur Company until his death in 1840. At that time Peter A. Sarpy took over ownership of the site. He developed a ferry and operated it along with the post until 1862. For a time the 2nd Nebraska Cavalry was billeted at the earliest Sarpy location, as they prepared for the Santee Sioux uprising of 1862 in Minnesota (see page 107).

The post's strategic location served trappers and traders well. In 1846 the first Mormon emigrants to cross the Missouri used Sarpy's ferryboat to make the river passage after Brigham Young had negotiated with Big Elk and other Omaha leaders for permission to camp on Omaha land for two years.

Meanwhile, Fontenelle's earlier post, sold to the Indian agency in 1832, became a center for the Pawnee, Omaha, Otoe, and Missouria

A display of U.S. Air Force missiles at the Strategic Air Command Museum in Bellevue, August 1995. The museum had plans to relocate to a site west of Bellevue.

The United States Air Force Strategic Air Command headquarters is in Bellevue, Nebraska.

tribes. In 1833 John Treat Irving Jr., nephew of author Washington Irving, traveled west and visited the agency at Bellevue, which he described this way: "The Otoe Agency is situated upon the banks of the Missouri river, at thirty-five miles distance from the Otoe village. It consists of half a dozen rough buildings, tenanted by as rough inhabitants. The most of these are half breed Indians, with full blooded squaws for wives, and an immense number of mongrel children. The latter may be seen from morning til night, lying on the ground in front of the agent's dwelling; and basking in the sunshine."

The location became a major river crossing in 1849–50 as gold seekers and emigrants headed toward California and Oregon made their way over the Missouri using Sarpy's ferry and two others then in existence. Bellevue's location on the Missouri and the continual presence of fur trading posts meant the community was well established when Nebraska Territory organized in 1854. The first territorial governor, Francis Burt, was sworn in at Bellevue October 16, 1854. He died two days later. That led to the appointment of Thomas B. Cuming as acting governor. He preferred Omaha as a territorial capital and moved the legislature there. The move so infuriated Bellevue residents that they demanded that Bellevue and Omaha be separated by a county line. Their insistence led to the formation of Sarpy County, with Bellevue as its county seat.

Offutt Air Force Base

In 1881 Congress agreed to replace Fort Omaha with a new facility. The government purchased 502 acres on July 23, 1888, but it took years to finish construction. The 22nd Infantry Regiment arrived at the new post, named Fort Crook, on June 20, 1896. Two years later, on April 18, 1898, the regiment left to fight in Cuba during the Spanish-American War. By January 1899, the regiment was in the Philippines, and Fort Crook became a recuperation and training center.

The first air unit to occupy Fort Crook, the 61st Balloon Company, started its service on September 10, 1918. Aerial reconnaissance started during World War I, and Fort Crook became a center for training and troop preparation. By the spring of 1921 the first permanent steel hangar and dirt runways were completed, allowing the landings of the first aircraft, two DeHaviland DH-4Bs.

On May 10, 1924, the air facilities at Fort Crook became Offutt Field to honor Omaha's first air casualty in World War I. In the summer of 1931, the field had improved runways and new floodlights. Just two years later the site became the Nebraska and South Dakota headquarters of the Civilian Conservation Corps. By October 1940, the 7th

Service Command had established itself at Fort Crook, and on January 4, 1941, the Glenn L. Martin Company leased five hundred acres and flying facilities for a bomber plant. The plant went into full production and completed the first B-26C on June 8, 1942. On October 25, 1943, production started on B-29 bombers, and two years later the site became an Italian prisoner-of-war camp. On June 11, 1946, the 7th Service Command transferred Fort Crook to the Second Air Force.

Because the Martin bomber plant operated as a full-scale B-29 production plant during World War II, it may not be surprising that its workers produced both the *Enola Gay,* which delivered the atomic bomb to Hiroshima on August 6, 1945, and the *Bocks Car,* which dropped the bomb on Nagasaki three days later. In fact, Col. Paul Tebbets, commander of the 509th Composite Group, piloted the *Enola Gay,* which is named for his mother, on the historic flight that dropped the bomb on Hiroshima.

Officials renamed the entire base Offutt Field on June 12, 1946, and it transferred to the air force on January 3, 1948. On May 28, that same year, Offutt became headquarters for the two-year-old Strategic Air Command. SAC bombers and intercontinental ballistic missile (ICBM) forces are controlled from an underground post at SAC headquarters at Offutt Air Force Base. The SAC commander has communications equipment that can put him in instant contact with forces at forty-six bases throughout the world. Since 1961 the *Looking Glass* flights have been flown from Offutt, although only limited flights occur now. The *Looking Glass* is a high-speed reconnaissance plane used to collect data for the U.S. military.

BOYS TOWN

Father Edward J. Flanagan, a Catholic priest, started a home for boys on the western edge of Omaha in 1917. The home—Boys Town— is now an incorporated community.

Fifteen days before Christmas 1917, Father Flanagan took $90 and rented a home at 2506 Dodge Street in Omaha, where he and two nuns started their first boys home. Father Flanagan had earlier operated a home for transient men, and he believed he could provide homeless boys a family-style environment that would give them an opportunity to become socially accepted. Father Flanagan emphasized moral, religious, and vocational education, a new approach to juvenile care. That first home evolved into a much larger operation and became the recognized prototype in public child care.

When Father Flanagan opened his first home, he had five residents, but within two months fifty boys lived at the home. Initially the boys attended Omaha public schools, but eventually the Sisters of Notre Dame taught them at the home. Residents arrived by personal choice, based upon recommendations from concerned citizens, or because they were sent to the home by the Omaha juvenile court. Father Flanagan operated on an unrestricted admissions policy, but the home soon had more tenants than it could handle, and in the spring of 1918 Father Flanagan moved to a larger facility. Just three years later the site was again too crowded, and Boys Town relocated to a seventy-acre poultry farm and an additional four-acre plot in the Florence area. But, as before, students overran the site. Local residents protested, and Father Flanagan decided he needed a larger and more isolated venue. In October 1921 he bought the ninety-four-acre Overlook Farm, which became the permanent Boys Town location.

Father Flanagan believed boys needed moral guidance, a homelike atmosphere in which to live, and the opportunity to learn a trade through hands-on experience. He organized a formal trades school in 1921, which expanded to include such disciplines as engineering, music, and electricity by 1932. Growth was boosted by visits from such national personalities as baseball players Lou Gehrig and Babe Ruth and western movie star Tom Mix. Father Flanagan combined vigorous publication and fund-raising activities. He implemented the *Father Flanagan's Boys' Home Journal* and launched Boys Town radio broadcasts that were heard from coast to coast. Those public activities helped

Father Edward Flanagan had this home built in 1927 as a refuge for boys. His refuge grew into Boys Town, an internationally known organization.

The most well-known sculpture depicting Boys Town, He's Not Heavy, He's My Brother.

to make Father Flanagan and the home nationally recognized symbols of successful juvenile care.

To combat the effects of the Great Depression and keep funding flowing, Father Flanagan launched a series of original public relations events, the most famous of them being a horse-drawn circus featuring Boys Town residents that played throughout the Midwest. The touring caravan didn't make any money, but it did raise public awareness and led later to the world-famous Boys Town choir.

In 1925 Father Flanagan turned over many of the routine operational tasks to a system modeled after the Omaha city government, with elected resident commissioners and a mayor. Nine years later Boys Town became a municipality; the student organization became the city authority and set up a system of urban government and municipal services. That provided yet another opportunity for student education, this time in the field of self-government and administration.

The Depression years provided great concern for the future of Boys Town—like the rest of the nation, the home struggled to make ends meet. But that decade also marked a turning point and catapulted the home into the national spotlight. The catalytic event was the 1938 release of *Boys Town,* an MGM hit starring Spencer Tracy and Mickey Rooney and depicting Father Flanagan's efforts to raise $1.5 million for expansion projects. The movie spread the message of Boys Town in a way no other publicity effort had been able to do. Soon state, national, and international officials started monitoring Boys Town policy on matters of juvenile care. The film led to increased donations on a national scale, making it possible for the home to expand and grow. Finally,

Cutting watermelon at a Boys Town picnic. —Nebraska State Historical Society

other child care institutions started modeling their operations after those of Boys Town.

Father Flanagan, meanwhile, became an expert on child care. He assisted in investigating accusations of malpractice and apparent suicide at the Whittier, California, home for boys. In 1947, at the request of Gen. Douglas MacArthur, he went to Japan and Korea to make recommendations about the establishment of youth and orphan homes there, and the following year he provided similar advice in Germany and Austria at the request of the War Department. By 1949, eighty-eight children's homes operated in the Boys Town style.

Father Flanagan died in Frankfurt, Germany, May 15, 1948, of heart failure, so leadership of Boys Town fell to Father Nicholas H. Wegner, who remained its director for two decades. During his tenure the home expanded its educational opportunities beyond vocational areas to more academic choices, with even more emphasis on college and career orientation.

By the early 1970s, Boys Town had more than 1,000 residents, and the grounds encompassed more than 1,300 acres. The teaching-family program implemented in 1975 by the new Boys Town director, Father Robert P. Hupp, who succeeded Father Wegner in 1973, involved husband-and-wife teams trained in social work. Each couple supervised one of the cottages housing eight to ten youths. The Boys Town Center for the study of youth development started in 1974, and in 1975 it established the Boys Town National Institute for Communication Disorders for Children, which treats between 4,000 and 5,000 youths annually for learning, speech, and related disorders.

Nearly two decades later the operation had expanded considerably, with facilities located in many metropolitan areas throughout the United States, including New York, Washington, D.C., Philadelphia, New Orleans, San Antonio, Orlando, and Las Vegas, Nevada. Other homes had been established in Glenwood, Iowa, Grand Island, Nebraska, Portsmouth, Rhode Island, and southern California. By 1993 Father Val J. Peter headed the board of trustees for Father Flanagan's Boys Town, with annual operating expenses totaling more than $86 million. The Boys Town National Hotline, established in 1989, is a toll-free crisis, resource, and referral service for troubled children and parents that answers calls around the clock, every day of the year. In 1993 alone the hotline received 501,434 calls, making a total since 1989 of more than 1.6 million calls.

GRETNA AND SPRINGFIELD

Numerous rest areas provide relief for travelers crossing Nebraska on Interstate 80 as it heads west from the Omaha metropolitan area. Nine of them include "sculpture gardens," and one is located at Gretna, organized by the Lincoln Land Company in October 1877 and incorporated on July 10, 1889. The Scottish name is probably from Gretna Green, Dumfriesshire, Scotland.

Springfield, west of Gretna, gets its name from the large number of springs that graced the area when the Missouri Pacific Railroad Company platted the town on land owned by J. D. Spearman in 1881. French fur trappers worked in the area during the 1700s. The Platte River is wide and sluggish from this point to its confluence with the Missouri at Plattsmouth.

FLORENCE

Mormons settled temporarily on the west side of the Missouri River in 1846 as they fled persecution in the East. By January 1847 some 5,000 Mormons lived at Winter Quarters, in what is now the community of Florence. The first entry in William Clayton's *Latter-day Saints Emigrants Guide* read: "Winter Quarters . . . the road good but very crooked, following the ridges and passing over a continual succession of hills and hollows."

Mormons established the Florence Mill during the winter of 1846–47 to supply flour and lumber for their people. That first winter on the west side of the Missouri was a bitter experience for the Latter-day Saints, with many dying in the frigid cold. The Mormons established

An Avard Fairbanks sculpture at the cemetery in Florence where some 600 Mormons who died during the winter of 1846–47 are buried.

The members of the Church of Latter-day Saints who perished during the severe winter of 1846–47 are buried in a hillside cemetery. Markers at the Mormon Cemetery in Florence are widely spaced, with only a fraction of the 600 graves delineated.

Interior of the Bank of Florence, Nebraska. —Nebraska State Historical Society

a cemetery on the hill at what is now State Street. The first party of Latter-day Saints left for Salt Lake in 1847 under the guidance of Brigham Young. The rest had no right to remain in Winter Quarters, as the land belonged to the Omaha Indians, and the U.S. government warned the Mormons to recross the river, which they did, building a town they called Kanesville at present-day Council Bluffs, Iowa. They then established a ferry to shuttle Mormons and gold rushers across the river.

In September 1854, following the creation of Nebraska Territory, the Mormons rebuilt Winter Quarters and renamed it Florence for the adopted daughter of promoter James C. Mitchell. Before long they had outfitted a saw and grist mill; signed long-term contracts for ferry services across the Missouri; built a warehouse, tavern, and houses; and advertised lots for sale. They chartered the town March 15, 1855. The site became a regular stop for Missouri River steamboats, and at one time promoters suggested the Mississippi & Missouri Railroad across Iowa would enter Nebraska at Florence. Town leaders attempted to get a federal subsidy to build a bridge across the Missouri, but they were unsuccessful, and the first bridge across the river in the region linked Council Bluffs and Omaha instead.

In January 1858 a majority of both houses of the territorial legislature left Omaha and reconvened in Florence, which immediately became a candidate for Nebraska capital status. The legislature convened in two vacant storerooms in Florence, but only a few meetings occurred there, and the legislature returned to Omaha.

Jacob Weber Sr., and his wife, Amalia, arrived in Florence in 1857 from Bavarios, Germany. Beginning in 1870 he, his son, Jacob Jr., and his grandson, Lyman, operated the Florence mill for half a century. In about 1880, Weber replaced the waterwheel with a steam-powered generator, and in 1920 the mill converted to electricity. The mill changed hands, and structures, through the years, selling to the Kenwood Feed Store in 1964 and remaining under that company's management until 1989.

Another long-standing icon in Florence history, the Bank of Florence, was chartered on January 18, 1856, by the territorial legislature. Owners were the Iowa financial firm of Cook, Sargent & Parker, with James Monroe Parker as manager. Employees lived in quarters above the bank's offices. The vault came in on a Missouri River steamboat from the Pennsylvania steel mills. It consisted of quarter-inch-thick sheet steel, and bank owners placed it inside an additional vault made of masonry three feet thick. The bank issued "wildcat" currency and speculated in land to the point that the economic panic of 1857 resulted in the institution's eventual failure in 1859. But that fate wasn't unique: All but one bank in Nebraska failed during 1859. The Florence Bank later reopened and remained in operation until 1904.

At various times since, the building has housed a grocery store, cleaners, and phone company. After the bank's failure in 1904, the state chartered a second Bank of Florence, which operated until 1930, when hard economic times caused a yet another failure. The building remains intact and is operated as a historical attraction by the Florence Historical Society. An Eagle Scout project by Mike Tomasik of Boy Scout Troop 73 provided concrete markers for various historical sites in Florence, and the town has two sets of street signs: brown ones depicting historic names, green ones for present-day names.

Omaha—Grand Island
148 miles

The earliest route west from Omaha to Grand Island followed the Platte River on a series of rutted wagon roads, with a portion of it known as the Ox-Bow Trail. The nation's first transcontinental auto route also ran along the Platte. US 30, recognized as the Lincoln Highway, still serves as a primary east-west route across Nebraska. In fact, although much of the original Lincoln Highway has since been overlain by other roads in other states, in Nebraska the earliest route remains in place. Running north of Interstate 80 and adjacent to the Union Pacific Railroad tracks, the Lincoln Highway gives travelers a better glimpse of Nebraska than does the interstate because US 30 still passes through the smaller communities. The interstate is the fastest way to cross Nebraska; the Lincoln Highway is the best way to learn about the state's history and heritage.

Two routes head west out of Omaha: Nebraska 64 and US 275. They pass through Boys Town, Elkhorn, and Waterloo (laid out in 1871 and named by the Union Pacific Railroad officials for the battlefield in Belgium) and provide access to Venice, Yutan, and Leshara.

The Otoe Indians occupied a village along the banks of the Platte River near the present town of Yutan at least as early as 1777, when they may have received gifts from the Spanish explorers, then headquartered in St. Louis. At that time La Balla (The Bullet) led the tribe, which had about one hundred warriors. But hostilities between the Otoe and Delaware tribes led the former to abandon the Yutan site in 1835 and move some fifteen miles to the southeast. Their Yutan earth lodges had been about twenty feet tall and some sixty feet in diameter. To the west of Yutan is Leshara, named for one of the three Pawnee chiefs known as Pitalesharo (sometimes Peta Lesharu or Pita Lesharu) in the tribe's traditional homeland. Burial sites and villages are known to have been used nearby.

FREMONT

In 1820 Maj. Stephen Long and his expedition traveled across Nebraska as part of a government exploration to the sources of the Platte and Red Rivers. The party camped during the winter of 1819–20 near Omaha, then headed west, roughly along the route of US 30, to the area of present-day Fremont, where they found the Otoes, close friends of the Skidis, one band of the Pawnee. The Pawnee believed that the *nahurack*, or spirit animals, lived along the high bluffs just

Fremont Brewery, Fremont, Nebraska, in 1905. —Wyoming State Museum, Stimson Collection

south of Fremont, and they initially tried to keep white settlers from moving into the region. The town itself is named for John C. Frémont, another early explorer.

One route of the Oregon Trail, the Mormon Trail, and the Ox-Bow Trail passed through the area south of the Platte River, and for at least two decades the trail along the north side of the Platte River was the major artery heading west. In 1847, when the military relocated Fort Kearny from its first site at Nebraska City to its second location farther west and south of the present-day town of Kearney, the main route from Nebraska City to Fort Kearny headed northwest to the Platte River, then proceeded to the western outpost, becoming one of the most heavily used trails. The present Fremont Historic District centers on the park in Fremont, which was platted in 1856 by the Fremont Town Lot Company. E. H. Barnard used the Military Road, Fremont's present-day Military Avenue, from the Missouri River to Fort Kearny as the baseline for the earliest town survey. The story goes that men conducted that survey using a wet rope, making measurements less than accurate and early maps inaccurate as well.

By 1866 the Union Pacific line had pushed through Fremont, and three years later the Sioux City & Pacific Railroad, serving Iowa and Minnesota, arrived. The Fremont, Elkhorn & Missouri Valley Railroad started construction in 1869, and the excellent availability of rail service made Fremont a center of agricultural trade. In 1888 the Chicago & Northwestern Railroad acquired the Sioux City & Pacific; even so Fremont's growth slowed during the 1890s. The economy rebounded in the early 1900s as the area became a feeding-in-transit center for livestock being shipped by rail. Livestock workers took animals off the trains at Fremont for feeding before reloading stock cars and sending the animals on to markets in Omaha or Chicago. With the arrival of the Chicago, Burlington & Quincy Railroad in 1906, Fremont had four rail lines. Automobile traffic really grabbed hold after 1913, when builders placed US 30 through this area, although the route west of Fremont remained unpaved until after 1920.

Today the Fremont, Elkhorn & Missouri Valley Railroad runs a dinner train as a tourist attraction. The city has a Masonic and Order of Eastern Star Home for children, and Valmont Industries is a major employer. That company builds pivot sprinkler systems, which are used throughout the farm belt. The state of Nebraska operates Fremont State Recreation Area, with picnicking, camping, fishing, and boating allowed.

Rawhide Creek near Fremont has an interesting story, albeit a completely false one. The tale is this: A man traveling west with a wagon train hated Indians and upon leaving his home in the East vowed to kill the first one he came across. The story goes that he did just that, shooting a young Indian girl along a creek in Nebraska. The girl's tribe, upon learning of her death, demanded that the man be turned over to them for torture and eventual execution, or the entire emigrant party would be massacred. After much hemming and hawing, so the tale goes, the emigrants agreed to leave the man to his fate with the Indians, who promptly skinned him alive—giving the nearby stream its name, Rawhide Creek.

The story is a good one for horror and alleged misdeeds, but it never happened in exactly that way. Similar stories crop up all along the western trails, from Tennessee through Wyoming, and the Legend of Rawhide is simply that, a legend most likely written and nurtured by a newspaper correspondent intent upon creating juicy copy, regardless of accuracy.

GRAND PAWNEE VILLAGES

The small town of Ames, located west of Fremont, is most likely named for Union Pacific Railroad developer Oakes Ames. At a location south of Ames and north of Cedar Bluffs is the site of Neapolis, which has a unique history. In January 1858 the territorial legislature decided to move the territorial capital from Omaha to a place "not less than 50 miles west of the Missouri and not more than six miles from the Platte River." Instead of selecting an existing town, the legislature formed a new one on paper, which they called Neapolis. Several legislators visited the proposed town site to evaluate locations for buildings. They envisioned the capitol building atop a tall hill, quickly dubbed Capitol Hill. The decision to move the capital from Omaha caused bitter division among territorial leaders, and after considerable wrangling it was agreed not to relocate to Neapolis. As a result, the town of Neapolis never materialized.

After the 1750s various bands of Pawnee Indians lived in this region along the three forks of the Loup River and near the Platte as far west as the junction of its north and south branches. In the early 1600s the Pawnees lived farther south, along the Red River, but when French trade with the tribes dwindled in that region the Native Americans had fewer supplies, particularly guns and ammunition, which forced them to migrate toward the north. It is Pawnee tradition that the first to move north were the Grand Pawnees, who roamed from Kansas and Quivara toward the Platte. The Pitahauerats followed suit, but the Kitkehahkis settled farther south, along the Republican River (see page 236).

The Grand Pawnees and the Skidi eventually had several settlement locations at sites near the present-day communities of Fremont, Linwood, Hordville, Fullerton, and Schuyler. The Pawnee villages generally sat on the north side of either the Platte or Loup Rivers. Southwest of Linwood are the sites of two, or perhaps three, Grand Pawnee villages and burial grounds. The Pawnee Indians occupied the site intermittently from about 1770 to 1859. Archaeologists recognize at least two different occupational periods. Studies show the remains of earth lodges, which appear as dark circles after farmers prepare their fields for planting. During the earliest periods of study, archaeologists could identify two deeply incised trails in the native sod extending from the edge of the Pawnee living areas up the northwestern face of the bluffs to the burial grounds, where shallow depressions mark the grave sites of the Pawnees.

Moravian missionaries Gottlieb F. Oehler and David Z. Smith visited the Linwood-area village in May 1851 to establish a missionary school and reported finding "between 140 and 150 lodges, the population amounting perhaps to 3,500. On approaching a village, the lodges have the appearance of so many hillocks, of a conical form, huddled up together in the closest possible manner, with only narrow passages between for walking, and the rest of the space filled up by pens, formed of stakes, for confining their ponies during the night."

71

The missionaries said each lodge frame had four to six evenly spaced large vertical posts about ten feet high and some twenty feet from the hearth. Willow wands, grass, and a thick layer of sod covered the frame, with a similarly constructed east-facing entryway that was about three feet wide and fifteen feet long.

SCHUYLER

The first Texas cattle shipped on the Union Pacific Railroad loaded into cars at Schuyler, a community named for Schuyler Colfax, vice president of the United States in 1869. Richland, to the west, originally went by the name Spitley, while Duncan (earlier Jackson) takes its present name either from a local resident or from the town of Duncan, Illinois, which got its name from James Henry Duncan, a Massachusetts congressman from 1849 to 1853.

COLUMBUS

Columbus was founded in 1856 near the confluence of the Loup and Platte Rivers by men who had come from Columbus, Ohio. The most well-known historic residents of the community are Frank and Luther North. The first organized showing of their longtime friend and associate William F. Cody's Wild West Show took place near Columbus because of his dealings with the Norths. Although Buffalo

Union Pacific Depot, Columbus, Nebraska. —Wyoming State Museum, Union Pacific Railroad Depot

Bill made a reputation for himself and helped to organize the original Wild West Show, his friends the Norths made their own contribution to the development of the West and to the show that perpetuated the grand myth of life in the region.

Thomas North arrived in Nebraska in 1855 along with his eldest son, James. The remainder of the North family migrated from Ohio to Nebraska the next year: Thomas's wife, Jane Townley North, and sons, Frank Joshua, who was born in New York on March 19, 1840, and Luther. Thomas North died in a blizzard on March 12, 1857, as he worked with a surveying party west of Omaha. Following their father's death, Frank and James moved to Columbus, to be followed there by the rest of the family in 1859. Frank obtained work as a clerk at the Pawnee Indian Agency in Genoa, where he made friends with many of the Indians and learned their language.

By 1864 Luther North had a freighting contract between Columbus and Fort Kearny. One day as he returned from the fort, a group of Indians approached him, making threatening actions. But the warriors departed, and North continued on his way without problem. Just two days later the Sioux raided emigrants near Plum Creek, to the west, beginning a series of attacks that launched the first Sioux War (see page 194). Word of the Sioux raid at Plum Creek (Lexington) reached settlers in the Columbus area, and they soon built a stockade for pro-

Luther North, 1867.
—Nebraska State
Historical Society

tection. Each night they herded their livestock within the enclosure, and two units of militia organized and provided night patrols. The risk seemed so tangible that the War Department even sent a detachment of cavalry to Columbus. When no raid occurred, the military eventually withdrew, and the people returned to their regular routines.

At the time Gen. S. R. Curtis commanded the 12th and 16th Kansas Cavalry and a company of the 2nd Nebraska Cavalry. He recommended that Frank North organize a company of Indian scouts to assist in the fight against the Sioux. The Pawnees were the logical pick for several reasons: They had a traditional enmity for the Sioux, they had not been involved in any major confrontations against American soldiers or settlers, and the majority were living at the Pawnee Indian Agency in Genoa, not too far from Columbus. Furthermore, Frank North knew many of the leading Pawnee men, and he spoke their language.

North accepted the assignment and headed to Pawnee Agency, where he quickly enlisted seventy-seven Pawnee warriors, who agreed to provide their own horses. At that time the use of Indian scouts to aid the U.S. Army was a new idea. North promised the scouts cavalry pay and an additional payment for the use of their horses. The Pawnees served in the initial campaign against the Sioux, but they never received any payment.

Nevertheless, when North received authority to expand the Pawnee Scouts, just three days after the initial group had returned to the reservation, he had little difficulty in finding interested men. North's commander ordered him to report to Omaha with the names of the one hundred new scouts. Although such a trek only takes an hour or so in an automobile today, in 1864 it took considerably longer. By the time North returned to Pawnee Agency, the warriors he'd recruited had left their village on the annual winter buffalo hunt.

Undaunted, Frank returned to Omaha and persuaded his eighteen-year-old brother, Luther, to track the hunting party and get the men to return and fulfill their commitment as Pawnee Scouts. Accompanied by a young Pawnee, Luther followed the trail of the hunters, nearly catching up to them in the area near Grand Island. But a winter blizzard struck, wiping out the trail, so the trackers returned to Columbus. Frank took another Pawnee guide and Charles A. Small in a second attempt to find the wandering Indians. They, too, failed. Eventually Frank recruited a new group of scouts from those Pawnees who had remained on the reservation.

By October 1864, North had the scouts ready for action. The officers included Frank North as captain, Charles A. Small as first lieutenant, and James Murie as second lieutenant. The company

Frank North, 1867.
—Nebraska State
Historical Society

mobilized at Columbus and proceeded to Fort Kearny, where they established winter quarters.

Training tested the mettle and wills of men on both sides. North attempted to instruct the Pawnees by using the army's "Manual of Arms." The Indians didn't understand English, and North had continuing difficulty translating the orders into Pawnee. Eventually authorities placed some Pawnees on picket duty and sent others to the Niobrara River country, under conditions so harsh it is surprising the Native Americans didn't quit and go home. They left Fort Kearny on foot, trudging through fifteen inches of snow, and they ran out of provisions long before reaching their destination and returning to Fort Kearny.

The following summer the Pawnee Scouts headed into Wyoming, where they pursued some of the Cheyennes and Sioux who had been involved in the two battles at Platte Bridge on July 26, 1865. In the first conflict, the Indians routed a military command under the direction of Lt. Caspar Collins, which was sent from the post at Platte Bridge to provide relief to a wagon train led by Sgt. Amos Custard. When Collins and his men crossed the North Platte River, headed toward the west, a large party of Sioux and Cheyenne Indians attacked in a short, furious fight that lasted only about ten minutes but left Collins and seven of his men dead. Later that day the wagon train guided by Custard came into sight of the fort, but the Sioux and Cheyennes attacked, killing twenty men.

The engagement was one of the events that launched the "Bloody Year on the Plains," as 1865 became known. The Sioux and Cheyennes took their actions in retaliation for the killing of Cheyenne families by troops under Col. John Chivington at Sand Creek, Colorado, in November 1864. The Sioux also sought to retain control of the lands in the Powder River country, which they considered theirs not only by right of possession but also under terms of the 1851 treaty signed at Fort Laramie.

The Pawnee Scouts accompanied Captain North to that region, where they avenged the deaths of Lieutenant Collins and his companions. In Pawnee tradition, warriors often change their names following battles, and after the conflict with the Cheyenne and Sioux in Powder River country, Captain North had a new one as well. Up to that point the Pawnees had called him White Wolf (Ski ri taka), but following that foray he became Pawnee Chief (Pani leshar).

Later that summer the Pawnee Scouts saw action in the Connor Battle along the banks of the Tongue River in present north-central Wyoming. Maj. Gen. P. E. Connor surrounded the Arapaho village of Black Bear and Old David on August 29, 1865, destroying Indian lodges and killing women and children. After the Connor Battle, the Pawnee Scouts returned to Nebraska and didn't see any major action in Nebraska until 1866 on the Republican River; we'll catch up to them there later.

Frank North continued to command various groups of Pawnee Scouts through the 1870s. His scouts served on patrol and guard duty during construction of the Union Pacific Railroad. In the summer of 1870 Yale University professor O. C. Marsh traveled throughout the West studying the fossil beds of the region. North, by then a major in the army, and two of his Pawnee Scouts guided the professor to the Loup Fork River, where he studied late Tertiary period fossil beds. Then they headed north from Fort McPherson across the South and Middle Loup Rivers, traversed the Sandhills, and returned to the fort by following the Dismal and Birdwood Rivers to the forks of the Platte.

In the winter of 1871–72, Major North served at Fort D. A. Russell, Wyoming Territory, and Luther, who had distinguished himself as an officer with the Pawnee Scouts, worked in a military camp on the North Loup River. In the fall of 1873 Luther guided paleontologist Marsh on a journey through western Nebraska and into northeastern Colorado, where the professor collected vertebrate fossils for Yale's Peabody Museum.

After spending the winter in Columbus, Luther joined Lt. Col. George A. Custer in his 1874 expedition to the Black Hills. Although Custer led that trek ostensibly to patrol the Sioux lands, to keep unauthorized individuals out of the region, and find a fort location, the exploration also determined the availability and extent of gold deposits in the Black Hills. The mission certainly accomplished that end, and by 1875–76 the rush to the hills had started.

The Sioux rightfully argued that the hills were their land. When encroaching miners ignored the tribes' protests, the military intervened, touching off the Great Sioux War. Best known for the Battle of the Little Bighorn in Montana Territory in June 1876, the war finally culminated November 26, 1876, at the Dull Knife fight at the western edge of the Powder River country. Pawnee Scouts served under General Crook in the fall and winter campaign of 1876–77. They assisted the military in bringing Red Cloud to Fort Robinson and Red Cloud Agency, where he put down his arms in October 1876. The Pawnee Scouts also participated in the November 1876 Dull Knife battle in Powder River country along the Bighorn Mountains in Wyoming. That engagement finally broke the fighting spirit of the Cheyenne warriors and ended the war.

Frank and Luther North returned to Columbus following the Indian Wars and later played a part in settlement of the Dismal River country, where they owned a cattle ranch along with their friend Bill Cody. In 1881, when Cody organized his first Wild West Show, the premiere performance took place at Columbus, and the North brothers had a part. When the show had a runaway with the Deadwood stagecoach, Frank North suggested that Cody use horses that were older and not so likely to bolt and Indians who had less enthusiasm.

GENOA

Founded as a trail camp by Mormons in 1857, Genoa became a way station for the Brigham Young Express & Carrying Company, which contracted with the government to provide mail service from Omaha to Salt Lake City. The town's name comes from Genoa, Italy.

Long before the Mormons passed through and settled the region, it was the home of the Pawnee Indians. When Coronado explored the Great Plains in 1540–41 searching for Cibola, the City of Gold, he ventured into Kansas and heard tales of a people he referred to as *Harahey* and who are generally regarded as the Lower Loup or prehistoric Pawnee. Coronado heard those people were residents of the Lower Loup village that stood near the present-day town of Genoa. That particular village, located about four miles southwest of Genoa on a level tableland overlooking the Loup River, was one of sixteen Lower Loup villages. Archaeological research shows fifty-seven mounds and middens covering between fifty and eighty acres. Evidence recovered at the site sets one period of use at A.D. 1630, and archaeologists believe early people occupied the site from 1500 to 1650.

In 1867 F. V. Hayden traveled through Nebraska and may have seen the village site. He reported: "On a recent visit to the Pawnee reservation on Loup Fork I discovered the remains of an old Pawnee village, apparently of greater antiquity than the others, and the only one about which any stone implements have not yet been found."

Another Pawnee village—known as the Wright site—is located a mile south of Genoa. Excavations in 1936 and 1950 showed there may have been 250 earth lodges covering forty-five acres and providing lodging for up to 1,200 people. It is believed to date back to 1680 and to have been used by Lower Loup people, the prehistoric Pawnee. Archaeologists excavated one lodge that was fifty feet in diameter. Within the site, researchers found the remains of fifty-five individuals, primarily women and children. The evidence suggests the village may have been attacked by enemies of the tribe, perhaps Plains Apaches, Omahas, or even a different band of the Lower Loup people.

Traditionally the Pawnees claimed much of present-day Nebraska as their territory. From 1300 to 1725 the various branches of the Pawnees had villages along the Missouri River from its confluence with the Kansas River in present-day Kansas to near the mouth of the Niobrara River along the Nebraska–South Dakota border. They also lived along the North, Middle, and South Loup Rivers, the Elkhorn River, the Platte River, and the Republican River. In 1675 French explorers reported seeing more than forty villages; in 1806 Lt. Zebulon Pike reported a population of 6,223 people. The numbers of Pawnee Indians fluctuated during the next two decades, with reports varying between 8,000 and 12,500 people until 1836. The first actual count of Pawnees occurred in 1840, when missionaries reported 6,244 people in the tribe. The Indian agent's report of 1846 placed the number at 12,500, but after that period the population steadily declined, if the various reports are to be given any credence.

By 1850 the tribe had dropped in population by half, to about 5,000 members, at least in part due to a cholera epidemic that swept the plains in 1849 and is blamed for the deaths of 1,234 Pawnees.

The Pawnees had many passions, chief among them buffalo hunting. The Skidi band also practiced the ancient rite of human sacrifice at least until the early part of the nineteenth century. They eventually abandoned the practice, in part because of the American view that such acts were heinous, barbarous, and not to be condoned in any manner. Perhaps the most recognized story related to sacrifice involves an Ietan girl and Pitalesharo, who later became a leader in his tribe.

In 1816 the Skidis captured the girl, intending to sacrifice her to Morning Star at planting time in 1817. Knowing the American opposition to such rites, Knife Chief (Lechelesharo) argued unsuccessfully against the sacrifice. Knife Chief had a son, Pitalesharo (Man Chief), aged about eighteen to twenty. On the day of the sacrifice he told his fellow tribesmen the sacrifice should not occur, that his father opposed it, and that it would occur only after they had first dealt with him. Young Pitalesharo then cut the girl free and led her from the area. He provided her with a horse and some supplies and accompanied her several days on a journey toward the southwest so she could find her people, which she did.

Pitalesharo accompanied a party of Pawnee chiefs as they traveled to the U.S. capital in the fall of 1821. While in Washington, a group of girls at a seminary pooled their resources and had made a silver medal recognizing Pitalesharo's efforts in rescuing the Ietan girl, according to an account by George E. Hyde in *The Pawnee Indians.*

The Pawnees entered their first treaty with the United States in 1833. Under its terms they relinquished most of their native lands in exchange for supplies and, most important to the tribe, protection from their enemies, the Sioux. The Pawnees agreed not to live south of the Platte River; the Americans already eyed that region for its potential as an overland route to the Pacific Northwest. Among those signing the 1833 treaty was Pitalesharo, although the man who made his mark was not the same one who had rescued the Ietan girl in 1817. The earlier Pitalesharo had already died when his tribe gave away most of its land.

The river valleys provided sustenance for the Pawnees, enabling them to raise crops and travel from their villages on hunting expeditions. But the country had a hostile presence in the form of Sioux Indians, who preyed upon the Pawnees. The Sioux from the north and west attacked Pawnee hunting parties and villages, with the greatest attacks occurring during the period 1842–46. Not feeling safe in their own country—in spite of promises of protection from the U.S. government in the 1833 treaty—the Pawnees wandered about, which perhaps explains why some of their villages have different occupational periods. Eventually they resettled along the Platte, hoping their enemies would let them be. The Pawnees established villages on the south side of the river, but that put them along the route of the Oregon Trail and in violation of the 1833 treaty.

Through the ensuing years the Pawnees and the emigrants, who had started crossing the plains in 1841, had various confrontations, but overall they shared the region rather well for the first fifteen years of

Indian students in classes at Genoa. —Nebraska State Historical Society

U.S. Indian School, Industrial Building, Genoa.

heavy overland migration. But by the mid-1850s eastern politicians were eyeing the Indian territory that encompassed all of present-day Nebraska, and efforts started to restrict further the Pawnee lands and lifestyle.

In mid-September 1857 the Pawnee chiefs attended a treaty council at Table Creek, near present-day Nebraska City, and on September 24 they signed away the remaining Pawnee lands. By 1859 the tribe had been relegated to a reservation in the Genoa area. In exchange for their lands, the Pawnee were to receive a $40,000 annuity each year for five years and then $30,000 annually into perpetuity. The government promised a school, sawmill, gristmill, blacksmith, and other shops at its agency. Finally, the government agreed (once again) to protect the Pawnee from the Sioux. Among the chiefs signing the treaty was another man named Pitalesharo (no relation to the earlier two Pawnees of the same name). But the tribe not only didn't receive promised annuities and other services but also hadn't heard the last of their enemies, the Sioux.

By 1859 the Pawnees lived primarily on a reservation north of the Platte in the region between Schuyler and Fullerton, with the agency at Genoa. The tribe remained in this area until 1875, when it relocated to Oklahoma. In 1884 the government established an industrial boarding school at Genoa, one of twenty-five bonded, nonreservation boarding schools of the Bureau of Indian Affairs charged with giving academic and vocational training to Indian children. It was the only school of its kind in Nebraska and remained in operation until 1933. During its peak operation, the school had 599 students from nineteen different tribes and reservations.

Omaha–South Sioux City
103 miles

FORT CALHOUN

This community sat on the banks of the Missouri when the town incorporated in 1858, but now the river has shifted to the east, leaving Fort Calhoun high and dry. Long before the community existed, the country was the domain of the Omaha Indians. When Lewis and Clark explored in 1804, they held their now legendary meeting with the Indians nearby, at a site they referred to as the Council Bluffs.

Governmental leaders in Washington recognized the value of trading with the western tribes. One story has it that after the War of 1812, Secretary of War John C. Calhoun proposed that a line of military forts be built near the U.S.-Canadian border to protect the U.S. fur trade from British competition. The British-owned Hudson's Bay Company and North West Company had a firm hold on the western fur trade, but the Americans owned the lands of the Louisiana Purchase after 1803, and they resolved to forge their own place in the commerce of the area. President James Monroe sent a military reconnaissance party to the western territory. One goal of the undertaking, known as the Yellowstone Expedition, was to develop a system of forts along the Missouri. The 6th Infantry left St. Louis in 1819 under the command of Col. Henry Atkinson. The Yellowstone Expedition initially attempted to ascend the Missouri in three steamboats, but that effort failed in part because of lack of experience with steamboats.

The Yellowstone Expedition arrived at Council Bluffs and started construction of the first fort: Cantonment Missouri. A shortage of supplies and harsh winter conditions created a miserable existence for the men stationed there during the winter of 1819–20. High runoff in the spring of 1820 caused flooding at Cantonment Missouri, so the troops relocated to the top of Council Bluffs, where they established Fort Atkinson. Prince Paul Wilhelm, the Duke of Wurttemberg, described the fort this way in 1822: "The fort itself was a square structure. Its sides were each 200 American yards long. There were eight loghouses, two on each side. There were three gates leading into this fort. Each house consisted of ten rooms, and was 25 feet wide and 250 feet long. The roof of the houses sloped toward the interior court. The doors and windows opened upon this court. On the outside, each room has an embrasure or loophole."

After the troops reached Council Bluffs, governmental officials recalled the expedition, so the only fort actually established was

Cantonment Missouri (Fort Atkinson). At the time it was the United States's westernmost outpost. Life at the fort took on an agrarian nature; troops fed and watered livestock and raised crops for their own food. The troops' primary goals, however, were to provide protection for fur traders, to maintain a peaceful relationship with the region's Indian residents, and to display the Stars and Stripes, thus establishing the region as U.S. territory.

Fort Atkinson may have been Nebraska's first modern-style town, with some 1,000 residents, including soldiers, trappers, Indians, traders, and hangers-on. Troops from Fort Atkinson took part in only one important military encounter, aiding trappers with William Ashley's company, which had encountered a hostile party of Arikara (Ree) Indians farther north. The June 18, 1823, battle occurred in present-day north-central South Dakota and resulted in the deaths of a dozen fur trappers and traders. The 6th Infantry under Colonel Leavenworth learned of the encounter from survivors who caught a ride down the Missouri on the keelboat *Yellow Stone Packet*. The troops and thirty of Ashley's surviving men headed north, where they enlisted the aid of another eighty white trappers and several hundred Sioux warriors, who were traditional enemies of the Rees. In the ensuing battle with the Rees, seven members of the 6th Infantry died; they are believed to be the first U.S. casualties of the West's Indian wars.

By 1824 Ashley had suffered tremendous losses in his effort to become a major player in the western fur trade. But that year he settled on a new way of doing business. Rather than relying upon a system of fixed forts, Ashley proposed trading in the mountains themselves. He sent a party overland, on a route up the Platte River to South Pass, a low gap that offered a break in the Continental Divide, enabling people to cross. In 1825, at a site on the Black's Fork of the Green River in what is now Wyoming, Ashley held his first mountain rendezvous and revolutionized the fur trade. In subsequent years fur trappers and traders conducted business along the western streams rather than at fixed forts. Even so, Fort Atkinson served as a refuge for trappers.

Several early expeditions to the Mexican settlements at Taos and Santa Fe started from Fort Atkinson, and the Council Bluffs site served as the Upper Missouri Indian Agency, managed by Benjamin O'Fallon and subagent John Dougherty. O'Fallon arranged for the Mexican treaty talks in 1825 and assisted Colonel Atkinson in negotiating peace treaties with the Indians of the Upper Missouri the same year, opening the way for U.S. involvement in the western fur trade.

Troops from Fort Atkinson also participated in treaty talks with the Ponca, Arikara, Mandan, Minataree, Otoe, Missouri, Pawnee,

Omaha, Crow, and Sioux tribes. Perhaps the most unusual pact was that of 1824, which was signed by representatives of the government of Mexico and the chiefs of the Pawnee nation. The Mexican government had asked for U.S. assistance in negotiating an end to hostile raids by the Pawnees. This was the only international treaty ever concluded with Native Americans in Nebraska.

Among the military leaders who served at Fort Atkinson were Maj. Steven Kearny, for whom a fort in central Nebraska is named; Lt. William Harney, who eventually led a retaliatory attack on the Sioux tribe in western Nebraska at Blue Water Creek; and 2nd Lt. Albert Sidney Johnston, who led troops in the 1857 "Mormon War" and who later fought and died for the Confederacy at the Battle of Shiloh.

The fort remained in use only seven years. After the troops pulled out in March 1827, Indians burned Fort Atkinson. The first settlers at Fort Calhoun in 1855 used what remained for building materials, but the grounds became a cornfield. In the mid-1950s, the Nebraska State Historical Society sponsored archaeological excavations to determine the exact location of the historic fort, and in the 1960s the Nebraska Game and Parks Division purchased a portion of the site. Further archaeological work in the 1970s led to reconstruction of the fort, which is now operated as a state historical park. Much of the history of Fort Atkinson is interpreted in the Harold Andersen Visitor Center, which was dedicated in 1986.

BLAIR

Blair is named for John I. Blair, a railroad magnate who owned the land on which the town is located. He came originally from New Jersey and once owned the Sioux City & Pacific Railroad. Danes settled both Blair and Dana, and Blair is home to Dana College, a Lutheran school established as a seminary in 1884 by the Danish Evangelical Lutheran Church.

On the hill above the college stands a symbol to a revolutionary Indian leader and the Nebraska writer who captured his story. The Tower of the Four Winds, designed by the Rev. F. W. Thomsen and dedicated June 27, 1987, honors Sioux holy man Black Elk and Nebraska poet laureate John Neihardt, who immortalized Black Elk in his classic book *Black Elk Speaks*. The monument represents the essential elements of Sioux belief. Decorated with mosaic tiles, the tower has a messiah figure standing against the tree of life. The crossed arms of the design represent the crossing of roads, with the black horizontal line indicative of the difficulties people must face as they travel through life and the red vertical line illustrative of the good road that leads from the

Great Spirit to Mother Earth. Black Elk received the vision depicted on the Tower of the Four Winds when he was a child, and he told it to Neihardt in 1931, saying, "The good road and the road of difficulties you have made to cross and where they cross—that place is holy."

De Soto National Wildlife Refuge

De Soto township gets its name from Hernando de Soto, a sixteenth-century Spanish explorer. The town was platted in 1854 but not incorporated until March 7, 1855.

Access to the De Soto National Wildlife Refuge is in Iowa, but the refuge borders the Missouri River. Part of it is in Nebraska, and one of its greatest offerings has its roots in the state. The refuge lies on a wide floodplain formed by the shifting course of the Missouri. Each spring and fall, at least since the last Ice Age, the area has been a migratory corridor for waterfowl. Much of the area is no longer river bottomland but rather fertile farm territory. That has altered much of the habitat; nevertheless, thousands of birds migrate to the region annually. During typical years, some 400,000 snow and blue geese rest and feed in the area from mid-September through November as they migrate from Arctic nesting grounds to Gulf Coast wintering grounds. About 50,000 ducks of various species (mostly mallards) also use the refuge grounds.

Waterfowl migrating north in March and April also use the area, although the numbers are far lower in the early season than in the autumn. Ducks and geese continue south in the fall after a layover at De Soto, but the bald eagles that follow them remain in this area. The refuge has 7,823 acres, about 2,000 of them farmed. A portion of the crops raised are left in the fields to serve as food for the migrating ducks and geese. Since 1965 about 1,500 acres have been converted to grasslands to provide nesting habitat and winter wildlife shelter. In order to maintain healthy stands of native grasses, refuge managers use both haying operations and fire.

Although waterfowl brings nature lovers to De Soto Wildlife Refuge, an attraction of historical interest came into view in 1968 when Jesse Pursell and Sam Corbino, both from Omaha, located the remains of a steamboat that sank in the Missouri more than a century earlier. The *Bertrand* went down April 1, 1865, en route from St. Louis, Missouri, to Fort Benton, Montana Territory. In addition to food, clothing, and agricultural and mining supplies, the *Bertrand* carried a small fortune in mercury to be used in gold refining. The boat was heading upstream toward Montana when it struck a snag about twenty-five miles north of Omaha at a location then known as "Portage La Force," a

Excavation crews look for artifacts on the steamboat Bertrand, *which sank in 1865 and lay under the sand and water of the Missouri for a century before being discovered in 1968.*
—Nebraska State Historical Society

few thousand yards below De Soto Landing. It sank in water on the Nebraska side of the Missouri.

That the *Bertrand* went down is not really unusual. As Jerome E. Petsche wrote in *The Steamboat Bertrand: History, Excavation and Architecture*: "For the amount of traffic that has been carried upon it, no stretch of water on the globe has swallowed up as much wealth as the Missouri River. Its shifting sands and numerous snags have sent many a boat to the bottom, and once located there, it is generally the work of but a short time for the wrecks to disappear from view and the approximate location of them is, in many instances, unknown."

The *Montana Post* reported on April 22, 1865, "The steamer Bertrand sank above Omaha while on her voyage hither. The passengers . . . are all safe and sound." The *Daily Missouri Democrat* reported that the $50,000 cargo, which was consigned to various Montana mining district businessmen, was insured. The boat, owned by Capt. James A. Yore and his brother and John G. Gopelin, quickly disappeared from view, but the location of the downing became known as Bertrand Bend.

Early salvage work commenced on the upper decks of the *Bertrand,* but then another ship, the *Cora,* went down a few miles upstream, and insurance company rescuers turned their attention to that wreck. Silt covered the *Bertrand,* and it disappeared under the murky Missouri, but not before crews recovered a large portion of the valuable mercury in the *Bertrand's* hold, although that fact wasn't widely known for more than a century. In 1967 salvage teams again started looking for the

Bertrand and the mercury they believed the ship still contained. After considerable effort they found the remains of the *Bertrand*—then in Iowa because the river's course had changed in the century since the boat went down—under a layer of topsoil that ranged from twenty to twenty-eight feet deep. Silt, clay, cottonwood logs, and other debris covered the boat. When workers dug through the layers of soil they found an amazing array of artifacts.

The boat had clearly been headed upstream when it swamped and struck bottom, as it still lay in that direction. By June 1969 the main deck had been exposed, and workers prepared to take off the decking, mud and steam drums, hog stanchions, and the cargo. Among the items recovered were Indian trade goods, including beads and bolts of red, brown, black, and burgundy cloth; rubber buttons from the Novelty Rubber Company of New Brunswick, New Jersey; and a variety of other items, including sewing supplies, hats, shoes, letter clips, pencils, ink, and bottles of William Brown's highly concentrated essence of ginger, Superior Bird pepper sauce. Canned items included tomatoes, strawberries, oysters, lemonade, gooseberries, and lard. The cargo had ale, champagne, and a variety of "bitters," including Kelly's Old Cabin Bitters, Drake's Plantation Bitters, and Dr. J. Hostetter's celebrated stomach bitters, made by Hostetter and Smith of Pittsburgh, Pennsylvania.

The goods on the *Bertrand* were bound for Fort Benton, Montana, to be sold to miners in the Virginia City goldfields and to farmers in Montana Territory. Therefore, cargo included everything from pots and pans to coffee grinders, gold pans, shovels, forks, ironstone pitchers and bowls, and oil lamps.

HERMAN AND TEKAMAH

Herman, located north of Blair, was a German and Danish settlement named for Omaha & Northwestern Railroad conductor Samuel Herman. On June 13, 1899, a tornado destroyed every building in town except for the school and the church, which sat at opposite ends of the town.

Tekamah is the county seat of Burt County, one of Nebraska's original eight counties, named for Francis Burt, the first Nebraska territorial governor. Tekamah, located on the riverfront, was established October 7, 1854, placing it among the earliest towns organized in Nebraska Territory. That year Benjamin R. Folsom and eight friends from Utica, New York, settled in the area, apparently naming the community for an area of California in which one of Folsom's compatriots had found gold. Some sources claim the origin of Tekamah isn't known. Some say it means "the field of battle"; others suggest it means "big cottonwood." Colonel Folsom may have called the town Tekamah because of the many cottonwood trees in the area; however, one report is that settler W. N. Byers named it for a place he had once visited in the East.

Indians often threatened during the period, and the Tekamah settlers sought military assistance and protection in 1855. A small, two-story log blockhouse was located on the southwest corner of the present courthouse site. The blockhouse doubled as a courthouse from 1857 to 1867 and functioned as a hotel until 1917.

An old stagecoach trail passed near Golden Springs, a historic spring west of Tekamah, and people carved their names on the sandstone bluff in that area. Indians claimed that some of the faintest scratchings on the bluff are those of the French and Spanish, who were in the area a century and a half before American pioneers.

DECATUR

Decatur got its start in 1855. It was organized by the Decatur Town and Ferry Company, owned by Benjamin R. Folsom, Peter A. Sarpy, T. J. Hinman, and Stephen Decatur. In 1927 a bridge went in across the Missouri at Decatur, but shortly afterward the river changed course, leaving the bridge high and dry until 1955, when the U.S. Army Corps of Engineers diverted the stream back to its earlier channel.

The Omaha Indians once ranged all along the Missouri River country in eastern Nebraska. The remaining members of the tribe have a reservation just north of Decatur.

The story goes that the most famous Omaha, Chief Blackbird, is buried in this area. Upon his death in 1800, Chief Blackbird's people tied him to his horse and took him to a bluff, where the horse was killed. The mourners then either piled rocks and stones around the bodies or buried them in a common grave.

Chief Blackbird distinguished himself in battle and in negotiations. He was as capable of driving a hard bargain as the French and Spanish fur traders with whom he dealt. Initially, Chief Blackbird welcomed the Spanish and French traders. He would view their trade goods, choose the best items for himself, and then allow the people of his tribe to trade. The practice not only made Chief Blackbird a rich man in the Omaha nation, it also made him some enemies. But he had good relationships with the French and Spanish. The story goes that one of them showed the chief a powerful substance: arsenic. When he learned its use, the chief controlled his people through intimidation and fear. If someone questioned his authority or leadership abilities, Chief

Blackbird predicted great harm would come to that person. He would outline when and where the individual would meet a horrible death. Because he had the arsenic, the chief could ensure that such a catastrophe always occurred as he had predicted.

In the early 1800s the dread disease of the white men, smallpox, reached the Omaha people, and hundreds of them died, including Blackbird himself. As he lay dying, Chief Blackbird asked that his body be placed upon his favorite horse and that the two of them be buried atop a hill from which it was possible to view a thirty-mile stretch of the Missouri. The Omahas complied with Chief Blackbird's request, and the hill thereafter became known as Blackbird's Hill. It is mentioned by Lewis and Clark and by artist George Catlin.

It is also the site of a legendary ghost story, which goes this way. Two men loved the same woman. One of them, whom the woman loved in return, went hunting, and members of his party said he had accidentally drowned in the river. The woman eventually married the other man. Some years later, the man who supposedly had drowned returned to the tribe. The husband, fearing he would lose his wife because she would go to her true love, cut her throat and jumped from the top of Blackbird Hill with her in his arms. The woman's blood covered the earth where they landed, and the story says the grass never again grew in that area. There have been reports of people hearing the faint screams of a man in this area. Those who believe the ghost story of Blackbird Hill think it is the sound of that man.

Robbers Cave, or Indian Cave, near Blackbird Hill served as a river hijacker's hideout.

MACY

Macy is the center of the Omaha Indian Reservation. The town was originally called Omaha Agency, but problems with mail delivery—postal people couldn't seem to keep straight which letters went to Omaha Agency and which went to Omaha—caused a name change to Macy (Omaha Agency.)

WINNEBAGO

This town takes its name from the Indian tribe and lies within the Winnebago Indian Reservation.

Known as the "people of the salt water," the Winnebagos occupied land around Lake Winnipeg in east-central Wisconsin and were one of the most respected tribes of the northern woodlands. Their first contact with white people occurred in 1634, when French traders moved through their homeland. The Winnebagos ceded the first of their lands

A Winnebago house and women. –Nebraska State Historical Society

in 1832 in exchange for $10,000 annually for twenty-seven years. The government also promised the tribe buildings, teachers, and funding for agricultural implements and livestock. Five years later the Winnebagos approved a second treaty in which they ceded the remainder of their lands east of the Mississippi River. They retained hunting rights, but two years later officials forced them to move to northeastern Iowa, the first of five forced relocations.

Eventually the tribe moved to its present reservation. By then the Winnebagos had developed an efficient agrarian lifestyle, but they'd faced one hardship after another on the way to Nebraska. From Minnesota they were forcibly removed to Crow Creek, South Dakota. In addition to leaving their crops and livestock behind, the Winnebagos had to pay $56,000 for moving expenses. At Crow Creek the Winnebagos shared land with the Santee Sioux, but more harsh times lay ahead. Three to four people died each day from sickness and fever, most likely caused by a lack of food. The Winnebagos never took a hostile stand against the government, but many returned to their ancestral lands in Wisconsin. About 1,200 finally settled on the Omaha reservation in 1864.

It took two years for the Omahas to cede some of their land to the government, land that ultimately went to the Winnebago tribe in exchange for their Dakota reserve. By 1874 many of the Winnebagos who had returned to Wisconsin were relocated to the Nebraska reservation. However, many simply went back again to the Wisconsin lands. Unlike other Native Americans, who were pursued and returned to their reservations by military authorities, the Winnebagos who left their reserve generally were allowed to remain in Wisconsin.

HOMER

The Omahas claimed the land all along the Missouri River, and Lewis and Clark saw the remains of a large Omaha Indian village, with perhaps 300 lodges, in the vicinity of today's Homer. The village, believed to be called Tonwantonga, or Large Village, had apparently been wiped out by smallpox.

Located along either side of US 77 about a mile northeast of Homer, the village was bounded on the west by Omaha Creek and on the south by steep bluffs. Now the Chicago, Burlington & Quincy Railroad parallels the highway and bisects the site. It's not certain when the site was first used. Lewis and Clark, in journal entries for August 4, 1804, noted that five members of their party visited the abandoned village. Other researchers show that the Omahas reoccupied the village from 1832 or 1833 until 1841 and again from 1843 to 1845.

James Mackay launched Fort Carlos IV, one of the earliest fur trading posts in Nebraska, near the village in 1795, which he operated for Spain. With a stockade, trading room, storehouse, and living quarters, the fort was a formidable place. Mackay sent Bernard Lecuyer upriver to seek a route to the Pacific, but Lecuyer had little success. Mackay later gave the same assignment to John Evans, who only made it as far as the Mandan villages in North Dakota before he ran out of supplies.

The Missouri Fur Company, for whom Mackay and his compatriots worked, couldn't continue the competition because of high start-up costs and mismanagement, and the company liquidated in 1807.

DAKOTA CITY

The Rev. Henry W. Kuhns answered the call of the Lutheran Allegheny Synod to serve Nebraska Territory in 1858. He organized a congregation the following year. In 1860 Augustus T. Haase, a member of the group, designed and constructed a church at a cost of $2,000. It remains the oldest church in the state.

Haase emigrated from his native Germany and settled in Dakota City in 1858, about the same time the Lutheran missionary arrived. The church served as the territorial county courthouse before Nebraska achieved statehood in 1867. Serving as pastor for the church after Kuhns was Dr. Samuel Aughey, who arrived here in 1864. He later made a name for himself as a natural scientist.

In its original form the frame church had one story, with a gable roof crowned by a bell tower. Native cottonwood timbers formed the framework. Few changes have been made to the church during the years, although some of the original siding has been replaced. The bell in the church's cupola is believed to be the original, which was cast in 1856. The Lutheran church is no longer used for regular worship services. In 1963 the deed passed to the Dakota City government from the Nebraska Synod of the Lutheran Church, and the local historical society rehabilitated the structure.

Today one of the community's primary employers is Iowa Beef Packers (IBP), one of the four major meatpacking companies in the United States in 1997. The company paid record finds of $5.7 million for meatpacking violations in the 1980s. The fines, imposed by the Occupational Safety and Health Administration, resulted because the company had ignored the hazards of repetitive motions by the packinghouse workers. Such motions can lead to disabling neuromuscular disorders such as carpal tunnel syndrome. In 1987, government officials said IBP had the most flagrant violations of record-keeping about job-related injuries it had uncovered in seventeen years of tracking occupational injuries.

SOUTH SIOUX CITY

South Sioux City spans three states: Nebraska, South Dakota, and Iowa. After Iowa officials endorsed Prohibition in the 1920s, the community got quite a reputation in the other two states as a good place to find booze, women, and cards. In 1995, when Nebraska had the nation's lowest unemployment rate for the sixth consecutive year, the South Sioux City Area Chamber of Commerce worked with officials in Nebraska, Iowa, and South Dakota on a "Come Home to Siouxland" brochure that touted the area's job opportunities and favorable living conditions.

Fremont—Walthill
52 miles

US 77 heads north-south between Fremont and Walthill, across rolling country filled with cornfields and cattle feedlots. Nickerson, just north of Fremont, is named for founder Reynolds K. Nickerson, a railroad contractor who directed the survey and layout of the town on January 13, 1871. The highway also passes through Winslow and Uehling, a relatively new town—it was platted on December 6, 1905, and incorporated the following November. Theodore Uehling lent his name to the community; he had been in Nebraska since 1860 and became the town's first postmaster.

Oakland still has an annual festival to celebrate its Swedish roots. Lyons takes its name from Waldo Lyon, while Rosalie is named for Rosalie La Flesche, a daughter of Joseph La Flesche—the last recognized French-Indian chief of the Omaha tribe.

BANCROFT

Located at the southern edge of the Omaha Indian Reservation, Bancroft is best known as the home of John G. Neihardt, western writer and author of such important works as *The River and I* and *Black Elk Speaks.*

Poet John Neihardt, as a young man sitting in his library in Branson, Missouri. —Nebraska State Historical Society

John Neihardt's study, in which he wrote portions of his epic The Cycle of the West *and other poetry and prose. It is located in Bancroft.* —Nebraska State Historical Society

Neihardt recorded the oral tradition of the Omaha longhairs (elders) and tales of leaders like Red Cloud and Crazy Horse, but his greatest contribution was his sharing of the vision of Oglala Lakota Black Elk with the world. Born January 8, 1881, Neihardt lived in Wayne, Nebraska, where he attended Nebraska Normal College. In 1900 he arrived in Bancroft, a town named for historian George Bancroft but known to the Omaha as Unashta Zhinga, or "Little Stopping Place."

Neihardt worked for J. J. Elkin, a trader on the Omaha reservation, where he studied Omaha history and culture. He became friends with several members of the La Flesche family, who were descendants of Estamakza (Iron Eyes). While in Bancroft, Neihardt reported for the *Omaha Daily News.* From 1901–3 he edited the *Bancroft Blade,* and he wrote a column for the paper until 1920. He became a literary editor for the *Minneapolis Journal* in 1912 and later also edited the literary page for the *St. Louis Post-Dispatch.*

His epic writing is *A Cycle of the West: The Mountain Men Trilogy,* which includes *Song of Hugh Glass* (written in 1915), *The Song of Three Friends* (1919), and *The Song of Jed Smith* (1941). He wrote *The Song of the Indian Wars* in 1925 and *The Song of the Messiah* in 1935. While working on the latter in 1930, Neihardt first met Black Elk. Speaking through an interpreter, the Lakota holy man said, "As I sit here I can feel in this man beside me a strong desire to know all things of the Other World. He has been sent to learn what I know, and I will teach him."

In 1931 Neihardt returned and listened to Black Elk's stories. At that time Black Elk named him Peta Wigmunke ("Flaming Rainbow") and gave Neihardt sacred articles that had been handed down to him by his own father. They included a sacred hoop, drum, goose's wing, pipe, and coup stick. In 1932 Neihardt published *Black Elk Speaks*. It received respectful reviews but now is considered a classic and is published in more than a dozen languages.

From 1942 to 1946, Neihardt directed information for the Office of Indian Affairs, U.S. Department of the Interior. He then lived in Columbia, Missouri, where he became poet-in-residence and a lecturer at the University of Missouri. He died in Columbia, Missouri, on November 3, 1973.

Neihardt is honored at Black Elk/Neihardt Park in Blair and at the Neihardt Center in Bancroft, which was dedicated in August 1976. The Bancroft facility features an interpretive center and a Sioux prayer garden that remains as a living symbol of the Hoop of the World vision told to Neihardt by Black Elk. The symbolism is described in detail in *Black Elk Speaks*. The garden has four quarters and colors: west/blue, with the power to live and to destroy; north/white to depict winter; east/red to depict light, understanding, and peace; and south/yellow to depict the power to grow.

Like the Tower of Four Winds in Blair, the Neihardt Center's prayer garden is styled after the Hoop of the World. According to Black Elk's teachings, all men start their journey of life in the east and travel toward the west, crossing the hoop in the process. The road they travel, which is depicted in black, is the pathway of worldly difficulties. People also have the option of traveling the red road of spiritual understanding that starts in the south and extends toward the north. The area where the good red road of spirituality crosses the hard black road of difficulty is holy. By offering prayers to each quarter in the Sioux prayer garden, one may gain the powers of each area.

PENDER

Pender was founded in 1886 two miles south of its present location and originally called Athens. The name was changed to honor Englishman John Pender, a director of the Chicago, St. Paul, Minneapolis & Omaha Railroad, which cooperated to move the town to its present location.

WALTHILL

Named for Walter Hill, son of James J. Hill, builder of the Great Northern Railroad, the town of Walthill was settled in the spring of 1906. Among the most well-known residents of the region is Susan La Flesche Picotte, who achieved recognition for her medical work among the Omaha Indians.

Susan was born in June 1866, a daughter of Joseph La Flesche (Iron Eyes), the last recognized chief of the Omaha nation. Her father saw the need for the Omahas to assimilate into the culture of the white people and therefore placed emphasis on education, sending Susan to the Elizabeth Institute for Young Ladies in Elizabeth, New Jersey. Upon completing her course work, she returned to the Omaha reservation in 1882 and spent two years working at the mission school. She then attended the Hampton Normal and Agricultural Institute in Hampton, Virginia, from which she graduated in May 1886, and the Women's Medical College of Pennsylvania in Philadelphia, from which she was graduated with a degree in medicine in 1889 to become the first Indian woman doctor in the nation.

Susan La Flesche first worked at the Women's Hospital in Philadelphia but soon returned to the Omaha reservation in Nebraska. She initially treated only children but eventually earned permission from Omaha agent Robert Ashley to provide medical service to the adult members of the tribe, making her responsible for the health care of more than 1,200 Omahas. An early concern, which became a lifelong passion, involved the alcoholism prevalent among Indian people. Susan called for laws to prevent crimes attributed to intemperance.

In 1893 she resigned as the government physician because of her own poor health, and in 1894 she married Henry Picotte. They moved to Bancroft, where she continued her medical practice, treating both Indian and non-Indian people, and became an active temperance speaker. When Henry died in 1905 because of complications of drinking, her temperance fervor only increased. She helped organize the Thurston County Medical Association, served on the health board for Walthill, and participated in other health-related activities. She supported the idea for a hospital in Walthill, which finally came to fruition in 1913, with funding aid from the Home Mission Board of the Presbyterian Church, the Society of Friends (Quakers), and various individuals. When completed, the hospital served both white and Indian patients, and its establishment capped a busy medical career for Susan La Flesche Picotte.

US 275
Omaha–O'Neill
183 miles

The route from Omaha to O'Neill follows the Elkhorn River, heading northwest through Valley and Fremont. Along the way it passes through Hooper, named after Samuel Hooper, a prominent Massachusetts congressman during the Civil War, and Scribner, named for New York publishing magnate Charles Scribner.

West Point was founded in 1857 by John D. Neligh and incorporated October 29, 1858. Neligh, who left a legacy farther west, had a brickyard and a sawmill in West Point, and a small war broke out between him and two competing businessmen, leading the opposition to set fire to the mills.

Cornfields, bean fields, and huge old cottonwood trees line the Elkhorn River valley as US 275 follows the river bottoms between West Point and Pilger. This is a major cattle feedlot area of Nebraska, with feeding operations on the hillsides, particularly north of the highway. Beemer originally went by the name Rockcreek but later changed names to honor A. D. Beemer, its founder.

Wisner settlement dates to 1865, and the community takes its name from Samuel P. Wisner, vice president of the local railroad company at the time. With a population of 1,253 in 1990, Wisner claims to be

A field of corn along the Union Pacific Railroad near Fremont. –Wyoming State Museum, Stimson Collection

Neligh Mill, April 1995.

A sampling of products made at the Neligh Mill, now operated as a state historic site.

the "Livestock Center of Nebraska." Like most Nebraska towns, the community has a grain elevator, and a flag flies from the top of one section of it; a Christmas star perches atop another area.

Peter Pilger left his name on a town, while Stanton got its moniker either from S. L. Halman, who platted the community in 1871 (his wife's maiden name was Stanton), or for U.S. Secretary of War Edwin M. Stanton, for whom the county is named. Stanton served in his official capacity during most of the Civil War (from 1862 to 1867). Stanton County organized in 1856, but officials redefined its boundaries on January 10, 1862.

NORFOLK

The name of this town is a contraction: The community lies on the *north fork* of the Elkhorn River. Orville Henry Carlisle lived here when he developed the first model rocket. He patented the design but lost the rights to it on a technicality. Even so, some of his rockets are on display at the Smithsonian Institute in Washington, D.C. Perhaps even more well known than Carlisle is Dr. Richard Tanner, the hero of the "Diamond Dick" pulp novels. The most famous Norfolk native of all is Johnny Carson, who grew up here and became a nightly guest in homes across the country as host of *The Tonight Show*.

The story goes that Battle Creek gets its name as a result of an expedition by the Nebraska militia commanded by Gen. John M. Thayer against the Pawnees in July 1859. Although there was no major battle, the town that developed in 1884 is called Battle Creek anyway.

Tilden gets its name from 1876 presidential candidate Samuel Tilden, who lost to Rutherford Hayes. Nearby Oakdale gets its name for the abundance of oak trees in the area. For a short time in the 1980s it housed the Tintern Monastery, founded by the Monks of Tintern (who follow the teachings of Father Clifford Frank). The monastery was the first order established since the thirteenth century and the first ever established in the United States.

NELIGH

The fertile farmland around Neligh ensured that the area would become a productive region, but it took the vision of John D. Neligh to establish a community and a business to support it—both of which took his name. In 1873 Neligh (pronounced NEE-lee) started construction of a flour mill on the bank of the Elkhorn River. His timing couldn't have been worse. No sooner had the initial structure been built than the national financial panic of 1873 struck. As a result, Neligh sold his mill to the firm Lambert and Gallaway.

The effects of a cyclone in 1909 near Neligh. —Nebraska State Historical Society

The first milling was done with the use of stones, but by 1886 the facility employed the roller process and a state-of-the-art dust-collection system. That was an important advantage, since the flour-making process created lots of dust; explosions even occurred in some mills as a result. The Neligh Mill expanded in April 1886 when the H. Beckman Company built an elevator nearby. The Elkhorn River provided power for the equipment, and mill owners added a warehouse to serve as a storage and sales area. By the 1930s the Neligh Mill Company produced wheat, buckwheat, and rye flour, wheat and rye graham, cornmeal, and livestock feed. Among the trade names were Neligh Patent Flour, Rose of Neligh, Pride of Neligh, Antelope, Verifine, Snow White, and Gold Medal. The best-known brand, So-Light Self-rising Pancake Flour, was introduced in 1906, and the last brand produced, Nancy Lee, went into production in 1939. Mill owners marketed one of the earliest flour products as Gold Medal flour, but in subsequent decades General Mills developed a flour product with that same name and purchased the trademark from Neligh owners in 1940, paying $5,000.

The mill was entirely automated with the exception of the flour-sacking machines and had a dozen employees at peak operation. Military forts and Indian reservations provided the main markets for the Neligh Mill. Generally, flour at Neligh was made in three grades. The lowest grade was sold to the military and Indians. Bakers' flour went to people for general use, and patent flour—often called cake flour—was the finest grade. The mill started bleaching flour after 1900, when farmers started raising more winter wheat. That grain created a flour more yellow in color than spring wheat, so millers bleached it using nitrogen peroxide gas.

At about that same time, the mill produced more electricity than it needed and sold it to the city of Neligh. The mill used water power until 1920 but never used a vertical waterwheel. A horizontal wheel was more practical because there was not enough drop to the river flows to create energy. During the war years of the 1940s, production started declining. Flour milling ceased in 1959, but the mill continued to produce livestock feed for another ten years. The mill and its original equipment remain intact, and it now serves as a historic site of the Nebraska State Historical Society. It is the best-preserved nineteenth-century flour mill, containing all its original equipment, in Nebraska.

O'NEILL

Irishman John O'Neill spearheaded a group of Irish American settlers, and the first town the group built was named for him. Born in Ireland in 1834, O'Neill was a U.S. Army officer from 1857 to 1864, when he became active in the Fenians—an American organization promoting Irish independence. He led several ill-fated Fenian raids against British military posts in Canada from 1866 to 1871. After the unsuccessful raids, O'Neill lost his leadership position in the Fenians.

By that time thousands of his countrymen and women were leaving Ireland and settling in crowded American cities. O'Neill, interested in founding agrarian colonies in the West, started one in Holt County, Nebraska. The initial colonists arrived in 1874. O'Neill died in 1878, but the town was already established as the county seat and growing.

Scandal rocked O'Neill in 1892 when Holt County treasurer Barrett Scott disappeared on the heels of rumors that his accounts had come up short. Authorities found Scott in Mexico and returned him to O'Neill for trial, but while he was free on bail forty masked and armed vigilantes kidnapped him. Authorities later found him dead, wrapped in a comforter near the Whiting Bridge over the Niobrara River. There was a rope about his neck and a boot mark upon his bald head. A dozen men suspected of the crime stood trial and won acquittal.

O'Neill Jaycees organized a St. Patrick's Day celebration in 1967, and two years later Governor Norbert Tiemann proclaimed O'Neill the "Irish Capital of Nebraska." Governor James Exon dedicated a marker at the 1972 St. Patrick's Day celebration denoting O'Neill as Nebraska's Irish Capital, and the Nebraska legislature got involved in 1977 by passing a resolution declaring the city as such. With two governors and a legislature making such proclamations, who's to argue with the title? The community's Irish heritage is marked with green shamrocks painted on city streets, storefronts, and sidewalks; the chamber of commerce promotes O'Neill as the Shamrock City. (Apparently being the Irish Capital of Nebraska isn't an adequate title for these folks.) On St. Patrick's Day and again during the July Summerfest celebration, residents paint the "world's largest shamrock" at the intersection of US 20, 281, and 275.

Central City—Neligh
60 miles

Nebraska 14 between Central City and Neligh crosses through the former domain of the Pawnee Indians. Burial sites lie at many locations near Fullerton and other communities in the region. Fullerton became a major stopping point for the Mormons after they started their migration to Utah in 1847. North of Fullerton is Belgrade, so named because its hilltop location reminded early residents of that Serbian city. The fourteen earliest settlers in Albion arrived on April 13, 1871, and they soon built a fourteen-by-eighteen-foot sod house, where all of them lived until further quarters could be constructed.

St. Edward began when A. T. Coquilliard obtained a tract of land in 1871 from the Union Pacific Railroad, which he and the earlier settlers named for Edward Serrels, a prominent man at Notre Dame University in South Bend, Indiana. In 1876 Coquilliard deeded the tract to the St. Edward Land and Emigration Company so public settlement of the village could begin.

About twenty-five miles north lies Elgin. When farmer William Eggleston filed papers with the U.S. Postal Service for an office based out of his home, he asked that his name be used for the site, but the Postal Service denied the request and returned the petition to the Oakdale postmaster, who selected the name Elgin from a list of Illinois post offices. The postal authorities agreed to the name and sent Eggleston the necessary documents to begin his work as postmaster.

Snyder—Albion
96 miles

Nebraska 91 between Snyder and Albion passes through fertile cropland and the communities of Dodge, Howells, Clarkson, Leigh, and Creston. Germans settled Madison in the late 1860s, and many of the trees in this region date back to the 1880s, when local farmers planted thousands of them. Nebraska took the lead in changing the character of the plains, as farmers and civic leaders planted trees throughout the state. Much of Nebraska has been turned by the plow and is now covered with row upon row of corn. The name for the town of Cornlea is a compound of *corn* and *lea*, which means "cornland" or "land of corn."

Wayne—Missouri River (St. Helena)
48 miles

Named for Gen. Anthony Wayne, a Revolutionary War figure, this community is known for its Chicken Show and for Wayne State Teacher's College, which was established in 1881.

In about 1900, a young boy named George Heady saw something fall from the sky. He watched the area where he thought the object landed and searched until he found a strange, donut-shaped circle of burned grass in the middle of a field. He found a large piece of metal or stone and told everyone he had found a star. Though they scoffed initially, eventually the people believed Heady; he kept the object throughout his life, giving it to a friend not long before his death. Now it marks his grave.

South Sioux City—Jct. 20/275
110 miles

The primary route across northern Nebraska is US 20. Starting in the east at South Sioux City, US 20 passes through Jackson, the site of St. John's Church, founded in 1856 by Irish Father Jeremiah Trecy and named to honor St. John the Baptist. St. Catherine's Academy was established in 1893 and run by Dominican sisters. The highway passes through Willis, Martinsburg, Allen, Dixon, Concord, and Laurel as it rolls up and down over the hills that characterize the Missouri River country in northeastern Nebraska.

Crop production in this area of Nebraska involves corn, sorghum, and hay, making it a primary location for honey production. Randolph, named to honor Lord Randolph Churchill of London, England, annually has some 16,000 colonies of bees (or about 160 million bees).

Farther to the west is Plainview, originally named Roseville for Charles Rose, the town's first postmaster. Settlers changed the name at the suggestion of an individual who had passed through a community called Plainview in Minnesota and thought it a pleasant place. The area is the first high land after leaving the Elkhorn River valley, and the voting precinct has the descriptive name Dry Creek.

Security Bank in Ponca, showing the classical styling of older buildings.

South Sioux City–Jct. US 281
117 miles

The northernmost highway that crosses Nebraska is Nebraska 12, which follows the Missouri and Niobrara River valleys. Between Ponca and Niobrara the road roller-coasters over a series of big hills, with the pavement creating a ribbonlike effect reminiscent of brightly colored holiday candy. Ponca State Park lies in the extreme northeastern portion of the state along the Missouri River bluffs. Named for the Indian tribe that used this land historically, the park encompasses 892 acres of heavily forested hills and offers camping, horseback riding, and hiking. It is one of the few locations on the Lewis and Clark Trail from which visitors can see three states: in this case, Nebraska, Iowa, and South Dakota.

PONCA

In May 1856 the first white settlers in the rolling hill country of Ponca camped on Aowa Creek. When the town was platted it became Ponca, named for the local Indians. Among the first settlers were the Stough brothers–John, Jacob, and Dr. Soloman B.–who built a flour mill on the creek in 1858. Solomon Stough worked as a surveyor and platted the town, which became a trade center for the agricultural development.

NEWCASTLE

Lewis and Clark passed a bluff not far from the present town of Newcastle on August 24, 1804. The party camped for three days at a site about three miles west of the future town, and on one point Clark

Lewis and Clark campsite in northern Nebraska, where the explorers spent August 23-25, 1804.

noted that the bluff appeared to be on fire. He saw signs of what appeared to be coal and perhaps cobalt. Fur traders later noticed smoke and fire in the region, which became known as the Ionia "volcano." In 1839 J. N. Nicollet attempted to prove the site wasn't a volcano; he thought it was a bed of iron pyrite that produced heat capable of igniting other combustible materials. Early settlers in the region feared the Ionia volcano, which took its name from the once-flourishing town that sat north of Newcastle.

In 1877 an earthquake shook in the area, and a year later a Missouri River flood undermined the bluff, causing a portion of the volcano to fall into the river. That same flood caused heavy damage in the town of Ionia, although the community wasn't abandoned until the post office was discontinued in 1907.

Meridian Bridge

The Meridian Bridge, built in 1924, provides the region's residents with access between Nebraska and South Dakota, crossing on US 81 from rural Cedar County to Yankton, South Dakota. Before the bridge went in, people traveling between the two states used a ferry service started in 1870 or a seasonally operated pontoon bridge that was installed in 1890. As a protection against ice damage, each year residents disassembled the pontoon bridge before the winter freeze and again prior to the spring thaw. They put it in only when the pontoons could be placed on the open water of summer or the firm ice of winter.

The Yankton merchants who counted northern Nebraska in their trade territory disliked any delays for people in crossing the river. In 1915 they organized a private bridge company and gained federal approval to build a permanent span across the Missouri, but the enterprise lapsed with World War I. In 1919 the project was revived with the full backing of Yankton's chamber of commerce. The road where the bridge would be built followed the 6th Principal Meridian from Mexico City, Mexico, to Winnipeg, Canada. It was an international highway commonly called the Meridian Highway, and the Yankton boosters simply named the bridge after the route.

Meridian Bridge, built at a cost of just over $1 million, opened in October 1924. It originally had a lower deck equipped with trackage, but it never carried the anticipated rail traffic. In 1946 the Meridian Bridge Company sold the structure to the city of Yankton for $700,000. After recovering the purchase price from toll collection, the city converted the bridge into a free facility, and operation later fell under the auspices of the state of South Dakota. In 1953 officials converted the lower rail deck into a highway lane allowing one-way traffic at both levels. At the same time, toll status dropped entirely.

The state of South Dakota partially rebuilt the south approach in 1969, and other approach spans were put into place in the early 1980s, creating the present configuration of seven steel-girder shore spans on the north and twelve on the south. The Nebraska Department of Roads supervised improvements on the Nebraska side of the bridge, but the structure itself remains in South Dakota ownership. The Meridian Bridge is the only example of vertical-lift design in Nebraska and South Dakota and one of the few remaining vertical-lift bridges on the Missouri River.

WYNOT

The story goes that once an elderly German in the area answered all questions "Why not?" and children soon started repeating his phrase. The adults of the area also picked it up. When the community had to have an official name, someone suggested, "Why not name it 'Wynot?'" and everyone agreed, according to Lillian Fitzpatrick in *Nebraska Place-Names.*

SANTEE SIOUX RESERVATION

President Andrew Johnson established the Santee Sioux Reservation in February 1869. Like the Winnebagos, the Santee Sioux had been removed from their traditional homeland. In their case the government forced them from Minnesota to South Dakota and eventually to Nebraska. Basically a Woodlands tribe, the Santee Sioux lived in permanent villages and practiced farming.

The Santees signed their first treaty with the U.S. government in 1805, ceding 1,000 acres in exchange for $2,000. A later treaty in 1837 led to cessation of their remaining lands east of the Mississippi River. In all the tribe relinquished some 35 million acres of land, an area larger than the state of New York. For it the government agreed to pay about eight cents an acre, but the Santees never saw most of the money: It was held in trust by the government, which failed to make annuity payments as promised.

When the Santees didn't get their annuities and other government support as promised, they revolted in 1862. The uprising stemmed from an argument among two young Santee men about whether they had the courage to steal eggs from white settlers. Their test soon became a challenge to kill the white people. Before long three white men and two women had been murdered. The Santees expected retaliation, and some of the young men convinced leaders Little Crow, Shakopee, Medicine Bow, and Big Eagle that they had to fight. Not all of the Santees participated; some even warned white people so they could escape.

The Santees attacked Fort Ridgely, but the army quickly quelled the uprising. Col. Henry Sibley and his troops arrested and imprisoned 1,800 Santees, many of whom expected fair and just treatment. An army commission formed to prosecute the Santees, who were denied legal counsel. At least three hundred members of the tribe faced charges of rape and/or murder. When each received a death sentence, missionaries protested and managed to get the attention of President Abraham Lincoln. Eventually Lincoln commuted all but thirty-eight of the sentences. Another five Santees also received a reprieve, but in December 1862 the remaining thirty-three Santees died in a mass execution in Mankato, Minnesota.

The following year the Santees were exiled from Minnesota, herded into boats, and moved to South Dakota, where they shared land with the Winnebagos on Crow Creek. Eventually the government carved out a reserve for the Santee Sioux in northeastern Nebraska. Initially the reservation had 115,075 acres, but it has since been significantly reduced.

NIOBRARA

Fur trappers started operating in this area in 1856, and the Ponca Indians claimed territory here until 1877, when the government forcibly removed them to Oklahoma.

Niobrara sits upon a hill above the Missouri, and approaching it from either direction on Nebraska 12 travelers follow the river; the western access road passes through Niobrara State Park. Initially the town sat closer to the river, but in 1881 a tremendous flood covered the town with up to six feet of water. By April 20 the river had flooded the town three times, and residents decided they should move the community. Two days later they picked up homes and businesses and relocated them on the higher benchland.

The Fort Randall Dam, upstream from Niobrara, was built in 1952 and reduced the periodic flooding of the region. However, the construction of Gavins Point Dam in 1957, downstream on the Missouri River, created Lewis and Clark Lake, which raised the groundwater table in the region and flooded many basements in Niobrara homes.

The townspeople had three choices: to abandon the town entirely, to build a system of levees and pumping stations, or to move the community again. They voted to move the town and completed the project in the 1970s at a cost to the federal government (which had built the Gavins Point Dam, creating the problem) of $14.5 million. That compared with a cost of $40,000 to move the community in 1881.

All the problems aren't completely resolved, however. During the summer of 1995 high runoff in the Missouri River basin forced officials to release water from the Fort Randall Dam in late August. They delayed the release because of concerns over endangered waterbirds that nested below the dam; when the water eventually was released, it flooded some property. Although some residents filed a lawsuit, it was dismissed without action. The entire region from Niobrara south to Neligh and east to Norfolk had flooding problems during August 1995 after an unusual late-summer storm dropped between six and seven inches of rain in a six-hour period. The heavy rain, combined with the increased water releases from Fort Randall Dam, closed Nebraska 12 between Niobrara and Verdel.

VERDEL

At a site just east of Verdel, a spur of land along Ponca Creek, the Ponca Indians built a fort they called *Na'nza* toward the end of the eighteenth century. The tribe occupied earth lodges at the fort at least by 1785 and likely engaged in various trading sessions with Spanish and French traders. However, by 1804, when Lewis and Clark trekked through the region, the tribal fort had been abandoned.

The view just east of Niobrara, Nebraska, a town that moved twice to avoid high waters of the Missouri River.

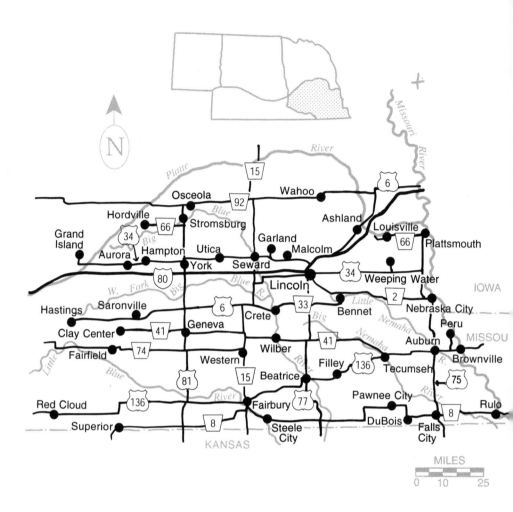

PART 2
RIVER COUNTRY

NEBRASKA IS SLICED IN TWO by the Platte River, which makes a long, slow S-curve through the state as it waters corn, alfalfa, sorghum, beans, and other crops. The river served as a conduit for early travelers, not because they found it particularly navigable (it wasn't) but because the fertile bottoms provided feed and water for their livestock and because the valley had an easy grade with few obstructions. In this book, southeastern Nebraska is called River Country because it is bounded by the Missouri on the east, by the Platte on the north, and includes the various branches of the Blue and Nemaha Rivers coursing through its interior.

The rivers not only provided the earliest methods of transport and commerce but also provided water for agricultural development and enterprise. The western boundaries of River Country are the Little Blue River and US 281, extending south from the Platte River at Grand Island to Hastings.

Long before Nebraska became a territory and before the United States tore itself apart in civil war, emigrants started crossing the region on their way to Oregon and California. Several routes across southeastern Nebraska provided access to the unclaimed territories of the West.

White settlement of Nebraska Territory began along the Missouri, then gradually spread west. Plattsmouth, Nebraska City, and Brownville were among the first prosperous Missouri River towns. Each had ferry service across the Missouri and promoted itself as the ideal location for settlement in Nebraska or from which to launch a western journey. Nebraska City and Brownville soon became the major communities.

Nebraska City's growth was spurred by freighting firms that hauled goods from the river west to Fort Kearny. First the freighters drove their oxen across the Ox-Bow Trail, which angled northwest to the Platte River, then moved along the southern bank of that waterway to reach

Freighters transported goods across the plains as these Middle Loup men did. Nebraska City grew rapidly due to freighting activities. —Nebraska State Historical Society, Solomon D. Butcher Collection

the fort. But heavily laden freight wagons had difficulty following the Ox-Bow Trail across the wet bottomlands along the Platte, so eventually a new, more westerly route, known as the Nebraska City–Fort Kearny Cutoff, became popular. Meanwhile, Brownville also boomed, becoming a major river port. Prominent residents helped push it to a position of considerable significance in the state. Brownville and Nebraska City remain vital communities, but they have been eclipsed by the region's largest city—Lincoln—which became the capital of Nebraska in 1867.

The entire Missouri River region from Plattsmouth to Rulo experienced turmoil in the years immediately preceding and during the Civil War. Only the Missouri River separated the slave state of Missouri from the free territory of Nebraska. Many slaves attempted to gain their freedom by crossing the river into Nebraska and then heading north. Tensions sometimes escalated to the boiling point over the issue. Many southeastern Nebraska residents worked as links in the Underground Railroad, helping the slaves to escape. At various locations in the hills along the Nebraska side of the river, slaves hid in cellars, caves, barns, and homes belonging to or built by Nebraskans. The problems of Jayhawking (antislavery guerrilla activity) spilled into Nebraska from Kansas.

After the Civil War, as the United States started its healing process, new transportation routes developed through eastern Nebraska Territory. The first, and certainly the most significant, came even earlier with the Pacific Railway Act of 1862, which provided for a transcontinental railroad. A number of communities promoted themselves as the best place from which to begin building the line west across the Great Plains. In the end, that old standby, the Platte River valley, proved to be the corridor choice, and Union Pacific construction started from Omaha in 1865. Work proceeded slowly at first, but, as crews became more efficient, the steel rails quickly advanced along the north bank of the Platte.

The presence of that new method of transportation attracted cowboys, who started driving Texas cattle north to the railheads for shipment to eastern markets. The lush valley along the Blue River served as a conduit for cattle, just as it had for emigrants. Although some small early herds pushed northeast to Plattsmouth, by far the majority of the animals headed due north, crossing the Platte between Columbus and Schuyler. The latter community became the state's first main shipping point, with between 40,000 and 50,000 head of Texas cattle being loaded there in the early 1870s. Later herds trailed to railroad shipping points farther west, particularly at Ogallala, and western Nebraska eventually became the state's primary cattle-shipping region.

That shift came in part due to settlement. In early years it was easier to ship from Schuyler than from Plattsmouth because fewer people lived in Schuyler and because there were fewer local herds susceptible to Texas fever; similarly, in later years there were fewer settlers to deal with farther west.

The settlement of southeast Nebraska spread along the rivers. The area now is characterized by its fertile fields. Orchards provided a livelihood for many of the early residents along the Missouri, and the land is still known for its fall apple harvest. Although some fair-sized cities dot the landscape, this is primarily agricultural country tied to orchards, alfalfa, dairies, corn, and soybeans, with an occasional feedlot thrown in to add a pungent scent to the air. This is good land, fertile and productive, and it's not anything like the popular stereotype of Nebraska—flat and covered with cornfields. The counties along the Missouri River have big, rolling hills and a diverse variety of trees that create a kaleidoscope of color in the fall. The river valleys along the Nemaha, the various forks of the Blue, and the Platte are a patchwork of crops, native grasses, and huge old trees.

We begin our journey through River Country in the east and first explore the region along the Platte north of that more modern but nevertheless important dividing line, Interstate 80. After traversing that region from east to west, we will return to the Missouri River and work our way downstream, following the major roads west as the emigrants and early settlers did.

The logical place to begin is Plattsmouth, where the muddy waters of the Platte pour into the roiling Missouri.

A dairy cattle herd at the State Hospital for the Insane at Ingleside. —Nebraska State Historical Society

Plattsmouth–Hordville
104 miles

PLATTSMOUTH

The Otoe and Pawnee Indians lived in the region of present-day Plattsmouth, which takes its name from the fact the Platte River empties into the Missouri here. That joining of the waters attracted early entrepreneurs such as Libias Coon, who had one of the first ferries across the Missouri. The first Mormon emigrants to cross the Missouri in 1846 probably used Coon's ferry, as he was a Mormon, but the religious group soon operated a ferry of its own.

By 1853 a trading post served westbound emigrants, Indians, and residents in the Plattsmouth area, but it wasn't much of a community until approval of the Kansas-Nebraska Act in 1854, immediately after which a number of enterprising men "boomed" cities. Leading the way for the development of Plattsmouth as a commercial and transportation center was Samuel Martin of Glenwood, who had a ferry across the Missouri and operated a trading post as well. The First Democratic Territorial Convention convened in Plattsmouth in 1858. In 1869 the Burlington Railroad started its westward journey from Plattsmouth, heading to Lincoln and eventually linking with the Union Pacific at Kearney in 1872.

By 1870 cowboys were trailing herds from Texas and Kansas to the railhead at Plattsmouth, and the community vied with Schuyler to become the region's main livestock shipping point. Although cowboys found a lot more to do in Plattsmouth, the route there had drawbacks, so the majority of the early Texas cattle followed the Blue River Trail to Schuyler. In all, perhaps 5,000 head of cattle moved through Plattsmouth, whereas Schuyler handled an estimated 40,000 to 50,000 head annually in the early 1870s. One factor that worked against Plattsmouth as it attempted to become a livestock shipping center was that by 1871 development to the south and southwest had restricted areas through which the cattle could be trailed.

Plattsmouth soon transformed itself from a livestock shipping location into an industrial center, complete with an ironworks foundry that manufactured much of the fancy metal used in construction projects in the eastern part of the state. For those more inclined toward social amenities, Plattsmouth also had a cigar factory. The first railroad bridge spanning the Missouri at Plattsmouth opened in 1880. That bridge was replaced in 1903, and the first wooden bridge for automobiles was installed here in 1911.

LOUISVILLE

The area between Louisville, South Bend, and Ashland includes Platte River State Park, the Louisville State Recreation Area, and Schramm Park State Recreation Area, which features the Ak-Sar-Ben Aquarium.

Opened in 1982, Platte River State Park comprises more than 400 acres of wooded terrain. It lies between and serves both of Nebraska's major metropolitan areas: Omaha and Lincoln. The park is a merging of three earlier preserves: the Harriet Harding Campfire Girls Camp, a 104-acre wilderness area obtained from Ole Sjogren, and Camp Esther K. Newman. The area has camping, hiking, horseback riding, swimming, fishing, boating, and various other recreational activities. Park development came with funds from a variety of sources, including some $2 million from the private sector and about $748,000 from the state.

Schramm Park State Recreation Area, located on the north side of the Platte, is the state's oldest recreational grounds, providing day-use activities such as hiking and picnicking. In 1879 the Nebraska legislature created the Board of Fish Commissioners, forerunner of the present-day Game and Parks Commission. That group contracted with the private Santee Hatchery, which was located at the site of Schramm Park, to provide fish to stock Nebraska waters. In 1882 the Board of Fish Commissioners authorized purchase of the Santee Hatchery at a cost of $1,200. Originally the operation was a natural hatchery that relied on spring water, but in 1914 the Board of Fish Commissioners replaced the original hatch house, which ultimately became the Gretna Fish Hatchery Museum.

Initially situated on a fifty-four-acre tract of land, the hatchery and recreation area expanded when University of Nebraska geology professor E. F. Schramm donated his adjacent farm to be used as an outdoor education center. The Ak-Sar-Ben Aquarium and World-Herald Theater feature a dozen large aquariums displaying both native and introduced Nebraska fish and sponsor a variety of educational programs. In 1977–78 the Youth Conservation Corps built three miles of recreational trail that are part of the National Recreational Trails System. They are used for hiking in summer and cross-country skiing in the winter.

The Louisville State Recreation Area provides an area on the south bank of the Platte River for camping, picnicking, fishing, bicycling, and other recreational activities. Like those at Schramm Park, the Louisville trails become cross-country ski trails when snow covers them.

ASHLAND

The Ox-Bow Trail forged by freighters in the 1850s as they hauled goods from Nebraska City to Fort Kearny crosses US 6 just south of Ashland. The trail followed the wet bottomlands of the Platte River valley, which soon became impassable to the heavy ox-drawn freight wagons. That caused freighters to find new routes west, and they generally followed the Nebraska City–Fort Kearny Cutoff, which avoided the soft country along the Platte. A Pioneer Wayside Area off Interstate 80 commemorates the Ox-Bow Trail near Mahoney State Park.

In the 1870s residents living along the Platte River near Plattsmouth often dug wells to meet their water needs. Because of the high water table in eastern Nebraska, most of the wells were shallow. That reduced risks to well drillers: There was less chance that a well under construction would cave in on them. But this area had a different problem. Sometimes a heavier-than-atmosphere gas called "damp" collected in the bottoms of a well, causing illness and even death to anyone who descended the well hole. The gas, also known as black damp, fire damp, and choke damp, was actually carbon monoxide, which robs a body of oxygen, causing death.

In August 1874 near Plattsmouth, John Livingston needed to make repairs to his well. He hired a Swede to descend to the bottom of the twenty-five-foot well. After a period of time Livingston became concerned because he could get no response from the hired man. Livingston enlisted the aid of other men, took a candle, and lowered himself into the well. As he descended his candle went out, and Livingston signaled to the men above ground to pull him up. Before they could get him out of the well, he dropped to the bottom. A rescue effort started immediately, and the neighbors soon had both Livingston and the Swede out of the well. It's not a happy ending, however—both men were dead. The Swede died from the "damp," while the fall killed Livingston, according to the August 13, 1874, edition of the *Nebraska Herald.*

Richard Hornby died on September 17, 1880, at the William Garland farm near Waverly when he descended a well to check its condition and died of suffocation. There are other reports of individuals falling victim to the underground gas, and they occur most frequently in eastern Nebraska.

This region relies on wells for agricultural production, with farmers in Memphis, Ceresco, Valparaiso, Dwight, Ulysses, and Polk raising a variety of crops. Ceresco gets its name either from *Ceres*, the goddess of corn and harvests, or from the Latin verb *cresco*, which means "I grow," according to Lillian Fitzpatrick in *Nebraska Place-Names.* Originally Valparaiso went by the name Raccoon Forks for the three streams that joined on the property of the earliest settlers, the Johnson family. But eventually they changed it to Valparaiso, "The Vale of Paradise."

NEBRASKA 92

Wahoo–Stromsburg

55 miles

WAHOO

There are several stories about the origin of this name. It may be an Otoe word for a berry bush that grew along the creek or for a tree with medicinal properties that was found here in pioneer days. Some

A view of Broadway in Wahoo. —Otto Berthold, private collection

Red Cross drive in Wahoo. —Nebraska State Historical Society

say it was the name of an Otoe medicine man, others believe it was the mispronunciation of an Otoe word meaning "without hills," and still others claim it means "elm trees." The community is located on an Indian burial ground, and the Otoes frequently camped nearby. The combination of camping and burial made this a particularly holy and spiritual place for the Otoes.

The Ox-Bow Trail wound its way along the Platte River bottoms southwest of the present communities of Ithaca, Swedeburg, Prague, Malmo, Colon, Weston, Bruno, and Abie. At David City the trail headed north a few miles to the area of present-day Nebraska 64, then it headed west and south to Grand Island and continued along the route now defined by I-80 to Fort Kearny.

OSCEOLA

While the Ox-Bow Trail was a renowned early freighting route, particularly for military supplies bound for Fort Kearny, the Blue River Trail was the first pathway for Texas cattle being brought to railheads. It came north through Kansas to Schuyler, the first heavily used cattle-shipping point in Nebraska. Although some animals moved through Plattsmouth, the majority followed the Blue River Trail, which crossed the Platte north of David City and Osceola. In later years the fertile lands around Osceola became a primary production center for broom corn, and a broom factory emerged in Osceola.

The drought that swept the Great Plains in 1873–74 spared no one. Dry conditions don't do a thing for corn growth, but they often spawn grasshopper production, and those winged insects became the terror of the plains. Farmers desperately tried to save crops, but the pests claimed more than their share. The *Osceola Homesteader* in July 1874 reported:

> Our foreign readers must forgive us for giving so much grasshopper news. We really cannot help it. The air is filled with them, the ground is covered with them, and people think and talk of nothing else. It rains grasshoppers, and snows grasshoppers. We cannot walk the streets without being struck in the face and eyes by grasshoppers, and we cannot sleep for dreaming grasshoppers, and if the little devils do not leave for some other clime soon, we shall go grasshopper crazy.

Thirteen miles west of Osceola on the bank of the Platte River is the site of a Pawnee village occupied from 1820 to 1845. In 1835 that village sat about fifty yards from the Platte, according to reports from fur traders.

When Polk County chose its county seat in 1916, Osceola vied for the distinction with Stromsburg, a community settled in 1872 by Swedes.

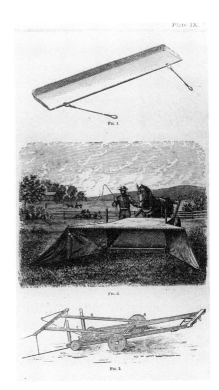

A horse-powered grasshopper trap from Report of the Commissioner of Agriculture, 1877. *When pushed forward by the horse's moton, the trap collected grasshoppers in its path.* —Nebraska State Historical Society

Osceola won the honor, some folks say, because it distributed cardboard maps, each with a small pin pointing to Osceola. People could balance the map on the Osceola pin, indicating clearly (at least to those making the claim) that Osceola was the center of the county.

US 34
Union—Lincoln
42 miles

The hilly country along the Missouri River flattens as it extends west from Union to Lincoln. The former got its name from people who sympathized with the Union during the Civil War, while the latter comes from President Abraham Lincoln. In its infancy Union had a neighboring community, known as Factoryville, that included such businesses as a flour mill, hotel, post office, and even a Methodist college.

WEEPING WATER

French explorers called the creek near this community *L'Eau qui Pleure*—"the water that weeps"—while the Otoe Indians called the creek *Ni-gahoe*, or "water that runs over a small falls."

The earliest reference to the creek's current name was a poem, "The Weeping Water," by Orsamus Charles Dake, the first professor of English literature at the University of Nebraska. His work appeared in *Nebraska Legends and Other Poems*, published in 1871. In his preface, Dake says he "developed" a legend that involved a fight between the Omaha and Otoe Indians on the battlefield south of the Platte River. In the conflict, all the warriors died. When the women and children came to the site looking for their husbands, sons, and fathers and found them all dead, the women and children sat down and cried. Their tears ran so freely that they formed into the little stream known as the Nehawka, or Weeping Water.

Another version of the genesis for Weeping Water comes from A. T. Andreas. In his *History of Nebraska*, published in 1882, Andreas says a powerful Indian tribe once lived in the region. The chief's daughter captured the "heart and brain of the ruler of a still more powerful tribe to the west," but her father refused to let the more powerful chief marry her. The rival tribe abducted the girl as she bathed with some companions, and the warriors in her tribe took off in pursuit. The two tribes met on a battlefield to the west, and the girl's warriors all died in the conflict that followed. As in Professor Dake's version, the women and children of the tribe eventually followed, found everyone dead, and sat down and wept the tears that became the creek.

Many other versions of the legend make up the folklore of the Weeping Water region. The earliest written evidence, however, indicates that French explorers and traders named the stream. In 1804, when Lewis and Clark passed this area, they called the stream by the French *L'Eau qui Pleure*.

After white settlement began, Weeping Water was dubbed "Stone City" for the limestone industry that provided an early economic mainstay of the area. Limestone quarry operations started in the 1860s, with men using hand tools. The town of Weeping Water incorporated on December 19, 1870, and milling operations provided the first source of employment, with the Weeping Water providing power for early mill wheels. The well-advertised mill drew farmers from a seventy-mile radius.

LINCOLN

Nebraska's capital city has a rich and unique political history, parks, industry, the state prison, and a widely respected university press. All manner of important people have called Lincoln home, including authors Mari Sandoz and Willa Cather (both of whom attended college in Lincoln), presidential candidate William Jennings Bryan, and a host of others. People once called it "Holy City" because it had so many churches (100, or one for every 700 people).

The salt flats west of the city attracted the first settlers to Lancaster County in the 1850s. Early residents thought perhaps the salt deposits could be the basis of a major industry, but that didn't occur. Instead, government became the region's primary economic engine. Communities such as Florence, Bellevue, and Omaha made bids to become the territorial capital, but after years of wrangling, the community known as Lancaster won out. It became Lincoln in 1867, when the city became the permanent capital, in honor of President Abraham Lincoln. The following year, construction began on a new capitol building, which stood until 1881, when a new edifice went up on the same site.

The present state capitol stands south of Centennial Mall, a few blocks from the University of Nebraska. Built of Indiana limestone between 1922 and 1932, it dominates downtown Lincoln. It took ten years to build the present statehouse because work progressed on a "pay-as-you-go" basis to prevent the state from incurring debt. Principal contractors for the $10 million structure were the J. H. Weise Company and Peter Kiewit Sons & Company, both of Omaha, and the W. J. Assenmacher Company of Lincoln.

Nebraska State Capitol, Lincoln.

The Nebraska State Capitol, designed by architect Bertram Grosvenor Goodhue, features eighteen bas-relief panels that depict great moments in the history of lawmaking. Scenes range from Moses' dispensation of the laws of God to the admission of Nebraska as a state, which occurred on March 1, 1867. Above each window are carvings with the names of each of Nebraska's counties. The tower rises four hundred feet above what once was the Nebraska prairie to the top of the dome, faced with gold tile and a nineteen-foot, eight-and-a-half-ton bronze statue of "The Sower," sculpted by Lee Lawrie.

During construction a seven-block rail line went in to transport materials to and from the construction site for the state capitol. The rail line soon had the nickname the "Capitol and H." Officials estimated that the line likely saved the state $100,000 in transportation costs.

As Lincoln grew the community annexed thirteen neighboring towns, including the villages of Havelock, Yankee Hill, and Bethany. In 1928, New York investment banker John F. Harris, a former resident of Lincoln, donated five hundred acres to the city as a Christmas gift. Two years later he donated another one hundred acres. The land forms the nucleus of Pioneers Park, which was dedicated on May 17, 1930. The city has a number of other parks, including the 1,445-acre Wilderness Park, with bridle, hiking, and biking trails covering more than twenty-two miles, and Antelope Park, with its sunken gardens and

O Street in Lincoln, about 1905. —Wyoming State Museum, Stimson Collection

Folsom Children's Zoo. The Nine-Mile Prairie is located nine miles south of the Lincoln town square and consists of native prairie. It is part of the Nebraska Statewide Arboretum, an association of affiliated sites throughout the state. There are fifty arboretums in Nebraska, a dozen of which are in Lincoln.

In addition to the University of Nebraska, Lincoln has three other colleges: Southeast Community College, Nebraska Wesleyan University, and Union College. Major industries are Archer Daniels Midland (fertilizer), Brunswick (aerospace products), Crete Carrier (trucking firm), Cushman Motors (industrial and commercial vehicles), Dorsey Laboratories (pharmaceuticals), Duncan Aviation (general aviation sales and equipment), Goodyear Tire & Rubber Company (V-belts and rubber hoses), Harris Laboratories (research and testing), Isco (scientific testing instruments), Kawasaki Motors (motorcycles, recreational vehicles, and Jet Skis), Selection Research (market research and opinion polling), SmithKline Beecham Animal Health (veterinary supplies), and Telex Communications (antennas and communications equipment).

Lincoln is also the site of the Nebraska State Prison. On February 11, 1912, the prison warden was stabbed to death. A month later his successor and two others also died in stabbing incidents, and in 1955 a riot tore through the prison.

Go Big Red

If Nebraskans have a collective passion, it is related to sports: football particularly, the University of Nebraska Huskers specifically. The red and white uniforms of the University of Nebraska Huskers (formerly the Cornhuskers) motivate the people of the state as nothing else. Mild mannered farmers, aloof insurance executives, and college students all come together at game time, donning their red and white sweatshirts and heading to the stadium. If they aren't lucky enough to have tickets (games always sell out), they gather in the parking lots. Husker fans support their team inside and out. All across the state fans gather before television sets; farmers listen to the games on their radios as they disk fields. Such devotion may seem a little silly, but not to Nebraskans. They stand behind their team every inch of the way. The athletes do their part to earn such devotion by bringing home national championships.

Coach Bob Devaney started the winning tradition in 1962, and since Tom Osborne took over in 1973 he has amassed 219 wins in 269 outings, making him the winningest coach in the nation. According to the university's sports information department, as of 1995 the Huskers had led the nation in consecutive winning seasons (thirty-three), an NCAA record; had gone to twenty-six consecutive bowl games, including fourteen consecutive New Year's Day bowls; and had earned eleven rushing titles (five in the last seven years). They won consecutive national championships in 1995 and 1996. Nebraska is only the third Division 1-A school to have back-to-back football coaches post 100 wins (Devaney 101, Osborne 219 and counting).

Winning on the field isn't the entire picture, however. Nebraska leads the nation in academic honors as well, with forty-eight first team Academic All-Americans and seven *NCAA Today's* Top Eight Award winners, the highest academic honor the NCAA gives to student athletes.

Prior to 1900 the Nebraska football teams went by the names Old Gold Knights, Bugeaters, and Antelopes. But that year Lincoln sportswriter Charles S. Sherman started calling them the Cornhuskers. The university adopted Herbie Husker as a mascot in 1974. By the early 1980s football recruiters started noticing that the name Cornhuskers (and Herbie Husker) didn't appeal to potential players. "We've found that Cornhuskers and Herbie just don't sell outside of Nebraska," Athletic Director Bill Byrne told the *Chicago Tribune* in 1995. University officials dumped Herbie and replaced him with the letter "N" as a logo. They also shortened "Cornhuskers" to "Huskers."

The University of Nebraska has much more going for it than football. One of its standout programs is the University of Nebraska Press, which publishes books related to the military frontier, Native Americans, women in the West, cattlemen, ranchers and cowboys, and blacks in the West. Titles include *The Log of a Cowboy* by J. Frank Dobie, *Love Song to the Plains* by Mari Sandoz, *The Galvanized Yankees* by Dee Brown, *Frontiersmen in Blue* by Robert Utley, *Letters of a Woman Homesteader* by Elinore Stewart Pruitt, *The Great Platte River Road* by Merrill Mattes, and novels by Bess Streeter Aldrich and Willa Cather.

Another type of book, particularly important for college students, had its genesis in Lincoln: Cliffs Notes. Started by former textbook salesman Clifton K. Hillegass in 1958, the company (now an $11-million-a-year business) produces the hottest-selling study guides in the country. The best-selling Cliffs Notes edition of all time is the guide for Hawthorne's *The Scarlet Letter,* although *Huckleberry Finn* and *Macbeth* sell well, too.

The Nation's Only Unicameral Legislature

As early as 1915 John Norton advocated a change in Nebraska's government from a bicameral, or two-house, legislature to a unicameral system. Norton advocated the change to reduce costs, to make lawmakers more responsible, and to limit the potential for political infighting and manipulation by special-interest groups. Although Norton had early support, his proposal took years to come to fruition, and it occurred only because a powerful U.S. senator became involved.

Nebraska's unicameral legislature in session, May 1995.

Senator George W. Norris is usually credited with ensuring Nebraska's move to a unicameral form of government. In 1923 Norris wrote a piece for the *New York Times* calling for a unicameral legislature in Nebraska, saying he saw little reason for two bodies when the requirements of members for each were the same. He dismissed the contention that two houses in the bicameral system acted as checks and balances for each other and once commented, "As a matter of practice, it has developed frequently that, through the conference committee, the politicians have the checks, and the special interests the balances."

The first constitutions of Vermont, Pennsylvania, and Georgia provided for unicameral legislatures. Pennsylvania's system remained in place from 1776 to 1790, Georgia's from 1777 to 1790, and Vermont's from 1777 to 1836. Other states had tried using a unicameral system, including New York, Ohio, Oklahoma, Oregon, and Arizona, but they'd been unsuccessful. Nebraska came close to enacting the single-house legislature in 1919, when a motion before the constitutional convention died on a close vote.

In 1934 Nebraska supporters of the unicameral legislature established the Model Legislative Committee, which included Norton, political scientists from the University of Nebraska, and other interested individuals. Norris wrote a proposal, which the committee accepted after making some revisions. Supporters then went to the people, circulating petitions and getting about 95,000 people to sign, making it possible to put the resolution before the voters as an amendment.

The state became bitterly divided over the proposed amendment. Proponents included members of the clergy, educators, and young people; opponents included politicians, attorneys, bankers, and other special interests. Most of the 440 newspapers in Nebraska opposed the plan; the only dailies to express support were the *Lincoln Star* and the *Hastings Tribune*. The powerful *Nebraska Farmer* rejected the idea as well.

Norris campaigned untiringly for the unicameral, traveling the entire state to address audiences. He particularly advocated having nonpartisan elections. In many cases the press refused to report on his appearances, and local opponents to the amendment tore down placards announcing his speaking engagements.

But when the people of Nebraska had their chance to vote, they endorsed the plan, 286,000 in favor to 193,000 opposed. Supporters recognized not only the potential for better representation but also the economic factors associated with a unicameral legislative body. The bicameral legislature, with thirty-three senators and one hundred representatives, had an annual budget in 1934 of $106,000; that dropped by about two-thirds under the unicameral form of government. Incidentally, in 1934 voters also approved measures related to the repeal of Prohibition and the establishment of pari-mutuel betting; some analysts think the fact that all three issues appeared on the same ballot may have influenced the outcome.

Nebraska launched its unicameral government in 1937 before a gallery of spectators, including members of the national media, who had come to Lincoln to report on the "Nebraska experiment," as the unicameral had become known by then. Initially, nonpartisan legislators served two-year terms, earning $872 a year. In 1962 legislation extended terms to four years, and the salary had increased to $12,000 annually, with representatives receiving expenses during the legislative session. Although other states considered unicameral governments, and Minnesota had one for many years, by 1997 Nebraska stood alone as the only unicameral government in the nation.

William Jennings Bryan

Standing next to George Norris in helping to shape Nebraska's political past is the man known as the "Great Commoner." It's likely more has been written about William Jennings Bryan than about any

Mr. and Mrs. William Jennings Bryan at the desk in the library of their D Street home in Nebraska City. —Nebraska State Historical Society

other Nebraska politician. He ran for president in 1896 and thereafter was known throughout the nation as a leader of both the Democratic and Populist parties. But it was his defense of the Bible in the 1925 Scopes "Monkey" trial that really struck a nerve with the American people.

Bryan was born in Salem, Illinois, in 1860. He and his bride, Mary Elizabeth Baird, moved to Lincoln in 1887, where he established a law practice. In 1890 he ran as a Democratic candidate for U.S. Congress, winning in the Republican community of Lincoln. He served two terms in the U.S. House of Representatives, advocating agricultural reforms such as tariff reduction and railroad regulation. He worked to find ways to ease credit problems for farmers, who had been hit hard by bad winters in the late 1880s and drought and grasshopper infestations in the early 1890s.

Bryan didn't run for reelection to Congress in 1894, instead becoming editor in chief of the powerful *Omaha World-Herald*. He went to work at the paper for a variety of reasons. Bryan wanted an avenue through which to espouse some of his beliefs and to "exert a considerable influence in the way of uniting these kindred forces against the common enemy—The Republican Party," he wrote *World-Herald* owner Gilbert Hitchcock on April 14, 1894. Hitchcock hired Bryan because he thought the politician would bring a fresh infusion of cash into the paper's operation, money the publisher needed to pay for new typesetting machines he had ordered. *World-Herald* Washington correspondent Richard L. Metcalfe also endorsed the idea of Bryan's involvement. But the deal had strings: Bryan became editor only when he agreed to purchase $15,000 worth of stock in the newspaper.

Although Bryan was a prolific writer, he seldom spent time at the office. Many of his ideas and partially completed pieces were put into final form by other staff writers, primarily by Metcalfe, and published under Bryan's name. When Bryan became a presidential candidate in 1896, the paper vigorously endorsed his return to politics, running the full text of many of his speeches.

In earlier years Bryan had differed with Democratic Party officials because of his support for free silver. At the 1896 Democratic Convention in Chicago, he had another opportunity to espouse his views, and this time he wowed his listeners. In his "Cross of Gold" speech, Bryan appealed for the opportunity to freely coin silver, saying, "Having behind us the producing masses of this nation and the world, we will answer their demand for a gold standard by saying to them: You shall not press down upon the brow of labor this crown of thorns, you shall not crucify mankind upon a cross of gold."

Bryan's marvelous oratory resulted in his gaining the Democratic nomination for the presidency. Further, the "Boy Orator of the Platte" had the support of the Populist Party because of his commitment to agrarian interests. He launched into his campaign, traveling 18,000 miles and making more than 3,000 speeches, but he lost the election to William McKinley. Democrats quickly alleged that the Republicans had purchased McKinley's position by conducting a massive propaganda campaign and spending ten times as much as did Bryan's supporters.

The Democrats nominated Bryan twice more, in 1900 and in 1908, but the splendid orator couldn't hold his own in a national campaign. By 1912 Bryan had lost some of his political clout (in part because the lifelong teetotaler had come out in favor of Prohibition in 1910), but he still had enough political power to assist in securing the nomination of Woodrow Wilson as the Democratic presidential candidate. Republicans divided their votes between William Howard Taft and Theodore Roosevelt, and Wilson slipped into the breach, capturing the White House for the Democrats.

Offered his choice of cabinet positions, Bryan became U.S. secretary of state. He helped shape progressive reforms, including creation of the Federal Trade Commission, adoption of the Federal Reserve System, and development of antitrust legislation. He had a role in the adoption of constitutional amendments that provided for the national income tax, direct election of senators, Prohibition, and women's suffrage.

Bryan and his wife, Mary, left Nebraska after World War I because her health was failing. They moved to Florida, where he became increasingly active in religious activities. Bryan decried the theory of evolution, and in 1925 he served as a member of the prosecution at the trial of Tennessee biology teacher John Scopes, charged with violating a state law that prohibited the teaching of Darwin's theory of evolution. Chicago attorney Clarence Darrow handled the case for the defense. The trial's climax occurred when Darrow placed Bryan on the stand and exposed his beliefs. Although Scopes was found guilty, the Tennessee Supreme Court eventually overturned Scope's conviction on a technicality.

Like most politicians, Bryan had his supporters and his opponents. Novelist Willa Cather noted that his conversation often was "absolutely overwhelming in its richness and novelty and power," and some scholars maintain that he was the "greatest moral force of his day." But Bryan had enemies who often criticized his speeches and his manners. One said he resembled the Platte River: "six inches deep and a mile wide at the mouth." The *Omaha Bee* editor called Bryan "Windy Jay."

But his legacy cannot be denied. Bryan helped mold and shape the Democratic Party, reorienting it from a party that opposed big government to one that advocated the use of government for social reform.

The Other Bryan

While William Jennings Bryan is touted as the Great Commoner and his deeds are recorded in the pages of history books, the fact is that his younger brother, Charles Wayland Bryan, had just as big a role in early Nebraska.

Seven years younger than W. J., Charles, or C. W., first became involved in politics during the 1896 presidential campaign, moving from Omaha to Lincoln to assume control of his brother's campaign office. During subsequent years the brothers worked together often. C. W. served as business and political manager for W. J. and worked as publisher and associate editor of the political newspaper W. J. started, *The Commoner*. The Bryans published *The Commoner* along with journalist Orlando Jay Smith from 1901 until April 1923. The staff included Will Maupin and Richard L. Metcalfe. Nationwide circulation peaked at 275,000. When *The Commoner* ceased publication, W. J. wrote, "My brother, as publisher, has from the beginning relieved me of all the work connected with this paper, except the writing of editorials."

Charles Bryan didn't enter Nebraska politics until his brother had stepped aside. But when C. W. entered the picture he did so quickly and decisively, serving as Lincoln mayor in 1915–17 and again in 1935–37. He served three terms as Nebraska governor (1923–25 and 1931–35), and in 1924 he followed his brother's footsteps in running (unsuccessfully) for national office as the Democratic vice presidential candidate.

The Starkweather Case

Charles Starkweather, nineteen years old in 1958, stood five feet, five inches tall, weighed 140 pounds, and had bow legs and pigeon toes. He wore his dark red hair cut short on top, and he had difficulty pronouncing his *w*s and *r*s. He had no juvenile record and wasn't a problem for schoolteachers, although he generally finished work in the bottom half of his class. Starkweather had a reputation as a hot-rod daredevil at the Lincoln Capital Speedways. He smoked too much, was a pretty good mechanic, and went by the nicknames "Big Red" and "Little Red," though he hated both of them.

Caril Ann Fugate wore her dark brown hair in a ponytail. She stood five feet, one inch tall and weighed 105 pounds. Though only fourteen years old in 1958, she looked eighteen and dreamed of becoming a nurse. A student at Whittier Junior High, Fugate lived with her mother, stepfather, and younger half-sister.

Lincoln police radios crackled about 4:30 P.M., January 27, 1958, when authorities found three bodies in some outbuildings at a home in Lincoln. Early reports identified the victims as Marion Bartlett, 57, his wife, Velda, 37, and their daughter, Betty Jean, who was just a couple weeks shy of her third birthday. The adults died of gunshot wounds, and the child had been killed by a blow to the head. Wanted for questioning were Mrs. Bartlett's daughter from a previous marriage, Caril Ann Fugate, and her boyfriend, Charles Starkweather.

In a front-page story with a headline blaring, "Belmont Family Slain," the *Lincoln Star* reported that police in a six-state area were on the lookout for Fugate and Starkweather, last reported headed south from Lincoln. They converged upon a farmhouse in Bennet, a small town southwest of Lincoln at the head of the Little Nemaha River. After firing tear gas into the home, police conducted a search, finding the body of August Meyer, an elderly bachelor who had been a friend of the Starkweather family. Police suspected Fugate and Starkweather had escaped in a car belonging to Robert Jensen, a seventeen-year-old Bennet boy. But before police could close in, the story took another grim twist. Everet Broening, a farmer in the Bennet area, found the bodies of Robert Jensen and sixteen-year-old Carol King in a cellar near an abandoned schoolhouse. The death toll on January 27—three bodies; the toll on January 28—six bodies. Police stepped up efforts to find Fugate and Starkweather, whom they always suspected was the instigator of the murder spree.

On January 29 authorities found three more people murdered: forty-eight-year-old C. Lauer Ward, president of Capital Bridge Company, his forty-six-year-old wife, Clara, and their fifty-one-year-old maid, Lillian Fencl. By that time Lancaster County residents feared the killers couldn't be stopped; stores that sold firearms did a brisk business as residents bought weapons to use for defense. The general panic led Mayor Abe Martin to ask Governor Victor E. Anderson to mobilize the Nebraska National Guard. Some one hundred to two hundred guardsmen soon patrolled Lincoln streets, assisting the Lancaster County Sheriff's Department. Police blocked all roads into and out of the city, and armed residents stood in their yards, watching for the suspects.

After the murders of the Wards and their maid, the suspects headed west, into the Sandhills. A truck driver reported seeing them at Mullen, Whitman, and Alliance. About 3 P.M. on January 29 in Douglas, Wyoming, Deputy Sheriff Bill Romer was traveling near Ayres Natural Bridge when he spotted the vehicle wanted in connection with the

Nebraska killing spree. A "running gun battle" ensued, according to an Associated Press report. It ended just west of Douglas, with the two teenagers in custody. Wyoming officials immediately learned the killing hadn't ended at the state line: Starkweather had shot Merle Collison, a Great Falls, Montana, shoe salesman, nine times near Douglas.

Before long both Fugate and Starkweather were extradited to Nebraska to face murder charges. Evidence quickly surfaced that Starkweather also had been involved in the death of Lincoln service-station attendant Robert Colvert on December 1, 1956. On May 23, 1958, following a two-week trial, a jury found Starkweather guilty in the death of Bennet teenager Robert Jensen and sentenced him to death. Although there were a number of delays, he died in the electric chair in Nebraska at 12:01 A.M., June 25, 1959.

Fugate, meanwhile, was held at the Lincoln State Hospital. Her trial for killing the Bennet teenager started October 27, 1958, and within a month the jury had a verdict: guilty of first-degree murder. However, the Fugate jury determined she should be sentenced to life in prison, not given the death penalty.

At age fifteen, Fugate went to the Women's Reformatory at York. She finished her schooling and studied to be a nurse. Fugate became a seamstress at the reformatory and made several bids for freedom before the Nebraska Parole Board. In 1973 the movie *Badlands* re-created the Starkweather-Fugate murder spree. A year later authorities paroled Fugate, and on June 20, 1974, she walked away from the Nebraska Center for Women (formerly the Women's Reformatory). Fugate left Nebraska for St. Johns, Michigan, where she had lined up a job. On September 28, 1981, the *Lincoln Journal* reported that Fugate had completed her five-year parole period. She had served eighteen years of a life sentence and always maintained she had been forced to go with Starkweather on the killing spree. In August 1996 she applied for a full pardon.

Other television programs and movies have focused on the Starkweather case, including the television series *Lie Detector* and the TV miniseries *Starkweather: Murder in the Heartland.*

Inside the Argus Automobile Company factory. —Nebraska State Historical Society

Lincoln—Grand Island
74 miles

Interstate 80 runs in a straight east-west line between Lincoln and Grand Island. Fields of corn and other crops are raised on farms both north and south of the highway. US 34 runs north of the interstate and provides access to many small communities (and a few large ones as well), including Malcolm, Garland, Seward, Staplehurst, Tamora, Utica, Waco, York, Bradshaw, Hampton, and Aurora.

German, Danish, and English immigrants settled the region, once the homeland of the Pawnee, Omaha, and Otoe Indians. Seward, named for William H. Seward, secretary of state under President Abraham Lincoln, became a trading center after 1873 when the Midland Pacific Railroad reached the town. Organizers platted York in 1869, but the rail line didn't reach the latter community until 1877. Nevertheless, York became a trading center, and early industry included a brick and tile plant, a foundry and engine works, and a factory that produced a variety of veterinary products for livestock. In 1890 the United Brethren in Christ established York College. The community also had an orphanage and the State Reformatory for Women, later renamed the Nebraska Center for Women.

In 1871 seven men from Chariton, Iowa, decided to start a town in Nebraska. They each gave $30 to David Stone, and he set out to find the site for the community. Not far from Grand Island he chose a place. Although their venture eventually failed, the town of Aurora, named for Aurora, Illinois, became established in the area.

Nebraska City—Lincoln
40 miles

NEBRASKA CITY

Long before Nebraska City existed, this area served as a military installation to protect emigrants as they started their migration to the Oregon Country. The city that now covers seven large hills developed into a prominent river and railroad center soon after the establishment of Nebraska Territory in 1854. Goods were transported on a variety of steamboats to landings on the Missouri River, then hauled west by dozens of companies. The city had a role in the purchase of Indian lands and reportedly became a stop on the Underground Railroad when abolitionists began spiriting southern slaves to freedom. Its greatest legacy for the nation, however, may be its role in the development of Arbor Day.

The Earliest Fort Kearny

Stephen Watts Kearny recommended that a fort be established on Table Creek near its confluence with the Missouri River in order to provide protection for emigrants traveling west on the Oregon Trail. The post at the Missouri, sometimes called the first Fort Kearny, was never actually a fort; it might better be labeled "Camp Kearny," which is what the first soldiers stationed there called it. The War Department generally referred to it as a "post" or "installation." General Kearny selected the site for the post in part because of its easy access to steamboat transportation on the Missouri River and in part because of the availability of stone and other building materials. Kearny suggested that the post be called Fort Nebraska or Fort Macomb, but it took his name instead.

In the spring of 1845 Capt. William McKissack was dispatched from Fort Leavenworth to obtain supplies to build the post. He originally estimated it would take $10,000 to complete the task, but in just a few weeks he asked for an additional $5,000 to cover expenses, including the purchase of 400 bushels of corn for the Otoe Indians. By mid-June 1845 McKissack had the blockhouse in place and a hospital foundation laid, but then the War Department issued an order to suspend con-

134

struction. The Mexican War had started, and men were needed for the Santa Fe campaign. At the same time Congress authorized construction of "military stations on the route to Oregon." The post along the Missouri failed to meet the obligation to protect overland emigrants; a new post farther west was needed to fill that bill.

On June 1, 1847, Secretary of War W. L. Marcy ordered posts to be built near the Grand Island on the Platte and at the fur trading post at Fort Laramie. It fell to Lt. D. P. Woodbury to select the site for the "new" Fort Kearny. He chose a place at the west end of Grand Island (see page 189). At about the same time the Oregon Battalion, formed of volunteers from Missouri, got orders to build and man the new forts. The 478-member battalion mobilized in the fall, but before it reached the site for the new fort near the Platte, inclement weather descended, and the battalion established winter quarters at Camp Kearny on Table Creek. Commanding officer Lt. Col. L. E. Powell referred to the camp as "Fort Kearny" on reports filed as that winter passed. When the grass started to sprout in 1848, the Oregon Battalion headed west and built the new post on the Platte. First called Fort Childs, it was later renamed Fort Kearny.

Freight Fuels a Nebraska City Boom

A number of towns boomed when Congress approved creation of Nebraska Territory in 1854, among them Nebraska City. The community was laid out by Hiram P. Downs, who had been responsible for

A sightseeing automobile in Nebraska City. —Otto Berthold, private collection

the government installation at old Fort Kearny. Breathing real life into the community, however, were the freighting companies that established headquarters on the hills above the Missouri. William Nuckolls is often given credit for founding Nebraska City as a trading post and riverboat stop on the rolling hills above the Missouri River.

Nebraska City quickly became a transportation center. It served as one of the earliest starting points for travelers headed west on the Oregon Trail. They followed the Nebraska City–Fort Kearny Cutoff, which angled west, roughly along the route of Nebraska 2, to about where Lincoln now sits. There it picked up the main road west. The Ox-Bow Trail also originated in Nebraska City's hills. That freighter and emigrant trail zigzagged across the country west of Nebraska City and angled northwest toward the Platte River, which it reached south of present-day Columbus.

Although some of the earliest travelers on both routes west were emigrants, the trails soon saw major commercial use, with goods hauled in a variety of freighting vehicles. The Missouri River landing at Nebraska City became a beehive as the city's sixty-four freighting companies loaded and unloaded their wagons. Prominent companies headquartered in Nebraska City included Coe and Carter; Wells, Fargo and Company; Hawke, Nuckolls and Company; H. T. Clarke and Company; Gilman Brothers; Ben Holladay; and the largest company of them all, Russell, Majors, and Waddell, which by the late 1850s dominated the industry in Nebraska.

Construction of Fort Kearny and Fort Laramie required the hauling of supplies from eastern river ports. In 1855 Alexander Majors and William H. Russell obtained a government contract to haul supplies from Fort Leavenworth to western outposts. Two years later, as Col. Albert Sidney Johnston took an army across the Oregon Trail to Utah in order to put down a revolt (the so-called Mormon War), Majors and Russell enlisted a new partner, William B. Waddell. At the same time, they recognized the need to haul freight from a point farther upstream on the Missouri, and when army quartermaster Maj. James G. Martin recommended Nebraska City, they moved their operation. The move transformed Nebraska City from frontier town to bustling river port.

The company purchased land for houses, foundries, warehouses, and boardinghouses. Hauling government freight required tremendous numbers of men and animals; Russell, Majors, and Waddell advertised for 16,000 yoke of oxen and 1,500 men to handle the lines. In separating their duties, Russell generally worked with Congress to obtain freighting contracts, Majors involved himself with the wagon trains, and Waddell handled the local financial affairs.

Several factors helped Nebraska City become a natural freighting location. The land gently sloped to the river, creating a good landing, and the direct route from Nebraska City to Fort Kearny was faster and drier than other trails to the western outpost. The *Nebraska City Newspress* of February 10, 1866, reported: "Nebraska City is eighty miles nearer Fort Kearney [*sic*] than any other freighting point on the Missouri river, and the best road running west, and as a matter-of-course freight can be transported from this point cheaper." Besides its distance advantage, the Nebraska City to Fort Kearny route—identified as the Great Central Route on a map drawn in August 1862 by Robert Harvey—had "every stream bridged, no fords, no ferries."

Russell, Majors, and Waddell headquartered their freighting firm at the present location of 14th Street and 3rd Avenue. Their presence helped Nebraska City prosper for nearly a decade, and there they launched the Pony Express. Nebraska City had three times as many freighting companies as Omaha during this period. Among others who freighted out of Nebraska City were Ben Holladay, who later operated the Overland Stage Line in western Nebraska and across Wyoming, and John M. Chivington, best remembered for the attack he ordered upon a camp of Cheyenne Indians in 1864 at Sand Creek, Colorado.

The Nebraska City–Fort Kearny route in the vicinity of Nebraska City became known as Steam Wagon Road in 1862 when J. R. Brown built a steam-powered covered wagon that had four engines. The unwieldy looking steam wagon featured four wheels in front, each six feet in diameter, and rear wheels that were twelve feet in diameter. Brown intended to drive the steam wagon from Nebraska City to Denver. He launched the venture July 22, 1862, but got only a few miles from Nebraska City before a drive shaft broke, stranding the vehicle. Brown didn't succeed in repairing the steam wagon, but the street where the vehicle headed out of Nebraska City is still called Steam Wagon Road.

The pontoon bridge over the Missouri, completed August 23, 1888, was the only way for wagons to cross until the community could raise the money for a permanent bridge. The pontoon structure zigzagged over the water because that design made it easier to adjust the bridge to the side when ships moved up and down the Missouri. A hundred or more flatboats made up the bridge, which had a main span 894 feet long. There was an 1,100-foot-long approach on the east side of the 24-foot-wide bridge. A round-trip cost forty cents for a double team, or a quarter for a horse and rider. That was about half of what it cost to traverse the river on the Nebraska City ferry. The bridge cost five cents for cattle or people on foot, ten cents for horses, and two cents for hogs. Though a rather remarkable engineering feat, the bridge saw use for only one season. The spring runoff in 1889 washed it out, and it was not replaced.

Civil War Activities and John Brown

Soldiers fought no Civil War battles in Nebraska, but the territory became bitterly contested ground nevertheless. The controversial Kansas-Nebraska Act set the stage for conflict in Nebraska. Located just across the river from slaveholding Missouri, Nebraska presented an attractive opportunity for slaves seeking to escape oppression.

Abolitionist John Brown was born in 1800 at Torrington, Connecticut. As a youngster he helped his father supply beef to U.S. troops during the War of 1812. During that period he started to notice the effects of slavery on blacks in the South. By the time John Brown had a wife and family of his own, the nation had started to tear apart as the rhetoric escalated over the issue of slavery. At age fifty-five, Brown left his wife and family at North Elba, New York, along with a small colony of fugitive slaves. He headed west to go to Bleeding Kansas, where he became Capt. John Brown. Soon he had several handles—John Brown of Osawatomie, John the Outlaw—and he became known as the Warrior or the Soldier of Freedom.

At about the same time John Brown arrived in Kansas, John Henri (Henry) Kagi (originally spelled Kagey) moved in with his sister, Barbara Kagi Mayhew, and her husband, Allen Mayhew, who had a small cabin

The Millar cabin at the John Brown Museum, Nebraska City.

at Nebraska City. Henry Kagi's father and younger sister Mary had a claim eight miles south of Nebraska City. Henry worked as a schoolteacher, lawyer, and correspondent for large eastern newspapers. On July 4, 1856, while reporting on the unsettled conditions in Topeka, Kansas, he met John Brown.

Before long Kagi became "secretary of war" in John Brown's "army." He fought in the August 30, 1856, Battle of Osawatomie and in other engagements in Kansas as tensions escalated. After the Battle of Osawatomie, where one of his sons died, Brown decided to help blacks escape the South, so he became involved in the Underground Railroad of the West, a network of people and places, including several in eastern Nebraska Territory, that hid fleeing slaves. The Mayhews became involved, and Nebraska City, strategically positioned at the edge of a free territory and on the Missouri River, became one station on the route.

According to local tradition, a series of man-made underground chambers served as hiding places. The slaves were ferried over the Missouri and hidden in a cave on the Mayhew property. It was known as "John Brown's Cave," although there is no concrete evidence that Brown had a personal and direct role in moving escaping slaves through Nebraska City. Nebraska State Historical Society staff are "increasingly skeptical of the whole story," according to senior historian R. Eli Paul. Nevertheless, a hard-to-kill legend says Abraham N. Kagey built the original cave, with an entrance in a ravine along Table Creek, west of the Mayhew cabin. The cave entrance was just large enough to crawl through, carefully concealed by brush, and marked by three oak trees near the cabin.

A replica of the Mayhew cabin and the underground tunnel and cave have been rebuilt near the original site in Nebraska City, and they now serve as a tourist attraction, along with the John Brown Cave Museum, which is built of wood from original Nebraska City buildings.

John Brown and Henry Kagi went on to other fights. Kagi and Aaron D. Stevens were the first of John Brown's nineteen men to cross the bridge to Harper's Ferry on October 16, 1859. There he was in charge of the government rifle works, which Lt. Robert E. Lee and 800 troops fought to protect. Kagi died at Harper's Ferry, and Brown was charged with treason, found guilty, and eventually hanged for his role in the raid that helped launch the Civil War. Both are buried on the Brown homestead near Lake Placid, New York, which is now a memorial to Brown and his comrades.

J. Sterling Morton and the Birth of Arbor Day

Another well-recognized Nebraska City landmark is the magnificent Arbor Lodge, now a fifty-two-room mansion. In 1855 it was the four-room, L-shaped house of J. Sterling and Carolyn Morton. J. Sterling claimed his land in 1855, paying $1.25 per acre, with the patent granted on May 1, 1860. By that time several important events had occurred on his property, including negotiations for the Table Creek Treaty between Pawnee chiefs and U.S. Indian Commissioner James W. Denver. On September 24, 1857, the Pawnees gave up an area that encompassed almost one-third of present-day Nebraska in exchange for a reserve along the Loup River that was only slightly larger than Otoe County. They also were to receive payments of $40,000 a year for five years.

The Mortons came to Nebraska Territory in 1854 and settled at Bellevue, then the only permanent white settlement in the newly created territory. Peter Sarpy and friends had officially organized the town on February 9, 1854. Morton quickly became involved in Nebraska politics, including the intense battle that brewed over the location of the territorial capital, and he served as clerk of the territorial supreme court during his first winter in the region.

In the ongoing saga of where to locate Nebraska's territorial (and eventually state) capital, Morton found himself on the opposite side of the Platte—south of it—from Thomas B. Cuming. The two men became intense rivals in a variety of political issues. Morton left Bellevue behind and moved to Nebraska City, where he edited the *Nebraska City News*. Morton had been involved with Thomas Morton (no relation) in publication of the *Nebraska Palladium* at Bellevue, the first newspaper in the region, and when Thomas Morton also relocated to Nebraska City, the two again joined forces. The *Palladium* had ceased publication by that time, so when the *Nebraska City News* started it absorbed the *Palladium's* subscription list.

In the fall of 1855 Nebraska City residents elected Morton one of their representatives in the 2nd Territorial Legislature, but he didn't support proposals many of his constituents favored—including numerous banking bills—and lost a reelection bid in 1856. The territorial economy skyrocketed because of some of those banking deals when wildcat institutions (which had little security and backing) issued paper money they used themselves for a variety of business enterprises. But then the bottom fell out of the economy, and it became clear the wildcat banks had no stability and few assets. Most of them failed in 1857, as the new Nebraska Territory faced its first economic downturn.

But the failure of the banks worked in Morton's favor; voters realized he might have been wise to oppose the banking bills and returned him to the territorial legislature. In 1858 Morton became secretary of the Territory of Nebraska, filling the position left vacant by the death of his former nemesis, Thomas Cuming, and he served as acting governor during the five months between the resignation of William A. Richardson in December 1858 and the appointment of Samuel W. Black on May 2, 1859.

Morton continued in various political capacities in subsequent years and eventually served as secretary of agriculture under President Grover Cleveland from 1893 to 1896. Morton's appointment came in part because of his past political experience and in part because of his agricultural knowledge. He had started farming almost as soon as he arrived in Nebraska City. From the very beginning he planted trees, moving small ones from along the Missouri River to near his home, which became Arbor Lodge. At the time the Mortons built their first home on the hills above the Missouri, they could see the shimmering ribbon of water from the front of the house. But over the years they planted so many trees near their hillside home that eventually the leaves and branches obstructed the river view.

Improving his home and grounds was an important part of Morton's life. "To fix up a home and beautify it is the pleasant part of living in this world," he wrote May 25, 1873. Just six years later he wrote, "We are building, renewing, and reforming. We dwell in shavings and water and amidst paint." The Morton home eventually had at least thirty rooms, and J. Sterling and Carolyn had four sons to carry on the work started in Nebraska. "They have the qualities out of which to mould [sic] fortunes and fame," Morton wrote of his sons. They lived up to his assessment. The eldest son, Joy, eventually started the Morton Salt Company; Paul worked with the railroad and served as secretary of the

J. Sterling Morton home (forerunner to Arbor Lodge). –Nebraska State Historical Society

navy under President Theodore Roosevelt; Mark worked as a farmer; and Carl established the Argo Starch Company. The Mortons retained Arbor Lodge until 1923, when they gave the land and their family home to the state of Nebraska for a park.

Although the lodge is a permanent part of Nebraska City culture, the major contribution of the Morton family is in its legacy of trees. J. Sterling Morton and his sons, particularly Mark, established large nurseries and apple orchards, and the elder Morton always believed in planting trees. The Nebraska State Board of Agriculture, with Morton as president, endorsed the importance of tree planting when it approved a resolution calling for Arbor Day in 1872. Initially the holiday was to be recognized on the second Wednesday of April; it changed to April 22—Morton's birthday—in 1885, when Arbor Day became an official state holiday.

Arbor Day has since been observed as a national holiday. Nebraskans planted more than a million trees the first year. In San Francisco such notables as Jack London and John Muir encouraged support for Arbor Day. In Oakland, California, a poet, Joaquin Miller, organized a celebration by getting schoolchildren to plant trees, and that city owes much of its greenery to Arbor Day.

"The cultivation of trees is the cultivation of the Good, the beautiful and the enabling in man," Morton wrote, adding, "Other holidays repose upon the past; Arbor Day proposes for the future."

Morton died in 1901, but his legacy remains in the form of the Arbor Lodge apple orchard and the millions of trees planted since the beginning of Arbor Day. In 1972 the National Arbor Day Foundation organized to recognize the centennial of Arbor Day. This nonprofit

Arbor Day two-cent postage stamp.
—Nebraska State Historical Society

Arbor Lodge view to the north. —Nebraska State Historical Society

Arbor Lodge, May 1995.

Harvesting grapes. —Nebraska State Historical Society

organization is dedicated to tree planting and environmental steward-ship through a number of education programs. The Arbor Day Farm includes the arboretums, windbreaks, apple and cherry orchards, and other agrarian interests on the original Morton farm. It is now a National Historic Landmark.

The apple orchard at Arbor Day Farm separates the region between Arbor Lodge and the Lied Conference Center, which was constructed using timber donated by the Oregon Small Woodlands Association. The National Woodland Owners Association appealed to its members for "a few good logs" to be used for the columns, trusses, and beams of the new facility. Among those who responded were the Lane County Chapter in Oregon, which contributed Douglas fir timbers from private woodlands, and Weyerhaeuser's Oregon Division, also in Lane County.

The center opened in 1993 and features ninety-six guest rooms. It is first and foremost a conference center, but a unique aspect of its construction and operation is a reliance on renewable resources. The carpets, for example, are made from recycled plastic pop bottles, while heating and cooling are provided by systems using wood chips. The center has sophisticated scrubbers on the heating and cooling air exhaust to clear the air of residue.

Wyoming: Ghost Town Near the Missouri

West of Nebraska City is the ghost town of Wyoming. In 1855 the settlement had a newspaper, two attorneys, two wagon repair and manufacturing shops, a lumber mill, a couple of blacksmiths, a doctor, and a saloon, which offered oysters for lunch. Many steamboats stopped to drop off supplies, and the town also served as a stop on the forty-eight-hour stage connecting St. Joseph, Missouri, and Omaha. Wyoming also served as the last official outfitting point on the Missouri River sponsored by the Church of Jesus Christ of Latter-day Saints. During a three-year period starting in 1864, church leaders sent wagons from Salt Lake City to Nebraska, where they loaded up with freight and provisions for Utah. During that same period some 6,500 people started their journey west with assistance from the emigrant agent at Wyoming. In 1867 Mormons started using the partially completed Union Pacific Railroad for transportation, abandoning river travel for faster rail services.

The completion of the Union Pacific led to a significant reduction in freighting business, but the death knell for Wyoming was construction of the Burlington Railroad in 1870, which bypassed the town by twelve miles. In 1860 Wyoming had ninety-nine people; by 1870 it wasn't even counted as a separate entity on the census, and in 1880 it didn't show up at all.

Lincoln–Hastings
99 miles

Like the area north of Interstate 80 between Lincoln and Grand Island, the country south of the interstate between Lincoln and Hastings is prime cropland. The west fork of the Big Blue River runs parallel to the two main roads headed west, I-80 and US 6. The interstate provides access to small communities such as Emerald, Pleasant Dale, Milford, Beaver Crossing, McCool Junction, Lushton, Henderson, and Glitner, all located between the interstate and the river. Meanwhile, US 6 and Nebraska 33 link Lincoln and Hastings, passing through or near Roca and Martell as well as through the "alphabet" towns named by the Burlington Railroad: Crete, Dorchester, Friend, Exeter, Fairmont, and Grafton. The land is open, characterized by crops and neat farmsteads with carefully groomed lawns and properly pruned trees.

CRETE
The earliest homesteaders in Saline County claimed land along the Blue River, using trails forged by Indians and later by emigrants headed west. The area drew many Czech settlers after Frank and Joe Jelinek arrived in 1865 from Wisconsin. Frank Jelinek eventually returned to

A man gets a meal at a bread line in Crete during the Depression.
—Nebraska State Historical Society

Wisconsin and wrote an article about the Nebraska country that appeared in *Slavie,* a newspaper with a wide circulation in the United States and Eastern European countries. That drew new Bohemian settlers to Nebraska.

In 1870 Jesse C. Bickle started a post office in his log house, calling the site Blue River City initially, then changing the name to Crete at the Postal Service's behest. The little town grew rapidly and by 1871 boasted a number of businesses, including attorneys, a doctor, department store, furniture store, drugstore, general store, grocery store, and newspaper, the *Saline County Post.* The community also had three saloons, a wholesale liquor house, a flour mill, a sawmill, two livery stables, and a number of other stores and businesses. The future of the town was secured when the Burlington & Missouri Railroad started operating between Lincoln and Crete in June 1871.

In 1872 the community established Doane College, which continues to operate on a modern, 300-acre wooded campus that is part of Nebraska's statewide arboretum. Three of the Doane College buildings—Boswell Observatory, built in 1883; Gaylord Hall, constructed in 1884; and Whitcomb Conservatory/Lee Memorial Chapel, built in 1906–7—are now listed on the National Register of Historic Places, as is the Jesse C. Bickle House, known locally as "The Maples," which serves the community as a museum.

All across the plains early settlers feared prairie fires. A tragedy occurred in this region on November 3, 1873, when flames raced across the land toward Pleasant Hill, which then served as the county seat. It was election day, and election officials had to close the polls so they could help battle the blaze, according to Annadora Foss Gregory in *History of Crete Nebraska, 1870–1888*. Once the threat to the town had been removed, the polls reopened. But the fire caused great damage and claimed the lives of two or three children and their grandmother as they tried to get home from school. Some other children, also caught in the blaze, managed to pull cornstalks from a large enough area that the fire circled around them.

SARONVILLE

Jarvil Chaffee claimed the first homestead claim in Hamilton County in May 1872 at a location where today's Nebraska 14 crosses the West Fork of the Big Blue River. Chaffee brought his family from Wisconsin and built a ten-by-twelve-foot dugout. Mrs. Chaffee died not long afterward. The story goes that the few women in the neighborhood didn't want to see her buried in a plain pine box, so they gathered wild grapes, crushed them, and used the dye to stain the box.

US 136
Brownville—Beatrice
52 miles

BROWNVILLE

Richard Brown crossed the Missouri River in late August 1854 to a natural landing in the newly organized Nebraska Territory. He started felling logs and building a cabin. The Tennesseean had emigrated from Nashville to Oregon, Missouri, where he had a wife and children. But the land across the Missouri River drew him, and when it opened for settlement Brown decided to move. He built his cabin, and other men did the same; they named the site Brownville, although it wasn't incorporated as an official town for another two years.

Official or not, Brownville expanded quickly. Brown became postmaster, and within a year the community had a sawmill, regular ferry services across the Missouri, and an official town plat. In February 1856 it incorporated, and town promoters touted it as the most logical place from which travelers headed west could begin their journey.

Emergency personnel monitor rising floodwaters at Brownville, May 1995.

Allen Coate prepared the town's official survey, writing on the plat in 1856: "The town site is a little uneven in a place or two & gradually ascending from the River to a distance of one and a half miles. . . . It is the nearest and most convenient place for Shippers to land Freight for the Forts & Annuities for the Indians. Also best crossing, nearest and best Route for Emigrants on their way over the Plains, and therefore bids fair to become the principal Town of Nebraska."

For a town to boom it needs forward-thinking residents, a good location helps, and a newspaper is almost a must. Brownville acquired the latter in 1856, when Dr. John McPherson arrived from Tippecanoe, Ohio, and started publishing the *Nebraska Advertiser.* Dr. McPherson brought with him an editor, Robert Wilkinson Furnas, who immediately started making his mark on the Brownville community. He went on to become a leader in Nebraska Territory and ultimately played a key role in the state of Nebraska.

Born near Troy, Ohio, Furnas was orphaned as a child and lived with his grandparents until he was old enough to become an apprentice printer. He helped with such projects as advertising flyers, posters, and routine business documents. Furnas also worked for a newspaper in Ohio. Before relocating to Brownville he also had jobs in the insurance and railroad industries.

In the premiere edition of the *Nebraska Advertiser,* Furnas placed an ad for himself: "R. W. Furnas, Land & Lot Agent, Insurance Agent and Agent for Agricultural Implements." Clearly, he didn't believe in putting all his eggs into one basket. Under his editorship the *Nebraska*

Advertiser had one primary goal: to promote the opportunities of Brownville. Articles touted the positive aspects of the community and encouraged new settlers, noting there were jobs for carpenters, bricklayers, shoemakers, tin- and coppersmiths, and a variety of other tradesmen. Cabins, houses, and businesses went up daily, and by 1856 the community even sported a fine new hotel, the Nebraska House, built by Taulbird Edwards and later leased by Albert J. Benedict. Other establishments quickly followed, including churches, a schoolhouse, and all manner of enterprises. Brownville had regular traffic crossing the river from Missouri on the ferry, and steamboats made the Brownville landing a regular stop. When a steamboat arrived, the entire community turned out to welcome it. J. H. Dundas wrote in *Granger History of Nemaha County*, published in 1902:

> When the loud whistle announced the coming of a steamboat, the boys hastened to the wharf. . . . And not only the boys, but the girls, young men, young ladies, businessmen, and even the aged and infirm came down to the river. . . . It is related that when the arrival of the first boat of the season had been announced that young men forgot decorum and hastened out of the church; the young ladies were restless and wondered if the preacher would ever quit, the deacons slipped out to look after the boys lest they fall in the river, and the preacher . . . hastened to the concluding paragraphs, made a short prayer . . . and then went to the river.

The steamboats brought passengers and freight, which meant profits and prosperity to the community. Some locals sold cordwood to power steamers such as the *Council Bluffs Packet*, the *Admiral*, the *Omaha*, the *Missouri River Packet*, and the *J. H. Lucas*, which set a record of just under sixty-one hours in making the trip between St. Louis and St. Joe.

Brownville wasn't all pride and prosperity, however. Early settlers often argued over claims. Sometimes claim-jumping disputes resolved themselves with little more than harsh words and strong-arm tactics, but other times one man or the other ended up dead. The community also had strong sentiments on both sides regarding slavery. Town founder Richard Brown owned slaves in Missouri, and many other residents also came from Missouri and supported slavery. Their sentiments showed up in various ways. At the Brownville Lyceum, Library and Literary Association, prominent men in the community often debated issues such as the Missouri Compromise, or this topic: "Resolved that the Indian has a greater right to complain of the whites than the Negro."

Pro-slavery sentiment manifested itself in other ways, too. It became most apparent whenever a report circulated that a fugitive slave was attempting to escape through Nebraska. In early September 1857, when

Archie Handley reported he had seen three armed blacks passing his house, a group of men—knowing that in Missouri there was a standing reward of $100 for anyone returning a runaway slave—quickly organized, racing out of town on horseback in hot pursuit. They caught up to the three not too far from town. Before the flurry of gunfire ended, one of the pursuing party, a man named Myers, lay dead in the trees, and the slaves were racing north on their pursuer's horses.

Later one of the three returned to Brownville suffering from a gunshot wound to the arm. The town's doctors consulted and decided to amputate the slave's injured arm. They did so and left him at the American House, guarded by Deputy Sheriff Ben Thompson. In the intervening time, word had spread across the river about the escaping slaves and the death of Myers. Before long a large party of men crossed the river from Missouri. Intending to retaliate for Myers's death, they went to the American House to get the prisoner. Ben Thompson refused to release the slave to the vigilante crowd. The Missouri slaveowners and slavery supporters ranted and raved about town. That caused a group of Brownville abolitionists to gather and arm themselves as well. The situation had all the makings of a disaster; each side flung threats and taunts toward the other. As dawn brightened the waters of the Missouri and filtered through Brownville's trees, Judge C. W. Wheeler appealed to Richard Brown to diffuse the situation. Brown told the Missouri crowd the status of the man in custody would be decided by the courts, not by a vigilante crowd. Eventually the Missourians eased away and went back to their side of the river.

At a subsequent coroner's inquest, one of the men who had ridden with Myers identified the man who had shot him as the "Big Negro"— not the man in custody at the American House. Eventually authorities in Iowa apprehended the "Big Negro," who himself died in another fight. Meanwhile, the man who owned the slave held at the American House arrived in Brownville. He threw a rip-roaring fit when he found the man's arm had been amputated, thus "devaluing" his property, but he reclaimed his slave anyway.

Life in early Brownville included performances by the Silver Cornet Band, dances at the Brownville House, and horse races at Newmarket Course. The town weathered the financial difficulties of 1857 and looked for prosperity in 1858 when the *Nebraska Advertiser* under the able leadership of editor Furnas started promoting Brownville as the logical place jumping-off point for "Nebraska's Gold Fields" on Cherry Creek. The route, estimated at 551 miles, would go through "one of the most delightful countries in Nebraska . . . with pure water, and lumber for camping," Furnas said. In spite of his efforts, Furnas couldn't get the people of Brownville behind his proposal for a road to connect Brownville with the Cherry Creek diggings and that new town springing up near the mountains—Denver.

Although the road project didn't get off the ground, hundreds of prospectors and freighters did outfit in Brownville before starting their journey to the goldfields. Furnas continued to make his mark on the community, and he started to expand his reach in 1859 with the establishment of the *Nebraska Farmer*, a monthly paper devoted to agricultural interests.

In 1860 Congress authorized a ten-year, $40,000 per year subsidy for a telegraph line from the western border of Missouri to San Francisco. Western Union president Hiram Sibley immediately started efforts to complete a line and get the subsidy. W. H. Stebbins started building up the Missouri River from St. Joseph to Omaha, and by August 29, 1860, the line reached its first Nebraska station at Brownville. The town's residents celebrated with "bonfires, illuminations, fire balls, music, burning gunpowder, speeches and toasts," according to the *Nebraska Advertiser*. The *New York Times* announced that the telegraph had reached "the half-peopled wilds of Nebraska."

When the Civil War broke out in 1861, Nebraska provided troops for the Union cause. The Brownville Union Guards had already formed several months before Acting Governor Algernon S. Paddock's May 9, 1861, proclamation asking for volunteers. Robert Furnas soon found himself in a new position exchanging the editorship of the *Nebraska Advertiser* for a military post. First Furnas was commissioned colonel of the 1st Indian Regiment raised in Kansas. But when Paddock asked him to assist in recruiting the 2nd Nebraska Cavalry Regiment, he returned to Nebraska and became captain of Company E. He eventually became the commanding officer of the 2nd Cavalry and served first in an expedition with Gen. Alfred Sully against the Sioux in Dakota Territory, then in other engagements to the east. In 1864 he became the Omaha Indian agent.

The Civil War had repercussions in Nebraska, particularly along the Missouri River. Although a free state, Nebraska had its share of individuals who supported the Rebel cause, and that led to conflicts at home. One concern in Brownville involved people who started stealing livestock, particularly horses, for the southern cause. The term "Jayhawking" came from Kansas and originally referred to abolitionists working against people considered "traitors to the Union." But eventually bands of thieves claiming to be Jayhawkers started robbing and plundering on a widespread basis. The situation around Brownville became so serious that a group of citizens organized a military-style defense committee. By paying an enrollment fee to the committee, citizens were protected from Jayhawking incidents.

Life in Brownville settled down after the war, and the community continued to grow. The first brewery opened, people formed a cemetery association, and in 1867 talk started about extending the Mississippi & Missouri River Air Line Railroad through Missouri. In May Brownville town leaders met with railroad officials, forming the Brownville, Fort Kearney (*sic*) & Pacific Railroad Company. In January 1868 local residents approved a bond issue to generate $350,000 for the railroad's construction, and the project appeared to hold great promise for the future. But estimated costs continued to rise, and it appeared Congress wouldn't approve a land grant for the line. The fate of the railroad appeared to ride on the wind. First it looked like a deal would happen, then the project appeared unlikely.

But those in support of the road persevered, and in October 1870 businesses closed and school classes were dismissed so everyone could attend the ground-breaking ceremonies for the railroad. Workers started grading and began laying track toward the west. However, by April 1, 1872, local control of the line ended. Residents' hopes and dreams were shattered when negotiations with those in charge of the railroad project fell apart, and workers started to tear up the track that had already been laid. By 1874 it became clear Brownville would have no railroad west to Fort Kearny, although a year later the Midland Pacific extended its Nebraska Trunk Line from Nebraska City.

Settlers who continued to make their way into Nebraska started moving farther from the Missouri River, toward the great open spaces to the west, and the population of the river towns started to decline. All the glory of Brownville didn't die, however. Longtime newspaper editor Furnas became Nebraska's governor. Long a promoter of tree planting, Governor Furnas proclaimed a state Arbor Day in 1873 although it didn't become an official state holiday until 1885. His political rival J. Sterling Morton had already succeeded in getting the State Board of Agriculture to pass a resolution establishing an Arbor Day—or a day of tree planting—in 1872.

Population decline in Brownville after 1873 was exacerbated by high taxes associated with the failure of the railroad project. Then, in 1876, county residents moved the county seat, and that seemingly sounded a death knell for Brownville. By 1890 the town had only 457 residents. Novelist Willa Cather wrote in the *Lincoln Journal* on August 12, 1894: "Even the Lone Tree saloon is falling to pieces, and that, in a western town, is the sure sign that everything is gone." Things only got worse. In 1903 a fire broke out in the main business district, destroying the Marsh Hotel and Opera House, the courthouse, and many other buildings. The fruit tree industry that had been established by such men as Robert Furnas did fairly well until the 1930s, when drought caused its demise. In 1951 the train depot closed. Most other businesses had ceased operation as well.

A less resilient town would have died. To be honest, Brownville almost did. What gave it a new lease on life was culture.

Early in Brownville's history the community had library debates and opera performances. Music and art also had long been important aspects of life in the river town. Artist Terence Duren breathed the first signs of new life into Brownville in 1956 when he wrote a series of letters encouraging people to take an interest in reviving the community. The Brownville Historical Society organized and immediately started working on preservation, restoring historic homes and businesses and promoting new opportunities. The Brownville Fine Arts Association organized in 1971. Activities today include summer workshops for music students, concerts, art shows and a gallery, and the Brownville Village Theatre, a summer repertory company.

Among the restored houses and buildings are the Captain Bailey House, the Cogswell House, Gates House, Nace House, Carson House, Tipton House, Thompson House, and the Brownville Methodist Church, the oldest Methodist church in Nebraska that still has regular Sunday services. Built as a Congregational church in 1859, the building was used for a brief period as Brownville College, but the Methodists bought

The Captain Meriwether Lewis, *a dredge now housing a steamboat museum at Brownville.*

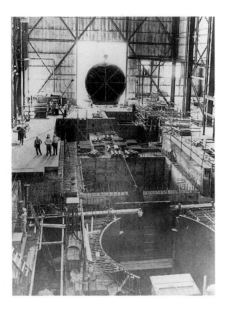

A fifty-ton steel containment vessel at the Hallam atomic site. Another atomic energy plant is on line in Brownville. —Nebraska State Historical Society

it in 1861, and there has been little change in it through the years. The church and the various other historic structures are scattered over Brownville's seven hills.

But the community's economy is not solely based on history and the arts. The $100 million Nebraska Cooper Nuclear Power Plant, one of two nuclear power plants in the state, went on line in 1974. It is operated by the Nebraska Public Power District.

PERU

Northwest of Brownville on Nebraska 67 lies Peru, the home of Peru State College, Nebraska's oldest state educational institution, which holds classes on its Campus of a Thousand Oaks. The college started in 1860 as the Nemaha Valley Seminary and Normal Institute. At one time the school was known as Mount Vernon College. Thomas Jefferson Majors, one of the early influential citizens of Nebraska, opened a general store in Peru in 1859. He ran the store until 1861, when he enlisted in the 1st Nebraska Infantry. Majors served throughout the Civil War, after which he returned to Peru and launched a career in politics.

Majors served first in the Nebraska Territorial Council, where he promoted the idea of using the Mount Vernon College as a State Normal School. In 1867 he succeeded in getting the property for the state. He later served several terms as a state senator, was a U.S. congressman in 1878–79, was Nebraska's lieutenant governor from 1891 to 1895, and ran unsuccessfully for governor. He had a successful farming and

A veterans' memorial at Peru.

stock-raising operation on his property adjoining Peru, became active in the Grand Army of the Republic, and even had a home large enough to accommodate meetings of that group.

Like other Missouri River towns, Peru is built upon a number of hills. Peru State College graces one hill, homes and residential areas another, and the cemetery the top of yet another. The community claims it offers a view of three states—Nebraska, Iowa, and Missouri—from an outlook near the cemetery. While that may be true, the sight isn't clear at least in part because of the large number and great variety of trees in this river country.

Indian Cave State Park

Indian Cave State Park lies south of Brownville and is reached by using Nebraska 67 through Nemaha and then spur route 64E to the park itself, which covers 3,000 acres of riverfront property. The park gets its name from a sandstone cavity at its extreme southeastern end, where Indian petroglyphs are etched into the walls. It is one of few places in Nebraska where such petroglyphs are known to exist.

The park has a large network of hiking trails (also used by horse-back riders) and several locations for picnicking and camping. Much of the park covers the high hills above the Missouri River, but some trails and roads run adjacent to the river itself. Most of the park is heavily forested with yellow oak, red oak, bur oak, hackberry, black walnut, cottonwood, butternut hickory, chokecherry, wild black cherry,

155

mulberry, basswood, wild plum, wild grape, sycamore, box elder, and panicled dogwood. The woodland floor is covered with wild strawberry, white dogtooth violet, goldenrod, elderberry, and wild touch-me-not. All those species result in an explosion of color at various times of the year, particularly in the spring, when they are blooming, and in the fall.

The heavy plant growth makes Indian Cave State Park an ideal setting for wildlife, including such species as opossum, beaver, red fox, raccoon, white-tailed deer, turkey, red-headed woodpecker, and great horned owl. In all there are 476 different species and subspecies of trees, shrubs, herbs and other plants, including two rare plants, the lady's slipper and the showy orchid.

ST. DEROIN

The first organized town site in Nemaha County was St. Deroin, started by Joseph Deroin, who had a trading post near the mouth of the Nemaha River in the 1840s in what is now Indian Cave State Park. His development probably came about in part because the 1830 Treaty of Prairie Du Chien provided for the establishment of an area for people of Indian heritage. It became known as "Half-Breed Tract."

Deroin himself was part Otoe, the son of an Otoe woman and French trader. He'd been born near Bellevue in 1819. In 1836 he moved to the main Otoe village at the mouth of the Platte River. He married an Omaha woman, Meek-ka-Ahu-Me, who in 1842 had their only child, a daughter named Mary. Soon after he started trading in the area south of the Nemaha River, his first wife left him; Deroin later married two other Indian women, a pair of sisters, Julie and Soula Baskette, the daughters of an Iowa woman and Frenchman Balone Baskette. With those two wives he had eight more children.

Deroin laid out the village that bore his name in 1853, though he no doubt traded at the location even earlier. The record isn't entirely clear, but legend has it that Deroin died of a gunshot wound he received on April 21, 1858, during a quarrel with James Beddow, a nearby landowner.

The population of Deroin included many Iowas, Omahas, Otoes, and Sioux. The shifting course of the Missouri may have affected its fortunes, but the town suffered most during a cholera epidemic. The cemetery high above the river in the state park is filled with markers of many people who died in 1869, in many cases several members of the same families. By the early 1900s the town—which at some point had the term *Saint* attached to its name—had about 300 residents. Eventually even they left, and only the town's name remains.

AUBURN

Now the Nemaha County seat, Auburn was created by the joining of two earlier communities, Sheridan and Calvert, in 1882. The town is named after Auburn, New York. The Otoe originally used the land in this region, and the river and county take their name from the tribal name *Ni Maha*, or "muddy river."

Auburn is near the location known as Half-Breed Tract, which the 1830 Treaty of Prairie Du Chien set aside between the Nemaha and Little Nemaha Rivers as a reserve for Native Americans. John C. McCoy surveyed the land in 1838, placing the boundary eight miles west of the river, rather than the ten miles approved under the treaty provisions. This mistake later caused problems when non-Indian people settled on the Indian lands. Nevertheless, in 1858 the McCoy Line became official, and on September 10, 1860, Louis Neal received the first patent. One of the original survey lines is now partly identified by Half-Breed Road, which runs in a southeasterly direction.

Tecumseh, also located on the Nemaha River, is recognized nationally as the location for the filming of the television miniseries *Amerika*. The Johnson County Courthouse and town square served as backdrops, and the film left a legacy in the form of a gazebo on the courthouse lawn, built by the production company.

FILLEY

Elijah and Emily Filley established Cottage Hill Farm in Gage County in 1867, living the first year in a tent. The next year the Filleys built a permanent home. They found an outcrop of limestone on their property. Emily helped haul it to the building site, where Elijah laid up the walls of a seven-room house that stood a story and a half high and in which they lived until 1883.

Elijah Filley quickly became a leading farmer and stock raiser in the area. He cultivated the land and planted miles of osage orange fence to keep his cattle on his property. That type of hedge plant had a sharp barb that effectively repelled even the most errant of livestock and kept the animals in the pastures. It was a popular fencing material prior to the widespread use of barbed wire, particularly in areas where wooden building materials were in short supply, as on the plains. Filley had been involved in raising livestock in Illinois, and he put his knowledge to work in Nebraska. He quickly expanded into feeding and breeding operations, having as many as 1,800 head of cattle at various feedlots in Gage County. He particularly worked with purebred stock, making him a leader in the Nebraska cattle industry in this area.

Hogs on the Jacob Stearly farm near Gibbon, 1903. —Nebraska State Historical Society, Solomon D. Butcher Collection

Some individuals find opportunities where others see only difficulties. Elijah Filley fell into the former slot. He purchased several yoke of oxen soon after arriving in Nebraska and used them to break ground for crops, hiring himself and his oxen out to neighbors. During the fall of 1868 Filley purchased his first threshing machine, which made it possible for him to gain work during the grain harvest, and he established an extensive freighting operation, hauling goods from Nebraska City and Brownville to Beatrice. He had an extensive cattle shipping business by 1872, and some sources claim he shipped the first carload of cattle out of Gage County on the newly completed railroad in 1871. Filley left his mark on Nebraska agriculture in other ways. He served six terms on the State Board of Agriculture and was a state representative and state senator. In 1924 he was inducted into the Nebraska Hall of Agricultural Achievement.

Ironically, the reason Filley is most remembered now is because he built a barn. In 1874 grasshoppers invaded Nebraska. Farmers and ranchers in Gage County not only lost their crops but also faced the loss of their livestock because they had nothing for feed. Elijah Filley stepped in and helped to save the day. He purchased thousands of hogs, shipping them and his own cattle to Iowa markets. Then he bought corn in Iowa and had it shipped to Nebraska, where he sold it to his neighbors and used it himself for work stock feed. But Elijah Filley wanted insurance against future feed shortages, so he built a barn. He had needed a substantial structure for some time and took advantage of the opportunity to hire workers at low wages. By paying lower wages he could actually hire more people for the same amount of money, thus helping more families. The limestone barn Filley and his cut-rate crew built is a monument to hard times and a testament to solid construction.

The three-story limestone barn is classified as a barn bank. It is built into the existing slope of the land, providing an entrance to the lower level from the east and access to the second level from the higher, west side. The lowest level provided stall space for cattle and oxen, while the second level served as storage for wagons, horses, and grain. There were horse stalls along both sides and hay storage above the main floor in two different levels. An opening in the west gable allowed hay wagons to enter the barn, and the hay itself was lifted to the mow from the rack with a horse fork.

The magnificence of the barn comes from the limestone, which is laced with elaborately cut diagonal patterns and surrounded by a smooth-cut border and arched openings. Now listed on the National Register of Historic Places, the Filley Stone Barn is one of the greatest in the state. It is the largest limestone structure identified by the Nebraska Office of Historic Preservation.

BEATRICE

Known as the place where homesteading started in the West, Beatrice also made a name for itself in bringing culture to the region. From 1889 to 1916 untold numbers of people from rural Nebraska and neighboring states enjoyed entertainment and education at the Beatrice Chautauqua. Featuring performances, discussions, lectures, and lessons in the fine arts and domestic sciences, the Chautauqua brought cultural opportunities to rural dwellers and promoted community spirit. Activities took place at the Assembly Hall, a large and impressive pavilion built in 1889 for the major events.

The Chautauqua took its name from Lake Chautauqua, New York, where a summer training session in 1874 attracted 142 Methodist Sunday school teachers. The Chautauqua format soon spread throughout the United States.

During the summer of 1888 five citizens who owned a tract of land adjacent to the Blue River made the first serious proposal to locate a Chautauqua facility in Beatrice. The Interstate Chautauqua Assembly formed to serve Iowa, Kansas, Colorado, and Missouri. The grounds were immediately improved, and the street railway company in Beatrice extended its tracks to the Chautauqua entrance. The corporation built an assembly hall that could seat 2,000 people for the June 8–11, 1889, session. The Beatrice *Daily Express* reported: "The entire Chautauqua interest of the state is centered on the Beatrice assembly. It is surely destined to be the most popular assembly in the state." Among the programs was a lecture on "The Bedouins of Arabia"; the largest crowd of the year, 2,500 people, gathered to hear a speech by Dr. Creighton, president of Nebraska Wesleyan University in Lincoln.

In subsequent years organizers built a number of cottages for participants and visitors; others camped on the grounds. The *Daily Express* reported in 1893, "The grounds are at their prettiest and today they are a scene of lively animation. Cottagers are moving in and a constant stream of vehicles is passing between the city and Riverside Park conveying baggage, household effects and passengers. The tents are about all pitched and are being taken rapidly."

Railroads serving the area offered special excursion rates to Chautauqua participants, and by 1905 attendance had swelled to 10,000 people on some days. After 1906 the railroads dropped their special deals, and attendance fell. By 1916 the Chautauqua had completed its run. That year the Beatrice Chautauqua Assembly was hopelessly mired in debt, and foreclosure proceedings were filed in county court. The city intervened in the case, paid all debts, and claimed the property, turning it into a municipal recreational facility known as Chautauqua Park. The Beatrice Chautauqua Pavilion is preserved at the park.

Homestead National Monument

The whole character of the West took a new face after 1862 because of landmark legislation approved by Congress. "In regard to the Homestead law. . . . I am in favor of cutting the wild lands into parcels, so that every poor man may have a home," President Abraham Lincoln said as Congress debated the provisions of the Homestead Act. The first claim under the 1862 law is believed to have been made in southeastern Nebraska Territory by Daniel Freeman.

But the development of the United States under various provisions of the homestead regulations started long before Freeman claimed his section. In 1841 Congress approved the Pre-emption Law, under which a settler could file on a 160-acre claim and purchase the land for $1.25 per acre after erecting a dwelling and meeting certain conditions. Just eight years later, in 1849, the Swamp Land Act was passed in an attempt to help states with poor land to lure settlers; however, the provision

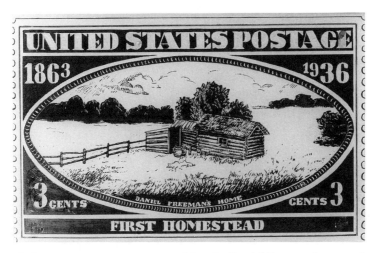

A three-cent postage stamp recognizing the Daniel Freeman homestead near Beatrice. —Nebraska State Historical Society

not only failed to satisfy the demands for free land but also led to wholesale fraud in certain portions of the country. In 1854 Congress approved the Graduation Act, which regulated the price of land based on quality, with some parcels selling for as little as twelve and one-half cents per acre.

From 1842 to 1853, the Donation Acts encouraged settlers to claim land in remote areas such as Oregon and later New Mexico by providing it free to emigrants who moved to those regions and began farming. Those provisions led the first great waves of people to cross the continent. Among the leaders in formulating U.S. land-development policies was Senator Thomas Hart Benton of Missouri. He believed the United States should sell land "for a reasonable price to those who are able to pay; and give without price to those who are not." Such a practice, Benton claimed, would provide a "race of virtuous and independent farmers."

A quarter of a century later, Representative Andrew Johnson of Tennessee backed several homestead bills. His arguments mirrored those of Benton. "Take one of these men, transplant him in the West upon 160 acres of its fat, virgin soil, and in a few years. . . you increase his ability to buy a great deal," Johnson said. Representative Galusha Graw of Pennsylvania, who authored the Homestead Bill that eventually became law in 1862, said, "Why should not the legislation of the country be so changed as to prevent for the future the evils of land monopoly, by setting apart the vast and unoccupied Territories of the Union, and consecrating them forever in free homes for free men."

Charles Shafer and family, homesteaders in Custer County, 1887. —Nebraska State Historical Society, Solomon D. Butcher Collection

As the Republican Party leader, Abraham Lincoln championed the cause; as president of the United States, he signed it into law. "I will simply say that I am for those means which give greatest good to the greatest number," Lincoln said. The cry "Uncle Sam is rich enough to give us all a farm" was finally heard, and on May 20, 1862, Congress approved the Homestead Act, which became effective January 1, 1863.

Many southern legislators opposed Homestead Act provisions and blocked several bills, but the onset of the Civil War assured passage. Other important legislation approved that year included the establishment of the U.S. Department of Agriculture and the Morrill Land-Grant College Bill. Both later played significant roles in the development of Nebraska.

The 1862 Homestead Act allowed men and women to claim up to 160 acres of land. Anyone who was twenty-one years old or the head of a family, who was a U.S. citizen or in the process of becoming one, and who had never fought in a war against the United States could claim a homestead. Up for grabs were hundreds of thousands of unappropriated public acres, primarily west of the Mississippi River. In order to gain title, an individual had to live on the claim for at least six months each year during a five-year period and make improvements, including building a twelve-by-twelve cabin. After a five-year development period, the land became the homesteader's property. For those

Homesteader Hannawald Merna and family of Custer County. —Nebraska State Historical Society, Solomon D. Butcher Collection

not wanting to wait so long, title could still be obtained under the process of preemption for $1.25 per acre.

The first man to claim a homestead under provisions of the 1862 Homestead Act, Daniel Freeman, located the land he wanted in 1862. Because he needed to return to his Civil War regiment, Freeman persuaded the land office agent to let him file for his homestead as soon as the new law went into effect on January 1, 1863.

Freeman was born in Ohio in 1826 and spent his early life in Illinois, where he practiced medicine starting in 1849. However, like many Americans at that time, he desired to own property, and in 1862 he made his way to Nebraska. Freeman paid his $12 filing fee for the land on Cub Creek, a tributary of the Big Blue River, fought in the Civil War, and in 1865 married Agnes Suita. They worked the land he had claimed in 1863, cultivating about thirty-five acres. Freeman built a stable, a one-hundred-foot-long sheep shed, and a corn crib, and he planted apple and peach trees.

Being an educated man himself, in 1871 Freeman built a school for his children using bricks made on the farm. The school remained in continuous operation until 1968. The Freeman Homestead is now a part of Homestead National Monument, located west of Beatrice.

Land laws continued to play a major role in the settlement of Nebraska. The Timber Culture Act of 1873, sponsored by Senator Phineas W. Hitchcock of Nebraska, allowed homesteaders to claim 160 acres. To "prove up" on a timber claim, the homesteader had to plant and keep growing forty acres of trees for eight years. That obligation was reduced to ten acres of trees in 1878. The Desert Land Act of 1877 allowed settlers to purchase or claim up to 640 acres that needed irrigation before it could be cultivated. The Kinkaid Act, sponsored by Moses P. Kinkaid of O'Neill and signed by President Theodore Roosevelt on April 28, 1904, affected thirty-seven counties of northwest Nebraska. It enlarged homestead tracts to 640 acres, with the provision that land that could be irrigated was not open to entry. By 1910 about 1,600 patents had been granted to approximately 800,000 acres of land in the Kinkaid area. Between November 1910 and July 1917 the government granted an additional 18,919 patents to more than 8 million acres in that region (see page 264).

It's not clear how many claimants carried through, received the final patent, and remained on the land. Certainly many of the Kinkaid homesteaders found even 640 acres too few from which to make a living. Only about 52 percent of homestead claimants earned the patent to their land between 1862 and 1900.

Homesteading continued until 1976, when the Federal Land Policy & Management Act replaced the Homestead Law, but by the mid-twentieth century most of the public land suitable for farming and grazing had been claimed. In all the government transferred more than 270 million acres—more than 10 percent of the entire United States—to private ownership under Homestead Law provisions. Montana had the greatest number of homesteads claimed: more than 150,000. North Dakota had between 115,000 and 120,000, while Nebraska was a close third, with about 105,000 claims.

Tecumseh—Clay Center
100 miles

Several east-west roads provide access to the farming communities of central River Country, including Nebraska 41. This highway cuts between cornfields and links Tecumseh with Clay Center, passing through such communities as St. Mary, Sterling, Clatonia, Wilber, Milligan, and Geneva.

The tremendous blizzard that swept across the plains in 1888 affected a large region from North Dakota to Kansas. In the area near Milligan, Mary Masek walked about two miles to get her sons, Charles

A Bohemian mural in downtown Wilber.

and Thomas, at the school. When she reached the schoolhouse, however, she found it vacant and headed for home. The icy whiteness of the storm engulfed Mary as she walked, and she became disoriented. When the storm cleared neighbors found her frozen body near a cottonwood tree. She was one of many killed in the storm, remembered as one of the worst ever to sweep across the plains.

WILBER

There is an Old World charm to the small town of Wilber, which calls itself the Czech Capital of Nebraska, a title bestowed upon it in 1963. Since 1987 it's also been known as the Czech Capital of the United States. Gift shops sell Czech heritage products, and a museum displays crafts, traditional costumes, doll collections, and replicas of early immigrant homes. Outdoor murals portray Czech scenes, and the names of businesses are written in the mother tongue. The Hotel Wilber hosts visitors for the annual Czech festival. During that annual summer event some 40,000 people congregate in this town, which otherwise has a population of only 1,600, to participate in the parade, enjoy ethnic dances, or partake of a Bohemian meal.

CLAY CENTER

As railroads developed across Nebraska, rail companies encouraged settlers to purchase land and move to the area served by their line. Settlers would ensure the railroads' prosperity by growing crops,

Cows graze near an abandoned ammunition storage area, now used as a livestock shelter. The ammunition shelters are being removed from their location near Clay Center.

raising livestock, or manufacturing goods that could be shipped on the line. As the railroads promoted an area, they helped organize towns and sometimes named them in alphabetical sequence. Clay County is an example, with towns named *C*lay Center, *D*eweese, *E*dgar, *E*ldorado, *F*airfield, *G*lenvil, *H*arvard, *I*nland, *O*ng, *S*aronville, and *T*rumbull.

Cattle graze in the region near Clay Center, where the U.S. Department of Agriculture has a meat animal research center. The center uses a number of World War II munitions bunkers as barns and storage areas. Although the bunkers are being removed, in the early 1990s they remained as large, grass-covered barns. Cattle grazed around, and sometimes even up onto, the sides of the bunkers.

NEBRASKA 8
Rulo–Superior
140 miles

RULO

Lewis and Clark camped a few miles north of Rulo on July 13, 1804, and Clark spent some time exploring. He traveled up the Nemaha River, where he found burial mounds, "which to me is a Strong indication of this Country once being Thickly Settled." The site he found was likely an early Otoe village and cemetery.

Rulo itself is named for the wife of Charles Rouleau, a Frenchman with the John Charles Frémont expedition in 1842. Rulo is near the lowest spot in Nebraska, 850 feet above sea level. The highest spot is in the panhandle at about 4,600 feet.

The approval of the Kansas-Nebraska Act opened vast amounts of land for settlement. In order for the settlement to proceed in a somewhat orderly manner, the new territory needed to be surveyed. On August 1, 1854, John Calhoun was appointed surveyor general of Nebraska and Kansas. The baseline for the surveys became the 40th Parallel, which also marked the division line between Kansas and Nebraska. The first official survey was authorized November 2, 1854, to include land extending for 108 miles west from the Missouri River along the 40th Parallel to the 6th Principal Meridian. On May 8, 1855, the surveying party put up a tall iron monument with the word *Nebraska* on one side and *Kansas* on the other at a point southeast of Rulo. When U.S. Deputy Surveyor Charles A. Manners set the iron monument, he set four witness stones and marked four black oak trees as well.

That monument near Rulo marks the initial point for the Kansas and Nebraska surveys, but all the official surveys are based from a location 108 miles west on the 6th Principal Meridian. In fact, all surveys for the states extending west to the Rocky Mountains originate from that point, which marks the intersection of the border of Jefferson and Thayer Counties in Nebraska with the Kansas state line.

Markers near Rulo recognize the campsites of Lewis and Clark in 1804 and welcome travelers entering Nebraska from Missouri.

Surveying was often dangerous work in the early years. Not only did the parties have to contend with difficult weather conditions, they also sometimes had to deal with hostile Indians. Members of the Nelson Buck survey party were attacked and killed by Indians in 1869 while surveying in central Red Willow County. The last general survey in Nebraska was on the Gates of Sheridan Reservation in Sheridan County, located in the northwestern portion of Nebraska, a survey completed in 1910. Also southeast of Rulo are the Iowa Indian Reservation and the Sauk and Fox reservations.

The Rulo bridge, constructed in 1938–39 at a cost of $651,296, started as a toll bridge project in 1933, promoted by John C. Mullen of Falls City. In 1934, however, Mullen assigned his "rights, interests, contracts, and franchises" in the bridge to Richardson County. The county agreed to take those rights, but only if it had a guarantee it wouldn't have to pay construction costs for the bridge. Mullen agreed and laid out a plan for the county to apply for a grant from the Reconstruction Finance Corporation of the federal government.

After years of negotiations, construction began in 1938, conducted by the Kansas City Bridge Company and the Missouri Valley Bridge and Iron Company. The Empire Construction Company of Omaha graded the approaches, and the Interstate Construction Company of Lincoln installed bridge lighting. Tolls collected through the years eventually retired the debt on the bridge, and in 1967 Richardson County worked with Missouri and Nebraska officials to turn over control of the bridge to the states. County officials noted, "It would be beneficial to the residents of Richardson County, Nebraska, and to the residents of northwest Missouri that the bridge be made a free bridge." At the time Interstate 29 was under construction in Missouri, and plans were under way to build an access road from I-29 to the Rulo bridge.

In 1969 Nebraska and Missouri assumed ownership of the Rulo bridge. The toll charges have since been discontinued.

DuBois

A large number of Czech people left their homeland and migrated to the United States, and many eventually settled in Nebraska along the Big Nemaha River. More people from Bohemia and Moravia settled in Nebraska than in the rest of the Great Plains states combined, according to Frederick C. Luebke in his article "Ethnic Group Settlement on the Great Plains" in the *Western Historical Quarterly*.

By 1920 more than 140,000 Czechs had settled on the Great Plains, with nearly half of them living in Nebraska. Most of the Czechs who migrated and settled in this region were free thinkers who had no ties with organized religion. The growth of such Czech free thinking in Nebraska and elsewhere on the Great Plains resulted in the rise of voluntary fraternal and benevolent associations. The first such society was founded in 1854 as the Cesko Slovensky Podporujici Spolek (CSPS), or Bohemian-Slovenian Benevolent Society, which started organizing on the plains in 1870s. Its members sought mutual life and health insurance as well as such benefits as fellowship, entertainment, community service, and both charitable and educational activities.

A dispute led to a new organization, Zapadni Cesko Bratrske Jednota (ZCBJ), also known as the Western Bohemian Fraternal Association. Its development came in 1897, and a key change was its admission of women as full members. Life insurance payments were based on age, and the organization also loosened its anticlerical stance.

The ZCBJ lodges have influenced the development of Czech-American society and have helped to promote and nurture Czech heritage in the United States. In DuBois the ZCBJ lodge is named for Jan Kollar, a pan-Slavic National Romantic poet. The lodge sponsored activities that promoted Czech schools, including history, language, drama, and music. For some years the lodge had its own Bohemian brass band and sponsored regular dances.

The ZCBJ Hall Kollar in DuBois is one of the finest examples of Czech Romantic design anywhere in United States. Other ZCBJ halls in Nebraska include Rad Sladkovsky in Pischelville, Rad Bila Hora at Verdigre, and Rad Slavin near Ord.

PAWNEE CITY

Pawnee City shows its patriotic spirit on holidays, when more than 200 flags fly as part of the city's Avenue of Flags display. The downtown business district includes forty-seven buildings that are listed on the National Register of Historic Places. Traveling west from Pawnee City, Nebraska 8 passes through or near Barneston, Odell, Steele City, Endicott, Reynolds, Hubbell, Chester, Byron, and Hardy before reaching Superior.

In the area southwest of Pawnee City and east of Nebraska 99 just near its intersection with Nebraska 8 is the Pawnee Prairie. Here visitors can see what this country looked like before a plow turned the soil. The Otoe Indians used this region in the 1800s, having a large village in the vicinity of Barneston.

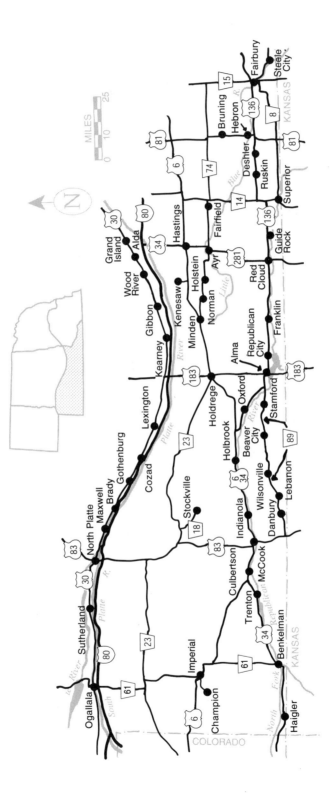

MILES

0 10 25

N

COLORADO

KANSAS

Fairbury
Steele City
15
Bruning
136
Hebron
8
KANSAS
Deshler
Ruskin
74
6
81
81
Superior
Fairfield
14
Hastings
136
Ayr
281
Guide Rock
Grand Island
30
Alda
80
34
Wood River
Kenesaw
Holstein
Norman
Red Cloud
Franklin
Gibbon
Minden
Kearney
Republican City
Alma
Lexington
183
Stamford
183
Holdrege
Oxford
Gothenburg
Cozad
23
Holbrook
Beaver City
89
Stockville
6
34
Lebanon
Brady
Maxwell
18
Indianola
Wilsonville
Danbury
North Platte
83
Culbertson
McCook
Sutherland
30
83
Benkelman
34
80
23
Trenton
KANSAS
Imperial
61
Ogallala
61
Champion
6
Haigler

Blue R.
Little
Platte River
Platte R.
South Platte River
Republican River
North Fork

PART 3
OREGON TRAIL COUNTRY

The Oregon Trail headed west out of Independence and St. Joseph, Missouri, cut across the northeast corner of Kansas, and entered Nebraska between Odell and Steele City as it struck the east bank of the Little Blue River. Emigrants followed the Little Blue to its northernmost point, then continued northwesterly across a dry stretch of country until they reached the bottomlands of the Platte River. From that point, west of Hastings, the overland travelers followed the Great Platte River Road west.

Fur trappers first used the route in 1812–13 as they headed from west to east en route from Astoria, Oregon, to St. Louis. A different fur party took the first wagons over the trail—heading from east to west—in 1830, and the first emigrant wagon train, the Bidwell-Bartleston party, crossed in 1841. The main period of emigrant travel started in 1843. From that point until 1859, thousands of travelers followed the road west. Their wagons carved ruts in the tall grasses as they crossed a land that was inhabited only by occasional Indian hunting parties.

After 1859 a number of stations developed to serve freighters, stagecoach passengers, and Pony Express riders. While most of the westbound emigrants had already passed through this region by then, a few stragglers continued to follow the trail west, and the various stations provided them with aid as well.

Zebulon Pike is the first U.S. explorer known to have seen this region, crossing it as he made his way toward Santa Fe in 1806. Pike entered the southeastern corner of present-day Nebraska and met with the Pawnees at their village near the present town of Guide Rock along the Republican River before continuing on his journey into Colorado and New Mexico.

This region is best known for its connection with westward travel, but the high plains along the Republican River also were historic buffalo range, which enticed Native American hunters for generations. In the 1870s, a different breed of buffalo hunters stalked the animals in this region. Not interested in killing the animals for their meat, the new "sportsmen" decimated the huge herds for their hides, in part to assist in the subjugation of the Plains Indians. By removing the buffalo from the range (and thereby taking away the livelihood of the tribes), the army could force the Indians to give up the warpath and settle on reservations. Some of the most famous—and mythical—western heroes of the eighteenth century, including Buffalo Bill Cody, Doc Carver, and Texas Jack, helped exterminate the buffalo.

After 1870 cowboys starting moving Texas cattle onto the range here, pushing the animals north across Indian Territory (Oklahoma) and Kansas on their way to northern ranges in Wyoming, Montana, and Nebraska. They scarred the land along the route, known as the Texas Trail.

Another kind of trail also crosses through this portion of Nebraska, although it leaves no permanent scars upon the land. It is the Central Flyway, an hourglass-shaped circuit used by millions of migrating waterfowl. Ducks, geese, and cranes head north each spring on their way to northern nesting sites and, like sands passing through the hourglass, fly south each fall. These migrations are awe-inspiring; the sky fills with the sights and sounds of honking geese, quacking ducks, and crying cranes. The birds flock to the Platte River, prairie lakes, and cornfields. This is the best region of Nebraska in which to hear the cry of wild Canada or snow geese or to glimpse a formation of sandhill cranes flying overhead.

For the purposes of this book, Oregon Trail Country is the region bounded by the Platte River on the north, the Little Blue River on the east, Kansas on the south, and Colorado on the west.

Fairbury—Superior
55 miles

The Oregon Trail enters Nebraska a few miles east of the Little Blue River. Highway 8 crosses the trail between Odell and Steele City. The emigrant path then turns northwest along the Little Blue River valley, with the highway to the west of the trail ruts. During the first years of overland travel (1843–54), before the creation of Nebraska Territory, several Indian tribes inhabited this region—primarily the Pawnee, although the Sauk and Fox may have had some very limited contact with the emigrants.

FAIRBURY

In 1859 stage stations went in along the route as the first overland stagecoach service started. The first Nebraska station appeared at Rock House, about three miles north of Steele City. Rock Creek Station stood a few miles up the trail, at a site some six miles southeast of Fairbury. As travelers headed west along the Little Blue River, they encountered, in order, the Virginia City, Big Sandy, Thompson's, Kiowa, Oak Grove (or Comstock's), Liberty Farm, Spring Ranche, Thirty-Two Mile Creek, and Sand Hill stations.

Rock Creek Station

S. C. and Newton Glenn built the original station at Rock Creek on the west side of the stream in 1857. They operated the Overland Stage station and trading post for two years before selling to David C. McCanles. Born in North Carolina in 1828, McCanles attended military school and worked as a sheriff in North Carolina, then decided to head west, leaving behind his wife, Mary, and four children. A cousin, James Woods, and several friends accompanied McCanles in a journey to the gold country. But by the time they reached Nebraska Territory, McCanles had abandoned his plans to seek gold; when he reached Rock Creek Station and found the property for sale, he ceased his westward journey.

David Colbert McCanles.
—Nebraska State
Historical Society

Rock Creek Station on the Oregon Trail, established by David C. McCanles, 1859. From a drawing by Phil Dawson, Fairbury, Nebraska. —Nebraska State Historical Society

Monroe McCanles, age twelve, witnessed his father's death. —Nebraska State Historical Society

James Butler Hickok.
—Nebraska State
Historical Society

Once he had purchased the Glenns' station, McCanles decided the location west of the creek deterred traffic, in part because the site lacked a good source of water. So McCanles relocated the station on the east side of Rock Creek and sent for his family. By the time they arrived he had started construction of a toll bridge across the creek, which had long been difficult for travelers to cross because of its steep, rocky sides.

McCanles's family was accompanied west by his brother, James. In 1860 the McCanles brothers made various improvements to Rock Creek Station and began farming operations on the Little Blue River. That year David leased the station to William H. Russell, Alexander Majors, and William B. Waddell, who were launching their Pony Express service. They used McCanles's Rock Creek Station as the second post in Nebraska, one of about thirty sites across the state.

The spring of 1861 brought a man who became one of the West's greatest legends: James Butler Hickok. The twenty-three-year-old Hickok worked for the Overland Stage Company (also owned by Russell, Majors, and Waddell) as a stock tender and stable hand. He'd been freighting on the Santa Fe Trail when he had a near-fatal encounter with a bear. He took the job at Rock Creek to convalesce from those injuries. In April the stage company agreed to purchase the Rock Creek property from McCanles, paying a portion of the selling price up front and agreeing to make monthly payments until the balance had been cleared. At about the same time McCanles sold his ranch, and in June he sold the toll bridge for $400 to Henry Bremmer.

When the first payment came due on Rock Creek Station, McCanles went to collect. Stage company station manager Horace Wellman told McCanles the funds hadn't arrived. Several weeks of delay occurred until Wellman finally agreed he would go to the company's headquarters in Nebraska City to get the money. Accompanying Wellman on the trip was Monroe McCanles, David's twelve-year-old son. The two left July 2 and returned ten days later. Upon their return home, young Monroe talked with his father at a neighbor's ranch; then the two of them, accompanied by McCanles's cousin, James Woods, and a friend, James Gordon, made their way to the station. And a legend was born.

McCanles and Monroe went to the kitchen door of the Wellman house, while Woods and Gordon headed toward the barn. When McCanles demanded to talk to Wellman, Mrs. Wellman said her husband wouldn't come out. McCanles replied that he would drag Wellman out. He may have intended to evict the stage company. But Hickok—whom McCanles called "Duck Bill" because of his protruding upper lip—stepped forward and shot McCanles as the man's young son watched. The gunfire attracted Woods and Gordon, who ran toward the cabin. Hickok fired at them, hitting both men. Woods ran to the north side of the cabin, where Wellman attacked and killed him with a hoe. Gordon made it to the brush about eighty yards from the cabin before a shot fired from Doc Brink's shotgun ended his life. Brink was a friend of the Wellmans. Young Monroe fled the scene, alerting his mother to the tragedy. She sent for her brother-in-law, James McCanles.

James McCanles headed to Beatrice to swear out warrants for the arrests of Wellman, Hickok, and Brink. Those three were already claiming that the killings were a simple case of self-defense. At a subsequent trial in Beatrice the three won acquittal based on their own testimony and that of Mrs. Wellman. The only other eyewitness to the events at Rock Creek Station, Monroe McCanles, was not allowed to testify.

Mary McCanles eventually married another area settler. James McCanles left Nebraska for Colorado, where he helped settle the town of Florence. Wild Bill Hickok went on to a storied career as a Union scout and Wild West gunslinger.

Rock Creek Station State Historical Park

Travel on the Overland Stage route declined steadily after the Civil War, and eventually the buildings that played a role in the Hickok-McCanles shooting deteriorated. Farmers worked the land for nearly a century until all that remained were deep ruts left by wagons pulling out of Rock Creek. In the 1960s interest in the area revived when the

Nebraska Game and Parks Commission started purchasing the land that encompassed the two old road stations.

In the 1970s the Jefferson County Historical Society and the Nebraska State Historical Society started researching the area. Advanced technology such as infared photography, proton magnetometer surveys, and photogrammetry helped show where various features had stood at Rock Creek a century before, and archaeological excavations of those sites yielded a wealth of information. Armed with such details as exact locations and the size of various structures, the Nebraska Game and Parks Commission then set about rebuilding Rock Creek Station, including the cabin where Hickok killed McCanles and a cabin depicted in a photograph taken at the original station (west of Rock Creek) in 1860. The state historical park also includes a picnic area, a campground, and a modern visitor's center, which provides information about the site, the Pony Express, Oregon Trail migration, and other area history.

The Oregon Trail followed the Blue River west from Fairbury. The Pony Express kept the same course, with periodic stations along the route, including the one at Millersville, west of present-day Hebron.

DESHLER

Just east of Deshler (which is known for its broom factory) is the site of the former village of Friedensau ("Peaceful Meadows"), established by Lutheran missionary pastor John J. Kern in 1874. His parishioners came from Indiana and Illinois to settle the town, and by 1885 about seventy people lived there. It had two German Lutheran churches, a school, post office, water-powered grist mill, lumberyard, hotel, and livery stable.

Residents expected that the Rock Island Railroad would extend from Fairbury through Hebron, Friedensau, Kiowa, Oak, and Nelson by the fall of 1886. But landowner John G. Deshler used his considerable influence to ensure that the line crossed to the east, through his property. That secured Deshler's future and sealed Friedensau's demise. In 1887 residents moved buildings over the fenceless prairie to Deshler. By the 1990s only the Trinity Lutheran Church and its cemetery remained in Friedensau.

Another nearby ghost of earlier days is Jansen, which was settled in 1874–75 by Mennonites led to the area by Cornilius and Peter Jannsen. They were descendants of Dutch emigrants who left Holland in the sixteenth century to found a colony in Russia. They eventually made their way to the United States and ultimately came here, purchasing 25,000 acres from the Burlington & Missouri Railroad.

The Mennonites' unique community organization consisted of a series of "line villages," each of which contained a number of dwellings located close together on both sides of a section line or road. About 1900 the village of Russian Lane reportedly had forty-two houses, a school, and a church situated along a stretch of road four and a half miles long.

Jansen, though spelled differently, took its name from founder Peter Jannsen and sat on land he platted in 1886. He raised sheep and became a Nebraska legislator in 1898, serving again in 1910 and remaining active in politics until his death in 1923. One of his descendants, David Jannsen, was born in Nebraska and went on to star in the television show *The Fugitive*.

RUSKIN

At a site near US 136 west of Ruskin, U.S. 2nd Cavalry C Company garrisoned between April and October 1870 at a temporary post called Camp Bingham. They'd been sent to protect early settlers from Indian attacks. In one incident, Sgt. Patrick J. Leonard and four other soldiers went to search for some lost horses. A group of Sioux and Cheyenne attacked, killing the horses and one of the soldiers. When Secretary of War William K. Belknap heard of the skirmish, he ordered medals of honor for the four surviving soldiers. Those medals represented the largest number of their type ever won in a military engagement in Nebraska. The fight took place in a large flat area marked now by large cottonwood trees.

NEBRASKA 74
Fairfield—Minden
48 miles

Nebraska 74 between Fairfield and Minden crosses the Oregon Trail and the Little Blue River, providing access to Ayr, Roseland, Holstein, and Norman. Spring Ranche, south of Fairfield, became the home of an interesting family and served as a stagecoach and trading post during the latter period of Oregon Trail traffic.

The Lynching of Elizabeth Taylor

Elizabeth Jones and her twin brother, Thomas, were born in Wales in 1854 and migrated with their family to the United States when they were about six years old. Elizabeth married James A. Taylor in 1869, and they settled in Clay County, Nebraska, at Spring Ranche, which sat adjacent to the Oregon Trail. Although most of the emigration had ceased by that time, a few travelers still used the trail, and they were served by a road ranch at Spring Ranche.

Elizabeth and James Taylor had three children, and by 1880 they were fairly well established along the Little Blue River. They loaned money to other people moving into the region, and in 1881 James started breaking new land for crops. Soon after that the family's problems started. They had difficulty with their neighbors' cattle getting into their crops, and their own animals seemed to get into the neighbors' crops. James Taylor apparently was a rather mild-mannered man, but his wife had a shorter fuse. He'd sometimes pay damages when his stock harmed other people's crops; she would not back down an inch. Eventually the strong-willed Elizabeth had James sign over all of the property—and outstanding notes he held on other people's goods and land—to her, and she took care of the business transactions.

Elizabeth demanded that people pay their debts, particularly those who had filed damage claims against the Taylors. When James Taylor died suddenly in 1882, neighbors suspected his wife had had a hand in the incident; they accused her of using rat poison to speed his demise. Not long afterward Elizabeth's father died, and a hired man, Ben Bethlemer, disappeared. In both cases the circumstances seemed a little out of the ordinary and people again became suspicious that Elizabeth had had a hand in the events. Nothing ever came to light to prove the allegations, however.

An abandoned building at Spring Ranche, near where Elizabeth Taylor and her brother Tom were hanged.

Eventually Elizabeth turned her business operations over to her twin brother, Tom Jones, and they expanded into cattle ranching. Some suspected their herds grew too quickly and that the siblings were engaged in a bit of rustling on the side, but still no one had any proof.

Tensions along the Little Blue River didn't ease. When neighbors started cutting trees and hauling them away from a timber claim owned by Elizabeth, she took them to court. Then her young sons got involved in the ongoing neighborhood feud. On January 8, 1885, Elizabeth saw Edwin Roberts headed toward her timber claim. She cursed him, knowing he probably intended to cut more trees. Later that day Taylor's sons met Roberts and Joseph Beyer as they returned from the timber claim. The boys may have spooked the team because it bolted, causing Beyer to fall from the load of logs. Not long afterward Beyer found Roberts in the wagon, dead from a gunshot to the head.

The two Taylor boys, only eleven and twelve years old, quickly found themselves in jail and facing murder charges, with trial set for May. The residents of the region, however, couldn't contain their anger, and perhaps as many as seventy-five of them went to the Taylor house demanding that Elizabeth and her brother come out. They were answered with a volley of gunshots that convinced the neighbors they'd best clear out.

But, like a blister on a heel rubbing against a new shoe, the situation just got worse. A couple of nights later the barn of neighbor John Llewelyn burned. Elizabeth and Tom moved from her frame house to the sod home they'd lived in earlier because the thick sod walls would be more likely to repel a bullet. On March 14, Elizabeth and her mother and daughter traveled to Hastings, perhaps to visit the two sons in jail. While she was away, neighbors went into her sod house and took her guns and ammunition.

That night a group of perhaps fifty men gathered, marched to the sod house, and ordered Elizabeth and Tom outside. When they emerged, Elizabeth and Tom were immediately grabbed and had their hands tied behind them. Then the vigilante mob marched them to a nearby bridge, where the two were hanged. Elizabeth Taylor is the only woman ever to be hanged in Nebraska.

Another Route to the West

Nebraska 4 runs between Bruning and Ragan, crossing the Oregon Trail between Oak and Lawrence. Deep ruts from the trail remain at several locations in the vicinity of Oak, reached by taking spur road 65A off Nebraska 4. There the trail passed through The Narrows, a bottleneck where wagons had to travel between the Little Blue River and a bluff. The Little Blue Station was one of only two stations between

Julesburg, Colorado, and Kiowa, Nebraska, not significantly affected by Indian raids in the summer of 1864. A massacre occurred nearby, at the Comstock Ranch, on August 7, 1864, perpetrated by the Sioux. The Eubanks and Roper families lived in this region, and Indian raiders captured Mrs. Eubanks, her four-year-old daughter, and sixteen-year-old Laura Roper (see page 194).

The Oregon Trail left the Blue River between Glenvil and Ayr, both located on Nebraska 74, and angled northwest, passing southwest of Hastings, Juniata, and Kenesaw before eventually reaching the Platte River bottoms, which then guided travelers through the rest of present-day Nebraska.

KENESAW

Travelers along the Oregon Trail had many hardships with which to contend, and perhaps the worst of all was cholera, which often struck early in the day and killed its victim before nightfall. Although the bones of hundreds of emigrants lie beneath Nebraska's soil, few of their graves are marked. One exception is the final resting spot of Susan Hail, who died June 2, 1852, most likely from cholera. Her headstone stands atop a little sand hill and is protected by a pipe fence. The story goes that when Mrs. Hail died, her husband, to whom she had been married just a short time, was heartbroken. But he refused to leave her in an unmarked grave, so he returned to St. Joe, where he bought a marble stone with her name upon it. Then he reportedly put the stone in a wheelbarrow and pushed it back to her grave site, where he placed it upon the fresh mound. The grave site is about four miles northwest of Kenesaw.

In a later era, the Summit Springs Stage Station operated at a location not quite two miles south of Kenesaw. The Muddy Station served travelers farther east at Juniata, on Thirty-Two Mile Creek.

Grand Island—Kearney
45 miles

GRAND ISLAND

The first white men to camp at the place that is now Grand Island may have been a group of Astorians en route from Oregon to St. Louis. The seven men—Robert Stuart, Ramsay Crooks, Robert McLellan, Ben Jones, Andri Vallee, Frances LeClerc, and Joseph Miller—left Astoria in June 1812. They lost most of their horses to raiding Indians in present-day Idaho, wandered aimlessly in western Wyoming, crossed the Rocky Mountains near South Pass, and camped near the North Platte River in central Wyoming. They intended to spend the winter at that camp, but when Arapaho Indians located them the Astorians left their shelter—believed to be the first white man's cabin ever built in Wyoming—and continued east. They spent much of the winter in camp in today's eastern Wyoming and near present-day Bridgeport, Nebraska, and continued eastward in March 1813.

As they journeyed they saw wild horses, hundreds of buffalo, and thousands of waterfowl. They reached Grand Island in the Platte River in early April and set up camp. Three days later an Otoe Indian guided them to his village, where the Astorians traded their old horse for a canoe, which they paddled to the Missouri River and eventually to St. Louis.

The next exploration of this region by white men came with the expedition of Maj. Stephen Long in 1820. But no settlement occurred for many years. A town south of present Grand Island organized in 1857 on the bank of the Platte, opposite the long island that French-Canadian trappers had called *La Grande Isle*. That village settled when the banking firm of Chubb Brothers and Barrows of Boston, Washington, D.C., and Davenport, Iowa, hit upon the idea of moving the nation's capital to the center of the nation. Some German emigrants led by William Stolley founded the colony with help from five Indians. The *Grand Island Independent*, reporting on Stolley's memoirs in April 25, 1932, said the colonists selected Grand Island because of the location's water supply and natural subirrigation. More Germans arrived from Davenport, Iowa, in 1858, and immigrants directly from Germany helped settle the area.

Grand Island nearly died during the financial panic of 1857 when some of the promoters withdrew their support. In 1859 an out-of-sorts gold miner who had a prejudice against Germans lit a prairie fire that burned most of the homes in the community. With assistance from residents of Omaha, Grand Islanders rebuilt.

In 1860 William Stolley started a tree-planting project, placing 6,000 small trees on his homestead claim. As the Grand Islanders farmed and developed their community, they had little trouble with Native Americans. But Stolley, a cautious man, began building a fortified log house near his own farmhouse, calling it Fort Independence.

Trouble with the tribes heightened in 1864, speeding the completion of Fort Independence and another fortification, the O. K. Store, in the eastern part of the community. In 1866 the Union Pacific Railroad

A scene on Stolley's Ranch at Grand Island. —Wyoming State
Museum, Stimson Collection

Hall County Courthouse, Grand Island.

reached the community, giving Grand Island Station, as the community was known until its incorporation in 1873, a measure of stability and prosperity.

The railroad left the community with an unusual legacy: Its downtown streets run at odd angles rather than north-south or east-west because they parallel the railroad tracks. The community soon had a clear division of social status, with churches, schools, the courthouse, and the fine houses of well-to-do citizens located south of the tracks. The area near the tracks had stores, homes, hotels, and principal businesses crowded together, while the industrial sector sat north of the tracks.

Industrial Development

Once the Union Pacific pushed through in 1866, Grand Island became an industrial center and a major railroad livestock-shipping point. A system of horse and mule streetcars provided transportation, and Blunk's Mill, which went into operation in 1877, provided milling services for farmers.

During World War II the Cornhusker Army Ammunition Plant headquartered in Grand Island, remaining in operation until the 1970s. The city also housed a military air base during World War II. The site of the plant now hosts an annual three-day irrigated-agricultural show, Husker Harvest Days. The show, presented by the *Nebraska Farmer* and the Agricultural Institute of Nebraska, features the latest irrigation equipment; field demonstrations of planting, harvesting, tillage, haying, and irrigation; craft shows; antique farm machinery; and even health checkups for farm families.

The Stuhr Museum of the Prairie Pioneer's frontier railroad town re-creates early Grand Island and includes many original buildings. Several motion pictures, including *My Antonia, Home at Last,* and Hallmark Hall of Fame's *Sarah Plain and Tall,* used the railroad town as a film location. Historic homes in the museum town include the small house in which actor Henry Fonda was born in 1905. US 34 heading east from Grand Island is the Henry Fonda Memorial Parkway.

US 30 heads west along the Platte River on a route parallel to the old Mormon Trail, passing through Alda, Wood River, Shelton, and Gibbon before reaching Kearney. US 30 to the east also generally follows the Mormon Trail route.

SHELTON

Shelton exists because a group of Mormons en route to Salt Lake City broke an axle and had to stop to make repairs. Edward Oliver was leading a group of English converts to Mormonism, and when the axle broke, his wife persuaded him to turn back from their intended destination far to the west. The Oliver family spent the winter in a log hut along Wood River. The following spring Oliver built a store to serve other Mormon travelers. The town didn't grow for some time, and when it did, it took its name from Nathaniel Shelton, another early-day settler.

The earliest groups of Mormons who went to Salt Lake City used wagons pulled by oxen, mules, or horses, but after 1856 many didn't have the money for such outfits. Between 1856 and 1860 Mormon travelers used wooden handcarts, which they pushed and pulled from the Missouri River near Florence to Salt Lake City. In all, eight handcart companies crossed the plains. Generally, each group of five persons had one handcart.

The family of Thomas and Sarah Moulton, originally from England, traveled with the James Grey Willie handcart company, which left Florence, Nebraska, in mid-August 1856. The company consisted of five wagons, twenty-four oxen, forty-five beef cattle, a tent for every twenty people, and 120 handcarts. The ten-member Moulton family had two handcarts, one open and one covered. Thomas and Sarah pulled one cart, filled with supplies and three children—Sophia Elizabeth, age three, Charlotte, age five, and Charles, a four-month-old baby. Four older children pushed and pulled the other cart, while eight-year-old Heber trailed along behind his mother, tied to her waist with a rope so he couldn't wander.

One traveler using wagons and draft animals on the journey west overtook a handcart brigade and wrote of the sight: There were two trains, one with thirty carts and the other with fifty. In most cases a man and three women pulled and pushed each cart, but sometimes only women moved the carts. The Danish, Swedish, Welsh, and English immigrants often had difficulty understanding the language of those they met. They'd suffered much hardship already, and a mile-long string of lame, sick, or needy people trailed behind the handcarts. Some were on crutches, and one woman carried a child and had several others hanging to her skirts.

In Nebraska the Mormons traveled on the north side of the Platte River to avoid conflict with non-Mormon travelers on the south shore. They'd had enough trouble in the east and sought to avoid further persecution. The Latter-day Saints formed supply points all along their route, with early travelers farming ground and planting crops that could be tended and harvested by other Mormons following the route West. The ruts carved by the handcarts and Mormon wagons remain at various sites in Hall County west of Grand Island.

GIBBON

Sixty-one settlers from New York, Pennsylvania, Ohio, Massachusetts, and other eastern states claimed homesteads near Gibbon when Col. John Sharp promoted a program to provide homesteads for U.S. Army veterans. Working with officials of the newly completed Union Pacific Railroad, Colonel Sharp offered free homesites and reduced railroad fares to the former soldiers. The men arrived on April 7, 1871, and each filed on a quarter section of ground, paying their $14 filing fees at the land office in Grand Island. The men determined who received which homestead by drawing numbers from a hat. The person who drew number one chose his section first, followed by the others in order.

Gibbon is centered on a forty-mile section of the North Platte River at the heart of the Central Flyway—a corridor from Mexico to Canada used by millions of waterfowl as they migrate from northern to southern habitats each year. Ducks, geese, and numerous other species follow the Central Flyway. The most magical of the birds are the sandhill cranes, which congregate in this area every year from early March through mid-April.

Historically, the Platte River had many strands flowing from west to east and few wooded areas upon its banks. There were numerous wet meadows to provide the sort of habitat cranes and other migrating waterfowl needed. The birds must stop to eat and gain weight so they can then continue their journey to the Arctic tundra, where they spend summers. But years of water diversion and increased upstream consumption by municipalities and farmers changed the river. Once, more than 200 miles of river provided the kind of habitat cranes like; now only about forty miles of prime habitat remain, situated roughly between Grand Island and Kearney. In this area the river sandbars are still relatively free of brush and trees, and the stream itself is wide.

Sandhill cranes have always migrated through this region, but since the restrictions on their primary Platte River habitat starting in the 1960s they have become more concentrated. Thousands of people come each spring to witness the migration of the big birds. Since 1970 the crane watch has become a combination tourist attraction and birders' paradise. This popularity has helped preserve the remaining stretches of pristine crane habitat. The proposed MidState Irrigation Project in the 1970s would have withdrawn water from the North Platte west of Overton, just upstream from the best remaining crane habitat. MidState promoters wanted to irrigate 218 acres of prime farmland in the Platte River valley, but concern over impacts to the cranes halted the project in 1975 when voters defeated a local referendum.

Sandhill cranes, both near and far, above fields south of the Platte River near Gibbon, March 1995.

A year earlier Gov. James Exon joined the U.S. Fish and Wildlife Service in announcing plans for a 15,000-acre wildlife refuge on Shoemaker Island southwest of Grand Island. Landowners protested, fearing condemnation of their land, and the proposal died. Even though Exon attempted a compromise in an effort to save the project, sentiment ran so strongly against it that he didn't have a chance. However, the National Audubon Society purchased some land southwest of Gibbon and established the Lillian Annette Rowe Wildlife Sanctuary. That was the first land along the Central Platte purchased solely for habitat for sandhill cranes and other waterfowl.

The next major development involved construction of the Grayrocks Dam on the Laramie River, a tributary of the North Platte in eastern Wyoming. Nebraska and the National Wildlife Federation filed a lawsuit to stop the project, and a court-approved settlement in 1978 called for creation of the Platte River Whooping Crane Habitat Maintenance Trust. Basin Electric, the operator of the Grayrocks Project, made a one-time payment of $7.5 million, which has been used to purchase more than 8,000 acres of prime waterfowl habitat along the Platte. Some of the money was used for easements on private land and for stream channel and bank restoration projects.

Platte River Bridge, One Mile long, Kearney, Neb.

A mile-long bridge across the Platte River at Kearney. —Nebraska State Historical Society

The Two Forks project to provide municipal water for the Denver metropolitan area had initial approval from the U.S. Army Corps of Engineers and regional Environmental Protection Agency officials, but a construction permit was denied in the late 1980s after concerns were raised about the project's potential effects downstream on endangered species such as the piping plover, whooping crane, and least tern. Other water development projects within the Platte River drainage and the Central Flyway are still on the drawing board. One of those projects, Wyoming's Deer Creek Reservoir, is one issue in *Nebraska v. Wyoming,* a lawsuit filed by Nebraska in 1986 and pending before the U.S. Supreme Court as of 1997. Wyoming did develop habitat for waterfowl as part of the mitigation for that project.

As water developers and conservationists continue to wrangle over development along the Platte, the sandhill cranes continue to flock through central Nebraska, and visitors still come to watch them. The annual migratory flocks constitute the largest concentration of any species of crane anywhere in the world. The cranes start arriving in early March and most are on their way north by mid-April. In all, between 450,000 and 500,000 birds use the Platte River as a staging area.

In March 1989 a boy from Shelton suggested there should be a Sandhill Crane Day, and the governor promptly designated March 15 as such. Some even suggested the western meadowlark should be replaced by the sandhill crane as the official Nebraska state bird, but so far that hasn't happened.

Because they are big and congregate in such numbers, the cranes have a sort of magic about them. When the Nebraska Council of Sportsman's Clubs in 1986 proposed open season on sandhill cranes, the public outcry reached fever pitch, at least in part because people have formed an emotional bond with the birds.

KEARNEY

The people who visit Nebraska during crane watch can view the birds at various places along the North Platte from Lexington to Grand Island. The largest concentration of cranes can be found in the vicinity of Kearney and Grand Island. Traffic snarls along bridges and roads as people pull over to watch the great flocks. Much of the land on which the birds feed is private, but there are public viewing areas such as the trail system at Fort Kearny. Cranes have been coming through this region for thousands, perhaps even millions of years; they certainly fed upon the banks of the Platte when soldiers built Fort Kearny.

Fort Kearny: Built to Protect Emigrants

The first fort built in the West to protect travelers on the Oregon Trail sat south of the Platte River near present-day Kearney. Mountain trappers and traders followed the Platte River road for nearly two decades before the first groups of pioneers took their wagons over the route. An earlier version of Fort Kearny sat at the Missouri River, near the present Nebraska City. Col. Stephen Watts Kearny recommended the Nebraska City site, which the military established in 1846 (see page

Re-created buildings at Fort Kearny State Historic Site.

134). But the increasing numbers of overland travelers made it clear to the military that some sort of government protection should be provided farther west, and in 1847, with a portion of the Nebraska City fort already built, Lt. Daniel P. Woodbury and about seventy men headed west along the Platte in search of a suitable site for a new fort.

Lieutenant Woodbury chose the new fort home "opposite a group of wooded islands in the Platte River" nearly two hundred miles west of Nebraska City's Fort Kearny and more than three hundred miles beyond Independence, Missouri. Construction started in the spring of 1848, with 175 men molding adobe bricks for the buildings of the rectangular fort compound.

Woodbury called the new post Fort Childs for his father-in-law, Col. Thomas Childs, but a War Department order provided that the post "established at Grand Island, Platte River, will be known as Fort Kearny."

The fort quickly became an important stop on the Oregon-California Trail. It served as a provisioning point and a place to leave and receive messages. In some instances emigrants bought supplies at cost, and on other occasions they received them free, with the fort acting as a type of aid station in the middle of the monotonous prairie. Westbound traveler James A. Pritchard wrote May 18, 1849:

> At noon we reached Fort Kearney, passed through the place 1 mile and stopped to grease & rest a couple of hours. Here we found a Military post established and some 80 or 90 Dragoons posted here— also a kind of Post office establishment, which gave us an opportunity of sending back letters. The Fort is about 12 ms above the head of Grand Island, and the houses are built of adobes or sun dried brick.

East of Fort Kearny, travelers headed west from various starting points: Independence, Fort Leavenworth, St. Joseph, Nebraska City, Plattsmouth, Bellevue, and Council Bluffs. The various trails from these places all joined at Fort Kearny, and the Oregon-California Trail beyond the fort followed one primary pathway. At times, however, it spread as wide as fifteen miles, as travelers sought to graze their animals or to get out of the dust stirred up by groups preceding them on the trail.

The Mormons headed to Utah from Council Bluffs and Winter Quarters (at Florence) kept their distance from the Oregon and California travelers by staying on the north bank of the Platte River. They maintained that separation until they reached present-day Casper, Wyoming.

Fort Kearny had regular mail delivery after 1859, and in 1860–61 it served as a stop on the Pony Express route. A *New York Herald* report in the 1850s noted that the fort "has no fortifications, but is merely a station for troops." It included a large open parade ground and five unpainted wooden houses as well as two dozen long, low adobe buildings. In 1869 frame buildings replaced the adobe structures. That year an official at Fort Kearny estimated a population of 1,500 in the trade area at Kearney, Wood River, and Grand Island.

There is no documentation that Indians ever attacked Fort Kearny, but the post did serve as a staging point for troops involved in conflicts in the region, particularly when fighting broke out over the plains in late 1864 and 1865. The military abandoned Fort Kearny on May 22, 1871, and in 1875 the buildings were torn down, with the materials taken to North Platte and Sidney Barracks. The Department of the Interior relinquished Fort Kearny's military reservation in 1876, and the area opened to homesteaders. It took only a few years for nature to reclaim the site. Except for the aging cottonwood trees that were planted soon after the fort's establishment and the earthworks developed during the Indian difficulties in 1864, for years the site was much as it had been prior to military occupation.

In 1928 the Fort Kearny Memorial Association formed, and on March 26, 1929, the site became a State Historical and Scenic Park and Bird Reserve. Replicas of the original fort buildings interpret the fort's history.

The town on the north side of the Platte near Fort Kearny, originally known as Kearney Junction, became Kearney. Like the fort, the town is named for Stephen Watts Kearny, but over the years the name has acquired an additional "e." In the 1880s local men promoted it in St. Louis as a location for the U.S. capital. Grand Island also sought that distinction. Both communities believed they should be so designated because of their location near the geographical center of the nation.

East of Kearney is the site of Hook's Ranch or Dogtown, a stage station and trading post at the junction of the Oregon Trail and the Fort Kearny Trail from Nebraska City. It is also the site of Valley Station, a later stage stop. The Pawnee Scouts under the leadership of Frank and Luther North headquartered in this area as they provided scouting services for the military during the Plains Indian Wars (see page 174).

A few miles west of Fort Kearny there arose a settlement of dubious distinction: Dobytown. Buildings of sod or adobe became saloons and gambling houses, places where military men could rendezvous and have a high old time carousing. Although locals attempted to bring respectability to the place by calling it Kearney City, its reputation as a hellhole carried through the years. As Irene Paden put it in *The Wake of the*

Prairie Schooner: "The place was a grisly combination of delirium tremens, stale humanity, and dirt."

In 1882–83 construction began on the Kearney Canal to provide irrigation to the region. It was completed in 1886. The Kearney Electric Company organized and installed the first waterwheel in the present powerhouse site. The town made extensive improvements in 1889, and three years later an electric streetcar system replaced the horse-powered service that had been in operation since 1888. In 1892 Kearney had a cotton mill, part of an ambitious scheme to link the cotton-producing South with the industrial North. Involved in the project were the Cumnock brothers—A. G., John, J. W., George, and Walter—who operated cotton mills in Massachusetts, Rhode Island, and Kentucky. They met with Kearney leaders in 1889 and laid out their plans. The mill would require a site of twenty acres plus $250,000 in capital—$100,000 in cash, the remainder in lots and acreage. In spite of what appeared to be exorbitant demands, the city put all its support behind the project. Within a month the community of 5,000 people had raised the necessary funds for the cotton mill.

In an article in the *Omaha Evening Dispatch* November 14, 1889, an eastern capitalist identified as Mr. Martin outlined the reasons for building the mill at Kearney:

> We can lay the raw cotton down in Kearney cheaper than in Lowell, Massachusetts. And, when we have it manufactured, it is in the market; whereas from Lowell it has to be shipped half way across the continent to reach the western market. We shall ship the goods from the South across the short side of the triangle to Kearney. In shipping from the South to Massachusetts and then back to Omaha, Denver, and Kansas City and all over the West and Northwest, we have to ship across two very long sides of the triangle, that is the difference in a nutshell.

The other key factor: an abundant source of water power. The *Omaha Bee* of January 24, 1892, reported:

> In many respects Kearney is far in advance of any other city of her population on either side of the Atlantic. . . . She has a water power that will make her one of the greatest manufacturing centers west of Chicago. The marvelous growth that has taken place in Kearney within the past few years is almost entirely due to the development of her water power, which has been achieved at a heavy outlay of local and foreign capital. Nebraska can justly feel proud of what may truthfully be called the gem of the Platte Valley.

Construction of the mill cost $400,000, including equipment. Production began in September 1892. The mill consumed 50,000 bales of cotton per year, with a capacity to produce 26,000 yards of unbleached

Road graders near the military school at Kearney. —Nebraska State Historical Society, Solomon D. Butcher Collection

Downtown Kearney, 1905. —Wyoming State Museum, Stimson Collection

white muslin annually. But the depression and drought that rocked Nebraska in 1893 hit Kearney hard. Like dominoes, the community's industries fell: the cotton mill, paper mill, oatmeal mill, plow factory, canning factory, woolen mill, cracker factory, and pressed-brick works.

Stephen A. Jenks purchased the cotton mill and reopened the business, which he continued to operate until 1901, when it closed. A lack of skilled laborers spelled the end for the Kearney cotton operation.

I-80 AND US 30
Kearney–North Platte
100 miles

Between Kearney and North Platte the Oregon-California Trail follows the south bank of the Platte River. The Mormon ruts are north of the river, located generally between Interstate 80 and US 30.

LEXINGTON

In early August 1864 Sioux parties raided through the plains, striking stage stations from Julesburg, Colorado, east to Fort Kearny, Nebraska. Although many places came under attack, none was so hard hit as Plum Creek, located about ten miles southeast of Lexington. The date of the raid is obscured by time, but it probably occurred on August 8, 1864. The Indians struck a train of eleven freight wagons on Plum Creek. Three of the wagons were driven by Tom and Nancy Morton; Nancy's brother, William Fletcher; and a cousin, John Fletcher. The Morton and Fletcher wagons were hauling freight to Denver when eight other wagons joined them at Plum Creek.

As the wagons slowly rolled across the prairie, Nancy Morton noticed movement, but before the teamsters had any chance to react the Indians attacked. In a short time they killed the eleven men and injured Nancy and a young boy, Dannie Marble, who had accompanied his father on the trip. The Sioux put Nancy, who was then nineteen years old, and Dannie on horses and headed away from the burning freight wagons.

In a later account of the raid and her capture, Nancy Morton said the Indian women threw green scalps in her face, tied her to a stake, and danced around her, threatening to burn her. Eventually the Indians held Nancy not far from Fort Lyons, Colorado, in a camp with Lucinda Eubanks, Laura Roper, and some children captured in other raids that summer. Traders eventually negotiated the release of Laura

Roper, Dannie Marble, and Isabelle Eubanks, the young daughter of Lucinda. As the traders retreated from the Indian camp, they believed they had reclaimed all the white captives. They didn't realize Lucinda and Nancy lay concealed by buffalo robes.

After the Sand Creek massacre in Colorado in November 1864, where Col. John Chivington killed dozens of Cheyennes under chief Black Kettle, the Indians who held Lucinda and Nancy struck north, headed for the Big Horn Mountains. Trader Jules Ecoffey, who had a post not far north of Fort Laramie, negotiated the release of the two women in late December. In exchange for many items, including thread, knives, tobacco, needles, blankets, coats, and some guns, the Indians released the women, who were taken to Fort Laramie and eventually returned to their homes.

The initial raids in August 1864 resulted in destruction of all stations between Julesburg and Fort Kearny, with the exception of Plum Creek Station, located near present-day Lexington. However, fourteen people were killed at Plum Creek Station during the raid there.

On August 7, 1867, Cheyenne chief Turkey Leg cut the telegraph line near Plum Creek, then lay in wait with his warriors to see who would come along the Union Pacific line to make repairs. In the dark the six men of the repair crew didn't see the ties Turkey Leg and his men had laid across the track, and when they struck them their handcar flew from the tracks. The Indians attacked immediately. Thinking they'd killed all six railroaders, the Indians tore up some of the rail track. Although scalped, William Thompson wasn't dead, and he started crawling toward Plum Creek.

Meanwhile, a freight train from the east pulling about twenty-five cars and a caboose hit the end of the track, and the collision killed the engineer and his fireman immediately. The Indians started looting the train as the remaining men from the train raced east toward safety at Plum Creek.

Thompson, with his bloody scalp in his hand, reached Plum Creek first and was immediately put on a train to Omaha, where a doctor attempted to reattach his hair (the operation was not a success). As dawn lit the sky, the remaining crew members from the wrecked freight train arrived; they could see the train burning in the distance. The army's Pawnee Indian Scouts, commanded by Maj. Frank North, rode to the rescue of the Union Pacific trainmen.

COZAD

In 1879 Maj. John Wesley Powell, in his report for the U.S. Geo-logical Survey, recognized the 100th Meridian as the natural demar-

*Irrigation changed the face of Nebraska as no other occurrence in
its history. Here a farmer sits atop a canal structure east of Cozad.*
—Nebraska State Historical Society, Solomon D. Butcher Collection

cation line between the humid east and the arid west. The 100th
Meridian passes through the center of the small town of Cozad. This
is the place, you might say, where East meets West. Farmers to the east
of the 100th Meridian operate differently than do those to the west.
The eastern operators have rainfall in excess of twenty inches per year,
while those to the west are lucky to see that much moisture every couple
of years. With less rainfall and widely dispersed streams and rivers, the
region west of the 100th Meridian appeared uninhabitable to people
who passed through in early years. Native Americans found the hunting excellent, particularly along the Republican River to the south,
because buffalo liked to concentrate upon this sea of grass. Stephen
Long in 1820 dubbed the region the "Great American Desert," and
it was widely agreed that the region had little use. Time and events
have disproven that perception.

When the Union Pacific rail lines reached Cozad on October 26,
1866, about 250 people, including railroad and territorial officials,
congressmen, and newspapermen, rode the first train in to celebrate
the event. A few settlers had claimed farms in the region, but it would
be years before large-scale irrigation development enabled the region
to start its climb toward prosperity.

The Pony Express

When Russell, Majors, and Waddell started the Pony Express in 1860, the "pony boys," those daredevil riders of the short-lived mail service, positioned themselves at stations spaced roughly twenty miles apart from St. Joseph, Missouri, to San Francisco, California. In Nebraska the route lay near the Oregon-California Trail and followed the Blue, Little Blue, and Platte Rivers. The pony riders carried the mail regularly from April 3, 1860, until October 24, 1861, linking East and West during a critical period in U.S. history. In the course of its eighteen-month life, the Pony Express had only one rider killed while on duty. The station tenders, who waited and watched for the riders to gallop over the ridge, faced the greatest danger, since they became sitting targets for the Indians, who became more aggressive toward white men as each year passed.

The Pony Express never would have come into being if Russell hadn't acted upon his own initiative in obtaining John Hockaday's stage line, which ran on the Oregon Trail. Russell's partners had no real desire to begin running the mail or to establish a stagecoach line on that central route. They thought it too expensive and risky. But when meeting with officials in Washington, Russell gave his word that the company would establish the route, and his partners backed his play. In a letter to Waddell in mid-summer 1860, Russell wrote of the company, "I was compelled . . . to build a world-wide reputation, even at considerable expense and also to incur large expenses in many ways, the details of which I cannot commit to paper," according to Raymond and Mary Settle in *Saddles and Spurs, The Pony Express Saga*.

Waddell and his partners could never meet their expenses, leaving one of their ventures, the Central Overland California & Pikes Peak Express Company (which operated separately from the Pony Express), with the unflattering nickname "Clean Out of Cash & Poor Pay." Despite the partners' fiscal woes, the Pony Express did successfully deliver the mail and did it faster than ever before in history. The key to achievement was the riding ability of some eighty young men (average age: nineteen), mostly orphans, who raced across the plains and mountains.

The Pony Express didn't actually use ponies. For the most part it relied on well-bred horses, often thoroughbreds, and sometimes on the endurance-tested mustangs of the West. Riders changed horses every twenty miles—if all went well. Once in a while marauding Indians or renegade whites stole stock, and the riders raced on, urging the same tired horse twenty more miles to the next station. That overuse occasionally killed the animals.

The riders might have been young, but they did everything they could to get across the continent with the mail, often breaking their own records and risking their lives in the quest. On one ride, Jim Moore, who later became a Nebraska rancher and for whom a small town in Wyoming was also named, rode at least 240 miles in less than fifteen hours, an average speed of eighteen miles per hour. His June 8, 1860, ride took him from Midway Station to Julesburg, Colorado. The feat was possible because Moore rode top-quality horses, which he switched at regular intervals.

Moore and his fellow pony riders carried the mail in a specially designed saddle called a *mochila,* which actually was a leather covering that fit over the saddle frame. At stations the pony riders simply jumped off their horse, grabbed the *mochila,* pulled it over the horn and cantle, repositioned it on a new saddle atop a fresh horse, swung into place, and took off in a cloud of dust.

The Pony Express made its first cross-country delivery from St. Joseph to San Francisco in ten days. The quickest crossing followed the inauguration of President Abraham Lincoln in March 1861. Then riders raced 1,966 miles in seven days and seventeen hours, an average speed of just over ten and one-half miles per hour, with the paper carrying the text of Lincoln's inaugural address.

Although a financial disaster, the Pony Express served a vital function, keeping people on the West Coast informed during the tense period prior to the outbreak of the Civil War. When southern states seceded from the Union, some Rebel leaders hatched a plan to force California out of the Union, according to Waddell F. Smith in *The Story of the Pony Express.* A vocal minority of California's population traced its roots to the South and sympathized with the Rebel cause. As southern eyes turned westward for support, the Pony Express raced cross-country with the word that California needed to be defended if it were to remain in the Union. Petitioners argued the importance of California to the Union and noted that it was much easier to retain a state in allegiance than to overcome disloyalty disguised as state authority.

Loyalists won a state election in September 1861, putting to rest the fears that California would side with the south. Throughout the crisis, news regularly passed between East and West, carried in the heavy leather *mochila* of the Pony Express. The demise of the Pony Express came from competition: William Creighton's transcontinental telegraph line spelled doom for the Pony Express.

Most sites of the various Pony Express stations have been definitively located. Gothenburg is unique in that a portion of what may be one of the original station buildings now stands in a town park used as a

Pony Express museum. Local residents moved the Gothenburg station from its original location about four miles east of Fort McPherson, where it had been built in the 1850s. Although some sources claim construction occurred in 1854, more likely it took place in 1858. It was a two-story structure, with stables located below. Its main purpose was to serve as a mail station after the Mormon War of 1857, and during Indian difficulties in the 1860s it could easily be defended because of its two-story design.

The station owners, brothers J. K. and Jud Gilman, traded animals to travelers on the Oregon-California journey. As Eugene F. Ware put it in his journal in 1863: "They now had a very fine and defensible ranch. They told us how they made their money . . . trade one well animal for two footsore animals. . . . They had a large stock of goods." The station served as a stage stop and eventually a ranch house until 1931, when residents moved the upper floor of the small log structure to Gothenburg.

Midway Stage Station

The Midway Stage Station, which served as a trading post, Overland stage station, and Pony Express home station, now sits on the Williams 96 Ranch about four miles south of Gothenburg. Jim Moore began his famous ride for the Pony Express from here. The station is located on a ridge not far from the Platte River; nearby springs provided water for the station. A portion of the cedar station house uses Canadian "post-and-sill" construction, while the remainder is of the more conventional "saddle-and-rider" style.

The log walls of the cabin originally sat on the bare ground, which served as the floor, but the entire structure has since been placed on a concrete platform. The wall spaces, originally daubed with mud, are now sealed with grout. Nebraska's most important extant building known to have served traffic along the Oregon Trail, it is one of the thirty-six buildings that served the Pony Express in Nebraska. Although it is claimed that three of those stations remain, only Midway is clearly a Pony Express station. The other two, located at Gothenburg and Cozad, may have served the pony riders, but their authenticity is not as clearly documented. Moreover, according to records of the Nebraska State Historic Preservation office, only Midway remains at its original site.

Although some suggest Midway was originally built as a fur trading post about 1850, it is more likely that the building was one of a series of fifteen stage and mail stations completed across Nebraska in 1859 by the Leavenworth & Pikes Peak Express Company to link the Missouri River with Denver and Salt Lake City. Soon afterward, Russell,

Majors, and Waddell acquired the station. In 1859 Midway was known only as U.S. Mail Station No. 17, but by 1860 it became known as Midway, apparently because of its central location between Atchison and Denver.

As a Pony Express home station, Midway housed riders and stabled their horses. After the demise of the Pony Express, the station continued to serve stage and emigrant travelers until the late 1860s.

Gothenburg's Industry

Gothenburg Water Power and Irrigation Company organized in the 1890s. By 1897 it had spent more than $800,000 for land, construction of buildings and reservoirs, and other improvements. The Holton Brass and Copper Company, formerly of Boston, also operated at Gothenburg. Germans, Danes, and Swedes settled the Gothenburg region, predominantly an agricultural area (it still has a weekly livestock auction). By 1990 alfalfa dehydration had become a major industry, valued at about $6 million annually. Dawson County produces an estimated 300,000 tons of alfalfa annually, and about half that is dehydrated in pellet mills located in Gothenburg.

BRADY

As early travelers made their way across the Platte River valley, they shared the land with the huge herds of buffalo that grazed the prairie lands. The buffalo often migrated toward the Platte River, lured by water. In 1847 the first group of westbound Mormon pioneers often killed buffalo; leader Brigham Young told them not to butcher any more until they needed food. Appleton Harmon wrote in his journal of the emigrants' difficulty getting through a herd of buffalo, which formed a line from their water hole on the river to a bluff some four miles back. Eventually the dogs in the train succeeded in driving the buffalo away from the river. Harmon wrote: "I could stand on my waggon & see more than 10,000 Buffalo from the fact that the Plain was purfectly black with them on both sides of the river & on the bluff on our right which slopes off gradualy [sic]."

Ten years later, in an 1857 *Rocky Mountain Life* article, Rufus B. Sage chronicled a hunting trip he had taken in the same vicinity, near the present town of Brady. After he shot an old cow, Sage recalled:

> They began by spurning the ground with their feet,—then, bellowing, gored the fallen beast, as if forcing her to rise,—then rolling upon the grass, in demonstrative sympathy,—and, now that she had ceased to struggle and lay yet quivering in death, they licked her bleeding wounds and seemed to exercise a kind of mournful rivalry in the bestowment of their testimonials of affection. She is encircled by her companions. . . . Meanwhile the hunter's rifle had been busily em-

ployed. . . . All hands were now summoned to aid at the work of butchery; but the fast-enshrouding darkness soon drove us back to camp. . . . Our withdrawal from the premises was the signal for possession by the eager wolves.

MAXWELL

The area near Maxwell served as a routine crossing for Native Americans traveling between Republican River country to the south and the Sandhills in the north.

The army established Fort McPherson along the Oregon Trail on the south side of the Platte River on October 13, 1863. The fort changed names more often than some of its residents changed their shirts during that period. It went by the names Cantonment McKean, Post Cottonwood Springs, Fort Cottonwood, and eventually Fort McPherson, the latter title bestowed in February 1866 for Maj. Gen. James B. McPherson, who was killed in Atlanta, Georgia, during the Civil War. It became the base for military scouting parties and field campaigns in 1865, 1866, and 1869, as Indians—particularly Cheyenne and Sioux—raised havoc all through the Platte River country.

Gen. Eugene A. Carr's 1869 campaign broke the power of the Cheyennes and largely cleared the surrounding area from Indian threats. The military abandoned the fort in 1880, but a portion of the site is now the Fort McPherson National Cemetery, established in 1873. Upon its establishment, the government removed the bodies of slain soldiers who had been buried at forts in South Dakota, Idaho, Wyoming, Colorado, and Nebraska for reinterment at Fort McPherson.

Perfectly lined tombstones at Fort McPherson National Cemetery. The earliest markers and graves are those of frontiersmen and soldiers, including those killed in the 1854 Grattan Massacre.

Many of the soldiers buried here died in the western country during the fur-trade era. Others perished in the Indian conflicts, including the 1854 Grattan fight at Fort Laramie, which precipitated hostilities along the Oregon Trail (see page 326). Originally the twenty-eight men who died in the Grattan battle were buried where they died near Fort Laramie, but in 1891 the military moved their bodies to Fort McPherson. They lie in a common grave marked by a large white marble monument. Lt. John Grattan, who led the soldiers to the rout, is now buried at Fort Leavenworth National Cemetery.

Some of the soldiers buried at Fort McPherson died in World War II at Chateau-Thierry, Omaha Beach, Saipan, Iwo Jima, and Okinawa; a few died in Korea. As with all cemeteries, there are unmarked graves. Those at Fort McPherson are unmarked not because it was impossible to identify the bodies but because natural forces erased the names. In some cases wooden crosses marked graves, and over time the weathering of wind, water, and temperature made names unrecognizable. In other instances the wood burned in prairie fires that swept the plains.

NORTH PLATTE

North Platte lies on a strip of land between the North and South Platte Rivers near the dividing line for the Central and Mountain Time Zones.

It started as a Union Pacific Railroad town. On November 9, 1866, William Peniston and Andrew J. Miller opened a trading post at the site. They'd heard it would soon be a construction camp for the Union Pacific, and they intended to capitalize on the boom associated with railroad work. Their foresight paid off, as Gen. Grenville Dodge soon laid out the town of North Platte. John Burke moved a log building from Cottonwood Springs, which he quickly put into use as a hotel. A man named Clark operated the community's first newspaper, *The Pioneer On Wheels*, from a boxcar, and by the winter of 1866–67 North Platte's population had swelled to 2,000 railroad workers and camp followers. The *Missouri Democrat* reported in May 1867:

> North Platte is a gay frontier hamlet; its citizens a motley crowd of construction camp denizens, roughs, and gamblers, emigrants but a few months from the countries of the Old world. Women from the dance halls, bullwhackers and teamsters would line the tracks to see the train in. Timid passengers, fearing to face so desperate appearing a multitude, were glad to follow hotel runners to a hastily constructed hostelry that charged a lot but gave little in the way of comfort. A gambling establishment was conducted in a large tent.

The Union Pacific Railroad affected the future of North Platte by making the city a "hump yard" for rolling stock. This 1874 view shows the windmill and shops near North Platte. —Nebraska State Historical Society

By June the railroad had extended its line west to Julesburg, Colorado, and the construction gang went with it, dropping North Platte's population to about 300. Any building that could be moved was, and the town's newspaper rolled on west as well.

North Platte might have slid into permanent small-town status if not for Union Pacific executives' decision to make the town at the forks of the North and South Platte a division point for the railroad as well. They built machine shops, a roundhouse, and a hotel, stabilizing the town population and leading to continued steady growth. By 1879 North Platte had 1,600 residents. By 1997 North Platte's Bailey Yards served as the largest and busiest train-switching station, or hump yard, in the United States.

Life settled during the 1880s, and North Platte vigilantes rid the community of any undesirable residents. The town built a $20,000 courthouse and a $16,000 schoolhouse, while the business district grew to include general stores, hardware, feed, and furniture outlets, a couple of blacksmith and wagon shops, and lumber and coal yards.

On April 7 a prairie fire started about nine miles west of town. A spark from a passing train ignited the tall grasses, and high winds drove the flames across the prairie from the northwest. The blaze ate everything in its path, including thirty-five homes in town and many farmhouses, barns, outbuildings, and other structures outside of town. Nearly

Buffalo Bill Cody and family. —Wyoming State Museum, Stimson Collection

everyone in the community responded to the emergency, pouring what water they had on buildings, and beat at the flames with anything they could find.

Today a prairie fire can be found in any North Platte tavern—a shot of tequila spiked with several drops of hot sauce.

Bill Cody's Scouts Rest Ranch

As a Pony Express rider, army scout and fighter, buffalo hunter, and showman, William F. "Buffalo Bill" Cody saw much of the West, and he had homes in several areas. One of them, his Scouts Rest Ranch, was at North Platte.

Cody worked in 1867–68 for the Goddard brothers, providing buffalo meat for workers on the Kansas Pacific Railroad. He earned $500 a month, and legend has it that he killed 4,280 buffalo in eight months. He killed sixty-nine buffalo in a contest against Bill Comstock (who shot forty-six), giving Cody his now-legendary nickname.

From 1868 to 1873 Cody worked as a government scout with the 5th Cavalry. He spent some time acting in a stage play about the frontier, then returned West to scout for Gen. George Crook through Wyoming. After 1876 the story of the man becomes so intermingled with myth it is difficult to tell the legend from the fact. One story goes that he

Bill Cody's house at Scouts Rest Ranch, North Platte.

claimed the first scalp for Custer when he killed Cheyenne chief Yellow Hair in northwest Nebraska just days after the Battle of the Little Bighorn (see page 368).

Cody ranched with Frank and Luther North along the Dismal River in north-central Nebraska and joined them to organize North Platte's "Old Glory Blowout" in 1881, which led to the Buffalo Bill Wild West Show. He toured with the show from 1883 to 1886 and took it to England in 1887, the same year Nebraska Gov. John M. Thayer appointed him aide-de-camp with the rank of colonel in the Nebraska National Guard.

Cody's Wild West Show and Congress of Rough Riders of the World featured cowboys and cowgirls who demonstrated their ability at bucking bronc riding, trick riding, and roping. The troupe also included a large number of Indians, many of them Sioux, whom Cody had opposed in battle in an earlier decade, and such celebrities as Annie Oakley, whom he called "Little Sure Shot."

Cody built Scouts Rest Ranch at North Platte during the heyday of his Wild West shows. It encompassed about 4,000 acres, upon which he raised cattle and horses. In 1886 Cody's sister, Julia, oversaw construction of the lavishly appointed, $3,900 house at Scouts Rest Ranch. It became a gathering place for Cody and his associates: businessmen, politicians, army officers, even royalty. Julia's husband, Al Goodman, managed the ranch.

Cody didn't limit his business interests to Nebraska. For a time he owned and managed the Sheridan Inn in Sheridan, Wyoming, and he helped build and promote the town of Cody, Wyoming. From 1900 to 1910 Cody continued his Wild West Show, eventually joining William Lillie "Pawnee Bill" and his Far East Show for a combined act commonly called the Two Bills Show. But Cody had a difficult time. His marriage was on the rocks, and his Wild West Show teetered as well. He borrowed money but couldn't managed to recoup his losses, and at the close of the 1911 season he sold Scouts Rest Ranch and some 3,000 acres to Pawnee Bill for $100,000. Cody moved his family to his other ranch near Cody, Wyoming, but he died in Denver in 1917 at the home of his sister and is buried on Lookout Mountain just west of Denver, Colorado.

In 1965 the state of Nebraska obtained Scouts Rest Ranch and designated it a state historical park. The state restored the house and barn and added displays that include many items related to Buffalo Bill's life.

North Platte Canteen

As troops headed to war during World War II, many rode trains that crossed the nation. At various sites local residents organized aid stations, called canteens, and the most famous in Nebraska was located at North Platte. The North Platte Canteen actually started because of

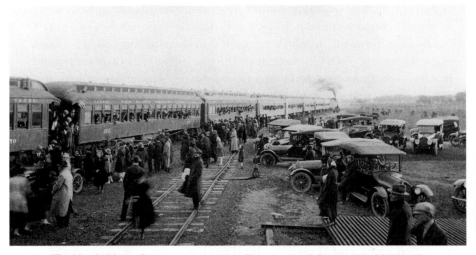

The North Platte Canteen was nationally recognized during World War II as a relief spot for troops headed to war. This troop train is near Camp Funston at Wahoo. —Nebraska State Historical Society

a mixup. A little more than a week after the Japanese bombed Pearl Harbor in December 1941, some local residents heard that Company D of the Nebraska National Guard would be riding a troop train through North Platte en route to the West Coast and potential action in the Pacific Theater. Townspeople gathered gum, cookies, cigarettes, cakes, and other items, then waited for the train to arrive, intending to pass out the supplies to their hometown boys.

But the Company D that rolled into town was from Kansas, not Nebraska. That didn't matter; the local residents handed out the items they'd collected. Rae Wilson, whose brother commanded Nebraska's Company D, led the move to keep the effort in place to meet all incoming troop trains. On Christmas Day 1941 the North Platte Canteen officially opened. Eventually people from communities all across central and western Nebraska helped support the canteen, which earned a nation-wide reputation as the best place for a troop train to stop.

The North Platte Canteen remained in operation until April 1, 1946. It came to life again in 1995 when Nebraskans celebrated the fiftieth anniversary of the end of World War II. In a statewide program called "Victory '95," Nebraskans staged the largest V-J Day fiftieth anniversary celebration in the United States, according to the Department of Defense WWII Commemoration Committee in Washington, D.C.

The celebration started in August with the recreation of the North Platte Canteen. On September 1 the Union Pacific Railroad operated a "troop train" across Nebraska, leaving from North Platte and headed to Omaha, with stops at Kearney, Grand Island, Columbus, and Fremont. In Omaha the activities continued with a special exhibit at the Western Heritage Museum in Union Station, a parade, a memorial dedication at the Heartland of America Park along the Missouri River, and air shows at Offutt Air Force Base.

I-80 AND US 30
North Platte–Ogallala
39 miles

Westbound emigrants had to make a major decision at the site that eventually became North Platte. One Oregon Trail branch crossed the South Platte to the south bank of the North Platte River, then followed a trail close to the present route of the Union Pacific Railroad. Most early travelers followed this branch toward Fort Laramie. However, after the establishment of Fort Sedgwick in May 1864, near present-day

Julesburg, Colorado, many travelers chose not to cross the South Platte. Instead they followed it to Fort Sedgwick before turning north toward Fort Laramie.

After 1862 Overland Company stages also followed the South Platte until they met the trail struck by the Cherokee as they headed to California after 1849. That Cherokee Trail also saw use from white travelers en route to California from Arkansas and Indian Territory. Most Overland Trail/Cherokee Trail travelers went into Wyoming and followed a route roughly parallel to US 30 and Interstate 80.

Sutherland Irrigation Project

The Dust Bowl days of the 1930s, particularly the drought years of 1934 and 1936, led Nebraskans to the realization that they needed to store some of the water that flowed down the North and South Platte Rivers each year. One of the earliest efforts—the Sutherland Irrigation Project—involved construction of Kingsley Dam with Lake McConaughy behind it, just west of Keystone. The separate 5,000-acre Sutherland Reservoir stores water for irrigation and production of electrical power. The Sutherland Project Power Plant, located south of North Platte, produces power for the region, with water flowing from the reservoir past the power turbines and back into the South Platte.

O'Fallon's Bluff

If you are driving the fast route across Nebraska—Interstate 80— one of the best places to view the Oregon Trail is at the eastbound rest area near Sutherland, which provides access to the area known as O'Fallon's Bluff. Because the topography here forced emigrants to draw their wagons close together and follow one behind the other, the ruts they carved into the land grew deep. The region right near O'Fallon's Bluff is not good farming ground, so whereas original trail ruts have disappeared under the plow in so many sections of Nebraska, they remain at this location.

Nebraska has done as good a job as any state in marking the route. At O'Fallon's Bluff the state placed large steel circles mounted on bricks right in the ruts to give visitors a sense of the trail and the wagons that carved it. Nebraska recognized the Oregon Trail in 1993 with a month-long wagon train, led by wagonmaster Joe Vogel, that crossed from Rock Creek Station to Mitchell.

OGALLALA

In many Nebraska communities with ranching roots, rodeo is still the biggest sport in town. Cowboys ride mile after mile over rolling hills gathering strays, just as they did more than a hundred years ago.

Early ranchers trailed their stock to railheads and loaded animals onto stock cars for shipping to markets in Omaha or perhaps even Chicago. Although many communities can rightfully call themselves rancher-friendly, perhaps none has as strong a claim to being the cowboy capital as Ogallala.

This town on the South Platte River at the southern edge of the Sandhills lies atop the ruts of the Oregon, California, and Texas Trails. It has a weekly livestock auction and a "boot hill" cemetery filled with cowboys and outlaws. A reconstructed Front Street still supports a saloon and dance hall/theater. Though the Oregon- and California-bound emigrants passed right through this area, Ogallala didn't exist during their era. It was the cowboys and the railroad who gave birth to the town, named for the Oglala Sioux.

Texas Trail

The high plains had natural grass and water sufficient for large numbers of cattle, and the best place to obtain them was in Texas. When Texans returned from the Civil War they found huge cattle populations grazing upon an overused range; the beef market was in the doldrums. Knowing there was plentiful grass to the north, the cowboys rounded up the animals and started driving them out of Texas.

Cowboys near Kennedy Post Office, Cherry County, Nebraska. –Nebraska State Historical Society, Solomon D. Butcher Collection

Moving cattle in central Nebraska. —Nebraska State Historical Society, Solomon D. Butcher Collection

An account by H. H. Bancroft says A. J. Williams brought 1,500 Mexican cattle to the Platte Valley in 1866, the first large importation of southern cattle to the northern plains. Some smaller herds had moved north earlier, and by 1867 cattle were moving into Colorado.

That year the Colorado Territorial Assembly approved a resolution that said, in part, "It shall not be lawful for any person or persons to import into the Territory of Colorado any bull, cow, ox, steer, or cattle of whatever description known as 'Texas cattle' for the purpose of sale, stock raising, growing, herding, feeding or for any purpose whatsoever." The ban sprang up to control a tick carried by Texas cattle. The tick didn't affect Texas animals, which were immune to it, but it spread fever among northern animals. Kansas passed a law similar to Colorado's prohibiting movement of the Texas herds.

The volume of northbound cattle grew from 1866 until 1884, when an estimated 416,000 animals moved onto the plains. In all, between four and six million cattle were brought north on the various cattle trails. One of the most important cattle trails, the Texas Trail, had a primary terminus in Ogallala, although it continued on through western Nebraska and Wyoming to Montana.

After 1884, cattle movement slowed because of the quarantine laws. That year cattlemen from twenty-seven states gathered in St. Louis, Missouri, to organize a national association and deal with various issues, including movement of herds. They adopted a resolution on November 18, 1884, urging Congress to establish a National Cattle Trail—a fenced lane, six miles wide, set aside as a permanent quarantine ground over which cattle could move unhindered from Texas to Canada. Noting that the government had turned millions of acres of land over to railroads, the resolution said Congress could hardly refuse "to donate some to the people in the interest of cheaper food." Texans supported the resolution, but cattlemen in northern ranges, particularly in Wyoming and Montana, opposed it because they didn't want additional Texas cattle moving onto their ranges. Ultimately Congress killed the proposal.

In *Trails of Yesterday,* John Bratt called Ogallala a "wide-awake, wild, and sometimes wicked town." He recalled seeing up to 50,000 head of cattle along the South Platte River in an area extending between ten and fifteen miles east, west, and south of Ogallala. An observer for the *Lincoln State Journal* wrote September 3, 1884:

> Today is a gala day with us here. More than seven thousand cattle crossed the river at this point today. . . . There are four thousand five hundred more on the south bank of the river to come over tomorrow. They are mostly fat cattle of graded Texas and improved stock that will be shipped from this point to Chicago. This makes in round numbers 400,000 received at this place of this season's drive. It is said that there are about 20,000 more on the trail expected to arrive here during the next ten days, and that will conclude the business for the season. Now bear in mind that to drive and handle these cattle required a force of about 2,500 to 3,000 men and fully 20,000 horses. . . . Ogallala is the terminus of the trail.

Cattleman John Clay wrote in *My Life on the Range* that the Texans worked their herds and filled contracts each day, with buyers driving out to view the herds. Afternoons found sellers and buyers meeting for drinks to negotiate deals. "Gradually the Texas crowd would concentrate, go across the tracks, all sit around in a circle and hold a council of war, smoking, chewing, whittling, comparing notes, and forming embryo trusts. . . . The buyers did the same only they were not so well organized as their southern neighbors," Clay wrote.

Eastern capitalists invested in the Ogallala Land and Cattle Company, with shareholders from Chicago, New York City, Washington, Kansas City, and Cheyenne. The main office was in Omaha, with branch offices in Chicago, New York, and Cheyenne. August Richard of New York was the first president of the company, which was capitalized at $1.25 million. It organized with 43,000 head of livestock in Keith, Deuel, and McPherson Counties and other areas.

Ogallala soon became one of the most famous of the "cow towns" in the Platte River valley, a well-known shipping point for cattle from Montana, Wyoming, Colorado, Texas, Oklahoma, and Nebraska.

Hastings—Holdrege
54 miles

HASTINGS

It's likely that Hastings has had an impact upon every state in the nation—all because E. E. Perkins started the Perkins Product Company in 1920. The company originally produced spices, flavorings, liniment, and other items, but in the late 1920s Perkins created the concoction that spread across the country: Kool-Aid. By 1931 the powdered soft drink commanded a large market, and Perkins, wanting to cut his freight costs, moved the company to Chicago.

To go back to Hastings's beginnings, it is necessary to rewind the clock to 1872, when the first settlers arrived along with the Denver & St. Joseph Railroad. The area soon boomed, in part because of its rail services; Hastings remains a busy rail center, with Amtrak making daily passenger stops in Hastings.

Hastings is a heartland town with a diverse commercial background. From the early 1900s through World War II the area produced millions of chickens, which were loaded onto trains and shipped to markets

Burlington Station, Hastings, designed by Omaha architect Thomas R. Kimball. —Nebraska State Historical Society

A woman feeds her chickens. —Nebraska State Historical Society

between San Francisco and Chicago. Because refrigeration hadn't been developed, the chickens were packed in crates and shipped live—"on the claw," as Harold Hamil put it in *Nebraska: No Place Like It.*

J. Oder founded the Hastings Poultry Company soon after his arrival in 1901. Oder had previously worked for the Swift Company, and he no doubt had an idea of the potential in poultry production and marketing. His company soon became the leading independent poultry dealer in the United States, with facilities in Julesburg, Colorado, Missouri Valley, Iowa, and North Platte and Loup City, Nebraska.

Trainloads of squawking chickens rolled across Nebraska until the mid-1920s, when companies started killing chickens prior to shipping them to markets. Part of the change in operation came because mortality rates for chickens shipped live tended to be high. Sometimes chickens pecked each other to death, and occasionally they developed a disease known as roup caused by drafty conditions in the train cars. And poultry shippers thought perhaps the employees in charge of the freight occasionally pilfered a hen for Sunday dinner.

By the 1930s most chickens went to market "New York style." That is, they were killed, bled, plucked, and refrigerated but not cleaned. That final step in chicken preparation fell to the retail meat dealer. After the switch from shipping live poultry to dealing with dead and refrigerated birds, Swift & Company opened a dressing plant near Hastings. Eventually the industry in Hastings dwindled; egg produc-

Hot air balloon ascension near Broken Bow. —Nebraska State Historical Society, Solomon D. Butcher Collection

tion shifted to the East and West coasts, and poultry production moved to Georgia, Alabama, Mississippi, and Arkansas.

The full force of the 1929 stock market crash and Great Depression didn't affect Hastings until 1931, and by then the town was already reeling from other factors. On May 8, 1930, a tornado ripped through Hastings, killing one person and causing more than $1 million in damage. The dry years of the Depression caused even more impact. Wrote Hamil in *Nebraska: No Place Like It:*

> Drought as a natural disaster is more subtle than a tornado or flood. It comes on slowly. People tend to postpone the reality. Finally, they act in disbelief, dismay, and sometimes, despondency. The end of a tornado or flood is usually definite and recognizable. The end of a drought, though, can be stretched through a whole succession of false signals and misplaced hopes.

Hamil reported on the situation for the *Hastings Independent.* Some of his stories read like a weather diary: February precipitation, .82 inches; March, .25 inches; April, .10 inches; April 11, dust storm; April 20, high temperatures in the 80s; May 5, wheat turning brown; May 11, a dust cloud estimated to be 1,500 miles long and 900 miles wide blots the sun in Chicago, the Twin Cities, Des Moines, St. Louis, and Kansas City; early June, rain falls in some parts of Nebraska, including two inches in Nebraska City, none in Hastings.

People withered, as did the crops. On July 28 attention turned skyward with the news that a balloon launched by the National Geographic Society and U.S. Army would record high-altitude weather conditions. The balloon, launched near Rapid City, South Dakota, drifted toward the southeast, carrying three men with various weather instruments. When the balloon reached an altitude about adequate for the men to begin their observations, the balloon's bag started to tear. The crew managed to descend to a safe landing in a field west of Hastings.

The economy of the community picked up during the years of World War II when a munitions plant opened in Hastings. The ordnance was stored in rural bunkers throughout the region, particularly in the area of Clay Center, to the southeast.

MINDEN

Minden residents call their community "The Christmas City" because of efforts since 1915 to display lights for the holiday season. City light commissioner J. W. Haws started the process when he stretched lights from the railroad depot to the town square in an effort to impress the state convention of the Grand Army of the Republic in 1915. A cold, freezing rain made it impossible to light the uninsulated lights, so Haws colored them and strung them on the courthouse dome. He eventually turned the lights on in time for Christmas Eve.

For years afterward Haws arranged the lights in Christmas shapes and displayed them at the courthouse. In 1942 the town presented its pageant, called "The Light of the World," climaxing with the lighting of some 10,000 lights.

The Making of Pioneer Village

Although Minden calls itself the "Christmas City," it is really more known for the incredible collection of an incredible man, Harold Warp. Warp was reared on a homestead not far from Minden. His father, John Neilsen Warp, immigrated from Skollenberg, Norway, and claimed land in the late 1870s. Later he married Helga Johannesen, a Norwegian immigrant who operated a nearby homestead with her brother.

The Warp homestead stood nine miles south of Minden, and there young Harold herded cattle. He attended school in a one-room building and watched as new inventions came along to make life better for his family: the automobile, the farm truck, the tractor, the telephone, and the radio. Warp eventually went to Chicago where, with $800 he had diligently saved, he started the Flex-O-Glass plastics company. That company went on to become an industrial giant, and Harold Warp became a rich man.

A full Conestoga wagon beckons visitors to Harold Warp's Pioneer Village in Minden. The Warp collection is an unparalleled array of materials ranging from collections of ballpoint pens and matchbooks to a steam engine, buildings, automobiles, airplanes, and household items.

One day he heard that the old one-room schoolhouse in Minden was going to be sold. Warp bought it and relocated it to downtown Minden, where he started the development of his Pioneer Village. The facility opened in 1953. Covering twenty acres, it has more than 50,000 items displayed in twenty-eight buildings, many of them original structures that have been relocated to the village. These include the Elm Creek Fort, likely the first log cabin in Webster County, constructed in 1869 and used as a dwelling and community fort; the Bloomington land office, moved from its site in Franklin County and containing old land records and John N. Warp's homestead title; the Lowell Depot, which served railroad passengers from 1872 to 1882; and the horse barn from the Warp homestead.

Other buildings display china, firefighting equipment, farm machinery, antique tractors and trucks, bicycles, motorcycles, automobiles, home appliances, and blacksmith items. The homes and shops building has kitchens, living rooms, and bedrooms for each generation since 1830. That building also has a music shop, doctor's office, print shop, drugstore, and barber shop, as well as shops for traditional crafts such as candle making, yarn spinning, weaving, and broom making. Around the Pioneer Village "town square" are the People's Store, the Lowell Depot (complete with a train engine), a sod house, a church, a merry-go-round, a livery stable, a Pony Express building and barn, a hobby house, and a home appliance building with nearly every style of washing machine ever invented. The entire Pioneer Village is a memorial by Harold Warp to his parents. On a plaque near the land office, he has written of the pioneers:

> *The cowards never started*
> *The weak died on the way*
> *Only the strong arrived*
> *They were the pioneers.*

Warp's 472-page book, *A History of Man's Progress from 1830 to the Present,* details all of the inventions, gadgets, and timesaving devices that have made life in the United States easier. It includes a description, and in many cases a photograph, of each item included in Harold Warp's Pioneer Village. One of the oldest pieces is Waterman's oxcart, built by Artimes Waterman in Deansboro, New York. A Conestoga wagon dates to the 1830s, and a stagecoach on display ran between St. Joe and Detroit after about 1850. Other early coaches are the Yellowstone Wagon, used in Yellowstone National Park between 1880 and 1916; a Concord coach built by the Abbott-Downing Company of Concord, New Hampshire; and a freight wagon built in 1857 by Henry and Clem Studebaker to transport goods across the plains.

Warp's Pioneer Village also has a locomotive built for the Burlington & Missouri Railroad by the Baldwin Locomotive Works in 1889; a horse-drawn streetcar used in New York City in 1832; dozens of buggies and other horse-drawn vehicles; a 1902 Cadillac; a 1903 Model A Ford; and dozens of other types of automobile. There is farm equipment, firefighting equipment, ice harvesting and refrigeration equipment, musical instruments, communications devices, firearms, mechanical toys, sculptures, and artwork; there are collections of china, buttons, zippers, matchbooks, and even ballpoint pens.

US 10, which provides access to Pioneer Village and Minden from I-80, is the Harold Warp Memorial Parkway. The road crosses the Oregon Trail just before it reaches the river, and a rural road, Nebraska L50A, follows the trail to Fort Kearny.

HOLDREGE

The area around Holdrege is prime farming ground, with acres and acres of corn raised annually. The opportunities in Holdrege in the 1990s came as a result of the irrigation projects developed along the Platte River decades before.

Irrigated winter wheat and oats. —Wyoming State Museum, Stimson Collection

The earliest farming in this region of Nebraska involved dryland development. But each year dryland farmers saw their soil blow into the air as plains winds scoured the ground. In 1905 George W. Holdrege, general manager of the Burlington Railroad, promoted the idea of an experimental farm—The Burlington Model Farm—that developed a method of packing the soil to improve production. The technique appeared to work. In the period between 1893 and 1904 an average of thirteen and a half bushels of wheat per acre were raised in Nebraska. On the Burlington Model Farm at Holdrege in 1906, the harvest came in at fifty-one and a half bushels to the acre.

Farmers throughout southwestern Nebraska soon utilized dryland farming techniques. Most often they chose to raise wheat, but some varieties of oats, including Sixty-Day, Kherson, and Swedish Select, also matured well under dryland conditions. Other farmers raised Tennessee winter barley, rye, potatoes, and even alfalfa, although they later found that crop did much better under irrigation. Corn never did well as a dryland crop, although some sorghum family products could withstand long dry spells without withering and dying.

The Central Nebraska Project's Kingsley Dam and Lake McConaughy brought irrigation water to farmers throughout south-central Nebraska in the 1930s, and the region became a virtual gold

Plowing near the North Platte, 1921. —Wyoming State Museum, Stimson Collection

mine. Farmers now could put every inch of their land to work. Although they raised many crops, corn dominated the landscape once there was adequate water for irrigation.

Corn has always been one of the state's staple crops. In 1862 *Nebraska Farmer* suggested thirty-three ways to cook corn, including hasty pudding (cornmeal mush), corn on the cob, apple cornbread, hominy, Virginia corn dodgers, pumpkin Indian loaf, corn muffins, griddle cakes, baked Indian pudding, boiled Indian pudding, maize, and white pot (milk, eggs, corn meal, sugar, and molasses). However, the homesteaders, who lived on an almost constant diet of food made with corn, maintained that any way you made it, it was still corn.

Corn continues to dominate the region's agriculture, although today farmers also raise significant amounts of soybeans and sorghum. The use of locally grown corn for livestock feeding operations is one of the mainstays of the agribusiness industry in this area.

There's more to the history of Holdrege and Phelps County than agriculture. Rock Falls, located southeast of Holdrege and Atlanta, started in 1873 on Spring Creek, a stream made wholly of springs. In 1886 Rock Falls developed into a resort. The *Holdrege Nuggett* wrote: "Above the falls the rowing is good and boats can be had at pleasure. A circular swing, which will accommodate eight persons at once, rope swings, rustic seats, and a large platform for dancing parties are all

A gathering of legends. Standing, from left: Deadwood Dick, Edgar Howard, Charles R. Nordin, W. F. "Doc" Carver, and Idaho Bill; seated, from left: Capt. Luther North, Pawnee Bill, and Diamond Dick. —Nebraska State Historical Society

provided on the grounds. And the waterfall itself is worth the ride which it costs to see it."

Atlanta, southeast of Holdrege on US 6/US 34, served as a major prisoner-of-war camp for Germans and Italians captured by Allied forces during World War II. The prisoners provided much-needed labor for local farms during the war years. The camp opened in 1943 and closed in 1946. Remnants of the camp include a smokestack, the silo-shaped water tower, and indentations in the land where buildings used to stand.

Northeast of Holdrege is the former site of Phelps Center. At its height that town had two newspapers, a couple of blacksmith shops, a hardware store, two drugstores, a general store, a harness shop, two hotels, two banks, a church, a post office, and a school, along with three doctors to serve the community. When the Burlington Railroad established Holdrege in 1883, Phelps Center's businesses pulled up stakes and moved to the new railroad station.

All of south-central Nebraska is a corridor for waterfowl migrations. Bald eagles start arriving in November and remain through mid-March. The Sacramento-Wilcox Wildlife Management Area is a waterfowl refuge with an area set aside for Canada geese. A portion of the area is used as a game farm, and some camping and hunting is permitted. The cornfields around Holdrege and to the east are alive during the spring season from mid-February through mid-April as sandhill cranes flock north from Mexico to the Arctic (see page 186).

(see page 186)

Holdrege–Colorado Border
158 miles

Nebraska 23 parallels the route taken by some travelers on the Oregon and California Trails, although generally the trail traffic kept farther north, along the Platte River. At times the wagons spread out for miles as they went west. Wherever the terrain allowed them to, emigrants traveled side by side rather than single file in order to keep out of one another's dust and to find fresh grass for their livestock.

A major Indian trail crossed this region as well, slicing south to north along the divide separating the Republican and Platte drainages. That route crossed the Platte in the area near present-day Maxwell and was well marked by Indian use by the time the military started following it (in 1863) as the main access route between the Republican River and the Platte. Even farther west, between Elsie and Madrid, Nebraska 23 intersects the Texas Trail, upon which hundreds of thousands of head of animals moved on their way to northern ranges in Nebraska, Wyoming, and Montana after 1870.

The country between Farnam and Moorefield is hilly, rising and falling between stream drainages. This area is part of the "dissected plains," old ground that has been heavily eroded by wind and water. In 1886 the Chicago, Burlington & Quincy Railroad established Ingham where its tracks crossed Deer Creek Canyon, one of the few level areas of this country. Initially a way station on the Burlington Highline (which connected Holdrege and Sterling, Colorado), Ingham soon served as a trading center for the dryland farms and cattle ranches in the area. The railroad also hauled locally mined and manufactured silica. The town had a post office by 1898, but not until 1924 did the first class graduate from Ingham High School.

The community's fortunes started declining in the 1920s. Dryland farming brought only marginal profits, and better roads and vehicles made it possible for farmers to haul their products to larger communities. In 1928 the silica mill relocated in Eustis, spelling the end of Ingham.

STOCKVILLE

Stockville, located south of Nebraska 23 on Nebraska 18, considers itself the oldest city in southwestern Nebraska. The original county courthouse, built in 1872, burned in 1884, along with most of the county records to that time. The new courthouse went up in 1888.

The Sioux particularly liked the Medicine Valley because of its location in the heart of buffalo country, and in 1870 the Cut-off Oglala Sioux band of Whistler settled near this area. The conditions that set up the last Indian-upon-Indian fight in Nebraska also developed in this area in 1872. Whistler's Sioux were the only permanent Indian residents in the region at that time. In August of that year the Pawnees left their reservation at Genoa to hunt along the Republican River. Accompanied by Texas Jack Omohundro, Luther North, and George Bird Grinnell, the party of about 2,700 Ponca and Pawnee Indians killed between 200 and 300 head of buffalo. As the Pawnee hunted toward the west, Whistler and his Sioux had gone to the Upper Republican, most likely in Colorado, for their own hunt, leaving their women and children in camp on the Stinking Water. During the course of the winter Whistler, Fat Badger, and Hand Smeller left the hunters and headed to Fort McPherson to seek supplies. On their way they visited a hunting camp of two or three buffalo hunters, where they asked for food. The hunters fed the three Indians but later had a confrontation when Whistler and his companions asked for more food. The incident ended with the deaths of the three Indians. Some Sioux initially blamed the Pawnees for the deaths of Whistler and his companions.

In a separate occurrence, some of the Sioux came upon a camp of Pawnees, raiding the camp and stealing many horses. The Pawnees were furious, in part because the horses reflected their main form of wealth. Those incidents led to disastrous events involving the Pawnees and the Sioux on the Republican River during August 1873 (see page 242).

Among the frontiersmen who frequented the region were Hank and Monty Clifford, John Y. Nelson, and Doc Carver. Buffalo Bill Cody and Texas Jack regularly guided the wealthy on buffalo hunts. Doc W. F. "Evil Spirit of the Plains" Carver, a scout for Gen. Henry Sibley in 1862, met Cody during that period and in May 1883 he joined Buffalo Bill's Wild West Show in an act known as the "Great Rifle Shot." It involved him riding horseback and shooting glass balls the size of quarters as they were tossed into the air. Later Carver and Buffalo Bill had a falling out; Carver started his own show and the two became enemies. Carver died in 1927 and is buried in Illinois.

Holdrege—McCook
72 miles

The town of Holbrook was originally known as Burton's Bend. With the influx of white settlers to the region after the Civil War, Indians followed the buffalo to the Republican River valley. Regular military patrols used the Fort McPherson Trail, which entered the valley a mile west of Holbrook. The largest military force to use the route was Gen. Eugene A. Carr's Republican Valley Expedition of 1869, which removed any remaining hostile Indians from the region.

In 1870 Isaac "Ben" Burton settled a mile southeast of the present town of Holbrook on a bend of the Republican at the edge of the West— the 100th Meridian. He was the region's first permanent settler and with partner H. Dice established the Burton's Bend Trading Post, which supplied necessities to buffalo hunters.

Now the Frenchman-Cambridge Irrigation District is headquartered at Cambridge, while the Medicine Creek State Recreation Area is located north of U.S. 34 between Cambridge and Bartley.

INDIANOLA
A German prisoner-of-war camp with more than 5,000 inmates swelled the population near Indianola in 1944. The prisoners worked on nearby farms. In all some 370,000 German and 50,000 Italian prisoners of war came to the United States during World War II, and about 12,000 were held at camps in Nebraska. Base camps were located at Scottsbluff, Fort Robinson, and Atlanta. The War Department established other POW holding sites at Morrill, Lyman, Mitchell, Bridgeport, Sidney, Ogallala, Palisade, Elwood, Lexington, Kearney, Bertrand, Alma, Franklin, Fort Crook, Weeping Water, Grand Island, Hastings, Hebron, and Indianola. Nebraska also had ordnance plants or depots at Grand Island, Mead, and Sidney, with the ammunition also stored in partially underground holding areas near Clay Center.

McCOOK
Currently the seat of Red Willow County, McCook originally went by the name Fairview, but it changed at the urging of Alexander Campbell, first superintendent of the Burlington Railroad. He suggested the town be named for his friend Brig. Gen. Alexander McDowell McCook, who had made a reputation as an Indian fighter. A graduate of West Point, McCook served in the Indian Wars, taught at his alma mater, and commanded troops during the Civil War at Bull Run, Perryville, Murfreesboro, and Chickamauga.

The city wrestled the county seat designation away from Indianola in 1896. The Burlington & Missouri Railroad's decision in 1892 to make McCook a division point on its line between Lincoln and Denver spurred the town's growth. The Lincoln Land Company purchased holdings for the city's development. Fairview was in a portion of the community now known as south McCook and included a three-room sod house that served as a post office, general merchandise business, and dining establishment. Three other shacks—two drugstores and a general merchandise store—comprised the settlement.

A number of men led McCook to prominence, among them Albert Barnett, who became known as "The Builder." He operated Barnett Lumber in McCook and other lumber companies in Scottsbluff, Curtis, Culbertson, and even Fort Morgan, Colorado. He also had a partnership in the McCook Cement and Stone Company, which paved many of the first streets in the town, and was involved in building the Masonic Temple, Keystone Hotel, Fox Theater, YMCA, Addams Hotel, Johnson Fruit Company warehouse, and many other businesses. Barnett was born in 1855 in Knoxville, Illinois, and worked as a country schoolteacher and dock laborer before moving to Nebraska.

Two other McCook residents stand out: George W. Norris and Harry D. Strunk. Their legacy is felt by not only the residents of McCook and the Republican Valley but by the entire nation.

George Norris: Fighting Liberal

Senator George Norris of McCook wrote the constitutional amendment eliminating the lame duck session of Congress, wrote the amendment to the Nebraska Constitution creating the unicameral legislature, supported legislation that created the Rural Electrification Administration (REA), and is known as the father of the Tennessee Valley Authority (TVA). He started his career as county attorney for Furnas County, served as a district judge, and was elected in 1902 to the first of five consecutive terms in the U.S. House of Representatives. He was elected to the U.S. Senate in 1912 and served thirty years there. He was elected to the Nebraska Hall of Fame in 1961. Norris, the "Gentle Knight of Progressive Ideals," was one of the nation's great statesmen. Norris Park is located on Main Street in McCook, and his home is operated as a state historic site.

Born in Ohio in 1861, Norris spent summers as a youngster working on farms. At age sixteen he became a teacher and put himself through college. He studied law and eventually moved to Beatrice, where he established a law practice. He married Pluma Lashley in 1890 and they had three children. In 1895 Norris was elected judge in the 14th Judicial

A farm woman, Mrs. Meredith, counting her eggs near Gretna.
—Nebraska State Historical Society

District, serving until 1897, and in 1900 he moved his family to McCook. His wife died in 1901 upon the birth of a third daughter, leaving Norris with the children to care for. His sister helped for a time; in 1903 he married Ellie Leonard, a McCook teacher.

Norris won his first election to the U.S. House of Representatives in 1902 and remained there through 1912. He quickly established himself as a progressive member of Congress and was often considered an outsider. In 1913 he made the switch to the U.S. Senate, where he continued to advocate reform measures.

His greatest contribution came in 1935 with creation of the REA, which provided power to farmers and ranchers; many city dwellers had had electrical service since the early 1900s. One of the New Deal programs implemented during the presidency of Franklin D. Roosevelt, the REA changed life for rural residents, particularly farm and ranch wives. Many believe Norris lent his unending support to the proposal because he saw his own mother, a widow living on a Nebraska farm, labor to provide for her children.

Prior to his success with the REA, Norris had sponsored legislation that eliminated the lame duck session of Congress. The Twentieth Amendment to the Constitution, known as the Lame Duck Amendment, was ratified on February 6, 1933. It abolished the lame duck session by moving the presidential inauguration from March 4 to January 20 the

Washday on the Trail Farm, Otoe County, before the Rural Electrification Administration provided power for country folks. —Nebraska State Historical Society

year after each election, and it stipulated that Congress would begin its session every year on January 3. It also established the procedure for succession in case a president-elect died before taking office.

The following year Norris helped push through the bill establishing a unicameral legislature for Nebraska. He particularly supported that style of government because he believed it reduced the potential for secrecy; legislative debate would be conducted in the open, rather than in private conference committee meetings. Norris made an extensive tour of the state, expressing his views on the unicameral legislature.

Earlier, Norris led the fight to create the Tennessee Valley Authority, which was charged with building dams and reservoirs for flood control, navigation, and the generation of electricity. The TVA also was to carry out reforestation, use marginal lands for power development, and provide for the social and economic well-being of people throughout the Tennessee River Basin. The TVA's greatest success came in the production and distribution of electricity. Approved by Congress in 1928 but vetoed by President Calvin Coolidge, the measure was again approved in 1930 but vetoed by President Herbert Hoover. In 1933 Congress passed the measure a third time, and President Franklin D. Roosevelt finally signed it into law.

Family furnishings and memorabilia from the forty years Norris spent in Washington fill his McCook home, now operated as a historic site by the Nebraska State Historical Society.

Harry D. Strunk: Newspaperman

The untiring efforts of newspaper publisher and editor Harry D. Strunk helped shape McCook and the entire Republican Valley. He became a thorn in the side of George Norris, in part because Norris strongly favored using watercourses to produce public power, while Strunk believed in using the water to promote irrigation, flood control, and reclamation.

The two had at least one thing in common: tenacity. Just as George Norris worked for years to develop such projects as the Tennessee Valley Authority and the REA, Strunk worked for reclamation along the Republican River, dedicating his life and his newspaper to that purpose. His efforts culminated in the naming of Harry Strunk Lake west of McCook.

Strunk had an eighth-grade education when he started working in the newspaper business at age fourteen. He was a publisher just two years later and opened the *Red Willow County Gazette* when he was seventeen. Although he supported many projects, his work for water development is his greatest legacy. He had been an early supporter of George Norris, but the two split when Norris refused to provide support for construction of dams to protect the Upper Republican River valley and its tributaries.

Strunk and Victor Westermark of Benkelman organized some thirty communities in southwest Nebraska and northwest Kansas in 1928 to form the Twin Valley Association of Commercial Clubs. Their goal was to control the Frenchman and Republican Rivers and their tributaries. The projects followed a roller-coaster development path, with some successes and more failures as the years passed. In 1935 the Republican River swept out of its banks, killing more than 100 people and leaving behind widespread damage, reaffirming Harry Strunk's belief that the river should be dammed. In 1940 Strunk revived the

Granite markers locate the water development projects along the Republican River.

Damaged track between Franklin and Republican City following the 1935 Republican River flood. —Nebraska State Historical Society

reclamation campaign, helping form the Republican Valley Conservation Association. That body eventually won approval for the proposal to dam the river, and six man-made reservoirs now lie upstream from Republican City in southwest Nebraska, northwest Kansas, and southeast Colorado. They prevent flooding and provide irrigation for about 67,000 acres of prime farmland.

Republican River Flood

After the prolonged drought of the early 1930s, the wet spring of 1935 was welcome relief for the area. But too much of a good thing is not a good thing at all. On May 30, 1935, torrential rains fell in eastern Colorado and southwestern Nebraska, causing the Republican River to run bluff to bluff along its upper reaches. The rains concentrated in the basin of the South Fork and extended into the valleys of the Arikaree, Frenchman, Red Willow, and Medicine Creeks.

Conditions had first become threatening on May 28, when the rising river neared the Nebraska Light and Power Plant in South McCook. Some highway and railroad bridges incurred minor damage as a result of those rising waters, but workers quickly made repairs. The rains didn't stop, however, and by the morning of May 30 the ground was so saturated the soil couldn't absorb the water. Instead it ran off the hillsides and into the streams, swelling the Republican to a raging cauldron of mud and water filled with all kinds of debris. The Republican River, normally 300 to 400 feet wide, swelled to a width of one to four miles. A wall of water variously estimated at three to eight feet in height roared down the valley. When the water subsided two days later, at least 112 people had died, and the area had sustained many millions of dollars in damage.

Some people had advance notice that the floodwaters were racing their way, but because past cautions had proved false they did not heed the warnings. Others were unaware of the flood's approach until they heard the roaring water and had time only to climb to their roofs or the second story of their homes. Some were able to ride out the floodwaters by staying in a high location, but the swirling waters took many homes down the river, drowning the occupants.

As in any natural disaster, ordinary people became heroes as they worked to rescue those in danger. Some of the Republican River flood heroes included Dale Miller and Clyde McKillip, who went to the aid of Mrs. Charles Miller Jr., Elizabeth Shook, Fred Swanson, Nels Nielson, and six Miller children. Those people took refuge on the roof of a farmhouse as the water rose around them. Swanson and Nielson were swept away; the former went under the raging waters, while the latter found refuge on top of the dairy barn.

Then the water picked up both the house and the barn. As the ferocious Republican swept them downstream, the adults made a plan. If the house started to tear apart, the women would each hold onto one child and the two men, McKillip and Miller, would grab a child under each arm. When the barn Nielson rode collided with the house, both structures started breaking apart, and there was little time to implement the earlier plan. Dale Miller grasped Nadine Miller, age five, and McKillip took hold of Charlotte Miller, age six. All four eventually made it to safety, and rescuers also saved Nielsen; the remaining occupants of the house drowned. Many similar incidents occurred all along the path of the raging water.

Three lesser floods raced down the Republican in a twenty-day period that spring. The series of disasters served as a catalyst, creating widespread recognition of the need for flood control along the river, as Harry D. Strunk had been arguing for years. To prevent repetition of the tragedy, the federal government built a series of six dams across the Republican and its tributaries, providing flood protection, irrigation, and recreation facilities.

McCook's Army Air Base

During World War II, a major air base was built just north of McCook. The McCook Army Air Base became active on April 1, 1943, one of eleven army air force training bases located in Nebraska during World War II, under the command of the 2nd Air Force Headquarters in Colorado Springs, Colorado. The base provided final training of crews for three types of heavy bombers: the B-17 Flying Fortress, B-24 Liberator, and B-29 Super Fortress. Cumulatively, 15,000 servicemen and 500 civilians staffed the base during the war. Its trainees included elements of the 8th, 15th, and 20th Air Forces, which saw combat in the European, Mediterranean, and Pacific Theaters. The 2,100-acre air base had three 7,500-foot runways, fire hangars, and barracks for 5,000 men. Housing for the base workers was an immediate and ongoing problem. Early on, the army operated a shuttle bus from McCook to the base, but the "old red school bus" wasn't reliable and created difficulties for those who depended upon it. Eventually fifty house trailers were brought in and put in place near the base to provide some housing for personnel.

Training involved both ground and air instruction in such topics as engineering, bombing, navigation, communications, physical training, air-to-air gunnery, formation flying, camera bombings, and bomb releases. Air Force public information officer Lt. Howard J. Otis wrote in July 1943: "It is truly an amazing sight to see these army air bases suddenly rise into view from farms, cattle ranges, or hayflats. As one drives across the state, there first appears an orange and black checkerboard water tank rising above the horizon. Then the blue-green glass windows of a control tower come into sight. Hangars housing big war birds were seen, their arched domes across the sky."

On May 5, 1944, the first of two training-flight accidents occurred near Scottsbluff when a B-24 piloted by 2nd Lt. O. A. Jones crashed into a hill, killing six of the eight men on board. Records indicated the pilot made two low-level passes over a gunnery and turned the third pass over to copilot 2nd Lt. Kenneth L. Hutzel, who did not pull the plane up in time after making the pass over the target. Both pilots died in the crash, as did bombardier Walter L. Johnson, engineer Sgt. Charles Runnion, gunnery Sgt. Billy Queen, and radioman Sgt. Robert Harris. Another gunner and the navigator were injured.

In December 1945 the army announced it would close the McCook Army Air Base, and most of the men stationed at McCook were transferred out of the area by mid-January 1946. There were still about 1,800 officers and enlisted men at the base in mid-January 1946, when base commander Col. Lewis Lyle announced it would be completely shut

A display at the McCook High Plains Museum includes original prisoner-of-war artwork and photographs of the McCook Air Force installation.

down by February 1. In 1990 some bomb squadron hangars, the water tower, and the quartermaster warehouse remained in place.

The war also brought another a German prisoner-of-war camp to the area. It stood east of McCook and north of Indianola. The prisoners decorated their barracks by painting the sheetrock walls. Many years later local residents removed seven of the paintings and relocated them to the McCook High Plains Museum. Three other paintings by German prisoners also are among the museum collection. The modern museum building is adjacent to the 1907 Carnegie Library (formerly the museum). Across the street stands the 1915 U.S. Post Office (now defunct) and the federal courthouse, which now houses an antique store.

Many Germans settled near McCook, and in 1970 the town started holding a German Heritage Days to honor them, in the same way Wilber holds Czech days. Each year members of the American Historical Society of Germans from Russia hold a pageant. An honored guest at the festivities in 1972 was George McGovern, Democratic Party candidate for U.S. President. A number of other presidential hopefuls have visited McCook during the years, including Franklin D. Roosevelt, who gave a speech praising the work of George Norris on September 28, 1932; Ronald Reagan on May 5, 1976; and Robert Kennedy, Eugene McCarthy, and Dwight Eisenhower. Various other well-known personalities also spent time in the community, including *Gunsmoke* cast members Milburne Stone (Doc Adams), Amanda Blake (Miss Kitty), and Dennis Weaver (Chester). Sports celebrities Jack Dempsey, world heavyweight boxing champion in 1919; Billy Martin, New York Yankees player and manager; Jesse Owens, 1936 Olympic track star; and Nebraska Cornhuskers head coaches Bob Devaney and Tom Osborne also have visited the town.

Superior–Oxford
99 miles

SUPERIOR

A post office launched Superior in 1872, but not until three years later did people survey and plat the town. Railroad builders put the line in to Superior by 1880, and four other rail lines quickly followed, along with substantial growth. The town population boomed from 458 in 1880 to 1,614 a decade later. Superior's commercial expansion happened nearly as quickly. In the 1880s the town had a bank and general stores, but over the years the number and variety of businesses increased with the arrival of several dry goods stores, a number of specialty stores, and eventually two chain stores: JC Penney and Hesteds. The entire downtown area is now a historic district and includes thirty-four commercial, governmental, recreational, and educational properties reflecting changes in Superior during the period from 1883 to 1937.

Superior likes to advertise the fact that a local girl, Evelene Brodstone, started her career as a stenographer and eventually became a millionaire. Brodstone studied stenography and accounting in Iowa, then returned to her hometown to work for Guthrie Bros., a flour milling firm, and then for Henningsen Produce. In 1895 she went to Chicago, where she obtained a job for the Vestey Cold Storage Company. One day manager Edmund Vestey called her into his office to take a letter. The young girl did her work efficiently and soon became Vestey's personal secretary. When the company moved its main offices from Liverpool to London, Evelene went to England to assist in setting up offices. By 1914 she had built an apartment in Superior in order to retire and return to Nebraska.

However, the outbreak of World War I led her to return to the workplace. The Vestey Company supplied meat to the Allied forces during World War I, with offices in England, Scotland, Russia, South Africa, South America, New Zealand, Australia, and China. Miss B, as she became known, was a formidable force within the Vestey operation, often traveling to Russia, South America, Australia, and other areas to arrange for meat purchases.

Following World War I Evelene retired again, moving back to Superior. Retirement didn't last long however, because, in 1924 William Vestey proposed marriage, and they were wed in September. Marriage altered many things for Evelene, including her first name, which she changed to Evelyn. She and William lived at Kingswood, the Vestey manor, in London, and she became Lady Vestey. Her husband's social position put her at the apex of British society. She participated in the coronation of King George VI and entertained at Kingswood and on the family ship, the *Arandora Star.*

But Lady Vestey never forgot her roots. She and her brother, Lewis, donated land and funds for a hospital in Superior, and she established a scholarship fund, purchased cottonwood trees, and paid for a bridge in the town's Lincoln Park. After her death in 1941, her ashes were buried in Superior. The community remembers her with an annual Lady Vestey Festival.

GUIDE ROCK

Zebulon Pike and his men camped in 1806 at a Pawnee village near Guide Rock. Pike attempted to persuade the Pawnees to provide assistance on a trading mission to the Comanches, but the Pawnees and the Comanches were warring at that time. Arriving at the Pawnee camp not long after some Spanish traders had been there, Pike convinced the Pawnees to remove a Spanish flag and replace it with an American banner. The Pawnees occupied the village site from about 1770 until 1830.

RED CLOUD

Although Pike and the Pawnees camped not far from Red Cloud, a woman really put the region on the map. Willa Sibert Cather spent her youth in Red Cloud, and she called upon her experiences there and the people she knew for scenes and characterizations in the novels that won her critical acclaim. Cather's writings have a regional flavor, but they express universal themes.

The common thread in most of her stories is the setting in the Red Cloud area. The community is the Sweet Water of *A Lost Lady,* the Frankfort of *One of Ours,* the Haverford of *Lucy Gayheart,* the Black Hawk of *My Antonia,* and the Hanover of *O Pioneers!* Willa Cather lived in Red Cloud from 1884 until 1890, when she ventured north to Lincoln, where she attended the University of Nebraska. The people of Red

Willa Cather,
author of
My Antonia,
of Red Cloud.
—Nebraska State
Historical Society,
Willa Cather Pioneer
Memorial and Educational
Foundation

Cloud and Webster County call this area Catherland. They promote it with an annual festival devoted to Willa Cather's work, and billboards depicting a sod-breaking plow lead to the community from all directions. Red Cloud residents have marked many of the locations Cather used in her books; they give tours and sell all of Cather's books at the Willa Cather Pioneer Memorial and Educational Foundation. The Nebraska State Historical Society has preserved Cather's childhood home.

Mildred Bennett in *The World of Willa Cather* wrote that when Cather's first hugely successful novel, *O Pioneers,* came out, she sent a copy to her childhood friend Carrie Miner, inscribing in the flyleaf: "This was the first time I walked off on my own feet—everything before was half real and half an imitation of writers whom I admired."

Cather's ambition was to be a surgeon, but the literary world is grateful she turned to the pen rather than the scalpel. She once remarked in an interview in 1921 that she had no ambition to write as a child and was glad that was the case. "I think it's too bad for a child to feel that it must be a writer, for then instead of looking at life naturally, it is hunting for cheap effects," she said. "I have never ceased to be thankful that I loved those people out in the Republican Valley for themselves first, not because I could get copy out of them."

Among the individuals who cropped up in her work, the best known is Annie Pavelka (from whom the character Antonia was drawn), while the Harling Family in *My Antonia* is based upon Carrie Miner's family.

In fact, so much of Cather's description—of both people and place—is so realistic that some people about whom she wrote accept it as fact. Mildred Bennett reported that one time Annie Pavelka's husband was in the hospital and, when asked his identity, told the attendant, "I am the husband of My Antonia."

Similarly, Cather used real places for her scenes and settings. The Garber Grove and Garber house in Red Cloud sit within a thick growth of cottonwood, which marks the original site of the Red Cloud Stockade, the Silas Garber house, and his earlier dugout. Cather wrote *A Lost Lady* about Lyra Garber, wife of Silas, the man who once served as Nebraska's governor. The homestead of Cather's uncle, George Cather, southwest of Bladen became the setting for her Pulitzer Prize–winning novel *One of Ours,* and the Pavelka farmstead, also located near Bladen, became a setting for *My Antonia.* That homestead, part of a Bohemian settlement in Webster County, is now included on the National Register of Historic Places because of its Bohemian influence and because of Cather's writings. Besides setting *My Antonia* there, she used the site in her short story "Neighbor Rosicky."

The Republican River itself became a predominant setting—almost a character—in several of Cather's works, including *O Pioneers, My Antonia, One of Ours, A Lost Lady,* and *Lucy Gayheart.*

Located just south of Red Cloud is the Willa Cather Memorial Prairie. This 600-acre area owned by the Nature Conservancy has never been broken by the plow. This is how Cather and her family found the land when they arrived in Nebraska, and it had a profound and lasting influence on the novelist. In Bennett's *The World of Willa Cather* she is quoted as writing: "This country was mostly wild pasture and as naked as the back of your hand. I was little and homesick and lonely and my mother was homesick and nobody paid any attention to us. So the country and I had it out together and by the end of the first autumn, that shaggy grass country had gripped me with a passion I have never been able to shake. It has been the happiness and the curse of my life."

US 136 runs on an east-west line between Red Cloud and Alma, following the north bank of the Republican River as it snakes down the valley. The route provides access to Inavale, Riverton, Franklin, Bloomington, Republican City, Alma, and Harlan County Lake, created by the Harlan Dam near Republican City.

FRANKLIN

Founded in 1870 by the Republican Land and Claims Association, Franklin was also called the Knight Colony. In 1881 the Congregational Church opened one of six academies in Franklin. The other five were located at Crete, York, Neligh, Weeping Water, and Chadron. Among the distinguished alumni of Franklin Academy were federal judge Robert Van Pelt and Dr. Frank Cyr of Columbia University, under whose leadership the standard yellow school bus developed. The area of the former Franklin Academy now serves the community as a park, with tennis courts and other facilities.

REPUBLICAN CITY

Harlan County Lake was one of six created along the Republican River for flood control following the devastating flood in 1935. The dams, which had the strong support of newspaper editor Harry Strunk of McCook, provide irrigation water to southwestern Nebraska. The Harlan County Dam, built in 1952, also created a recreational area for the region.

Tradition holds that the Grand Pawnees were the first to migrate to the Platte River country from Kansas. The Pitahauerats followed, but the Kitkehahkis ventured no farther north than this river country. Apparently the French traders and Spanish officials in Louisiana viewed the situation as a revolt and they started calling the Kitkehahkis "Republicans." Hence the name of the river.

Traditionally this was buffalo country. The Pawnees always hunted buffalo in this region, usually making one summer hunt and another winter hunt. Millions of animals roamed the prairie until the 1870s, when white hunters systematically decimated the huge herds for their hides and to deny Native Americans a source of subsistence.

NEBRASKA 89
Stamford–Marion
58 miles

Nebraska 89 provides access to several small towns between Orleans and the Kansas border, including Stamford, Beaver City, Hendley, Wilsonville, Lebanon, and Danbury. This is the type of agricultural country Senator George Norris had in mind when he worked so hard in the 1930s to get approval for the Rural Electricfication Administration. The REA provided power to remote, rural ranches, making life infinitely easier for the families living in such areas. Norris understood their situation; he'd grown up on a farm and lived in Beaver City prior to moving to McCook. In fact, Norris served as the district attorney for Furnas County before he served Red Willow County, where he earned such recognition in later years.

Another early resident of Beaver City was Dr. Frank Brewster, who bought a Curtiss-Wright JN4D biplane in 1910 for $8,000 and began making rounds. Ranchers in remote areas of the state welcomed the sound and sight of the doctor's plane.

US 6

McCook—Colorado Border

97 miles

CULBERTSON

Alexander Culbertson, a fur trader on the Upper Missouri, left his name to this community, which W. Z. Taylor started as a trading post in July 1873. It became the county seat when Hitchcock County was organized August 30, 1873. The community included Taylor's store and J. E. Kleven's blacksmith shop and post office until 1875, when thousands of Texas cattle were brought into the four southwest Nebraska counties. Culbertson was the only town in the region, and

A proud farmer, John Spellmeyer of Sumner, with his triplet calves. He also had sixteen living children, including three sets of twins, shown at left. —Nebraska State Historical Society, Solomon D. Butcher Collection

the ranchers made it their headquarters, many serving as county officials. During the years of "open range," ranchers spent summers on the range and winters in Culbertson.

The railroad arrived in 1881 and thousands of homesteaders came into the county, displacing the ranchers. During this period Culbertson became a pioneering irrigation center. In 1893 the county seat was moved to Trenton, near the center of the county.

A military road, which had earlier served as an access route for Native Americans, connected the Kansas buffalo country with Fort McPherson, crossing US 6 near Palisade. The military road roughly followed the route of Nebraska 25, which provides access to Hayes Center, a community known as the Windmill City because each family had its own windmill (the town also had one for public use).

HAYES CENTER

This was the front line of one really wild prairie fire. It started some seventy miles to the west. Near-tornado-force winds drove the fire across thousands of square miles of western Nebraska, Colorado, and Wyoming, reaching Hayes County April 1, 1893. The fire left drifts of ashes against fences and houses and blacked out the sun for a time. Amazingly, it only claimed two lives, though it burned most of the land between the South Platte and the Republican Rivers.

Plains residents dreaded prairie fires. The blazes sounded like freight trains as they roared across the land, high winds whipping the flames. Residents hated prairie fires almost as much has they abhorred grass-hoppers and drought. In fall and late summer cattlemen and farmers plowed fire guards—four furrows about thirty feet apart—then burned the grass between them in order to keep the entire range from burn-ing. When fires did break out, men, women, and children hauled buckets and barrels of water and used wet sacks to beat out flames that jumped the fire guards.

Year after year newspapers throughout the region urged residents to plow breaks and prepare for the fire season. In November 1860 the *Nebraska Advertiser* told readers:

> The horizon is now, every evening illuminated by the burning prai-rie—sometimes shedding more light over limited districts than the full moon, and rivaling the aurora borealis in beauty.
> We hear of numerous instances of loss from fire in various por-tions of the country. Some have lost their hay, some their corn, and others their fences.—The loss sustained from prairie fires is very great every year; and yet, *every year*, farmers neglect to protect their prop-erty! . . . Reader, if your hay, fences, corn, buildings, or any other property is unprotected from the prairie, attend to it immediately.

Do not wait until tomorrow. Those who have lost the most property, both this year and last, were *"a-going to plow round it tomorrow,"* but they delayed it one day too late.

In the fall of 1872 the *Beatrice Express (Oct. 24)* castigated farmers:

> Prairie fires are again sweeping across the country making their annual havoc with the grain stacks and buildings of careless settlers who have neglected to provide means of safety until too late. . . The results of a year's work are swept away in a flash of flame, . . . and yet the next year finds just as many procrastinators unprepared. They know the fire is sure to come and they mean to get ready for it, but they wait until the fire is in sight, and then it is too late.

Perhaps the people of Beatrice finally heard the editor's warning, because in the fall of 1873 the Beatrice mayor organized a group of men and boys, then lit a fire to burn a strip eight to ten rods, or about 440–550 yards wide. The October 30 *Beatrice Express* lauded his efforts, saying, "Citizens may sleep as sound o'nights as though a Chinese wall girded the city."

US 6 follows the Frenchman Fork of the Republican River, splitting to the northwest near Culbertson and passing through Palisade, Hamlet, Wauneta, and Enders. This was prime buffalo country; Stinking Water Creek got its name from the piles of buffalo carcasses left by white hunters in the late nineteenth century. Buffalo Bill Cody, Doc Carver, and others killed hundreds of buffalo here for the railroad in 1868–69, making their reputations as buffalo hunters.

Grand Duke Hunts with Buffalo Bill

In January 1872 Russian Grand Duke Alexis visited the United States on a goodwill tour arranged by his father, Czar Alexander II of Russia, and U.S. President Ulysses S. Grant. Because the Grand Duke enjoyed hunting, Grant assigned Gen. Phil Sheridan the duty of entertaining the Russian. Sheridan in turn sought aid from his chief scout, Buffalo Bill. The party arrived in North Platte in early January, where the Russian dignitary was greeted by such men as Lt. Col. George Armstrong Custer, Maj. Gen. E. O. Ord, Maj. Gen. Innis N. Palmer, and Brig. Gen. George A. Forsyth, who had distinguished himself at Beecher Island.

Along with his servants and many wagons filled with supplies, Cody and the Duke traveled south to a camp on Red Willow Creek, where they celebrated the Grand Duke's twenty-second birthday. Spotted Tail's band of Brulé Sioux had a camp nearby, and upon the invitation of Cody they joined the birthday celebration. Cody expected a small number of warriors to do some dancing for the Russian's entertainment, but nearly 1,000 arrived for the big powwow.

In the hunting expeditions that followed, the Brulés demonstrated their skill and bravado, but the Grand Duke had difficulty hitting his target. Eventually he killed a large bull, which he had skinned for a robe. He also took the head back to Russia with him. From North Platte, Grand Duke Alexis toured other areas in the West before returning to his homeland.

The Pawnees named the Frenchman River for a lone trapper; the Sioux called it the White Man's River. The Pawnees often hunted in this region during summer or winter pilgrimages to get meat. The Sioux also used this land; in the 1870s Whistler and his small band of Cut-off Oglala had a permanent camp to the northeast near present-day Stockville.

CHAMPION

Chase County and the town of Champion are named for Champion S. Chase, Nebraska's first attorney general. In 1886 work started on the Champion mill, located on the Frenchman River near a three-foot natural rock falls that provided a prime power site. The mill company built a dam across the Frenchman in 1887 and unsuccessfully attempted to lease the mill site. In 1888 the company finally gave the land and water rights to Thomas Scott after he agreed to build a fifty-barrel roller flour mill. Scott's mill started producing flour and feed in 1889, providing Champion with an economic advantage over other southwestern Nebraska communities. The local newspaper noted: "As a residence, milling, manufacturing and business center, Champion will increase in favor and in the future no man of intelligence and good judgement [sic] will have aught but words of praise to speak of the 'Little Giant City.'"

Flour milling became an important part of the Nebraska economy after the 1860s, but the earliest grist mill operated at Fort Atkinson in 1821. That mill used draft animals for power and could grind up to 150 bushels of grain each day. It served an important purpose in an area where soldiers had to be relatively self-sufficient. A storm destroyed the Fort Atkinson mill in 1825, two years before the military abandoned the post itself.

Most of Nebraska's earliest mills—those developed between 1860 and 1890—used water power. Very few used traditional upright waterwheels; most had a vertical wheel or turbine. In most cases mill owners constructed a dam to provide the power, but water power wasn't totally reliable. In drought years streams dwindled, and sometimes there wasn't adequate water to produce the power needed for mill operations. On other occasions the mill pond washed out, and work had to be suspended until a new dam and pond could be established. Some mills used wind power.

In the earliest days of Nebraska's settlement, flour mills were few and far between, requiring farmers to haul their grain many miles for processing. Some had to travel a hundred miles or more to a mill, where they would either wait to have their wheat ground or exchange it for flour from wheat the miller had previously received and ground. The earliest operations involved millstones for grinding, but in the 1880s most mills converted to more efficient steel rollers.

Once railroads pushed through the territory, milling became an easier process; now farmers could transport their wheat on rail cars rather than hauling it with horse and wagon. By 1870 Nebraska had sixty flour mills (compared with nineteen in 1860) with a total of 183 employees, making it the leading industry in the state. By 1880 some 177 flour mills operated in the region. Flour production increased dramatically after the introduction of steel rollers after 1880. Those rollers could process wheat more finely, making it possible for millers to better use the wheat brought in by farmers.

Communities with a mill enjoyed many advantages over those without one. Not only would farmers from outlying areas come to town to bring their wheat, but many early mills produced excess power, providing their communities with electricity. The Neligh mill provided power to local residents after 1899, and the DeWitt mill provided power for its region after 1919.

Another side benefit was the mill pond, which served as a recreation center for many communities. In the summertime people could fish, swim, or have a picnic at the site, and during winter the ponds froze, making them ideal places for ice skating or harvesting ice for summer.

The Champion mill pond was the recreational hub of southwest Nebraska through the 1940s. Few bodies of water existed in the region, and the Champion town-site company actively promoted the site, holding the first county fair in 1886 just west of the mill pond. Other fairs took place west of the pond and a horse racing track went in as well. The county fair moved to Imperial, the county seat, in the 1890s, but the Champion mill pond continued to host Fourth of July celebrations. In 1887 that event included tub races on the mill pond by local business-men. The peak recreational use of the Champion mill pond occurred in the 1920s, when a bathhouse and concession stand provided ameni-ties (including rental of black wool bathing suits). The mill pond had a boat dock, a diving tower, and rental cabins.

In the 1930s the Nebraska Game and Parks Commission purchased the area for Champion Lake State Recreation Area. The mill and the mill dam remained in private ownership until the 1960s, when the state acquired them for a historical park. It became a state historic site on September 26, 1966.

The twentieth century witnessed a decline in small mill operation, for several reasons. The three most recognized ones are the demand by housewives and bakeries for a uniform quality in flour, the general advantage of large-scale production, and the high costs of new milling equipment. The number of mills started to drop. By 1931 the state had eighty-one mills, and in 1958 it had only twenty. Just two decades later only five mills produced flour in the state, four of them large-scale plants whose production eclipsed the volume produced by dozens of nineteenth-century mills.

US 34
McCook—Kansas and Colorado Borders at Haigler
93 miles

TRENTON

Sioux and Pawnee warriors fought each other at various times and in various locations throughout Nebraska, but their final big battle occurred in a canyon near the Republican River between Trenton and Culbertson. The massacre of Pawnees by the Sioux is commemorated with a granite marker at a highway wayside area on US 34 east of Trenton. The canyon where the battle occurred is about a mile south of the rest area. The granite monument, erected in 1930, has two faces, one of a Sioux Indian warrior, complete with feathered headdress, the other of a Pawnee.

The sloped hills of the Republican River sheltered the Sioux warriors in 1873 as they planned their attack, which represented the worst sort of treachery. In the first place, the Pawnees had provided assistance to the U.S. military for years and had never engaged in war against white people. Many had served with the Pawnee Scouts under Capt. Frank North in the Plains Indian wars against their primary enemy, the Sioux. Because they had helped the military, the Pawnees believed they'd be protected in turn. It often happened that when Indians thought they had government protection, they were most likely to be whipped.

The 350 Pawnee men, women, and children involved in the battle were on a sixty-day leave of absence from their reservation near Genoa, north of the Platte River, on a hunt. The Pawnees had traditionally left their reservation to hunt the Republican River country. In 1872

The two-faced monument to the Pawnee, right, and Sioux Indians, left, near Trenton where the last battle between Pawnees and Sioux occurred.

they'd been accompanied by John Burwell (Texas Jack) Omohundro of Fort McPherson. He acted as their trail agent, making decisions as needed. But in 1873 Texas Jack was off with his friend Buffalo Bill, performing onstage in New York, and the Pawnees were assigned a new trail agent, John Williamson. Under his guidance the Pawnees headed south from Genoa in early July.

At about the same time, Pawnee Killer and his band of Cut-off Oglala arrived on the Republican River along with their subagent, Antoine Janus. A separate party of some 700 Brulés under subagent Stephen F. Estes arrived at the end of July and camped on Stinking Water Creek. On August 3 the two Sioux parties combined and the 1,000 or so warriors headed down the Frenchman toward its confluence with the Republican just east of the new trading post at Culbertson. Almost simultaneously the Pawnees moved in that direction, too. By the morning of August 5, 1873, the two enemy tribes were headed directly toward each other.

The Sioux definitely knew of the Pawnees' presence, and the Pawnees probably knew the Sioux were in the region, although they may have miscalculated the numbers of their enemy. The fight began when the Pawnees sighted some buffalo on a ridge and headed toward them. The Sioux lay in wait and killed the advance hunters. The Pawnees ordered their women and children into the canyon as their warriors prepared for a defense. Williamson and Ter-ra-re-cox, a chief for the Skidi band of Pawnees, wanted to withdraw down the canyon to take shelter in the cottonwood and ash trees, but Fighting Bear of the

Kitkehahkis argued they should make their stand where they were. He convinced the Pawnees his way was best; out of arrogance, or perhaps simple ignorance, agent Williamson agreed with the plan.

The Sioux quickly divided their forces and had the Pawnees nearly surrounded, shooting down upon the Pawnees in the canyon. Williamson attempted to negotiate a truce, but his efforts were unsuccessful. A Sioux warrior even shot Williamson's horse out from under him.

The Pawnees threw off their trail packs (which contained robes, meat, and equipment) and raced with Williamson away from the battle scene. Eventually they reached the military camp of Capt. Charles Meinhold. The chiefs requested military protection and permission to accompany the army in a search for the Sioux. Captain Meinhold refused both requests, instead ordering the Pawnees to continue down the Republican.

Captain Meinhold and his cavalry troop then rode to the massacre site. It has often been suggested that the cavalry caused the Sioux to flee when they arrived, although it now seems pretty certain the Sioux had already left the area when the army came upon the scene. A survey by Captain Meinhold and later counts taken at the Pawnee reservation showed twenty men, thirty-nine women, and ten children of the Pawnee nation died at the battle. Probably six Sioux were killed. The canyon where the fight occurred was first called Massacre Canyon by Royal Buck, founder of the little settlement at the mouth of Red Willow Creek thirty miles to the east.

The 1873 tribal buffalo hunt that ended in such tragedy for the Pawnees signaled the end of an era: The tribe made no more buffalo hunts in Nebraska. Two years after the battle at Massacre Canyon the Pawnees, once Nebraska's most powerful tribe, ceded their remaining reservation land and moved to Indian Territory (Oklahoma).

In 1923 the citizens of Trenton organized a Massacre Canyon Powwow with Sioux survivors, and in 1925 both Sioux and Pawnee survivors participated, with some tribal members on both sides sharing a peace pipe. The powwows continued until the 1950s, with a hiatus during World War II.

In 1920 Asahel L. Taylor started his effort to obtain a monument to the last Indian battle in Nebraska, but the state legislature denied his request for $500. Then, with the aid of Bill Otis, he organized the annual powwow, and eventually Congressman A. C. Shallenberger sponsored legislation to appropriate $7,500 for the monument, which is made of pink Illinois granite. The monument was dedicated on September 26, 1930.

US 6 follows the Republican River, crossing the Texas-Ogallala cattle trail at Trenton, passing the Swanson Reservoir between Trenton and Stratton, and continuing through Max to Benkelman. This rolling hill country is good for cattle—just as it once was prime pasture for buffalo—and alfalfa is a prime crop raised along the cottonwood-lined river valley.

BENKELMAN

From June 22 to 30, 1867, Lt. Col. George A. Custer, commanding troops A, D, E, H, K, and M of the 7th Cavalry, camped near what is now the southern edge of Benkelman. While in this area Custer's men were involved in several skirmishes. On June 24 Pawnee Killer led a dawn attack on the camp, killing a sentry. Some of the troopers rode out of camp and into an ambush laid by the Indians, but they managed to fight their way clear. Almost simultaneously, Sioux attacked Custer's sixteen-wagon supply train on its way from Fort Wallace, Kansas. That fight took place near Black Butte Creek, Kansas, and left sixteen Indians dead. Another military party carrying orders from Fort Sedgwick, Colorado, missed Custer's camp, and all of the messengers died in a fight near Beaver Creek. On July 12 Custer's men found and buried their bodies.

The Hiawatha Academy, organized by the Society of Friends (or Quakers) in 1888, operated only a short period; poor economic conditions and crop failures in the mid-1890s forced it to close. A sign at the entrance to Benkelman proudly portrays the community as the home of Wagonmaster Ward Bond, the Hollywood actor.

HAIGLER

Herds of Texas cattle passed through this area in the 1870s and 1880s. A checkpoint was established four miles east of Haigler, at an area known as Texas Trail Canyon, by 1881. There cattle were inspected for trail brands and disease, as cattlemen in the northern ranges didn't want the Texas fever to spread north. Concern about that fever, caused by ticks in the southern regions, eventually led to closure of the great cattle trails. About 150,000 cattle moved through here in 1886, the last year of the trail drives.

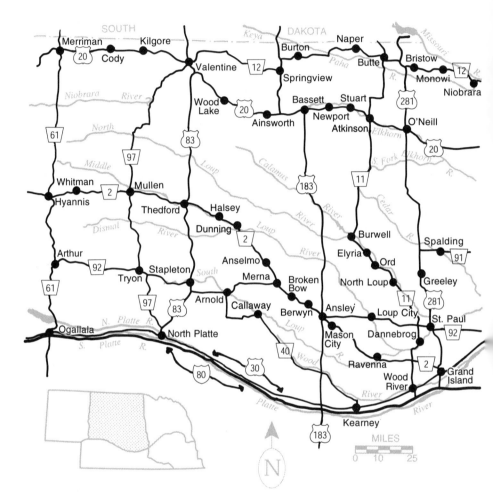

PART 4
SANDHILLS COUNTRY

NEARLY A QUARTER OF NEBRASKA'S LAND is rolling prairie, characterized by tall grasses and a water table just beneath the surface of the sandy soil. The Sandhills are a diamond-shaped region bounded by the fertile bottomlands of the Platte River on the south and the South Dakota border on the north. The eastern boundary for our purposes is a line drawn from Grand Island north to the Missouri River along US 281. Another north-south line following Nebraska 61 lops off the Nebraska panhandle on the west.

The boundaries may be delineated with respect to the lands of American Indian tribes, with the Ponca and Omaha to the east, the Pawnee to the south, the Cheyenne on the west, and the Sioux to the north.

It is a land of isolated beauty and rare power. To spend time in the Sandhills is to return to a time and place little changed in centuries. The soils are stabilized sand dunes held together by the western grasses: blue grama, buffalo grass, Indiangrass, and big and little bluestem. In 1806 Zebulon Pike wrote that much of the area was "barren soil, parched and dryed [sic] up for eight months of the year." He suggested the land would "become in time equally celebrated as the sandy desarts [sic] of Africa." And if the homesteaders who moved into Sandhills Country in the latter half of the nineteenth century had plowed the soil and attempted to grow crops, that might indeed have happened.

Most of this country kept its natural blanket. The grasses that supported millions of buffalo in the early 1800s nourished hundreds of thousands of head of cattle after the 1870s. They still do. Perhaps the most unique aspect to the Sandhills region is its isolation. Many of the counties cover hundreds of square miles yet contain only one town.

The people who lived here in the 1800s were self-reliant, as are the people who remain here today. This region of grasses and rolling hills has a climate to challenge weak hearts. Hot summer winds cure the grasses, and sunshine plays over the humps and bumps of the terrain, creating dancing shadows. There are brilliant wildflowers, but this land changes its appearance with the weather. Low, gray clouds make the spring gloomy and somber, in sharp contrast to the bright days of high summer. When winter winds and spring storms blow in from the north, the hills disappear into the white of blowing snow, isolating the residents even more than usual.

Nebraska doctor Mary Canaga Rowland, born in 1866, wrote in her journal as a young physician: "In Kansas and Nebraska one must always fight the elements. It always seemed too hot or too cold or too dry or too dusty. I have always thought that the reason the Sioux Indians were the strongest of all the Indian tribes was that they had to fight the midwestern weather."

Labeled the Great American Desert by Stephen Long in 1820, the region, like a shy man, hid its best attributes—nutritious prairie grasses and an underground aquifer—until the latter half of the nineteenth century, when the first settlers came to a region just barely perceived as the West. Thousands of families from Iowa, Illinois, and other areas east of the Missouri claimed land in central Nebraska in the early 1870s. They found a land that could provide adequately, with homes and outbuildings made of the earth itself, grass for cattle, and a temperate climate that made growing crops relatively easy.

However, calamitous events of nature made everything difficult; great raging wildfires swept across the grass-covered hillsides, and icy blizzard blasts prohibited winter travel. Often the isolated homesteaders made it through a period of bad weather by grinding grain in a coffee grinder and drinking brewed rye. In 1881 winter blizzards struck in October, covering the plains with snow that filled gullies, making it impossible to go to Grand Island or Kearney for supplies. Another winter storm took huge tolls on livestock and schoolchildren in the winter of 1888, and the drought of 1894 left most homesteaders and ranchers with no crops at all, forcing them to take aid sent from other parts of the country.

Useful aid came in the form of necessities like flour, sugar, coffee, and salt. However, some eastern families sent clothing, most of it totally inappropriate—fancy dresses, fine suits, and top hats. Berna Hunter Chrisman wrote in *Pioneer Stories of Custer County* that some of the clothing suited parties and banquets better than farm fields. The people accepted the handouts, though it did seem odd to see a man plowing sod while wearing tight pants, yellow pointed toe shoes, a dress shirt, and a plug hat or to watch a woman working in her garden while gowned in a pink silk party dress and slatted sunbonnet.

Much of the photographic heritage of early Nebraska is told through the lens of Solomon D. Butcher, who made this image of himself near his first house in Nebraska, 1880. —Nebraska State Historical Society, Solomon D. Butcher Collection

The insects of the plains played their own part in the region's development. Grasshoppers intermittently governed the earth and ate the crops of industrious pioneers in the 1870s and 1890s, while many stories written by early settlers recall difficulties with fleas. Although no one clearly says why there were so many fleas in central Nebraska and the Sandhills, the pesky insects caused problems for most residents.

By the time homesteaders claimed land along the Dismal River and the north, middle, and south forks of the Loup, the buffalo that populated and fertilized this natural grazing area had been nearly exterminated. Their bleached bones remained among the grasses and were exposed after prairie fires. The early settlers had to contend with gray wolves and mountain lions that preyed upon their calves. Elk were abundant upon the northern Sandhills, and rattlesnakes fed upon the towns of prairie dogs. Various species of cranes migrated through the region, and the Niobrara River country became a main stopping place for whooping cranes every year. By 1995, when only 131 whooping cranes were known to live in the wild, the habitat along the Niobrara became critical to the survival of the species.

Many homesteaders staked claims under the Timber Culture Act of 1873, and as a result thousands of trees sent their roots into the Nebraska soil. Box elder predominated, but the strength of fruit tree species such as wild plum satisfied requirements for some claims.

Shaw's unusual round sod house on Gordon Creek in Cherry County.
—Nebraska State Historical Society, Solomon D. Butcher Collection

Farmers also planted chokecherry trees or gooseberry and currant bushes to meet the letter of the law.

The Oglala and Brulé Sioux followed the great buffalo herds through this region and lived from the land, but by the late 1860s they'd been pushed to the west, fighting a series of desperate battles in Wyoming to hold Powder River country. By the late 1870s they'd been moved onto reservations. Sandhills Country then became the domain of cattlemen and homesteaders, who broke the fragile soils and eked out a living. They came and stayed, perhaps, because the land claimed them.

The Sandhills are a symphony of sound. The rustle of the wind mingles with the cries of ducks, geese, and other birds. The bawl of a cow, yip of a coyote, and sharp trill of a yellow-bellied meadowlark might be obscured by the eerie creak of windmill blades. To best know this land, sit on a hilltop and listen to the voices of the hills in the early morning or late evening.

The hills themselves take various forms: long, massive ridges almost a mile across and up to ten miles long; circular mounds; tall, towering forms some 400 feet high. The steepest slopes of the long ridges generally face toward the south and southwest; often the dunes rise above shallow lakes. The entire region has the appearance of being

The Nebraska Sandhills. —Nebraska State Historical Society, Solomon D. Butcher Collection

a huge golf course, complete with long fairways, putting greens, water hazards, and sand traps.

Geologists aren't certain how the Sandhills formed. Some believe they were molded during the last Ice Age; others think strong northerly winds created the dunes, but they suggest the phenomena occurred during a desert period. Either way, the Sandhills probably formed about 25,000 to 60,000 years ago.

We begin our journey through Sandhills Country along its southern border, with access provided by Interstate 80. Because the earliest white settlers in Sandhills Country came from the east, we will travel east to west.

US 281
Grand Island—O'Neill
149 miles

Recognized as American Legion Memorial Highway, US 281 traverses a region initially settled by Danish emigrants. The first community north of Grand Island, St. Libory, was founded in the early 1870s by the Danish

Land and Homestead Colony of Milwaukee, Wisconsin. The first settlers included Lars Hannibal and six other Danes, who claimed land in 1871 along Oak Creek northwest of St. Libory. Others soon followed at Elba, Dannebrog, Dannevirke, Nysted, and Ord.

DANNEBROG

Dannebrog, west of St. Libory on Nebraska 58, may be the best known of the Danish communities, in part because a retired college professor chose to settle there. Roger Welsch isn't just any retired professor, however, he is the author of numerous books, most related to Nebraska's folklore, and he reports from the town (and other rural areas) on the CBS television program *Sunday Morning.* Welsch's "Postcard from Nebraska" also airs in Denmark, and Dannebrog claims it is the "Danish Capital of Nebraska."

The community works hard to live up to that title. The annual Grundlovsfest (a Danish festival) occurs each June, and many specialty stores carry only Danish goods. Native traditions also get attention during the Christmas season, when a number of events recognize the Danish roots of many of Dannebrog's residents. At a program in the downtown Dansk Hall, residents in traditional Danish costume hear the Christmas story read in Danish; eat Danish kransekage, krumkage, and other confectionery delights; and visit with Denmark's Old Father Christmas.

ST. PAUL

Nebraska's largest Danish community—St. Paul—became an agricultural trading center and shipping point. In 1871 Maj. Frank North rode through the area with James N. Paul, a surveyor who liked the area and considered placing a town where the North and South Loup Rivers join. He shared the idea with his brother Nicholas and eventually founded the town along with thirty-one other settlers. They originally called the place Athens but changed its name to St. Paul when they found out there was another Athens, Nebraska. The first railroad arrived in St. Paul in 1881, and by the following year the Union Pacific had completed its line from St. Paul to North Loup. By late 1886 the line had reached Ord, and branches served surrounding towns.

St. Paul houses the Museum of Nebraska Major League Baseball Greats, featuring Grover Cleveland Alexander of St. Paul, Dazzy Vance of Hastings, Sam Crawford of Wahoo, and Bob Gibson of Omaha. The community likes to point out that the Howard County courthouse is constructed of the same marble as that used to construct the Tomb of the Unknown Soldier in Arlington, Virginia.

The earliest restrictions to development near St. Paul were caused by Indian attacks, storms, and grasshopper plagues. The Sioux frequently traveled the North Loup Valley on their way south to raid the Pawnees. By 1872 settlers had moved into the valley, but in October 1873 Indians stole horses at Sioux Creek valued at $1,500 and killed Marion Littlefield of Clay County at Pebble Creek in January 1874, leading the settlers to ask for military protection. That request led to establishment of Fort Hartsuff, fifty-five miles upriver, to protect white settlers and the friendly Pawnees from Sioux depredations. In June 1937 the Burwell Wranglers Club built a memorial to Marion Littlefield, with dedication ceremonies held in conjunction with the region's Old Settlers Picnic. The monument itself is near the spot where Littlefield died, located between Burwell and Calamus Lake.

GREELEY

The Irish Catholic Association first settled O'Connor, on the east side of Greeley, in 1870. The town of Greeley itself was well established by the 1880s, when the Sisters of Mercy opened a school with a musical academy and retreat house. They placed the first school on wheels so it could be moved from one site to another.

Once thousands of buffalo grazed this area, and wolves ranged here as well. But the wolves took a toll on domestic livestock, and by the 1890s hunters could earn a $3 bounty for each pelt. During one

A common scene on J. K. Regier's dairy ranch. —Nebraska State Historical Society

Students and teachers at a sod schoolhouse. —Nebraska State Historical Society, Solomon D. Butcher Collection

week in July 1894 bounty hunters delivered 328 wolf pelts to the courthouse at Greeley. There is a legend about a ghost dog that roams the hillsides looking for his master, a seven-year-old boy attacked and killed by wolves.

Another legend of the area involves the howling blizzard that swept across the plains in 1888. Known as the School Children's Blizzard, because it started just when the children were to return to their homes after a day of lessons in remote schoolhouses, the storm completely covered a barn in this area, forcing the owner to chop a hole in the roof in order to feed and water his horses. Some schoolteachers and children died as they tried to return to their homes; others became heroes as they saved lives. More than one person took shelter in a haystack (see page 164).

SPALDING

Spalding, east of US 281 on Nebraska 91, saw great devastation in 1873 when grasshoppers chomped their way through the area, eating every blade of vegetable material for miles around. The town takes its name from Bishop Spalding, president of the Irish Catholic Association that founded the community. Just across the Cedar River from Spalding is the site of a large Pawnee village used until the mid-1870s. By 1910 a dam placed across the Cedar River provided power for a flour mill, with the excess sold to the town of Spalding. The town still gets a small amount of its power from that supply. The community in 1994 received money from the Nebraska Environmental Trust Fund to rejuvenate the Cedar River Dam and surrounding area.

Grand Island–Hyannis
208 miles

BERWICK

Angling from southeast to northwest, Nebraska 2 cuts through the heart of the Sandhills, slicing between the South Loup and Middle Loup Rivers from Grand Island to Dunning, then following the Middle Loup as it heads west through a sea of grass.

Berwick, once located just south of Cairo, started as a farming community in the 1880s. It had an interesting organization in 1886 called the Berwick Eating Society, which gathered every few weeks. Perhaps getting together to eat and visit reduced the isolation early Nebraska settlers felt, and it also may have eased the monotony of hard work. The nearby Prairie Creek area was one of the hardest hit by the

Drilling sugar beets, 1921. –Nebraska State Historical Society

Appian Avenue in Ravenna. —Nebraska State Historical Society

grasshopper plagues of 1873 and 1875. As the grasshoppers destroyed crops, farmers used sulphur to try to smoke the pests out of the corn.

Because life was so harsh as farmers initially broke the soil and started making their way in this region of Nebraska, they had little compassion for people who caused difficulties. In 1878 a prairie fire swept the area, and not long afterward two men were found shot to death with cards on their shirts that said: "Shot for setting the prairie fire." That type of swift justice may seem harsh, but residents had little time and less compassion for people who made their lives more difficult.

Ravenna takes its name from a city in Italy, but originally it went by the title Beaver Creek. The older streets in Ravenna have Italian names, and the main street, now Grand Avenue, originally was Appian Way. When Erastus Smith settled here in 1874 he brought with him the first herd of registered Shorthorn cattle.

The nearby town of Hazard once went by the name Bunnell. Someone called a conference to choose a new name, and the story goes that one delegate invited those present to "hazard some new name"—to which another replied, "That's it. We'll call it Hazard."

MASON CITY

The "Queen City" of the Muddy Valley sat adjacent to the Grand Island & Wyoming Central branch of the B&M Railroad. The Lincoln Land Company located the town site in April 1886, and by November the town was well established. A fire that month razed a store building owned and occupied by Mack & McEndeffer. Three people died in the blaze—J. J. Hoagland, Malcolm Miller, and Malcolm McEndeffer. Another catastrophe occurred on July 2, 1892, when a cyclone tore through the area, destroying the schoolhouse, two churches, and many other buildings.

ANSLEY

Ansley, at the intersection of Nebraska 2, US 183, and Nebraska 92, first settled in the summer of 1886. Before long the Grand Island & Wyoming Central Railroad pushed through the community. Besides three churches, Ansley had a Modern Woodmen Hall. The first floor housed a meeting room, dining room, and kitchen. The upper story was home to an opera house with porch and vestibule, two reception rooms, and a large audience room with seating for 400 people. A gallery that would seat 150 people sat over the reception rooms. The building featured painted stage scenery and acetylyne gaslights.

Ansley is named for a woman who invested considerable money in real estate in the newly laid-out town. The first school building on the uncultivated prairie came from Westerville, seven miles distant.

BERWYN

On June 5, 1884, I. C. Reneau, a boy living near Berwyn, saw the outlines of a cavalry barricade on Muddy Creek, directly south of where the town of Berwyn is now located. In 1936 Reneau returned to the area and made a diagram of the barricade, which had some fifteen rifle pits along the south side of the creek and a similar system of pits on the west bank, where the creek runs south against the high bluff. Reneau's drawing showed how Muddy Creek angled through the soldier barricades, and it detailed the location of Indian relics found in the area as well as a hermit's dugout and about ten graves. These features were located in a narrow area known as Horse Gulch.

Reneau wrote in *Pioneer Stories of Custer County* that a "better class of farmers and young single men from various parts of the eastern and middle states" settled this area of Nebraska. He further maintained that if someone analyzed feuds, killings, and shootings in the region, he would likely see that more "were the result of division lines and roads between homesteaders, than [conflicts] between cattlemen and homesteaders."

The South Loup in early years was essentially cattle country from where the river enters the valley on the west to where it leaves toward the southeast corner, a distance of more than fifteen miles. The Middlesex Ranch eventually became the Buckeye Land & Cattle Company. And although there were some difficulties between homesteaders and cattlemen in this area, the primary trouble lay with the Olive family from Texas, as we'll see on down the road.

BROKEN BOW

In 1880 Wilson Hewitt homesteaded near present-day Broken Bow, petitioned the government for a post office, and sent in a name for the site. The Postal Service granted the office but rejected the first name selected and a couple of succeeding ones. Hewitt, a blacksmith and hunter, one day had found a broken bow and arrow on an old Indian campground. He put them in a box and thought nothing more of them. When postal officials rejected his third choice for a town name, he suggested the name Broken Bow. The Postal Service gave the nod. Hewitt prized his broken bow, but apparently a cleaning girl threw it in the fire one day along with some rubbish.

Jesse Gandy located the town site and filed the plat in June 1882. A dozen families soon had homes and businesses, and Broken Bow became a business hub for the region. By 1884 the town had tripled in size, with more businesses, a Methodist church, and a courthouse. With the construction of a school and even more businesses, as well as a Baptist Church, Broken Bow became a permanent and prosperous town.

The railroad pushed its tracks into Broken Bow, with the first train arriving on August 26, 1886. By 1900 the population had increased to 1,345 people, and the town became the seat of Custer County, named for Lt. Col. George Armstrong Custer.

The Nebraska Farm Movement

In 1867 the National Grange of the Patrons of Husbandry organized in Washington, D.C. During the 1870s it became the major voice of the American farmer, and its social, education, and fraternal activities brightened farm life. Farmers in Orleans, Nebraska, organized the first Nebraska Grange in 1872, and within two years the state had 596 such institutions, including one at Broken Bow.

Nationally the Grange worked to promote social and educational opportunities, but farmers in many states, including Nebraska, relied on the organization to improve their economic conditions and to push their own political agenda. The Grangers lobbied for farm legislation and formed cooperatives that bought supplies, marketed produce, and manufactured farm machinery. The Nebraska State Grange organized in 1872 and worked as an independent agency in helping find relief funds for farmers hit hard by grasshopper plagues and drought in subsequent years.

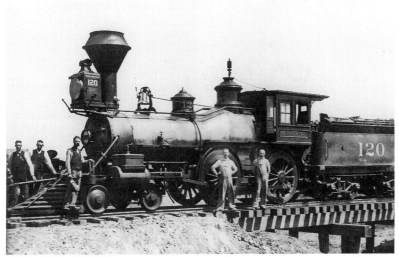

Burlington engine at Broken Bow, 1886. —Nebraska State Historical Society

Plowing with a six-horse hitch. —Nebraska State Historical Society

Rolling a cigarette in Gage County, 1938.
—Nebraska State Historical Society

After a decade the Granger movement in Nebraska started to decline, at least in part because farmers often sold to the highest bidder rather than supporting cooperative ventures. By 1876 the Nebraska Grange movement had shifted away from its cooperative marketing mission and again became more interested in serving a social and educational role.

Tough times rode the plains in the late 1880s. A variety of factors (low prices, drought, blizzards, prairie fires) quickly culled homesteaders. Those not able to withstand the pressures scurried east, leaving behind broken dreams and deserted farms. Those who remained demanded relief. Freight rates west of the Missouri far exceeded those in the eastern states, and credit had virtually dried up for western farmers. The Grange declined in popularity, and homesteaders turned to a new organization, the Farmer's Alliance, formed in 1880. The first Farmer's Alliance started in southeastern Nebraska near Filley, but within two years the movement had spread widely; at least 2,000 alliances with about 65,000 members existed throughout the state.

Mirroring the earlier efforts of Granges, the Farmer's Alliances established marketing cooperatives and became active in politics, supporting independent candidates. Agrarian interests successfully launched the Populist Party in 1892 at a convention in Omaha, and Populist presidential candidate James. B. Weaver won 8.5 percent of the vote in the 1892 race for president. In Nebraska, 42 percent of the vote went to Weaver.

The Farmer's Alliance declined in the early years of the twentieth century, and the Farmers' Union organized in 1911. Its goal was to eliminate marketing middlemen and thereby increase profits for producers. The economics of farming improved considerably during that period, at least in part because World War I increased the demand for American products—particularly food. But commodity prices fell quickly after the war, and many farmers filed for bankruptcy. The Great Depression put an even greater burden on farm families. By 1932 they earned only 13 cents for a bushel of corn, while grain went for 9 cents a bushel.

As they had in the 1870s and in the 1880s, Nebraska farmers took drastic steps to help their industry. Along with representatives from seven other states, they formed the Farmers' Holiday Association in Des Moines, Iowa, in May 1932. They threatened not to sell their produce if they didn't get fair prices. Pickets halted crop shipments near Sioux City, Iowa, in August, and a week later some 500 farmers organized the Nebraska Farmer's Holiday Association at Dakota City. They closed roads leading into Sioux City from the west and even halted a train on its way to that market center.

The protest swept south as Iowa farmers closed roads leading to Omaha. Policemen and farmers fought on the eastern edge of the city, causing Iowa Farm Holiday leaders to halt the embargo. But the movement had gained too much momentum to stop quickly, and in Newman Grove, Nebraska, Andrew Dahlsten led a local Farm Holiday Association, which had a connection to the American Communist Party. His group wanted to prevent land foreclosures and turned bank foreclosures into "penny auctions" that helped protect farm property. In one of those sales, in Elgin, bidders paid no more than 5 cents for each item sold at the foreclosure of a local widow's property; the Farm Holiday Association prohibited anyone else present from bidding higher. When the sale had concluded and every item had sold—the bank raised only $5.35—the new owners proceeded to give everything they had bought back to the widow. Such "penny auctions" served their purpose by making banks and mortgage companies reluctant to foreclose on property.

After the election of Franklin D. Roosevelt as president in 1932, farmers called for a halt to extreme actions, hoping Roosevelt would support their need for better prices. But in February 1933 some 3,000 farmers marched on Lincoln, where they called for legislation that would prohibit foreclosures for up to two years. Later that fall, in a final, desperate act, the Farm Holiday movement again embargoed crops. Iowa farmers blocked roads leading into Omaha, and Nebraska farmers halted a train headed into Sioux City, burning bridges that provided access to the community.

Harvesting wheat near Lexington, 1905. —Wyoming State Museum, Stimson Collection

Subsequent federal legislation provided support for farmers throughout Nebraska and other midwestern states. There have been fewer agrarian protests since the 1930s. The need for agricultural commodities during World War II boosted farm incomes. An economic downturn in the 1980s mirrored that of a century earlier as farmers made an exodus from the land, forced out by the high costs of doing business and low prices. Beginning in 1985 entertainers led by country star Willie Nelson staged a series of "Farm Aid" concerts. Among the headliners: John Cougar Mellencamp, Neil Young, Kris Kristofferson, Merle Haggard, and Bon Jovi.

Nebraska lawmakers, in an effort to keep the land in the hands of individuals, adopted legislation in 1984 prohibiting corporate farming by other than family groups. However, farmers have become increasingly dependent upon the government for price supports and federal subsidies. From 1985 to 1989 Nebraska farmers received almost $4.3 billion in federal subsidies. That represented nearly 45 percent of their net agricultural income and was well above the national farm average of just more than 33 percent of net income from price supports.

ANSELMO

On April Fools Day, 1887, a couple of cowboys rode the construction train on the B&M Railroad out of Liscott to Anselmo. They intended to have a high time, but word got to the community before the cowboys did. Billy Frischauf closed his saloon that morning, and John Anderson also kept the doors closed to his tavern. But during the afternoon Anderson turned his keys over to brother Frank, who let the brew flow.

The cowboys knocked back a few drinks and then took target practice at the railroad pumphouse. One trainman wired the railroad company, saying the locomotives could get no water in Anselmo that day because filling the train could mean getting a backside full of buckshot. Although one cowboy kept pretty calm, the other let everything go. He put tin cans on the tops of hitching posts in the street and shot holes in them. He shot a hole through the stovepipe of a furniture store, narrowly missing the man working inside.

Anselmo citizens decided not to send for the sheriff but to hold off and hope the rowdies would settle down. Then one of the cowboys' errant bullets hit a resident in the toe, and word immediately spread that a man was shot. "Cowboys are terrorizing the citizens of Anselmo, and one man has been shot through the foot. We ask your protection," Walter Scott and C. D. Pelham wrote in a telegram to the Custer County sheriff in Broken Bow.

Meanwhile, the cowboys found some horses and rode into the Pelham store, where they supplied themselves with cigars. They visited other stores in town, including the saloon, but when they learned the sheriff had arrived they raced away, firing their guns as they went. Just outside of town, the sheriff and several men with him caught up to the cowboys. When the cowboys refused to surrender, the lawmen shot and killed both of them. An inquest found that the cowboys were killed while resisting arrest.

HALSEY

A railroad surveyor working in the area, Halsey Yates, left his name on this community near the Nebraska National Forest, created in 1902 by President Theodore Roosevelt. Encompassing 93,000 acres, the Bessey section of the forest near Halsey is the conception of botanist Charles E. Bessey, who believed the Sandhills, and the aquifer that lay under them, could support a large forest. The earliest plantings occurred in 1891, when Bessey obtained permission from the U.S. Department of Agriculture's Division of Forestry (the parent of the U.S. Forest Service) to plant trees near Swan Lake (midway between Burwell and Atkinson on Nebraska 11). By the late 1890s Bessey had further support for his tree planting program, and in 1902 President Roosevelt established two forest reserves in the Sandhills, the Dismal

The Nebraska National Forest is the only entirely man-made forest in the country. Here workers plant seedlings near Halsey. —Nebraska State Historical Society

River Reserve and the Niobrara Reserve, together totaling 206,000 acres. The Dismal River Reserve eventually became the Bessey Division of the Nebraska National Forest near Halsey.

Between 1903 and 1921 some 13.5 million seedlings, including both jack and yellow pine, were planted. During the first fifty years of the forest's existence workers planted about 200 billion seedlings. The reserve now contains hackberry, red cedar, cottonwood, willow, green ash, and aspen as well as nonnative varies such as jack pine, American elm, white fir, honey locust, catalpa, blue spruce, and black locust. It provides habitat for a variety of wildlife, is a popular recreational area, and local residents cut firewood here.

The productive forest has suffered several natural setbacks, including a 1910 fire that destroyed several hundred acres. The drought of the 1930s affected some trees, particularly the jack pines, and another major fire in 1965 burned at least a third of the forest, killing about 2.5 million trees. Since its start in 1902, the Nebraska National Forest has twice been expanded, with new divisions in northwestern Nebraska.

THEDFORD

A major change in the 1862 Homestead Law occurred because of efforts by the Thedford Livestock Association, which petitioned Congress to allow homesteaders to claim up to two sections of land rather than one quarter section (160 acres). With the support of the Livestock Association, Nebraska congressman Moses P. Kinkaid of O'Neill got approval for changes in the Homestead Law. The Kinkaid Amendment

Trench planting trees in the Nebraska National Forest.
—Nebraska State Historical Society

to the 1862 Homestead Act went into effect June 28, 1904. It provided that anyone who had never taken a homestead could file on 640 acres of land, and if he had taken a claim of less than 640 acres, he could claim more ground up to a maximum of 640 acres. Those people who already had homesteads had first right to claim lands adjacent to their original homesteads.

To make final claim on a Kinkaid Act land section, the owner had to live on the land for five years and make at least $800 in improvements. The law applied only to Nebraska and only to lands that couldn't be irrigated. Some nine million acres met the criteria for Kinkaid homesteads.

When the time came to file for the claims, Nebraska towns throughout the region affected by the Kinkaid Act saw mini-population booms. More than 600 people flocked to O'Neill; Alliance reported 3,000 people in town for the land division; and Valentine was avalanched by would-be homesteaders. Late on the afternoon of June 27, 1907, the Reverend Samuel Holsclaw took a position at the Valentine land office door in order to be the first to enter the next morning. Soon other men and a number of women got in line behind him, and by that night the queue extended more than two blocks. Several of the men in line agreed to hold places for the women during the night. In Broken Bow cattlemen sent their cowboys to town with instructions to claim a tract under the Kinkaid Act, but the range riders created such a disturbance that the National Guard had to be called in to restore order.

The Kinkaid homesteads went to married men and their unmarried adult sons, ranchers and their cowboys, and even some schoolteachers. In almost half of the cases the homesteaders eventually sold their claims to bosses, friends, neighbors, or family, giving birth to many of the large cattle operations in the region.

Even though many of the Kinkaid homesteads eventually changed hands, the law achieved some of its original purposes. It allowed farmers and ranchers to expand their holdings so they could make a reasonable living turning the open range to closed range, helped to settle the heretofore nearly vacant country, and increased Nebraska's tax revenues by putting more ground into production.

There were few trees in this area, yet homesteaders needed wood for various projects, so many claimed land under the Timber Culture Act of 1873. Under that provision of the law, land ownership came with cultivation of trees (see page 163).

Lost on the Prairie

A tragedy occurred north of Thedford in May 1891 when two young girls wandered from home picking wildflowers for their mother. Eight-year-old Mathilda "Tillie" Haumann and her sister, Retta, age four, asked their mother if they could walk to meet their older sister, Hannah, who worked for a nearby neighbor. The girls picked wildflowers as they wandered, but they became disoriented, and soon the hills all looked the same. With no landmarks, they couldn't find their way home. Although they heard people calling to them after night fell, the girls wouldn't respond because they feared Indians.

After four days, searchers found Retta, alive but severely sunburned and suffering from exposure. It took several more days for the searchers to locate Tillie, who had taken off her apron and spread it over a wild rose bush to form a spot of shade in which to lie. She died there upon the prairie on May 17, 1891. During their roaming over the hill country, it is estimated the girls walked about seventy-five miles. The two girls are memorialized in many poems and stories that are part of the folklore of this area.

MULLEN

Mullen is in the heart of Sandhills Country. At first settlers thought the Sandhills were good only for grazing cattle, but then the Ogallala Aquifer, an enormous underground sea of water stretching under most of Nebraska and going as far south as Texas, was tapped, and farmers began growing crops. Controversy exists over the best management of the land. Some say the use of pivot irrigation systems is leading to depletion of soil nutrients; others say the ranchers and farmers who have made their living from the land for generations ought to know what's best for their country. Not all of the land falls under irrigation systems; some is in dryland production. In such cases farmers plant different fields each year, allowing for a period of nonuse for every section of land on a rotating basis. They also plant species of crops that are best equipped to survive and produce with little moisture.

The North and Cody Ranch

After their years as military leaders during the Indian Wars from 1864 to 1877, Maj. Frank North and Capt. Luther North joined forces with their old friend and fellow Indian fighter, Col. William F. Cody, in a ranching venture on the north fork of the Dismal River. It became the North and Cody Ranch and always served a welcome to honest travelers.

The North brothers and Cody bought a cattle herd at Ogallala and drove the animals north in 1877. In 1882 Maj. Frank North won election to the Nebraska legislature. He died at Columbus three years later, leaving a wife and daughter. Capt. Luther H. North also eventually settled at Columbus, where he died April 16, 1935, at age eighty-nine.

WHITMAN

This area was settled at the hands of Kinkaiders and was the last area of free land in the state of Nebraska given away in 640-acre tracts. A weeklong lottery was held in 1913 in Hyannis. As the time for the drawing grew near, Whitman streets were overrun with tents serving as temporary quarters for people hoping to win some of the free land. In 1892 a prairie fire started on the Monahan Ranch, consuming hundreds of acres of native rangeland and making it one of the worst natural disasters in Nebraska's history.

HYANNIS

Hyannis became the seat of Grant County in 1897 after a group of people broke into the county courthouse, took all the records, and brought them to Hyannis. Dr. A. J. Plummer started the Dumbbell Ranch, which eventually had 52,000 acres, then moved to Montana. (He is no relation to A. H. Plummer, who had a long career as both an outlaw and a lawman in California, Nevada, Idaho, and Montana, where he died at the end of a vigilante rope.) This is still ranching country, with cattle and in some cases buffalo dotting the hillsides.

Locals drive pickups pulling trailers filled with livestock. They wear cowboy hats and boots and might be on their way to the home ranch, the livestock sale barn, the county fair, or a rodeo.

Ashby, just west of Hyannis, started as a railroad town. The first road heading southwest of town was pioneered by a local man who headed his car toward Denver, marking his route by painting the fenceposts blue.

Wood River–Burwell
72 miles

Nebraska 11 crosses through the Platte River valley to the north, providing access to a number of small communities first established by homesteaders. From Wood River the highway heads through Cairo and provides access to Boelus, located west of Cairo on the Middle Loup River. (Boelus may be named for Belus, a small river in Palestine described by Pliny.) Following the Middle Loup to the east, Nebraska 11 takes travelers to Dannebrog, one of the many Danish settlements in this region (see page 252), then turns north through Farwell, Elba, Coatsfield, and Scotia.

SCOTIA

Early settlers in the fertile North Loup Valley were greeted in 1872 by Jack Swearengen, a trapper, guide, and government scout. He lived in a dugout in the white chalk bluffs that rise above the valley. The highest hill became known as "Happy Jack's Peak" and served as a lookout point to guard against Indian attacks.

The hills took on added importance after 1877 when Ed Wright began mining the chalk. He built a general store in Scotia in 1887. Other residents used chalk in the foundations of their buildings. The mine stood idle for a number of years but reopened in the 1930s under the management of a paint company based in Omaha. The chalk was used in paint and whitewash, cement, polishes, and chicken feed. In 1967 the formations of calcareous rock, which can be seen throughout the North Loup Valley, were included in a wayside park operated by the Nebraska Game and Parks Commission.

North Loup, with its popcorn processing factories, claims to be the popcorn capital of the world and celebrates an annual Popcorn Day.

Restored officers' quarters at Fort Hartsuff, August 1995.

Fort Hartsuff

Midway between Ord and Burwell is the small community of Elyria. Nearby stand the remnants of Fort Hartsuff, which is now Fort Hartsuff State Historical Park. Originally designated "Post on the North Fork of the Loup River," Fort Hartsuff was established September 5, 1874. The location was chosen by Gen. Edward Otho Cresap Ord, a West Point graduate who scouted the area that year. On December 9, 1874, military officials renamed the post for Maj. Gen. George Lucas Hartsuff. The War Department established the fort to protect white settlers and Pawnee Indians, who had provided much assistance to the military since 1864. The Teton Sioux considered the land along the North Loup their territory, and they attacked both white and Pawnee settlements.

Fort Hartsuff also served as an important link in the central plains military fort system. Built as an open fort, with no protective barriers around the various buildings, Fort Hartsuff cost $110,000. The military made its nine buildings of grout (which is similar to concrete) because there was a local supply of gravel and lime nearby. Men using horses hauled gravel from Gravel Creek, four miles to the southeast, and brought lime from Doc Beebe's ranch, forty miles to the south.

Upon its completion, Fort Hartsuff became a symbol of government order and "civilization" in a land "decidedly ungoverned, unruly and uncivilized," according to one early account. It became the center of social life in the valley, and during the droughts and grasshopper invasions of the early 1870s, officials dispersed supplies from the fort.

The fort generally had one infantry company of less than one hundred men from the 9th, 14th, and 23rd Infantry Regiments, who scouted for hostile Sioux along the Loup and Cedar Rivers. They sometimes ranged as far north as the Niobrara River and assisted civil authorities in chasing horse thieves, train robbers, and murderers.

The fort's major military engagement came at the Battle of the Blowout in April 1876, when a detachment from Company A, 23rd Infantry, responded to reports of Sioux harassment of settlers at a location some five miles north of the present town of Burwell. In the battle 1st Sgt. William Dougherty died, but troops commanded by Lt. Charles Heath Heyl routed the Sioux. Lieutenant Heyl, Cpl. Patrick Leonard, and Cpl. Jeptha L. Lytton earned Medals of Honor as a result of their actions during the encounter.

The military abandoned Fort Hartsuff May 1, 1881, replacing it with Fort Niobrara, near present-day Valentine. The Union Pacific Railroad paid $5,000 for the property but sold it when company officials decided not to build their line on the north side of the river. For years the fort buildings did duty in a farming operation, with hogs housed in the guardhouse and grain stored in the main house. Farmers dug an irrigation canal around the fort location and planted corn on the parade ground.

Dr. Glen Auble and his wife, Lillian, started the preservation efforts of Fort Hartsuff during World War II when they bought a half-interest in the site. In 1960 they acquired the other half-interest and deeded fifteen acres containing the remains of the old fort buildings to the Nebraska Game and Parks Commission. The commission has restored and reconstructed the buildings and uses them to interpret the seven-year history of the fort. Many of the original buildings remain, including the headquarters, officers' quarters, barracks, laundry, and other facilities.

During Fort Hartsuff's existence, the camp-follower community of Calamus grew about a quarter of a mile to the southeast. The town had a school, newspaper, law office, blacksmith, shoemaker, saloon, and general store, but after the military abandoned Fort Hartsuff the community withered. A tornado that tore through the area in 1885 wrecked the school and sealed the town's fate.

BURWELL

Richard McClimans filed a claim September 29, 1875, on a site east of Burwell under the Timber Culture Act of 1873. The act, sponsored by Sen. Phineas W. Hitchcock of Nebraska, allowed homesteaders to claim up to a quarter section of additional land by agreeing to cultivate timber.

In 1960 the family of Osceola and Laura McClimans Cram donated a portion of the original McClimans timber claim to the Nebraska Conference of the United Church of Christ as a memorial. The church obtained additional acreage for the memorial, named Kamp Kaleo, in 1961. Many of the Kamp Kaleo trees are survivors of the original McClimans timber claim, and thirty-two acres of forest are managed as a nature area by the Soil Conservation Society of America.

From Burwell, Nebraska 11 runs almost due north across the eastern point of the Sandhills, crossing the Cedar River, passing Swan Lake, and following a short stretch of the South Fork of the Elkhorn River on its way to Atkinson. This rich agricultural land is used for cattle range south of Atkinson, but north of there farmers raise corn, sorghum, and other crops. They utilize pivot sprinkler systems for irrigation. As the highway descends toward the Keya Paha River, the land changes from flat, primarily treeless farmland to rolling hills with big trees.

Mr. Fisher cultivating his farmstead windbreak. —Nebraska State Historical Society

St. Paul–Ansley
49 miles

The Isaac Merchant family settled on Victoria Creek (at the site of Victoria Springs State Park east of Anselmo) in April 1875. At the time there were only two other families in the valley—the Caswells and Rosses. Fear of attack from Indians kept the early settlers on the alert, and eventually they built a fort not far from the Merchant place. The fort stood a short distance from the Merchant family barn, and a winding tunnel connected the two structures. The fort was twenty feet square and built mostly in the ground with the exception of two logs, through which holes had been made for shooting. The fort provided some protection from Indians, and in 1876 the government provided guns to all the region's men and several of the boys.

A former Custer County judge, Charles R. Matthews, homesteaded the area that now makes up Victoria Springs State Recreation Area. The sixty-acre area gets its name from a natural mineral spring, which once drew visitors who believed in the therapeutic value of the waters. At one time Matthews bottled and sold the spring water. Established as a state recreation area in 1925 (the third designated in Nebraska), Victoria Springs has a campground, picnic area, and nonmotorized boating. The cabin that served as Judge Matthews's home and another small building, Custer County's first post office, remain at the site.

Kearney–Arnold
89 miles

From Kearney to Oconto, Nebraska 40 follows the Wood River through Riverdale, Amherst, Miller, Sumner, and Eddyville.

Frederick Schreyer settled on the South Loup River in 1875, the first homesteader in the valley between Callaway and Arnold. Schreyer built a dugout to serve as his first home. Such habitations were literally dug out of the ground, often into a hillside, with a roof of boards covered with sod at ground level. Early residents used such houses because they had no other building materials. Cooking often took place at open fires out of doors, so the dugout mainly served as a place to get in out of the weather, a place to sleep, and a place to store supplies and what limited possessions early residents had with them.

The Peter M. Barnes sod house near Clear Creek, Custer County, 1887.
—Nebraska State Historical Society, Solomon D. Butcher Collection

Because dugouts were dirty, generally filled with bugs and insects, and often fairly enticing to rodents and rattlesnakes, Schreyer eventually built a house of bricks made from clay, grass, and straw, with a second story built of lumber hauled in from elsewhere.

Schreyer had many a run-in with cowboys who tried to frighten him from the land, but he had fortitude and refused to budge. He operated a small grocery store and opened the Triumph post office in 1877. As the years passed it became clear that a railroad would push into the area, and in the early 1890s Schreyer decided to build a flour mill. He surveyed the area and made plans to build a dam of sandstone from a nearby outcropping. With a crew of men, Schreyer mined the sandstone using picks, shovels, and dynamite. Before Schreyer could complete his flour mill, however, he realized the railroad would extend only to Callaway, not to his location. An early proponent of water development, Schreyer later built a dam near his home, creating a small lake on the South Loup River from which water could be diverted for cropland irrigation.

Nebraska's Range War: Homesteaders vs. Cattlemen

Throughout the West in the late 1800s, conflict arose about land use. The most riveting incident in Nebraska involved people with roots in Texas and took place all across the prairie, from Callaway to Broken Bow.

Isom Prentice Olive, known better as Print Olive, moved to Nebraska from Texas, where he had a reputation as a cattleman who never backed down from trouble. Olive's family settled along the San Gabriel River in Texas prior to the Civil War. His father, James, gathered wild longhorns and started building an empire for himself and his sons: Prentice (Print), Thomas Jefferson (Jay), Ira, Robert (Bob), and Marion. In those days the fortunes of the daughters of the family were left to the men they married.

James Olive started gathering longhorn cattle for a herd, and by the time Print was ten he began working the annual roundups. He had a natural ability with animals and developed into a first-rate cowman. After fighting for the Confederacy, Print returned to Texas to gather large herds of Texas longhorns. When difficulties arose with other men intent on starting herds of their own, Print took to regularly carrying a pair of six-shooters, which he used to solve any disputes over cattle ownership.

One day Print rode the Yegua Creek bottom south of the ranch when he encountered a couple of cowboys driving a small herd downstream. Print circled to the front of the herd and asked the men if they had proof of ownership, as some of the cattle wore the Olive brand. As one of Print's cowboys rode up to the herd, one man moving the cattle drew on Olive. But the Civil War veteran responded, drilling the cowboy with bullets in his breast and shoulder. The man he shot, Rob Murday, didn't die, and he hadn't been stealing Olive cattle; he eventually went to work for Print on the Texas ranch.

That shooting was Print's first as a civilian, but it wasn't the last in his family. By 1867, word filtered into Texas of the planned construction of the Union Pacific Railroad across the Platte River country. Print Olive looked north at the potential market for his longhorns and during the summer of 1868 sent his first herd up the Chisholm Trail to Kansas. In 1869 he extended the movement to the Platte in Nebraska. The Platte country became the key to Olive's expansion plans. It offered a moderate climate, plenty of water, and hip-deep grass for fattening cattle. Moreover, the railroad provided a ready form of transportation to Eastern markets.

In 1870 Print had another run-in with cowboys moving cattle wearing the Olive brand. One, named Dave Fream, drew on him, but Print fired off a couple of quick rounds and killed the man. This time, however, Print himself was hit. He survived the shooting, and eight months later Texas authorities charged Print with murder. As the case got under way it became clear that Fream led a gang of cattle-rustling outlaws, so the judge dismissed the charges against Olive.

In 1873 Olive furthered his reputation as a man not willing to back down from any threat: During a card game in Ellsworth, Kansas, an opponent shot him three times, while Olive was unarmed.

The tempo of violence along the San Gabriel increased in 1874 and 1875. One day Print met with his father and brothers telling them they either had to pull up stakes and head north to new range or put their six-guns into use. They decided to stay and fight. As a first course of action, they required buyers of Olive cattle to brand the animals with the new owner's mark before leaving the ranch. That way if the Olives came upon cowboys trailing cattle with the Olive brand, they could easily prove they'd been rustled. Then they printed a large ad in the newspaper giving notice that anyone with horses or cattle bearing only Olive brands would be shot on sight.

Having given notice, the Olives started to enforce their rules. It is not known how many men they killed in Texas, but certainly several died at their hands. Print's younger brother Bob became perhaps the most dangerous of the brothers, often hunting down men suspected of stealing or injuring Olive stock.

In 1876 the Olives were trailing a herd north toward Nebraska when a message came from Jay back in Texas that Print needed to return home immediately. He did, only to find death threats against him and his brothers: a reward of $500 for the person who killed "any Olive male." In an August 1 attack, Jay Olive fell under a bombardment of bullets and died a few weeks later. The death of the most peaceable of the Olives—Jay was never known to have killed a man and had never ridden north with the cattle—forced the family to evaluate life in Texas. Eventually Print rounded up his herds and headed to Nebraska for a new beginning.

In 1877 Print started ranching on the Dismal River about four miles from Callaway, north of Plum Creek. In Nebraska, Bob used the last name Stevens, one he'd taken after killing Cal Nutt, leader of the San Gabriel rustlers and the man who'd once shot Print (and who likely had been involved with the killing of Jay Olive).

Trouble found the Olives in the north.

Blacksmith Luther Mitchell and bachelor Ami Ketchum claimed adjoining homesteads and in 1878 built a sod house, with half on Mitchell property and the other half on Ketchum property. Ami Ketchum and Mitchell's stepdaughter, Tamar Snow, planned to marry at Christmas. The homesteaders settled near Johnny Bryan, who had already claimed land, and they plowed the bluestem grasses under in order to plant corn. As summer wore on, the corn rapidly grew, and it appeared as if they would have a bumper crop.

The Luther Mitchell sod house, where Mitchell and Ami Ketchum had a shootout with riders associated with the Print Olive ranch, and where Bob Olive was shot and killed in 1878. Mitchell and Ketchum later were hanged by vigilantes. —Nebraska State Historical Society, Solomon D. Butcher Collection

The Olives, however, had cattle running on range near the homesteads along Clear Creek, and the sight of homesteaders with cornfields protected by wire fences festered like a splinter of wood under the skin. One night longhorns got into Bryan's cornfield, ruining much of it, and before too many additional nights passed the cattle completely destroyed the crop. Later, as the corn started to ripen, longhorns trampled the Mitchell-Ketchum field as well. As the homesteaders inspected the damage, it quickly became clear the fence had been cut. They suspected the Olives.

The Mitchell family had nowhere to go and Ketchum no desire to leave, so the men devised a scheme to hunt for meat and sell it in Kearney, some fifty miles to the south. By killing animals early in the day and then driving hard for Kearney, they could take the meat to markets without any loss from spoiling in the hot sun. Although they purportedly intended to kill elk, actually much of the "game" harvested wore the brand of Print Olive. The rustling that had created such problems for the Olives in Texas wasn't unknown in Nebraska, and when Manly Carple was arrested and charged with throwing a long loop, he implicated Ami Ketchum.

The Olives had taken strong and decisive action in Texas, and they did the same in Nebraska. They had information pointing to Ketchum and decided to arrest him. Sheriff David Anderson, who was in Print Olive's pocket, set the stage for the big showdown when he named Bob (Olive) Stevens a deputy sheriff and sent him to the Mitchell homestead to arrest both Mitchell and Ketchum.

On November 27, 1878, Bob Olive rode to the Mitchell place along with four other men: Pete Beeton, Barney Armstrong, Fred Fisher, and Jim McIndeffer. Beeton rode in alone to determine whether Ketchum was at the homestead. He asked to have a horse shod but was told to come back a few days later. Ketchum immediately suspected Beeton was a front man for a gang bent on treachery.

Before long Beeton returned with Bob Olive and the other three men, all of whom had been appointed official sheriff's deputies. With little discussion to precede it, the gunfight began; Ketchum was shot in the arm, and Mitchell defended his friend by shooting Bob Olive. Tamar Snow entered the battle on the side of her fiancé. She loaded his guns and helped steady him as he fired at the Olive cowboys. After the shooting of Bob Olive, the posse quickly retreated, but the wounded man died before they could reach a doctor. Two other members of the sheriff's party received minor injuries in the fray.

Mitchell and Ketchum, quickly assessing the danger in remaining, left for their former home in Merrick County, so the large party of cowboys who visited the Mitchell homestead the night of the shooting found it deserted. Once in Merrick County, Ketchum had a doctor treat the gunshot wound to his arm. Then he and Mitchell found a safe place for Mitchell's family before they decided to give themselves up.

As they headed back to Custer County, they stopped at Loup City, where Judge Aaron Wall told them not to continue their journey. If they did they'd likely be lynched, he said. Mitchell and Ketchum remained in Loup City until Merrick County Sheriff William Letcher and Howard County Sheriff F. W. Crew—who like Judge Wall supported the homesteaders' rights to be on the land—arrived and arrested them, with a goal of protecting them by keeping them in the jail. They were taken to the Buffalo County jail at Kearney, where sentiment ran against them; most people believed Bob Olive was acting as a lawman at the time of his death.

Print Olive wanted to deal with the two in his own manner. Olive had offered a $1,000 reward for the arrest of Ketchum and Mitchell. Now he said he would only pay the reward if the two men were brought to Custer County, where the killing of Bob Olive had taken place. As they had in Texas, the Olives enjoyed support from law officers in

Nebraska, most notably Sheriff David Anderson of Kearney. Anderson said he would transfer the men to Custer County only if he had enough money from the reward to hire extra guards for the prisoners.

It seems that every law enforcement officer in that region of Nebraska, regardless of county lines, became involved in the situation, and eventually Keith County Sheriff Barney Gillan agreed to transfer the prisoners. He agreed because Olive offered to give him the full reward if he turned the prisoners over to Olive once they were in Custer County.

Gillan and deputy Phil DuFran took Ketchum and Mitchell from the jail and boarded the train to Plum Creek—the heart of Olive country. They put the prisoners into a wagon, and the trip north started. At South Loup, about ten miles southwest of Broken Bow and some five miles southeast of Callaway, Olive and his men took charge of the prisoners. There, on December 10, 1878, they hanged Ketchum and Mitchell. Eventually some men burned their bodies. After the lynching Olive paid Gillan the reward money he'd promised; then they parted ways.

Eventually warrants were issued for the arrest of the men who were suspected of being involved in the lynching. Nebraska attorney general–elect Caleb J. Dilworth and numerous deputies went to Plum Creek and arrested Print Olive, Fred Fisher, Barney Armstrong, Bion Brown, William Green, and John Baldwin. Olive assembled a group of top attorneys to defend him against the charges. Because tension was high—and there was the very real fear that either Sheriff Anderson, a known friend of the cattleman, or some of Olive's cowboys would stage a release from the jail—the prisoners were transferred to the state prison at Lincoln.

In January 1879, Judge William A. Gaslin ordered a change of venue in the case, moving the trial from Kearney to Hastings, and he secured warrants for the arrest of several additional Olive accomplices, including Dennis Gartrill, Pete Beeton, Pedro Dominicus, Jim McIndeffer, Deputy Sheriff Phil DuFran, and Sheriff Barney Gillan.

In February 1879 a grand jury linked the November raid on the Mitchell-Ketchum home with the December lynchings of the two homesteaders. Trial was set for March 31. It quickly became the most newsworthy event in Nebraska, as the kingpin of the cattle business went head to head against the state to determine the fate of the Platte country west of Kearney. The question to be settled was whether the land would be controlled by the big cattlemen or by the homesteaders.

The trial got under way April 1, 1879, in Liberal Hall in Hastings, the largest building in the community (it could seat up to four hundred spectators). Phil DuFran turned state's evidence, building a strong case, particularly against Print Olive and Fred Fisher. By April 10, tension in Hastings was as tight as a drumhead, and Sheriff S. L. Martin sent a telegram to Governor Albinus Nance requesting troops to provide extra protection:

> SEND COMPANY OF TROOPS IMMEDIATELY, THE CRITICAL TIME HAS ARRIVED. DO NOT FEEL SAFE WITH SUCH GUARDS AS I CAN GET. SEND TROOPS FROM OTHER POINTS THAN THIS COUNTY, FOR REASONS THAT YOU KNOW. HAVE THEM HERE BY SPECIAL TRAIN AT NOON TOMORROW (FRIDAY). FOR GOD'S SAKE DON'T FAIL.

Early the next morning Brig. Gen. George Crook sent troops from Company H, 9th U.S. Infantry, from Omaha to Hastings. The trial resumed that day, with one change in Judge Gaslin's manner: He placed his gun, which he had formerly held in his lap, on the bench before him, in plain view of all in the improvised courtroom.

On April 11, Brig. Gen. Crook sent a telegram to Governor Nance asking that he obtain permission from the president himself for the continued presence of the federal troops in Hastings. The governor wired President Rutherford B. Hayes, who refused the request. Because of the tenseness of the situation in Hastings, however, Crook left the troops in place several more days.

The trial continued, and Bion Brown added direct testimony that confirmed the state's case against Olive. After deliberating only about an hour, the jury returned its verdict: Olive and Fisher were guilty of second-degree murder. Gaslin sentenced them to life imprisonment.

Olive appealed, and two years later the Nebraska Supreme Court ruled that Judge Gaslin had improperly organized the trial. Olive and Fisher were freed, subject to a new trial to be held in Custer County. The hearing there had a different ending: The two men were released, and the case was never reopened. The other men indicted in 1879 had already had charges cleared against them. It was never clearly shown who set the bodies on fire.

After the killing of Bob Olive, Ami Ketchum, and Luther Mitchell, Ira Olive remained in Nebraska, living south of Plum Creek and the North Platte River, where he became a leading citizen in the town of Plum Creek, which later became Lexington. Print left Nebraska in 1882 and headed for Kansas, and within four years he had operations in both Kansas and Colorado. He died in Trail City, Colorado, late in the summer of 1886 when Joe Sparrow, a Texas cattleman who had borrowed some money from Olive, shot and killed him over an unpaid bill of $10.

New Callaway vs. Old Callaway

In 1887 George M. Mair moved to Custer County from Chicago. With a career as a job printer behind him, Mair quickly became involved in the newspaper business in Nebraska. He did his work in New Callaway, just a mile from Callaway. The *New Callaway Courier* rivaled the *Callaway Standard*, and the papers had quite a time promoting their own communities. Callaway had a population of about two hundred, New Callaway only about fifty, but that didn't dampen the spirits of the newspaper editors.

The *New Callaway Courier* issued forth from a barnlike structure built of boards with knotholes, which provided air conditioning in the warmer months but let in the cold during the winter. Although the initial plan was to heat the office with coal hauled from Cozad, that fuel was expensive, so Mair and his partner, Jake Horn, made routine trips out to the cornfield of N. M. Morgan, a vice president of the town-site company. One day Morgan visited the newspaper office with a notice he wanted published. It warned thieves to keep off his premises under threat of severe penalty. The newspapermen duly printed the notice and thereafter obtained their fuel supply of corn from other fields in the area.

Although officially known as New Callaway, the town usually went by its nickname, "Podunk," and the residents became known as "Mud Hens," according to an account of the early days by Mair in *Pioneer Stories of Custer County Nebraska*. When railroad progress stopped, most Podunk businessmen moved to Callaway, leaving Mair and Horn as the only residents of New Callaway. They moved into an abandoned school building, a sod house that had the advantage of being cooler in summer and warmer in winter. However, it had the disadvantage of a dirt roof that leaked profusely when it rained. As a result, Mair often found himself setting type with an umbrella perched above his head and the type cases.

Eventually only Mair lived in New Callaway/Podunk, but he continued to operate the paper and had reasonable success, at least in part because the area was a trade center for many of the rural families living in the Sandhills country to the north and west. The people read both the *Courier* and the *Standard* because "they greatly enjoyed the verbal tilts between the two town site organs," Mair wrote in *Pioneer Stories*.

Not all of his dispatches kept strictly to the facts. Mair admitted he liked to stretch the truth, as a sampling of his news stories attests:

> As Ira McConnell was crossing Wiggle Creek yesterday he was wondering which of the two towns would win out when the railroad came, when a big bullfrog stuck its head up out of the water and

croaked "Podunk." He is going to invest in several corner lots on the strength of the tip.

A brindle dog with one ear came to town last Monday and viciously attacked our champion high jumper of the Podunk Athletic Club, Jack Rabbitson, injuring him so seriously that a match he had arranged with a claim jumper from Stop Table had to be postponed.

The late sleet storm made the grass on our sidewalks so slippery that one of our prominent jackrabbits fell and sprained one of his ankles so badly that he walks with a limp.

Eventually the *Standard* and the *Courier* had competition in the form of a third paper, the *Headlight*, to serve the community of three hundred people. No doubt editor Mair's lively "make-believe news" kept readers interested. Because many of the area residents were bachelors, he had a running report on an imaginary "Callaway Bachelor's Club."

The disagreements between the *Standard* and *Courier* editors notwithstanding, the two Callaways finally became one community when Mair moved to the larger town and let New Callaway die a graceful death. But that didn't put an end to the conflict, because when the railroad at last moved through the region organizers platted a new town midway between the two Callaways.

Once again Mair had a role in the town-site development. When it became clear to him that the railroad addition would prevail he moved there, taking with him the post office, which he ran. Townspeople in Callaway didn't want the post office moved, and they posted a guard on Mair, but one night he gave them the slip and with help from several friends moved the mail to a temporary location at the new town. Callaway residents were furious and succeeded in getting the post office reestablished in Callaway, marking the occasion with demonstrations and bonfires.

US 183

Elm Creek–Springview

162 miles

Elm Creek had a frigid beginning, with blizzard after blizzard wiping out cattle herds soon after the town's genesis in 1873. In 1906 things turned torrid when a raging fire swept through town, destroying all of the buildings along main street. US 183 passes through Miller and intersects with Nebraska 2 at Ansley, then continues north to Westerville.

The Seneca post office was established February 6, 1879. However, when James H. Westervelt began homesteading south of town, near

Elm Bridge, at the site of a sod schoolhouse across Clear Creek, the Seneca post office moved there, and the settlers started calling the place Westerville in honor of the man who founded it. When William Baillie became postmaster on August 28, 1882, he had the name of the post office changed from Seneca to Westerville.

Westervelt platted the town August 11, 1880. The town grew rapidly until 1886, when the railroad moved through the region. Then many of the houses were placed upon wheels and taken to Ansley. But Westerville claimed many firsts in Custer County, including publication of the first newspaper, the *Custer County Leader* (established June 13, 1881), site of the first county fair, and location of the first church. The town had a free circulating library, started in 1888, and a brass band. Because Broken Bow was more centrally located, Westerville lost its bid to become the seat of Custer County.

SARGENT

Sargent, laid out in 1883 on the north side of the Middle Loup River, sat about a mile from the stream and had the earliest bank in Custer County. The first building erected at the town was J. K. Spacht's general store, which went up in the middle of a wheat field in the summer of 1883. By 1901 the town had a two-story frame school, two newspapers, two banks, two grain elevators, a creamery, and other businesses.

The first white man to settle in what is now Sargent was Joseph A. Woods, who located in Wood's Park in the spring of 1874. Other early settlers included Davis S. Groff and three of his sons. Bachelor Job Semler settled in the valley six miles below Sargent and freighted cedar from the Dismal River and goods from Grand Island, then the nearest railroad town.

The Wilson Dye family lived near Sargent during the winter of 1880 when Dye found it necessary to go to Wood's Park on an errand. He left his wife and three small children at home and set off on his trip. As Dye readied for his trip home, a prairie blizzard embraced the land, howling with such intensity that Dye dared not start his journey back from Wood's Park. At the homestead, Mrs. Dye had the three children to care for as well a cow and calf. While the storm howled, she became concerned for the animals, which were tied to a picket rope outside. There was no stable for their shelter, and Mrs. Dye feared the storm would be too much for the cow and calf to bear. She did what she had to do and brought the animals into the house. There, in a single room homestead sixteen by twenty feet, Mrs. Dye, her three children, the cow, and the calf passed the storm.

Homesteaders near Westerville, 1877. —Wyoming State Museum/ Denver Public Library, Western History Department

Wilson Dye homestead and family near Sargent. Mrs. Dye once saved the family cow by bringing it into the homestead during a blizzard. —Nebraska State Historical Society, Solomon D. Butcher Collection

North Platte—Valentine

156 miles

Ogallala—Merriman

135 miles

Three highways cut through the heart of the Sandhills on a north-south axis. US 83 connects North Platte and Valentine, passing through only two other towns—Stapleton and Thedford—in that 156-mile stretch. Nebraska 97 runs to the west of the US 83 route, connects North Platte and Valentine, and also goes through only two communities, Tryon and Mullen. The western edge of our Sandhills Country is formed by Nebraska 61, which connects Ogallala with Merriman, passing through Arthur and Hyannis en route.

All three highways traverse rolling hill country used today for cattle range and historically as buffalo pasture. In recent years some livestock producers in the area have started raising buffalo.

In the early 1960s the Nebraska Department of Roads began using more native grasses and legumes to stabilize roadside soils. By 1974 the highway workers had started including wildflowers in the mix. These plants bind the soil, provide food for livestock and wildlife, and help control blowing and drifting snow during winter storms. After workers complete road construction projects, they plant native grasses (buffalo grass, switchgrass, big bluestem, Indian grass, and blue grama) and twenty-three species of wildflowers, including blue sage, prairie wild rose, sawtooth sunflower, white aster, prickly poppy, plains coreopsis, yarrow, black-eyed susan, plains prickly pear, ironweed, and the state flower (adopted in 1895), late goldenrod.

Merna—Arthur

108 miles

In the southern portion of Sandhills Country, Nebraska 92 connects Merna, located on Nebraska 2, to Arthur, passing through Arnold, providing access to Gandy, and then heading to Stapleton, Tryon, and Arthur. One of the horrible wild prairie fires of the 1890s burned thousands of square miles near the Thomas County/Logan County border, north of Stapleton, destroying barns and livestock. More recent fires stopped just short of Nebraska National Forest lands, south of Halsey. A blaze that started March 6, 1972, scorched 100,000 acres in a patch thirty-two miles long and a dozen miles wide and destroyed many ranches in the area.

ARTHUR

Deep in the heart of the Sandhills, both the town and county of Arthur get their names from President Chester Arthur. In 1913 a large tract of land near Arthur that had been set aside for a forest preserve was opened to homesteading, one of the last areas in Nebraska available to men and women seeking free land.

The people of this region showed their inventiveness in 1927 when they built Pilgrim Holiness Church—of baled rye straw. From the outside, the church doesn't look all that unique, just a small rectangular structure covered with white stucco. The interior, too, is rather simple, with plastered walls and wooden pews on the slightly sloping floor. Two small rooms, a parlor and a kitchen, sit behind the altar, and a staircase provides access to two small sleeping rooms in the attic area. But between the stucco and the plaster are rye straw bales nearly two feet thick. The Pilgrim Holiness Church may be the most unique form of folk architecture in all of Nebraska. It certainly represents its region well. There are few trees in this grassy Sandhills Country, and the sandy

Pilgrim Holiness Church, made of baled hay, covered with stucco.

soil did not lend itself to good, tight sod for construction. Local residents, longing for a church, made do with what they had. The era of baled hay construction coincided with the Kinkaid Act period.

The Arthur County Historical Society now owns the Pilgrim Holiness Church. In 1976 the society restored the exterior with assistance from a grant from the Nebraska Bicentennial Commission, putting on a new roof and new outside stucco and painting the exterior.

O'Neill–Merriman

192 miles

The country between O'Neill and Bassett is Nebraska's best-known hay-producing region. Natural meadows line US 20, particularly between Stuart and Bassett. Ranchers stack sweet-smelling hay in loose piles, pour it into square metal cages, and then remove the cage when it is full. Small stacks are sometimes placed under trees, but many are simply left in the fields, reminiscent of a group of checkers on a board. Although much of the hay raised in this region is sold and shipped away for use in other areas, that which is needed for local livestock is loaded onto hay movers that take it to feeding grounds.

Haying operations in central Nebraska. –Wyoming State Museum, Stimson Collection

Spring Valley Park, near Newton, perhaps the first roadside rest area established in Nebraska.

NEWPORT

A prairie fire threatened Newport in 1904, burning a pathway more than ten miles wide through the natural hay meadows that lie to the south and west. The large amount of hay produced here made Newport a hay-shipping center in the early part of the twentieth century, and it is still a major beef-producing area.

In 1938, just west of Newport, Vic and Maude Thompson established Spring Valley Park, believed to be the first roadside rest area in Nebraska. In 1966 the Thompsons dedicated their Centennial Memorial Forest, in which the rest area is located, and proclaimed their ranch a wildlife refuge. Large shade trees and a playground area beckon travelers to take a break from driving.

BASSETT

Just south of Bassett, named for the man who brought the first cattle into the region, is the ghost town of Harrop. John Harrop filed a Kinkaid homestead claim west of the Calamus River in 1908. Four years later he operated a post office and mercantile store. In 1927 Harrop platted and dedicated the town site that carried his name.

Harrop and his son, Roy, provided primary leadership in the establishment of the Calamus Irrigation District. They wanted to dam

David C. "Doc" Middleton and his horse at the finish of a 1,000-mile race from Chadron to Chicago, photographed at the Buffalo Bill Wild West Show. —Nebraska State Historical Society

the Calamus River to provide irrigation water. The irrigation district proposition didn't have unanimous support in the region and eventually ended up in the courts, and in 1929 the Nebraska Supreme Court dissolved the district. A year later John Harrop died, and with him went the support for the irrigation district and eventually the town. By the mid-1990s residents in the area had started developing Harrop Park, situated east of the earlier town.

The Legend of Doc Middleton

In the period after the Civil War many men left Texas headed north because they'd had a scrape or two with the law. Among those who did so was D.C. Middleton. Middleton went by the name James Riley in Texas, where he is known to have shot three men. One had an affair with his sister, the second was a black cowhand, and the last was his own brother-in-law (from his first marriage in Texas), whom Riley found beating his grandmother in an attempt to have her reveal the location of her money.

In 1872, in Coryell County, Texas, Riley/Middleton faced his first charge for horse theft, and two years later Gillespie County, Texas, authorities handed down an indictment against him for stealing a gelding. Authorities eventually dismissed the charge, but Riley/ Middleton couldn't resist the lure of good (and bad) horseflesh, and in 1875 he went to prison for horse theft, sentenced to eighteen years. He quickly escaped but was recaptured and sent to Huntsville; however, on April 1, 1876, after serving less than a year, he escaped again. He headed north, working with an outfit driving cattle from San Angelo to Dodge City. To avoid capture he changed his name to David C. Middleton. The "C" may have stood for Cherry, his mother's maiden name. He quickly became known as "Doc," perhaps because his initials somewhat resembled that name or perhaps because he was a good horse doctor. In 1876 he cared for a cowboy with a broken leg, and he was particularly adept at "doctoring" brands on stolen horses and cattle.

Once Middleton arrived in Nebraska, he worked as a freighter, and many people believed he was a medical doctor, perhaps in part because of his cultured appearance—he was tall, dark haired, and well mannered—and had obvious signs of education.

By the fall of 1876 Middleton worked as a night herder for the Sidney-to-Black Hills freight route operated by Pratt and Ferris. After one trip Middleton and some of his freighting buddies stopped in Sidney at Joe Lane's dance hall, known as the Saratoga House. The men had been on a long and dusty road and were ready for a night on the town, but they found it was soldiers' night out, and many men from Sidney Barracks were entertaining themselves in the saloon. The rule was that on soldiers' night only the men wearing blue uniforms could participate in the dances.

Middleton and a friend sat at the bar near a soldier, Pvt. James Keefe, and his girlfriend. The woman taunted Middleton about not being able to join in the dance. She may have been flirting a bit, as well, and her soldier companion quickly picked a fight with Middleton. "In a moment everything was confusion and uproar in the place and the two men were locked in a fierce struggle," S. D. Butcher wrote in *Pioneer History of Custer County*. When other soldiers joined Keefe, Middleton fired a shot, and his tormentor fell.

Middleton raced into the night. From the saloon he made his way on foot to the first stage station north of Sidney, where he caught a ride on top of the coach headed north. He didn't have proper clothing, but local legend says one of the North brothers, who'd supervised the Pawnee Scouts, gave him a ride. At Fort Robinson, Middleton left the stage and promptly disappeared.

The Fifth Judicial District Court in Nebraska filed second-degree murder charges against Middleton April 7, 1877, but authorities never caught him on that warrant. He likely left Nebraska for a time and probably rustled horses. By 1878 he had a loose-knit gang of associates who preyed upon horses throughout the Nebraska Sandhills. Although they took some from settlers, by far the majority of the horses they swiped belonged to the Brulé Sioux led by Spotted Tail, who had settled near the confluence of the Niobrara and Missouri Rivers. Some also came from the herds of Oglala chief Red Cloud and his people, who settled farther west, near Fort Robinson.

During 1878–79 Middleton's gang stole about 3,000 horses, which they sold in Nebraska, Dakota, Iowa, Wyoming, and Colorado. Though they took horses from settlers along the Niobrara and Elkhorn Rivers, they also assisted some of those people. On occasion they gave a horse to someone in need, and they paid settlers in cash for food and lodging. In the tradition of Robin Hood, Middleton and his gang of thieves stole from some but helped others, often the poor settlers who had little. That earned them a circle of friends and protectors. When authorities made any attempt to stop the rustling, Middleton usually had a tip from a friend so he could escape.

Like the stories associated with many western figures, the Middleton tale grew with each telling, so it is now difficult to tell fact from fiction. According to one story in the book of Middleton legend and lore, he once found an immigrant family stranded by the trail and, learning that their horse had died, gave them a horse. This incident happened near O'Neill, or Long Pine, or in western Nebraska—take your pick. Another time he and a cowboy companion supposedly rescued a mother and baby from drowning in the North Platte River.

Middleton charmed the ladies by bringing them thread and other incidental items. He was good on the dance floor and could saw a fiddle better than anybody in the Sandhills. One Sandhills resident recalled that Middleton "had many, many friends and was generally well liked because of his good deeds, especially among the ladies." At dances his Montana boots had a bright shine, and his corduroy trousers and fancy shirts were neat and clean.

Middleton had had a wife in Texas, but he was single again on May 28, 1879, when he eloped with eighteen-year-old Mary Richardson. She swore she'd stand behind him, no matter what happened. But in July 1879 William Henry Harrison Llewellyn broke up the happy marriage when he arrested Middleton in a raid at Wyman Creek.

Doc went to prison to serve an eighteen-year sentence, and two years later Mary "divorced" him, although there is no legal documentation of the divorce. She then "married" Sam Morris. Doc served less than four years and was a model prisoner the entire time. He walked free from the Nebraska penitentiary on June 18, 1883, and went to

Colorado. Not quite a year later Middleton was back in the Sandhills country, where he married Rene Richardson on June 1, 1884. She was the younger sister of his second wife. On July 3, 1884, The *Fremont Daily Herald* reported: "Doc Middleton and bride returned to O'Neill last week. A grand ball was given in the evening in honor of the arrival of the distinguished couple. Let him steal a few more horses and they will want to send him to Congress."

After his period of incarceration in Nebraska, Middleton did mend his ways. He and Rene eventually settled in Gordon, where Middleton operated a saloon and gambling parlor. He traveled extensively, engaging in gambling at various locations. He even worked for a time as a deputy sheriff in Gordon. Middleton filed on a homestead but sold it before proving up. By 1893 Middleton and Rene had moved to Chadron.

That year a newspaper promoter launched the idea of a horse race from Chadron to Chicago. John G. Maher had become a correspondent for several Eastern newspapers, generally writing half-truths and downright fiction in his dispatches. The story of the horse race started as a fabrication—there were no plans for such an event—but when interest in the idea grew, it became a reality. Buffalo Bill Cody put up some prize money, and Chadron promoters added more. Although Middleton was a favored contender in the race, he didn't win. The headlines Middleton garnered during that race were among the last of his illustrious career.

He and Rene had five children. From Chadron they moved to South Dakota, spending many years in Ardmore, where he operated a saloon. By 1913 Middleton had moved to Douglas, Wyoming, where he operated a saloon at nearby Orin. When one-armed sheepherder H. L. Plunkett stabbed George Spencer while they were in the tavern, they were arrested, and so was Middleton—for selling whiskey illegally. He pleaded guilty to the charge and was fined $150 plus costs amounting to about $50. But Doc didn't have the money to pay the bond and ended up in jail, where he became ill with erysipelas and pneumonia. He died December 27, 1913, and is buried in an unmarked grave in Douglas Park Cemetery.

Outlaw Kid Wade

While Doc Middleton may have been the most well-known outlaw to use the Nebraska Sandhills as a base of operations, Albert "Kid" Wade runs a close second in prominence. Wade was a rustler, gambler, and outlaw gang leader of the Pony Boys. Wade took over much of Middleton's territory after Doc landed in the penitentiary in 1879. Wade

Settlers stage taking the law into their own hands in this 1885 reenactment.
—Nebraska State Historical Society, Solomon D. Butcher Collection

first crossed the law by stealing a horse in Iowa in 1880 and spent a year in prison there before heading west to Nebraska, where he continued stealing horses.

Authorities—and, more important, vigilantes—soon had him labeled as a leader of the outlaws. In January 1884 vigilantes had word of a couple of missing horses, likely taken by Wade and his accomplices, Henry Brockman and Frank Ellison. Those two didn't provide any information about Wade, however, so the vigilantes continued searching and eventually nabbed Jim Smith, whom they heard knew where to find Wade. Smith at first refused to cooperate, but when he realized the vigilantes intended to hang him, he squealed and told them to look for the Kid in Le Mars, Iowa.

Before long the vigilantes had Wade in custody. They first took him to Long Pine because residents there had given the vigilantes a cash contribution to help with their search for the outlaw. Eventually they intended to return Wade to Holt County to stand trial. The story goes that Wade provided the vigilantes with quite a lot of detail about his outlaw escapades and that much of it implicated prominent people.

It's not entirely clear how Wade ended up in Bassett, but he was taken there and kept under guard, either in the Martin Hotel or in an old store building. About midnight February 7, 1884, masked men stormed the location and took Wade to the whistle signal post along the railroad just east of town, where they hanged him.

AINSWORTH

Ainsworth, named for Missouri Valley Railroad construction engineer J. E. Ainsworth, is in the Bone Creek Valley, so called because once there were thousands of buffalo and cattle skeletons scattered toward the pine-covered canyons of Plum and Pine Creeks and the Niobrara River to the north. This region is also replete with fossilized remains of camels, rhinoceroses, mammoths, and prehistoric horses.

John Berry drove the mail and stagecoaches from Fort Niobrara to the area of his homestead, the future site of Johnstown, which is named for him. Berry earned recognition in 1893 when he won the 1,000-mile race from Chadron to Chicago during the World's Fair.

WOOD LAKE

A lake surrounded by cottonwood trees gave its name to this community, originally known as Cottonwood Lake. By 1882 the railroad had reached the area, making Wood Lake the oldest town site in Cherry County. Originally little more than a railroad section house and depot, the town soon had a store operated by Charles A. Johnson and Washington Hone, and a post office gave a sense of real community to the small gathering of homes and businesses. By November 1883 a school had opened, and a bank was established three years later. Eventually the community had three banks, two cafes, a meat market, a livery barn, a blacksmith shop, two lumberyards, and several other businesses.

Wood Lake's location helped it become the major trade center for miles around. The steep hills of the Niobrara River country formed a formidable barrier to cattlemen. As a result, they took their herds to the railhead at Wood Lake, and it became the largest cattle-shipping station on the Chicago & Northwestern Railroad. Ranchers crowded the railroad siding with freight wagons as they met incoming trains to pick up supplies.

Among the earliest settlers in the Wood Lake vicinity were a number of Germans, who built sod houses and farmed the fragile though fertile soils. While they had little in the way of money, they raised good crops, in part because the region received abundant rainfall in the 1880s.

Dozens of men from this area served in the Home Guard during World War I, and local residents raised $110,050 for the Red Cross, putting Cherry County $94,000 over its quota. The advent of better

An unusual two-story sod and wood homestead. —Nebraska State Historical Society, Solomon D. Butcher Collection

highways and modern vehicles reduced travel time to other areas and restricted Wood Lake's purpose as a supply center. By 1980 the community had eighty residents, a service station, a bar and cafe, two churches, a school, a post office, a rural fire department, a Masonic Lodge, and a small grocery.

A number of other small communities grew up in Cherry County during the 1880s, including Goose Creek, about twenty-five miles southwest of Wood Lake. One of the most destructive prairie fires of the region occurred in the Goose Creek valley March 3, 1943. The blaze raced before high winds, traveling about twenty-five miles before firefighters contained it. The firefighters included men, women, high school students, and soldiers from the army air base at Ainsworth. The fire reduced more than 5,000 tons of hay to ashes and burned one barn, but it damaged no houses and caused no injuries. As the firefighters controlled the blaze in the evening, they started toward their homes and "beheld a scene which will remain in their memories during the rest of their lives," Charles S. Reece wrote in *Early History of Cherry County*. "From places of elevation they could see the 1,000 stacks of hay still burning. In the darkness they lighted up the valley for many miles. It made a weird and beautiful sight, reminding one of the lights of a great city."

Scene on the Middle Loup River. —Nebraska State Historical Society, Solomon D. Butcher Collection

Other Cherry County communities included Cascade, on the north bank of the Loup River; Purdum, located downstream from Cascade; and Brownlee, also located on the Loup. When a number of families moved in to an area between the Middle and North Loup Rivers from Virginia, their town became known as The Virginia Settlement.

De Witty Colony, located northeast of Brownlee and fifteen miles west on the Loup, became known as the Colored Settlement. Clem Deaver claimed the first Kinkaid homestead in 1904; by 1912 seventy-nine African Americans had homesteads in the area. The community soon had a school, church, and post office. The Depression-era drought took a heavy toll on De Witty Colony, and by 1945 the homesteaders had relinquished their claims.

Cherry County Namesake

On May 11, 1881, 2nd Lt. Samuel A. Cherry led a detachment of troops on a mission to track down three robbers, or perhaps three army deserters who had taken some government horses with them. When Cherry and his men caught up with the three, a fight ensued, resulting in the death of the lieutenant, at the hand of Pvt. Thomas W. Locke. The military returned Locke to Fort Niobrara, where he was convicted of murder and sentenced to eighteen years in prison.

The first settlement in Cherry County took place a few years earlier, in 1878, when the government moved the Rosebud Sioux tribe to its reservation in South Dakota, which borders the county and Nebraska on the north. As part of the Indian relocation, the government needed to provide the tribe with beef, so large numbers of cattle moved into Cherry County. One of the first herds came from Dodge City, Kansas, driven by A. J. Abbott and other cowboys. The area's natural grasslands made it an excellent place to raise cattle, and before long large herds used the open range.

Relations between the cowboys and the Sioux were not always peaceful. One altercation took place May 6, 1879, when James Williamson, a twenty-six-year-old cowboy, and Felix James, both riding for the McCann Ranch, assisted on a horse gather along the Snake River and Boardman Creek. Williams changed mounts just before they reached Steer Creek, but his new animal wasn't in good condition, and soon after he switched horses a party of Indians appeared on the scene. They chased Williamson and James, and the former lost the race and his life. James, meanwhile, reached safety at the ranch, where he organized a rescue party to search for Williamson. They arrived too late to save the cowboy, and the Sioux had fled the scene.

Cherry County, the largest in Nebraska, is 96 miles long and 63 miles wide, for a total area of 6,048 square miles. It is larger than Delaware and Rhode Island combined. Charles S. Reece wrote in *An Early History of Cherry County*: "It could devote a space the size of the state of Connecticut to meadows and summer pastures and still have as many acres for winter range as the greater part of Rhode Island."

The 1895 cattle population of Cherry County numbered 56,327, but by 1905 the county only had 14,324 head of cattle, the decline coming in part due to general economic downturns, particularly after the drought of 1893. On March 14, 1913, a severe blizzard struck the area, killing hundreds of head of livestock, many of which wandered into lakes and drowned or froze to death. By 1915 ranchers reported only 12,815 head of cattle to agricultural census takers, but ranchers quickly increased their herds and a decade later the region had 187,225 animals, and by 1935 the region boasted 210,262 head of cattle despite of a severe drought in 1934 that forced some ranchers to cull herds by selling some animals.

The 1934 drought left a hay crop only 10 to 50 percent the size of a normal one, and prices plummeted as the country fell into the Great Depression. The federal government tried to relieve the crisis by purchasing a large number of animals, paying $8 for calves, $12 for

Sioux Chief Sitting Bull.
—Wyoming State Museum

A Custer County farm. —Nebraska State Historical Society, Solomon D.
Butcher Collection

yearlings, and $20 for cows. The government buyout served two purposes: It allowed ranchers to reduce the size of their herds to numbers that could be fed adequately, and it helped them dispose of old and inferior animals. In Cherry County alone, 25,605 cattle were sold to the government for a total of $388,764, an average of $15.18 each. The meat obtained by the government under the program was processed by packing companies and distributed to areas heavily affected by the drought. In some areas of the West beef couldn't be processed efficiently, so cattle purchased under the government plan were shot and the meat destroyed.

VALENTINE

The arched cantilever truss bridge located just east of Valentine on US 20 is connected in the center with a single pin. It is the only bridge of its kind in the United States. Josef Sorkin, who immigrated from Russia in 1923 and graduated from the University of Nebraska College of Engineering in 1929, designed the bridge, which is 289 feet long and has a 24-foot-wide roadway. It cost $55,564 when built by the Department of Public Works in 1932. The American Institute of Steel Construction selected the Bryan Bridge as the "Most Beautiful Steel Bridge of 1932 in Class C," the first bridge between Wisconsin and the Pacific Coast to receive such an award. In 1988 the bridge was listed on the National Register of Historic Places, and in 1995 the Nebraska Section of the American Society of Civil Engineers designated it a State Historic Civil Engineering Landmark. That same year work started on a new bridge across the Niobrara.

From its modest beginnings as a cow town in 1882, Valentine, named for congressman E. K. Valentine, has become one of the most prominent towns in north-central Nebraska. It sits on the homestead tract originally claimed by railroad surveyor D. Y. Mears, who became postmaster when the Postal Service established an office December 4, 1882.

Today the Niobrara River provides all types of water recreation for local residents, who particularly like floating down the slow-moving stream on inner tubes during hot summer days. However, early residents had trouble dealing with the region's the lack of water. For the first seven years of its existence the community got its water from a spring on Minnechaduza Creek. A "water man" made daily trips to the spring with a water wagon, filling each citizen's barrel for a 25-cent fee. In 1889 the community built an elevated wooden tank, with water pumped from Minnechaduza Creek. Although that system never worked well, it remained in effect until 1928, when the community drilled a

Lake Minnechaduza near Valentine, a recreation spot in summer and a place to harvest ice in the winter. —Nebraska State Historical Society

deep water well. A local flour miller dammed Minnechaduza Creek in 1892, creating Lake Minnechaduza.

Lake Minnechaduza served another important need from the mid-1890s to 1936: ice harvests took place each winter. The Chicago & Northwestern Railroad, which reached Valentine in 1883, instituted the ice harvest and built a 1,000-foot ice chute from the lake to a storage building and the railroad track. Workers loaded an average of twenty-five railroad cars daily, each car holding twenty-five tons of ice. The final ice harvest took place during the winter of 1935–36, with Bill Roe in charge of seventy men using twenty-three teams and wagons to haul the ice. The pay: 35 cents per hour for each man and 15 cents a ton for each team. The greatest production occurred in 1909, when crews harvested 10,000 tons of ice from Lake Minnechaduza.

Valentine was the end of the railroad until 1885, when the line was extended into South Dakota and eventually into Wyoming. During the early 1880s Valentine received between 3,500 and 5,000 tons of supplies for distribution on the nearby Rosebud Sioux Indian Reservation.

While the railroad was being constructed, Valentine had a reputation as a rough-and-ready town. Saloons outnumbered stores, and the Hog Ranche just outside town drew cowboys from Nebraska, Wyoming, and South Dakota, who sought a bit of pleasure. Such establishments sprang up near most military installations (and other towns as well) during the frontier period. They catered to the lusty desires of men stationed at the various forts and usually dispensed liquor, which was banned from sale at military posts by President Rutherford Hayes in February 1881.

The stories of shootings, fights, brawls, and other altercations at the Valentine Hog Ranche grow with each telling. One involved Cherry County Sheriff Johnny Key and a friend of his, Sam Earnest. The two were at the Hog Ranche when a group of Wyoming cowboys from the OW Ranch near Manville arrived. One of the cowboys, Clarence Hand, held a grudge against either Earnest or the sheriff. During the afternoon they had one minor tiff, but then the Wyoming boys left. Key and Earnest remained at the Hog Ranche, expecting no more trouble. But while Key relaxed in the arms of one of the women, the cowboys returned, threatening to ride their horses into the saloon.

The bartender loudly protested, but that didn't stop the OW hands. The first cowboy attempting to ride into the saloon fell with a bullet from Key's gun in his body, and the other cowboys bailed from their mounts and took up defensive positions around the building. Key quickly assessed the odds and, knowing he was no match for so many guns, slipped out the back door and disappeared.

Townspeople soon armed themselves, closed all the businesses, and prepared for an all-out assault, certain the cowboys would quickly avenge the death of their partner. The next morning Key turned himself in and was arrested, but a subsequent coroner's jury ruled he had shot the cowboy—who turned out to be the troublemaker Clarence Hand—in self-defense. It never became entirely clear what precipitated the problem in the first place.

The railroad operated as the Sioux City & Pacific until 1885, when it became the Fremont, Elkhorn & Missouri Valley Railroad for a two-year period. In 1887 it became part of the Chicago & Northwestern system, which operated it for the next century. The C&NW discontinued passenger service in 1958 and made its last freight run in November 1992; by 1994 work had begun on the dismantling of the abandoned rail line. The right-of-way is now a hiking, biking, equestrian route known as The Cowboy Trail.

One of the most exciting days in Valentine history occurred during the presidential campaign of 1944. Republican candidate Thomas E. Dewey came to town September 13 at the invitation of former Nebraska governor S. R. McKelvie, campaign manager for the western states. McKelvie owned the By the Way Ranch, where he hosted a barbecue. The following year the Metro-Goldwyn-Mayer Company used the ranch as a location for their feature film *The Sea of Grass*, which included a large number of local residents as cast extras.

Fort Niobrara

After 1878 the U.S. government had confined most western Indian tribes to reservations and the military had implemented a new policy of locating forts and posts nearby. When the Spotted Tail Agency relocated in south-central South Dakota, settlers feared the Indians might go on raids off the reservation. The military responded to the concern by agreeing to built a post to guard the Rosebud Reservation and provide security for settlers and cattle ranchers. On June 23, 1879, Congress appropriated $50,000 for the post, with Gen. George Crook to select the site. He chose a location south of Spotted Tail Agency on a broad plain south of the Niobrara River. Troops from Companies, B, C, and F of the 5th Cavalry and Company B of the 9th Infantry arrived and started construction of the fort's adobe buildings on April 22, 1880. The soldiers used locally available clay for the adobe bricks. The fort protected settlers and provided markets for cordwood, hay, grain, poultry, and dairy produce. Some women of the area laundered clothes for the soldiers to make extra income, and area settlers received an added bonus when soldiers sold their military-issue clothing to residents at extremely low rates.

A large ox team fording the Niobrara River. —Nebraska State Historical Society

Mail and supplies for the fort came in from Neligh, more than 150 miles to the east, which was the end of the railroad line at that time. George Jewett's bull train handled the chief freighting duties. The train consisted of from ten to twenty teams made up of a dozen yoke of oxen each. A stage line also operated between Neligh and Fort Niobrara. The railroad moved west during subsequent years, reaching O'Neill in 1881 and advancing to within six miles of Fort Niobrara by 1883. The military reserve initially encompassed a ten-square-mile area, but in 1881 officials enlarged it to fifty-five square miles in order to add a timber and wood reserve for the post. From 1880 to 1885 between two hundred and three hundred members of the 5th Cavalry and the 4th and 9th Infantry served at Fort Niobrara. Cavalry troops scouted the surrounding region for potential trouble, while the infantry soldiers served as guards and escorts for freight haulers.

Black cavalrymen and white infantrymen served at Fort Niobrara from 1885 to 1890, and few problems arose during the period, although occasionally members of the black 9th Cavalry had disagreements among themselves. The Valentine *Democratic Blade* on December 1, 1887, reported: "Too great credit cannot be given [Bvt.] General [August V.] Kautz and the officers and men of his command for the gentlemanly and soldierly way they have treated the people of Valentine and its surroundings. Upon every hand is said that the soldiers of the 8th Infantry and the 9th Cavalry are all that could be deserved as soldiers for the protection of the people hereabouts. Race or color does not enter here." That report is particularly interesting because that year a mob hanged a black civilian, who had given his name as Jerry White, after he reportedly attacked and raped a white woman.

In the late 1880s a major duty of Fort Niobrara troops involved moving supplies and beef from the post to the Rosebud Agency. Troops had little in the way of excitement, and they spent much of their time on scheduled practice marches and in field training exercises, perhaps wondering if they'd have any need for the instruction. By the summer of 1890, though, things started to change, as Sioux living at the Rosebud Agency and farther west at Pine Ridge became involved in the Ghost Dance movement. Settlers in the area expressed fear that the Indians would revolt and launch full-scale attacks. The concern mounted, and troops from Fort Niobrara became involved in the "Sioux Campaign" of 1890, which culminated with the killing of Sioux at Wounded Knee, South Dakota, on December 29, 1890.

That confrontation, known as the Wounded Knee Massacre by white people and as the Chief Big Foot Massacre by Native Americans, is generally regarded as the last major bloody fight between the

U.S. Army and Indians. It broke the fighting spirit of the Sioux for good; by April 1891, when military officials from Fort Niobrara went to the Rosebud Reservation, they were able to recruit men to serve in Troop L of the 6th Cavalry. The goal of the troop: to become a bridge between cultures.

Buffalo soldiers also served at Fort Niobrara. Those black soldiers became a part of the regular army as the 9th and 10th U.S. Cavalry and the 24th and 25th Infantry Regiments. The 9th Cavalry Regiment served at Fort Niobrara in the 1880s and again in 1902 after a difficult tropical campaign in the Philippines. The government abandoned Fort Niobrara October 22, 1906, retaining a 16,000-acre tract of land as a preserve for buffalo, elk, deer, antelope, and Texas longhorn cattle. The remainder of the military reservation later opened for homesteading, with a drawing in Valentine to determine who would get the land. Special trains brought in thousands of land seekers, and between October 13 and October 26, 1913, more than 20,000 people entered the homestead land drawing.

Once the military abandoned the fort, President Theodore Roosevelt placed the reserved land under the U.S. Department of Agriculture to be used as a wildlife refuge and breeding ground for native birds. In 1912 that facility expanded its scope when J. W. Gilbert donated his private herds of deer, bison, and elk. Valentine residents helped fence the land, and in 1913 the animals moved to their new range. The refuge now maintains a herd of about 225 buffalo and 275 Texas longhorns. Because these are breeding herds, Fort Niobrara National Wildlife Refuge sells the excess animals each year.

Valentine National Wildlife Refuge

The Valentine National Wildlife Refuge, located south of Valentine adjacent to US 83, developed during 1932 and 1933 when the U.S. Fish & Wildlife Service purchased about 70,000 acres of land in Cherry County. The Civilian Conservation Corps in 1935 brought in some 200 workers to begin refuge development. They camped on the west end of Hackberry Lake. The work program included 125 miles of five-strand barbed-wire fence, roads and trails to provide access to major lakes, and artificial potholes to serve as potential nesting sites for waterfowl and to collect water during dry seasons.

The CCC workers planted shrubs and fruit-bearing trees to increase the food supply and improve cover conditions for upland game and songbirds. They abandoned their CCC camp October 1, 1939, but Works Progress Administration projects in 1938 and 1940 augmented development work on the refuge. During World War II bomber

crews used certain portions of the refuge as practice ranges to prepare for combat duty.

CROOKSTON

Taking its name from W. T. Crook, yard master for the Northwest
Railroad in Valentine, Crookston incorporated as a village on April
21, 1890. Minnechaduza Creek flows past the town, and the railroad
already existed, so soon the community flourished. Much of the business for the town store, owned by F. H. Baumgartel and Max E. Virtel,
came from Indians living on the Rosebud Reservation. Minnechaduza
is an Indian word meaning "murmuring water."

When a large number of Germans moved in 1883 to the area
between Crookston and Kilgore, their village soon became The German Settlement. By 1889 a broom factory operated in the town, using
broom corn as the main source material for the final product. Post
offices established in the area went by the names McCann and Reige,
with mail carried from Valentine for distribution.

Crookston made headlines on October 23, 1928, when two eastbound cattle trains left town about fifteen minutes apart. Some three
miles west of town the lead train uncoupled, so engineers stopped to
reattach the cars to the engine. While they attempted to do that,
however, the other train slammed into the halted cars, killing cattle
buyers T. J. Harris and W. J. Mansfield and about sixty-five head of
cattle. A fire broke out, further damaging the two trains. The following
morning some 200 residents of the Rosebud Sioux Reservation came
to the site, where they butchered the animals that had died.

KILGORE

Residents of Kilgore had a tough time deciding on a name for the
community. First it was Boulware, for original postmaster Ira Boulware;
then it became Georgia; and finally it received the moniker Kilgore
for early residents Scott and Columbus Kilgore, the first section fore-
men for the railroad in the region, and their sister Alice, a pioneer
schoolteacher.

NENZEL

In 1885 George Nenzel homesteaded thirty miles west of Valentine. He built a frame building that served as a store, post office, hotel,
and living quarters for his family. On June 23, 1899, the community
officially incorporated as Nenzel. By then the founder had become the
postmaster and had built the first school. The town had no water supply

initially, so settlers packed in water from nearby ranches, some located up to a dozen miles away, or from the Niobrara River. In 1886 Nenzel and his sons dug a deep well on their homestead, and soon other residents also dug wells.

The Niobrara Division of the Nebraska National Forest is near Nenzel. Although the larger nurseries are in the Bessey Division, near Halsey (see page 263), this forest division has more than 115,000 acres along the Niobrara River. The forest has windmills and tool caches spread throughout the region for use in fighting fires, and in the 1930s spotters in a lookout tower in the western corner of the division guarded the trees.

CODY

Although some assume that this community gets its name from that famous frontiersman Buffalo Bill Cody, it actually comes from a more obscure fellow, Thomas Cody, who was foreman of the water supply crew when the railroad was built through this area. The town was established with the coming of the railroad in 1885 and represented the end of the line for many years, giving it a distinct advantage over neighboring villages. It became an officially incorporated town on November 5, 1886, and served as a trading post for the Rosebud Indian Agency in South Dakota.

MERRIMAN

Settlers of Merriman, like those in other nearby communities, felt great fear in 1890 as word of an Indian uprising spread throughout northern Nebraska. When told the Indians were on their way to burn the town, residents decided to evacuate. They congregated at the railroad station watching for the train's belching smoke. But when the train chugged into the station it was so overloaded it didn't even stop at Merriman. The scared residents grimly returned to their homes and prepared to defend themselves from an attack. But the Indians failed to arrive; the worry and defense preparations had been unnecessary.

Arthur Bowring Sandhills Ranch

Henry C. Bowring laid railroad track across Iowa and South Dakota before claiming a homestead near Gordon in 1885. He and his wife, Jane, had a large family, and in 1894 their seventh son, Arthur, claimed a 160-acre homestead near Merriman. He later added a 480-acre Kinkaid tract, purchased other land from the government, and added even more from his family, which had claimed land nearby. Bowring expanded his holdings to 7,200 acres and started raising Shorthorn cattle, eventually switching to the more popular Herefords.

The old sod house at the Arthur Bowring ranch near Merriman.

In 1908 Arthur Bowring married Anna May Holbrook, who had been teaching at the local school. A year later she died in childbirth. Not until 1928 did Arthur take another bride, marrying Eve Kelly Forester. Born in Missouri, Eve had already been married once, had divorced, and had four sons, one of whom died in infancy. By 1924 she was living with her boys in Lincoln. She started working for the Norfolk Steam Bakery as a traveling saleswoman and covered a large area, extending as far west as Merriman. While on the job one day, she had trouble with her automobile and drew the attention of Arthur Bowring.

They married and together they increased the size of the ranch to 12,000 acres. Although Eve Bowring once said all she knew about ranching she had learned from Zane Grey novels, by the time Arthur Bowring died in 1944 she had enough knowledge to manage the ranch herself, which she did until 1985.

Both Arthur and Eve gave many years of public service. He was a state legislator, member of the school board and county commission, and a deputy of the Nebraska Game and Fish Commission, among other duties. He also was a member and officer of the Nebraska Good Roads Association, one priority of which was to build better farm-to-market roads. In the state legislature Bowring called for doubling the

Eve Bowring Visitors Center on the Bowring Sandhills Ranch at Merriman.

gasoline tax from two to four cents, with the proceeds to be used for road improvements. In 1929 he introduced legislation creating the first Nebraska driver's license. The lifetime permit cost a dollar, including a 25-cent processing fee for the county clerk.

When Arthur Bowring died in 1944, newspaper editors remarked on his work to improve roads in Nebraska, particularly US 20, which they called a monument to him.

Eve, meanwhile, served in various offices of the Nebraska Republican Party and was a member of the National Institute of Health and the U.S. Board of Parole. But she is most remembered for the inroads she made for women in Nebraska when Governor Robert B. Crosby appointed her to fill a vacant seat in the U.S. Senate in April 1954. Upon arrival in Washington, Senator Bowring told the press she would "ride the fences a while until I learn where the gates are."

Eve Bowring was a remarkable woman, and as she neared the end of her life she wanted to preserve the ranch she and Arthur had built. She outlived her husband and her three sons and didn't want to see the ranch divided among her family, which had no relationship to Arthur. Further, such a ranch division would fragment the holdings. So Eve Bowring made arrangements to donate the Bar 99 Ranch to the Nebraska Game and Parks Foundation. She had only three stipulations: That the county receive annual tax payments, that her private collections be kept intact, and that the Hereford cattle herd be retained so the ranch could function as a living history museum. She wanted to help support the county and give visitors a glimpse of what an early-twentieth-century ranch looked like.

The Arthur Bowring Sandhills Ranch State Historical Park now documents the cattle industry in Nebraska with displays related to the history and geology of the Sandhills as well as the cattle business. The Eve Bowring Center focuses attention on life in the Sandhills through exhibits related to farm equipment, windmills, barbed wire, road ranches in Nebraska, and the cattle barons of the region.

Niobrara—Valentine
142 miles

The northernmost route across the state, Nebraska 12, runs between the Missouri and Keya Paha Rivers from Niobrara to Monowi, travels along the Keya Paha to Mills, angles toward the Niobrara River valley, and follows it to Valentine. Just west of Niobrara the highway provides access to Niobrara State Park and closely follows the Lewis and Clark Trail just before the explorers' route leaves Nebraska north of Lynch and Bristow. It is a stunning hill-country drive. Boyd County residents overwhelmingly defeated a proposal in 1992 to create a five-state nuclear waste dump in this area. Evidence of the campaign remained in 1995 in the form of signs on abandoned buildings, fence posts, and even trees blaring, "No Dump!"

Nebraska 12 follows the north bank of the Keya Paha River through Bristow, Spencer, Butte, and Naper, then crosses to the south bank and continues to Mills. From there the highway remains on high benchland, with periodic roadside rest stops, and provides access to Burton and Springview, the Keya Paha County seat and the main trading center in north-central Nebraska.

After the death of Mormon leader Joseph Smith, a party of sixty-five Mormon families headed out of Nauvoo, Illinois, in 1846 and formed a camp at the Missouri River. An advance party of 150 wagons continued west but stopped at Pawnee Station (now Columbus, Nebraska) and prepared to raise small amounts of grain and corn as part of a government contract. While they were there, new Mormon leader Brigham Young sent word that they shouldn't continue west but instead should develop a winter camp. A band of Poncas who were visiting the Pawnees told the Mormons of a good site to the north, between present-day Niobrara and Monowi. The Mormon party made their way north and stopped along the banks of the Missouri River. They spent the winter under harsh conditions, and some seventeen members of the party died before spring flowers bloomed. Then Young called the advance travelers to return to the main camp on the Missouri, and from there he led them to the Great Salt Lake Valley (see page 64).

Monowi means "flower" and perhaps represents a type of spurge known as snow-on-the-mountain. The town reportedly received the name because there are so many wildflowers in the area.

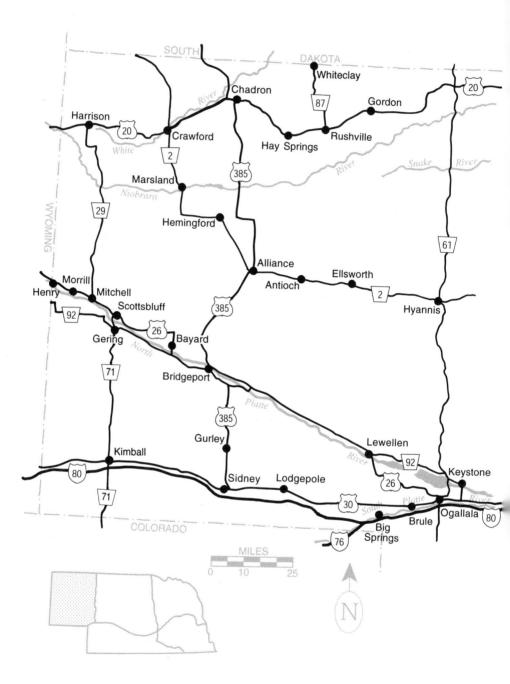

SOUTH DAKOTA

Whiteclay

Chadron

87

Gordon

20

Harrison

20

Crawford

Rushville

Hay Springs

White River

2

385

Marsland

Niobrara River

Snake River

29

Hemingford

WYOMING

Alliance

Ellsworth

Morrill

Antioch

2

Henry

Mitchell

Scottsbluff

Hyannis

92

385

61

26

Gering

Bayard

North

71

Bridgeport

Platte

385

Gurley

Lewellen

Kimball

92

Keystone

80

Sidney

Lodgepole

26

Ogallala

71

30

South Platte River

80

COLORADO

Brule

Big
Springs

76

MILES

0   10   25

N

PART 5
PANHANDLE COUNTRY

THE PRAIRIES OF NEBRASKA METAMORPHOSE into the high plains of the Rocky Mountains in the panhandle; the grass-covered Sandhills on the east give way to sagebrush-covered hills and breaks to the west.

In its earliest days this land was the home of the Gatakas or Kiowa Apaches and later of the Cheyennes and Sioux. The tribes gathered annually along the Moonshell River, as the Lakota called the North Platte. Their summer powwow became the first rendezvous of the region. The bluffs and breaks sheltered the Sioux from their enemies: the Pawnees, who ranged northwest from their lands along the Republican and Platte Rivers, and the Crows, who came from the northwest. Some of the greatest Indian battles in Nebraska occurred in the Panhandle Country. The Sioux and Pawnee warriors fought many battles along the Moonshell near the site of a later horrific encounter between the Sioux and the U.S. Army in the vicinity of Blue Water Creek. The Sioux and Crows raged against each other farther north, along the White River.

Although military-Indian conflicts in present-day Nebraska were less numerous and less significant than the battles fought in Wyoming and Montana, this region witnessed a cataclysmic event for the Sioux. Here the government forced them to live on reservations and to accept their first handouts, at Red Cloud and Spotted Tail Agencies. And here their greatest leader died: Crazy Horse.

Most of the mountain fur trade occurred much farther west. However, high up in Nebraska's northwest corner, along the White and Niobrara Rivers, trappers worked the streams for beaver from the early 1820s until the mid-1840s.

Robert Stuart and six companions headed toward St. Louis from Astoria, Oregon, in 1812–13 and camped along the Platte for part of the winter. When another early explorer, Hiram Scott, died near a large bluff in 1828, it took his name. Fur traders established supply posts, which served mountain men and Indians and, much later, the emigrants traveling the Platte River road to Oregon or California.

When gold was discovered in the Black Hills in 1874–75, prospectors raced for the area by the most direct routes possible. Cheyenne, Wyoming, became the earliest provisioning and jumping-off point for the Black Hills, primarily because in 1875 the U.S. Army built an iron bridge across the North Platte River near Fort Laramie. However, when a new bridge went in not far from Courthouse and Jail Rocks near present-day Bridgeport, the miners traveled directly north from the railhead at Sidney to Deadwood, South Dakota.

At one time much of present-day Wyoming was part of Nebraska, and the panhandle of Nebraska could just as easily have become a leg of Wyoming. Today the farmers of this region share the North Platte River water with Wyoming's growers, and the politics of that water have grown contentious. The farmers can't bear watching corn or sugar beets wither from lack of irrigation water as they listen to state officials argue about water rights.

The Oregon Trail travelers who cut through this country after 1843 called the panhandle region, particularly the land near Scotts Bluff, the Valley of Monuments because of the strange and distinctive natural rock formations. After weeks on the prairies, they welcomed the diversity of the landscape, particularly the trees at the bottom of Ash Hollow, the breaks of the Wild Cat Hills, the distinctive shapes of Courthouse and Chimney Rocks. Others remarked on the strange conglomerations of Toadstool Park. Short buffalo grasses wave in green splendor in early spring and summer and wither to a golden glow by fall; yucca and cactus bloom in the spring before fading.

For our exploration of Panhandle Country we will travel from east to west, as the emigrants did, and from south to north, as the miners did.

I-80 AND US 30
Ogallala—Wyoming Border
126 miles

Two highways and a railroad line mark the southern boundary of Panhandle Country. Interstate 80 and US 30 both cross the gently rolling land between Ogallala and the Nebraska-Wyoming state line. The two highways are usually visible from each other. US 30 provides the slower

Pioneers faced many difficulties when traveling the emigrant routes to Oregon or California, such as the prairie windstorm depicted here.
—Nebraska State Historical Society

glimpse of the terrain; I-80 is the fast way through. Nebraska was the first state on the interstate route to complete its section of highway that now stretches from coast to coast. A gold-colored metal bar across the highway between Kimball and Sidney, known as the "Golden Bar," calls that fact to the attention of drivers. The "Golden Bar" is immediately north of a highway rest area on the eastbound lane of I-80.

BRULE

Gold seekers on their way to California's diggings in 1849 wanted to reach their destination as quickly as they could, so many of them used mules to pull wagons. Not only did the mules make much better time than the oxen so common on emigrant trains, they also got by with less forage, so the gold rushers could travel earlier in the spring and spend more hours per day on the trail. Although many emigrants continued along the south bank of the South Platte River until they reached Julesburg, most of the 49ers crossed the river either at North Platte or a mile west of present-day Brule, at a spot known as the Upper Crossing or the Old California Crossing. The travelers then struck a line almost due north. Pulling out of the South Platte River bottoms, the emigrants first faced steep, cactus-covered California Hill. Once they topped the rise they had a dry run across present-day Deuel County to Ash Hollow, where they struck the North Platte River, which they followed for weeks.

Other emigrants and gold seekers continued along the South Platte to the site of Julesburg, Colorado, then turned northwest, following a line between I-80 and US 30 on the Lodgepole Creek Trail. The Pony Express used the same route. After the various Indian conflicts of 1864–65, that southern route saw heavy traffic as a segment of the Overland Trail, which proceeded due west from Julesburg, entered Wyoming at Virginia Dale, south of present-day Laramie, and continued across the southern portion of Wyoming parallel to the Union Pacific Railroad line and modern-day Interstate 80.

BIG SPRINGS

Nebraska's most famous train robbery took place near Big Springs on September 18, 1877, when Sam Bass and five companions stopped Union Pacific express train No. 4 and grabbed about $60,000 in $20 gold pieces and currency. They captured station agent John Barnhart and destroyed the telegraph, then made their getaway. With Bass at the Big Springs robbery were Joel Collins and Bill Heffridge (both later killed at Buffalo Station, Kansas, west of Hays), Jim Berry (killed near Mexico, Missouri), Tom Nixon (who reportedly went to Canada), and Jack Davis (later whereabouts unknown, although he initially went to Texas).

Bass was in Texas by the fall of 1877, where he teamed with Henry Underwood and Frank Jackson to hold up the stage from Concho and Granbury a few miles west of Fort Worth just four days before Christ-

Railroads provided many opportunities for people of the plains, particularly in serving as freight transportation methods. This scene of the Union Pacific is near Elm Creek. –Nebraska State Historical Society

mas. Then, on January 26, 1878, he and Jackson robbed a westbound coach en route from Fort Worth to Weatherford and Breckenridge. They rode away with four gold watches and some $400 in cash—but they didn't fare so well in their next robbery attempts.

In July the Bass gang headed to Round Rock, Texas, for a bank job. One of the outlaws turned on his companions and tipped lawmen of the plans in an effort to reduce other charges against himself. On July 20, 1878, a day before Bass and the boys planned to make their move on the Round Rock bank, they rode into town for another check of the layout, and the Texas Rangers who'd been laying for them dropped the net. In the gunfight that followed both Bass and compatriot Seaborn Barnes received mortal wounds. Bass didn't die instantly. Frank Jackson helped Bass into the saddle and led his horse out of town through a hail of bullets. After they made their initial escape, Bass insisted Jackson leave him and strike out alone. Lawmen found Bass the next day; he died July 21, 1878. Jackson's fate remains a mystery.

Meanwhile, no permanent settlement occurred at Big Springs until 1883, and it was another year before the Union Pacific Railroad platted the town. It became a main station on the line because the nearby spring was a critical source of water for the trains. In 1885 Sarah Phelps opened the Phelps Hotel. It became the UP station and a travelers' rest spot and now is on the National Register of Historic Places.

West of Big Springs, Union Pacific official John Chappell helped lay out the community that bears his name. The Lodgepole Creek Trail headed northwest from Julesburg, crossing present-day I-80 near the Chappell exchange, then proceeding west to Sidney.

There are few fences around the croplands in this area. Sometimes when the wind blows hard—which it does more than sometimes—the skeletons of plants race before the fury of the gusts. With no fences to slow their run, the tumbleweeds roll and bounce across the prairie; sometimes they are loners and bounce along at a canter, but at other times they gallop across the prairie in great herds, leaping ditches and the highway, bucking and tearing over the landscape.

Dust clouds boil up here partially because this is farming country, the primary wheat-producing region of the state. The growers generally rely on natural moisture, so they plant alternating fields in alternating years. When a field lies fallow, winds can catch the topsoil and fling it about. Some farmers have planted trees around the edges of their fields to mitigate the destructive action of the plains gusts. The highways through this region also have some shelterbelts, with even rows of trees set at angles to I-80. Those natural windbreaks not only slow the breezes but also serve as snow fences.

Wind erosion piled dust into drifts during the Dust Bowl. This scene is near Neligh, 1938. —Nebraska State Historical Society

During the Dust Bowl days of the 1930s, the soil swirled like the tumbleweeds, forming great clouds and turning day to dusk. This is a fickle country. Where one day the tumbleweeds take flight and the soil billows, the next they may lie sluggish under inches or feet of snow. The same soil that swirled over the region in March 1995, closing some highways temporarily for lack of visibility, became saturated by constant rains in April and May. By June, farmers who'd watched the soil sail past just a quarter of a year earlier lamented the fact that they couldn't plant crops because it was too wet in the fields.

LODGEPOLE

Lodgepole gets its name from the Indians' custom of gathering timber for tipi poles along the creek. There was little permanent settlement until the early 1880s. However, a company of U.S. soldiers from nearby Sidney Barracks camped at the spot to guard the railroad against Indian attack, and the Pony Express had a station a few miles to the east.

Developers platted the town in 1884, and within two years the population included 200 people, most of whom raised livestock. The Union Pacific built a depot in 1887 that remained in use until 1968. It now houses the Lodgepole Depot Museum.

SIDNEY

The Lodgepole Creek branch of the Oregon Trail turned north at Sidney, then followed a route now on the west side of US 385 toward Bridgeport. Although the site of Sidney served as a major turning point for the emigrants, the town didn't come into its own until many years after the pioneer era. It is named for Sidney Dillon, a New York attorney who worked for the Union Pacific Railroad. The town developed around Fort Sidney, called Sidney Barracks when it started as a subpost to Fort Sedgwick.

In 1867 Sidney Barracks was a temporary camp with only one permanent structure, a blockhouse to the north. Two years later it relocated to a site at the eastern edge of present Sidney to provide protection for UP crews, and in 1878 Sidney Barracks became Fort Sidney. Troops escorted freighters delivering supplies to the Red Cloud and Spotted Tail Agencies in northwestern Nebraska after 1873, and they protected miners headed to the goldfields in the Black Hills after 1875.

Sidney had a fair share of the traffic to the South Dakota mining camps, so the dance halls, gambling house, and twenty-three saloons in town did a roaring business. Shootings became fairly common occurrences. One story goes that someone was shot during a dance one night. Those present paused long enough to prop the body in the corner. When another fracas broke out, revelers placed a second body near the first. Only when a third shooting claimed a life—and partygoers propped the body beside the two earlier victims—did the party final wither.

Union Pacific Railroad Depot in Sidney, 1906. —Wyoming State Museum, Stimson Collection

*The Cheyenne
County Museum
in the former
officers' quarters
of Fort Sidney,
March 1995.*

In one shooting David C. Middleton killed a soldier from the Sidney Barracks, launching him on an outlaw career and making him a legend in Nebraska as Doc Middleton (see page 288). According to local legend, after Middleton killed his man, he left Sidney on a freight wagon driven by either Frank or Luther North. Whether or not one of the North brothers actually aided Middleton in his escape, Sidney's rough reputation quickly spread, and Union Pacific train crews often warned visitors either to avoid Sidney or to watch their backside if they debarked in the town.

There were occasional incidents involving Native Americans in the area near Fort Sidney, the last of which provided the most drama. In 1878 the Cheyenne under Dull Knife broke from their reservation in Indian Country (now Oklahoma) and staged an epic flight across Kansas and Nebraska to return to their old territory on the northern plains. As the Cheyennes headed north, federal officials kept a special train at Sidney to be rushed either east or west to intercept them when they reached the UP line. On October 4 the train raced to Ogallala, but the Indians eluded authorities and escaped into the Sandhills. Before winter authorities recaptured them in western Nebraska (see page 368). The post at Fort Sidney closed in 1894, and army officials sold the buildings in 1899.

Early in its development Sidney became a regional legal center, the place for landowners to pay their taxes and for lawbreakers to face the courts. In 1884 Frank Abbott noted that about twenty criminals were awaiting trial in Sidney, "all expecting to come clear as usual for lack of evidence." North Platte Judge Gaslin tried the cases and surprised everyone by sentencing the criminals to various jail terms. In later years Sidney became an important cattle trail town and railhead.

Sioux Ordnance Depot

During World War II, a major ordnance depot went in at a location about nine miles northeast of Sidney: the Sioux Ordinance Deputy Fire & Guard Headquarters. The Brownson Viaduct provided access to the site. Designed by the Nebraska Department of Roads and Irrigation, the 352-foot-long, thirteen-span bridge was built of treated timber trestles and cost $30,927. The Defense Highway Act of 1941 directed construction of access roads to defense plants, and the federal Priorities Critical List directed use of materials in highway construction; both affected the planning and design of the Brownson Viaduct. "The defense activities, the declaration of war, the construction of Army and Navy ordnance plants, air bases, satellite airfields, and other defense plants brought about a decided change in the highway program for the past two years," the Bureau of Highways reported in 1942.

Construction crews arrived March 20, 1942, to begin building the Sioux Ordnance Depot, and by December 28, 1942, the $27 million facility had been completed. The depot included several hundred ammunition storage igloos and 300 mobilization buildings. In 1943 a temporary prisoner-of-war camp opened at the Sioux Ordnance Depot. The Department of Defense kept the depot in operation after World War II, eventually closing it June 30, 1967. It now is the location of the Western Nebraska Vocational Technical School.

Home of Cabelas

The Cabelas Sporting Goods store draws people from throughout the region to Sidney. People drive hundreds of miles for the outlet's annual "Garage Sale Day."

Cabelas, which proclaims itself "the World's Foremost Outfitter," got its start at the kitchen table of Chappell residents Dick and Mary Cabela. Dick decided he could turn a profit on flies he had purchased in Chicago, and he ran a newspaper ad in the Casper, Wyoming, newspaper advertising "12 hand-tied flies for $1." Orders started rolling in almost immediately. As Dick and Mary filled those first orders, they included a mimeographed "catalog" of other outdoor products. By the fall of 1962 the Cabelas realized they couldn't keep up with the business themselves and encouraged Dick's younger brother, Jim, to join them in the venture. Cabelas moved three times in the Chappell area before eventually moving permanently to Sidney.

Cabelas Sporting Goods, Sidney.

Keeping up with the company growth was difficult. By 1968, in need of more space, the Cabelas found an opportunity in Sidney when a vacant John Deere building was donated to the local hospital as a tax write-off. The hospital wanted to dispose of the building and sold it to the Cabelas, who remodeled it and opened the retail store, with added room for the ever-expanding catalog business.

By the mid-1980s it became apparent the company needed to expand again, and when a former Rockwell International Plant in Kearney became available, the company bought it and transferred the telemarketing operations there. A full-time staff produces the Cabelas catalogs, which are distributed throughout the United States and to ninety-five foreign countries. In 1991 Cabelas circulated more than 40 million catalogs.

That same year the company opened a new retail store at Sidney designed to "bring the outdoors inside." It features a cathedral ceiling supported by huge pillars covered with Colorado moss rock. Opposite the main entrance is a rock "mountain" with forty life-size mounts, including wolves, bears, cougar, elk, moose, deer, and a variety of game and birds, depicted in their natural habitats. Suspended in the air between the entry and the "mountain" is a flock of sixteen Canada geese. Scattered throughout the 75,000-square-foot building are some 500 other wildlife mounts (polar bear, African elephants and lions, and pheasant) and a large aquarium full of trout, bass, catfish, and other species. Hunters and fishermen know they've reached Cabelas when they see "The Royal Challenge," an elk sculpture created by T. D. Kelsey, of Kiowa, Colorado, which weighs three tons and is sixteen feet tall and thirty-four feet wide.

Sidney—Bridgeport
47 miles

US 385 generally follows the route of the Sidney-Deadwood Trail between Sidney and Bridgeport. About three miles northwest of Sidney, Deadwood Draw formed a natural avenue for wagons pulling out of the Lodgepole Creek valley as they left the Union Pacific railhead at Sidney Barracks. Well-defined trail ruts follow the bottom of the draw and form three parallel lines of what was once part of the Sidney-Deadwood Trail.

In 1874 Lt. Col. George A. Custer led an expeditionary force to the Black Hills, to view the area and locate the site for a fort. In actuality, Custer's objective was to confirm the discovery of gold in the Black Hills; rather than keeping miners and prospectors out of the region, the expedition paved the way for the rush to the hills.

The major impediment to mining activity in the Black Hills centered on the Sioux refusal to sell their territory. In May 1875 the Sioux rejected the first government offer. At a second meeting in September, Red Cloud demanded $600 million plus government annuities to support his people for seven generations. The government offered $6 million plus an additional $400,000 each year as a lease for mining rights. Red Cloud refused, but the government simply announced the "unofficial" opening of the Black Hills to development. By late 1875 the gold rush was under way.

Even before that "opening," fortune seekers had started for the Black Hills. In Fremont, A. M. Blakesley, owner of the Pacific House, made plans for an expedition to the gold camps. The *Omaha Weekly Bee* reported on March 31, 1875: "The route to the Black Hills country is well known to him, and he says he will start from Fremont as soon as there is grass for his mules. He wants company and is making arrangements to supply board and haul baggage for 100 men, which he offers to do for $30 each. . . . Uncle Sam will have his hands full when he undertakes to stop top western miners from hunting gold."

Several communities quickly realized they could profit from the rush to the hills by becoming supply centers: Cheyenne, Wyoming; Yankton, Dakota Territory; Sioux City, Iowa; and Sidney, Nebraska. The route between Sidney and Camp Robinson in northwestern Nebraska already was well marked, as government contractors had been hauling supplies to the Red Cloud and Spotted Tail Indian Agencies since their establishment in 1873. By the summer of 1874 Pratt and Ferris were handling most of the freighting.

The presence of Sidney Barracks at one end and Camp Robinson at the other ensured that the route had military protection from any marauding Indians or renegade whites. But a significant impediment to travel occurred each spring when floodwaters swelled the North Platte River. Although the Sidney-Deadwood route was slightly shorter than the Cheyenne-Deadwood Trail across eastern Wyoming, more people used the Wyoming route because the iron bridge across the North Platte River near Fort Laramie enabled heavy freight wagons and stagecoaches to cross easily.

In the spring of 1876 a toll bridge over the North Platte opened about three miles west of present-day Bridgeport. Built under the supervision of Henry T. Clarke of Bellevue, the bridge enabled Sidney to rival Cheyenne as the main jumping-off place for gold seekers heading to the Black Hills. The sixty-one-span truss bridge also provided easier access to the Indian agencies, and the U.S. War Department protected it by establishing Camp Clarke at the north end of the bridge.

Clarke, meanwhile, established a store, post office, and livery barn at the south end of the bridge. He also organized a Pony Express–style mail delivery service: Clarke's Centennial Express. Initially he had an army contract to deliver mail sent between Sidney Barracks and Camp Robinson; later he set up stations and made letter deliveries to Custer City and Deadwood. Like the earlier Pony Express of Russell, Majors, and Waddell (see page 197), Clarke's Centennial Express failed financially, even though the mail volume became so heavy that Clarke had to contract with the firm of Marsh and Stephenson to haul the mail in coaches pulled by four-horse hitches. The profits Clarke made on his toll bridge more than countered the losses he suffered with his mail service. Eventually so many people headed toward the Black Hills from Sidney that a stage line opened. J. W. Dear, Indian trader at the Red Cloud Agency, started the line in the spring of 1876, charging a first-class fare of $12.50 between Sidney and the agency. (Incidentally, Dear also built numerous stations on the Cheyenne-Deadwood route that same year.) The Marsh and Stephenson coaches used to carry mail for Clarke's Centennial Express also hauled passengers, with service provided three times each week, as compared with once-a-week service on Dear's line.

From 1875 to 1881, the 267-mile trail between Sidney and the Dakotas served as one of the major routes to the goldfields. The main freighters were Pratt and Ferris, D. T. McCann, and A. S. Van Tassel; a number of smaller operators, known as "shotgun freighters," rounded out the industry. During 1878–79, more than 22 million pounds of freight moved over the Sidney–Black Hills Trail. Gold shipments worth up to $200,000 each moved south from the Black Hills to Sidney and the railroad. The route eventually had stopping places at Water Hole, Greenwood, Court House Rock, Camp Clarke, Red Willow, Snake Creek, Point of Rocks, Running Water, Red Cloud Agency, Carney's Station, and various other points extending to Custer and Deadwood.

Of course, not all travel on the Sidney-Deadwood Trail was a piece of cake. Stagecoaches and freight wagons didn't provide the smoothest ride, and there was always the distinct possibility a band of robbers would stop travelers and lighten their load. Among the outlaws who worked the routes to the Black Hills were Sam Bass, Joel Collins, and Duncan (Dunc) Blackburn and his partner, a man remembered only as Wall.

In October 1880 the Chicago & Northwestern Railroad reached Pierre, Dakota Territory, and soon most of the traffic was diverted away from Sidney.

GURLEY

The first oil well in western Nebraska came in three miles south of Gurley on August 9, 1949, at a depth of 4,429 feet and pumping 225 barrels per day. Operated by Marathon Oil Company, the well ended sixty years of unsuccessful searching in western Nebraska. The first reported exploration for oil occurred in 1889 near Crawford, and the first drilling was done near Chadron in 1903. Western Nebraska has little mineral development, however; most of its economic base is in

An oil derrick at Shelton.
—Nebraska State Historical Society, Solomon D. Butcher Collection

agriculture. The area west of Sidney, including such communities as Brownson, Ordville, Potter, Dix, Kimball, Bushnell, and north toward Gurley, is prime wheat and potato country.

Long before the Sidney-Deadwood Trail became a major access route or any farmers broke the land, native people lived near Potter. The most striking tipi ring site in Nebraska is about seven miles east of Potter on the north edge of the Lodgepole Creek valley. Known as the Wes Stevens site, it comprises twenty-five clearly defined stone rings between twelve and twenty-one feet in diameter. There are other well-preserved semicircular and linear scatterings. The site sits on a grass-covered terrace near a limestone outcrop, from which the stones for the circles came. Arapahos, Cheyennes, and Sioux lived in this area of Nebraska, but archaeologists aren't certain which tribe used the Stevens site.

Among the earliest people known to have lived in western Nebraska are the Gatakas, who made their home in the Upper White River valley. By 1682 the Gatakas had acquired animals from southern tribes to trade on the northern plains. The Kiowas started migrating into northwest Nebraska about 1730, and they became friends of the Gatakas, who eventually became known as the Kiowa Apaches, according to James Austin Hanson, writing in *Northwest Nebraska's Indian People*.

An Indian woman with a travois and a place for two children to ride. —Wyoming State Museum

Kiowas, Kiowa Apaches, and Crows settled in the valleys of northwest Nebraska. About 1730 the Crows moved north; the Kiowas and Kiowa Apaches remained in northwest Nebraska until 1803. At about that time the Brulé Sioux moved into the region from their eastern tribal lands. Although the Kiowas, Crows, Gatakas, and Cheyennes attempted to repulse the Lakota onslaught, it was too great, and the more numerous Lakotas forced the other tribes out. The Kiowas and Gatakas migrated south, the Crows headed farther west, and the Cheyennes became allies with the Sioux, moving first to the Black Hills and later even farther west. From that time forward, various bands of Sioux, including the Brulé and Oglala factions, considered much of the region that now makes up western Nebraska their territory. They also swept into central Nebraska, engaging in various battles with the Pawnees.

US 26 AND NEBRASKA 92

Ogallala–Scottsbluff

126 miles

The North Platte River between Ogallala and Scottsbluff served Native Americans, white emigrants, and fur trappers as the primary route west. The water and prime grazing habitat along the river bottoms gave travelers and their livestock sufficient support and ensured the presence of wild game such as deer, elk, and bison.

The route to Oregon and California extended west out of Ogallala, crossed a stretch of dry country, then descended Windlass Hill and dropped into Ash Hollow along the south bank of the North Platte River. The Mormon Trail followed the opposite bank. Its ruts lie in the area now marked by Nebraska 92 as it makes its way around Lake McConaughy.

KEYSTONE

The tiny town of Keystone, located east of Lake McConaughy on a rural road, has a unique house of worship built in 1908. Eleven teenage girls joined together into a club and held a series of oyster suppers, bake sales, and bazaars to raise money so they could build a church. They raised $300 and brought their community together in the effort. When the fund reached $714.50, the Bill Paxton family agreed to provide additional money so the town could have a church.

Both Protestants and Catholics lived in Keystone, and there wasn't enough money to build two churches, so the obvious thing to do was to build one and have both congregations use it. As a result, the Little Church has two altars—one for Catholic worship, the other for Protestant services. It took a special dispensation from Pope Leo XIII to have dual faiths in the same building. His permission was given to the American cardinal and then delivered to church officials in Omaha on September 15, 1908.

The Catholics worshipped at the north altar, and Protestants turned the hinged pews so they could hold services at the south altar. Presbyterians met at the church until December 12, 1926, when they moved to a new facility. The Catholics celebrated their last mass at the Little Church on October 13, 1929. Lutherans met at the church until June 1949.

Though no longer in service, the church is opened upon request and used for special occasions such as weddings. It is cared for by the local community and the Keystone Extension Club with funding from freewill offerings.

LEWELLEN

Just west of Lewellen, US 26 crosses Blue Water Creek and passes near the site of a confrontation between Sioux under Little Thunder and U.S. troops commanded by Gen. William S. Harney. The military attacked September 3, 1855, as retaliation for the Grattan Massacre, which had occurred near Fort Laramie the previous year. The battleground sweeps up the creek toward the hills to the north; it is not far, although not visible, from the highway.

In the fall of 1854 the Sioux gathered near Fort Laramie and waited for U.S. officials to arrive and dispense the tribe's annuities, as stipulated in the 1851 Treaty of Laramie. While they awaited the authorities' arrival, a Miniconjou Sioux killed an emigrant's cow. The army sent twenty-five privates under 2nd Lt. John L. Grattan to arrest the guilty individual, and a full-scale battle broke out. Grattan and twenty-four of his men were killed.

A full year later, the army took its revenge. Brig. Gen. William S. Harney left Fort Leavenworth with about 600 men and orders to restore peace on the trail. On September 3, 1855, at Blue Water Creek, a hundred or so miles east of the spot where Grattan and his command died, Harney encountered Little Thunder's band of Brulés. In a confrontation known as the Bloody Blue Water, the Battle of Ash Hollow, the Battle of Blue Water, or the Harney Massacre, between 90 and 136 people died, most of them Brulés. It didn't seem to matter to the attacking Harney and his men that the Indians they fought weren't necessarily those who'd been at the Grattan fight a year earlier.

The Little Church, with a Protestant altar at one end and a Catholic altar at the other, served everyone in Keystone.

The pews in The Little Church are specially designed with hinges so they face one direction during Protestant services and the opposite way during Catholic gatherings.

Harney proceeded to Fort Laramie, then to Fort Pierre, where he forced the Sioux to sign a treaty restating their willingness to permit white travel along the Oregon Trail and allowing the establishment of a military road from Fort Laramie to Fort Pierre.

Those two events—the Grattan Massacre of 1854 near Fort Laramie and the Harney Massacre of 1855 near Ash Hollow—set the stage for conflict between the encroaching whites and the plains tribes.

Ash Hollow

The depression along the North Platte River known as Ash Hollow once served as habitat for prehistoric rhinoceroses, mammoths, and mastodons. Some 6,000 years ago, Paleo-Indians camped at the site, and Native Americans used rock shelters in the area for at least the past 3,000 years, camping in such places as Ash Hollow Cave. Among the more recent people to use the area were the ancestors of the Plains Apache. Only in the past two hundred years have white people been here.

The first whites known to reach this area are Robert Stuart and six companions en route from Fort Astoria in Oregon to St. Louis in 1812–13. The Astorians had started west from St. Louis in 1811 under the sponsorship of John Jacob Astor. It was the second sizeable party of Americans to cross the lands of the Louisiana Purchase. The westbound Astorians ascended the Missouri River, skirted the Black Hills, crossed the Bighorn Mountains, and eventually reached the Snake River (which they called the Mad River). The Astorians followed the Snake to the Columbia and floated downstream to its mouth.

Where the Columbia poured into the Pacific, the overland Astorians joined forces with compatriots who had traveled by ship, and together they built Fort Astoria, the first American trading post in the region. In 1812 Robert Stuart and six companions started back to St. Louis with messages for Astor. They journeyed up the Columbia to the Mad River, following it to present-day western Wyoming. Then they wandered around somewhat aimlessly before stumbling upon South Pass, becoming the first white people to cross it. They continued down the Sweetwater River valley to the North Platte River. They camped at Scotts Bluff in December, but severe storms forced them to retrace their steps, and the Astorians eventually spent most of the winter in camp near present-day Torrington, Wyoming. In the spring of 1813, Stuart and his party resumed their eastward course, passing near the canyon at Ash Hollow on March 26, 1813. They probably camped in the area, which later became known for its abundant game, good source of water, and fine stand of trees. Stuart called the region Cedar Creek because of the cedar trees in the vicinity.

The Astorians' trek was a remarkable one, not only because Stuart and his companions crossed uncharted land and spent a winter in total isolation but also because they forged a route from Astoria to St. Louis—much of which later became the Oregon Trail.

Fur traders and explorers passed through the area during the next thirty years, further defining the route. The first emigrants headed west in 1841—the Bidwell-Bartleson party—followed the south side of the North Platte River until they reached a swamp at the foot of a bluff east of Ash Hollow. They forged a route over the hills and down into the hollow. Most emigrants went down Windlass Hill, the steepest descent they faced in Missouri, Kansas, and Nebraska. They left deep ruts in the soil, which have eroded naturally in the ensuing years.

Before too many years of pioneer travel, a trading post opened at the south end of Ash Hollow, with an abandoned trapper's cabin serving as a post office. Four different trading posts served travelers in the area during the 1840s and 1850s. Historically, the protected hollow served as a popular camping spot for Native Americans, and in 1835 the Sioux and Pawnee fought a pitched battle upon the valley floor. An early journal, according to the WPA guide to Nebraska, said:

> The affray was commenced early in the morning, and continued til near night. A trader, who was present with the Sioux on the occasion, describes it as having been remarkably close. Every inch of ground was disputed—now the Pawnees advancing upon the retreating Sioux; and now the Sioux, while the Pawnees gave way; but, returning to the charge with redoubled fury, the former once more recoiled. The arrows flew in full showers,—the bullets whistled the death-song of many a warrior. . . . At length arrows and balls were exhausted upon both sides,—but still the battle raged fiercer than before.
>
> War-club, tomahawk and butcher-knife were bandied with terrific force, as the hostile parties engaged hand to hand. . . . Finally the Pawnees abandoned the field to their victorious enemies, leaving sixty of their warriors upon the ensanguined battleground. But the Sioux had paid dearly for their advantage;—forty-five of their bravest men lay mingled with the slain. The defeated party were pursued only a short distance, and then permitted to return without further molestation to their village, at the Forks of the Platte.

Since 1962 the Nebraska Game and Parks Commission has acquired the land around Ash Hollow and now operates the largest state park in the area, offering interpretation of the emigrant era as well as the prehistoric age. On a knoll by the river at the hollow's mouth is the site of Fort Grattan, a frontier post built of sod.

Cattlemen established ranches near Oshkosh, but the area didn't have a post office until 1886. Now the Crescent Lake National Wildlife

Refuge includes 41,000 acres operated initially by the U.S. Bureau of Biological Survey (now the U.S. Fish and Wildlife Service) as a sanctuary for the thousands of ducks that nest in the area every year.

BRIDGEPORT

In 1812–13, when Robert Stuart and his companions headed east across Nebraska on their way from Astoria, Oregon, to St. Louis, they camped near present-day Bridgeport and viewed the natural sandstone rock figures that became known as Jail Rock and Courthouse Rock to hundreds of thousands of travelers on the Oregon-California Trail. After the wearing monotony of the prairie with day after day of undulating grasses and hills, westbound migrants delighted in the landmarks they could see as they followed the river west. They called the area from Ash Hollow to Scotts Bluff the "Valley of Monuments" because of the strangely shaped rocks.

It is said that some travelers from St. Louis named Courthouse Rock because it resembled the courthouse in their hometown. Missionary Samuel Parker called the rock a castle, while James Clyman in 1844 referred to it as an Old World ruin. The smaller formation, now known as Jail Rock, is said to have been named by cowboys, but since overland pioneers referred to the rock by that name it is unlikely the title originated with the men of the range, who came later.

Another rock formation became known as the Post Office, and early travelers wedged messages in the rocks for later travelers to find. In 1841 emigrant Rufus B. Sage wrote:

> Upon the south bank of Bonneville's creek, ten or twelve miles from the river, is a singular natural formation, known as the Court House, or McFarlan's Castle, on account of its fancied resemblance to such a structure. It rises in an abrupt quadrilangular form, to a height of three or four hundred feet, and covers an area of two hundred yards in length by one hundred and fifty broad. Occupying a perfectly level site in an open prairie, it stands as the proud palace of Solitude, amid here boundless domains. Its position commands a view of the country for forty miles around, and meets the eye of the traveller for several successive days, in journeying up the Platte.

An Indian legend about the area tells of a young Pawnee who rescued his aged grandmother by riding a magic horse. He then rode the same steed into battle against his tribe's traditional enemy, the Sioux, and performed such feats of valor that he won the chief's daughter as his bride. Between his rescue of his grandmother and his battle with the Sioux, the Pawnee retreated to these rocks to commune with his spirits.

Main Street, Bridgeport. —Wyoming State Museum

The Camp Clarke Bridge on the Sidney-Deadwood Trail opened a direct route from the railheads of western Nebraska to the gold mining camps in the Black Hills (see page 322). The bridge saw little use after 1900, when the Nebraska, Wyoming & Western Railroad rolled through the country. In 1996 the pilings remained in place, located on private ground near Bridgeport; however the river itself had changed dramatically, and the water no longer touched the pilings.

Camp Clarke is a ghost as well; all its businesses moved three miles downstream to become the present-day Bridgeport. But during its early existence Camp Clarke served as an important supply center. In 1884 all area people living on the North Platte River and its tributaries went to Camp Clarke to vote in the presidential election, according to a 1941 letter by area resident Frank Abbott.

Abbott cowboyed in the area. His family traced its roots to England, where his grandfather was a miller and his father a carpenter. The Abbotts moved to the United States after 1845, and Frank was born in Jackson, Michigan, on February 7, 1857. In 1871 Frank's brother Sam moved to Exeter, Nebraska, where he took a homestead. The rest of the family followed in the spring of 1873. A few years later Frank and Sam trailed cattle and horses over the Oregon Trail from Portland, Oregon, to Cheyenne, Wyoming, and Grand Island, Nebraska. Frank then cowboyed in Montana, but in 1884 he took a job with the Eligh Tussler Ranch northwest of Sidney, which he called a "red hot cow town." Abbott recalled: "This was a rainey wet year, the South Platte River bottom was one bog after another. Wood was scarce, the Buffalo chips wouldn't burn. We had a hard time to get anything to eat, our beds were wet all of the time and the sun only came out at intervals.

There were about a half dozen wagons with about 12 men each." The cowboys rounded up the 5,000 head of cattle and then branded 1,500 calves in a two-week period.

In the spring of 1885 Frank and Sam joined forces at Camp Clarke and claimed land on Pumpkin Creek, near Bridgeport. They started a small ranch and bought a six-horse freight team with two wagons, just in time to watch a constant stream of homesteaders select claims in the region. Many lost everything they had, but a few managed to hold on amid the large cattle outfits that ran on the western Nebraska range.

BAYARD

Thousands of travelers along the Oregon, California, and Mormon Trails died as they headed west, and most lie in unmarked graves driven over by wagons or walked upon by travelers and livestock so Indians and wild animals wouldn't find them and dig up the bodies. Some claim there are four graves for every mile of trail in Nebraska, and most are unknown. One of the few marked graves in Nebraska, that of Rebecca Winters, is located not far from Bayard. By far the most common cause of death upon the trail was Asiatic cholera, a disease that often struck in the morning and killed its victim—by dehydration—by evening. That is what killed Winters, the wife of a Mormon Church president, in 1852. The words carved upon an iron wagon tire that lay upon her grave said simply, "Rebecca Winters, age 50 years."

When engineers for the Chicago, Quincy & Burlington Railroad surveyed through this area they found the single grave and its wagon-wheel marker directly in their path. According to a report, the head engineer commented:

> Boys, said the leader, we'll turn aside
> Here, close by the trail, her grave shall stay,
> For she came first in this desert wide,
> Rebecca Wright [sic] holds the right of way.

So the CQ&B rerouted the line to the west to avoid her grave. In 1995, however, Rebecca was disinterred and her remains relocated in a new grave near the original site. Among those present for the event were her relatives from Utah.

Chimney Rock

Like Courthouse Rock to the east, Chimney Rock fascinated travelers for days, its slender-looking spike visible long before they reached it. From a distance Chimney Rock looks like an upside-down funnel, but up close it looks more like a child's sand castle and appears broader that it does from afar. Formed of clay and sandstone, Chimney Rock is the most noted landmark on the Oregon Trail. Merrill Mattes, writing in *The Great Platte River Road*, says fully 97 percent of all emigrant diarists mention Chimney Rock. Only 77 percent of the writers tell of Scotts Bluff, while Independence Rock and South Pass in Wyoming are written about in 65 percent and 51 percent of the journals, respectively.

Fur trappers called the outcrop "the Chimney," and in 1830 Warren A. Ferris, a clerk with the American Fur Company, referred to it as "Nose Mountain." As fur trappers and emigrants headed west along the North Platte River, they saw Chimney Rock long before reaching the site. To some it looked like a thin pencil; others likened it to a smokestack. "The chimney might pass for one of the foundries in St. Louis were it blackened by burning stone coal," Virgil Pringle wrote in 1846. William Riley Franklin wrote in May 1850: "This rock is 200 feet high and can be seen at a distance of 20 miles and when seen from this distance it resembles some tall monument, erected on some well contested battle field in memory of the brave dead who sleep beneath its towering summit." Mattes summarizes the monument's effect this way:

> The significant thing about Chimney Rock was the powerful impact of this strange and spectacular phenomenon on the mind and emotions of the traveler. Ash Hollow had created some excitement, with its "perpendicular descent" and its oasis-like canyon. Court House Rock had elicited admiration for its solitary grandeur and its mirage-like qualities. But Chimney Rock was the great scenic climax, a spectacle of such rarity that it seemed, like Niagara Falls, to rival the Seven Wonders of the ancient world.

In 1992 lightning struck the rock, knocking a section from its top. Undoubtedly natural elements have whittled the chimney through the years. "It is, I should say, 500 feet high. . . . It appears to be fast chipping and crumbling away," English journalist William Kelly wrote in 1849. However, the pioneer estimates have no consistency; two years earlier Mormon William Clayton wrote that Mormon elder Orson Pratt had found Chimney Rock to be 260 feet high, and Rufus Sage in 1841 estimated it was 200 feet tall. In 1849 five different men headed to California estimated the landmark at 360 feet, 150 feet, 600 feet, and 150 feet. The fifth diarist, Franklin Starr, reported on June 6: "The Chimney is rough and looks as if it would not stand a week." In 1862 Hamilton Scott wrote: "June 16. Passed Chimney Rock. This rock stands on a sand bar and is thirty feet high and about six feet in diameter at the top."

The Nebraska State Historical Society's visitor center, which opened in 1994, has a viewing area where people can attempt to guess the rock's height.

In 1837 Alfred Jacob Miller sketched the rock, probably the first artist to do so. William Henry Jackson also made numerous drawings and watercolors of Chimney Rock, some of which are on display at the nearby Scotts Bluff National Monument. Chimney Rock itself is a National Historic Site. In 1993 a wagon train that crossed Nebraska as part of the commemoration of the sesquicentennial of the Oregon Trail camped at Chimney Rock. The people of Bayard and the surrounding region had a celebration at the rock, complete with a concert by Michael Martin Murphey, who sang old cowboy songs while standing on a flatbed trailer with Chimney Rock as a backdrop.

Scotts Bluff

A few miles west of Chimney Rock, Scotts Bluff juts into the sky. The rugged cliff is easily seen from Chimney Rock, while the pointed spire of the Chimney appears as a mystical image, almost a mirage, when viewed from the top of Scotts Bluff. These two natural landmarks guided overland travelers and no doubt served Native Americans as reference points for centuries, before emigrants ever saw them.

Scotts Bluff gets its name from Hiram Scott, an employee of the Rocky Mountain Fur Company, who died at the bluff in 1828. Robert Stuart and seven companions returning from Astoria to St. Louis had camped at the bluff in 1812. Stuart wrote, "The Hills on the south have lately approached the river, are remarkably rugged and Bluffy and possess a few Cedars."

That Scott died at the bluff that bears his name is fact. How it happened is the stuff of legend. Washington Irving, in *The Adventures of Captain Bonneville*, first published in 1837, gave an early account of Scott's death. He said the party of trappers with whom Scott was traveling overturned their boats on the North Platte River. In doing so they ruined their powder, making it impossible to hunt for food. They lived on roots and wild fruits, but eventually Scott became ill. His companions halted so he could recover, but as they waited they found the tracks of other white travelers, whom they thought they might be able to overtake.

Irving wrote: "Should they linger they might all perish of famine and exhaustion. Scott, however, was incapable of moving; they were too feeble to aid him forward, and dreaded that such a clog would prevent their coming up with the advance party. They determined, therefore, to abandon him to his fate." Scott's companions told him they were going to search for food and would return; instead they deserted him and struck out for the other trappers, whom they eventually overtook, saying Scott had died.

However, according to Irving's account, Scott didn't die at the spot where his companions abandoned him. Irving claims Scott walked, hobbled, or crawled nearly sixty miles before he eventually gave out. The following summer his former companions found his bones at the base of the bluffs.

An 1830 account by American Fur Company clerk Warren Ferris, however, gave a different view. He agreed that Scott's companions abandoned him but said they did so at the bluffs where he died; he didn't force the poor man to crawl sixty miles in order for him to die at the proper place.

It's not certain who accompanied Scott on his last fateful trek toward the east, but Merrill Mattes in *Scotts Bluff* suggests it may have been William Sublette who led the party in 1828. Mattes says it certainly was Sublette who found Scott's skeleton the following summer.

The earliest wagons passed Scotts Bluff in 1830 as part of a caravan headed toward rendezvous. After the great migration started over the Oregon route in 1843, a steady stream of travelers passed and camped at Scotts Bluff. A paved road now runs between Scotts Bluff and South Bluff, but earlier emigrant traffic originally went around them to the south, crossing over Robidoux Pass. Later traffic used Mitchell Pass, along the route of Nebraska 86.

Robidoux Trading Post

In 1849 the American Fur Company sold Fort John to the U.S. military for the site of Fort Laramie and moved east to the vicinity of Scotts Bluff. Company traders are believed to have spent the winter of 1849–50 in temporary quarters on Robidoux Pass, southwest of Scotts Bluff. In 1850 the company relocated at Helvas Canyon, directly south of Scotts Bluff, and built a new trading post, also called Fort John, managed by Maj. Andrew J. Drips.

Also in 1849–50, Joseph Robidoux himself started a trading post and blacksmith shop at the eastern edge of the pass that bears his name. He later moved south to a location near the mouth of Carter Canyon. Both he and the fur company probably chose their respective locations in order to be near the Oregon and Mormon Trails, which were in heavy use by 1849 with the discovery of gold at Sutter's Mill, California, the previous year. The new locations sat far enough from the main trails to be out of the way of the massive streams of people and animals and their resulting noise and dust. However, the posts were close enough to provide service. When travel shifted in later years to Mitchell Pass, the two trading posts ceased operation.

In addition to selling supplies to emigrants, Major Drips traded with the Indians, who produced fine buffalo robes from raw hides. One report shows that at the close of the 1852 season he had 380 packs of fine robes, each pack holding ten robes.

Fort Mitchell sat about two miles northwest of Mitchell Pass, the only practical wagon route through the rugged terrain around Scotts Bluff. It is about four miles west of the city of Scottsbluff. Col. William O. Collins drew the plans for the fort, which the army established in 1864. The soldiers' quarters sat on the south and west sides, with stables to the north and a stockade of vertical posts on the east. The fort featured sod and adobe quarters. Sibson's road ranch sat just south of the fort. John Bratt worked there in 1866–67 and described the road ranch in 1921 in *Trails of Yesterday*:

> The road ranch was large, built of cedar logs, and had seven fair-sized rooms besides the store. It had dirt floors and roof. It had a large corral built out of cedar logs set closely together, some three . . . feet in the ground and standing eight feet high above the ground, with port holes on all sides. . . . We milked a number of cows, butter selling readily from fifty cents to seventy-five cents per pound. There were also a good sized bunch of ponies and some work cattle and horses. These were kept for trading purposes. . . . The store carried the usual stock of a ranch—clothing, provisions, including canned goods, and plenty of whiskey, much of which was adulterated behind closed doors by Mr. Sibson. He would never let me into this secret but I think, from observation, much of the adulteration was tobacco juice. He also sold buffalo robes, elk and deer skins, harness, saddles, guns, revolvers, ammunition, and many other articles too numerous to mention.

Many travelers left descriptions of Scotts Bluff and Mitchell Pass. William H. Jackson, traveling through the region in 1866, drew a scene at Fort Mitchell. His drawing, and many other Jackson sketches and paintings, are among the collection at Scotts Bluff National Monument, which Congress created in 1919. The national monument now encompasses about 3,000 acres. A narrow, winding, paved road leads up the west side of the bluff to a parking area on top, and a hiking trail also links the bluff's top with the monument's interpretive museum and other facilities. The American Pioneer Trails Association donated Jackson's artwork to the National Park Service in 1943. The Jackson Room received a $10,000 donation from Julius F. Stone, with other money provided by public contributions.

GERING

Named for Martin Gering, a Civil War veteran, banker, and member of the original town-site company, this community organized in 1887 and is a division point of the Union Pacific Railroad. Half a century earlier, on July 17, 1830, William Sublette's fur trade expedition camped near this site, and the town now commemorates the event and the Oregon Trail with a celebration every July.

Stagecoaches traveling between Kimball and Gering crossed the Wildcat Hills through Helvas Canyon, a minor gap in the hills, and the highway crosses Stage Hill, so called because of the early-day stagecoach traffic. The hill is now a part of the Wildcat State Game Preserve.

SCOTTSBLUFF

Although there was a trading post nearby as early as the 1840s, the community of Scottsbluff was created by the Burlington Railroad. The town site was laid out by the Lincoln Land Company, a subsidiary of the Burlington, in December 1899, and the tracks themselves arrived in February 1900. By March of that year Winfield Evans started construction of the community's first store, owned by E. H. Kirkpatrick. Before long the Emery Hotel went up, and the Carr & Neff Lumber Company relocated from nearby Gering. The railroad led to steady development over the next four years; then work began on construction of the huge irrigation canals to transfer water from eastern Wyoming and the North Platte River to panhandle farm country.

The Laramie and Tri-State Irrigation Canals brought in thousands of construction workers, who did much of their business in Scottsbluff, making it difficult for local merchants to keep up with the demand. When construction of the "big ditches" started to slack off, the Great Western Sugar Company built a beet sugar factory in Scottsbluff, completing the work in 1910. That ensured the future of the community, as farmers who relied on water from the North Platte in Wyoming grew surplus crops for processing in Scottsbluff.

Over the years potatoes and beans put down their roots in the western soils as well, forming a crop triumvirate in an area Stephen Long had dismissed as the Great American Desert. The farming is possible only because of irrigation projects funded partially by the farmers themselves but primarily by the federal government. The area has sometimes been called the "Valley of the Nile," as the water turned a desert landscape into an oasis. In 1889 farmers irrigated only 2,700 acres of land in the region. By about 1950 some 230,000 acres had water flowing to them regularly.

Kingsley Dam holds back the waters of Lake McConaughy and provides release, shown here, for irrigation operations downstream.

The Laramie and Tri-State Canals are part of the huge North Platte Project, first started in 1904, which involves seven major storage reservoirs in Wyoming and more than 1.3 million gallons of water every year. The U.S. Supreme Court in 1945 delineated allocation methods for each of the three states in the North Platte River drainage (Colorado, Wyoming, and Nebraska). That court decree specified exact amounts of water for each state every year and the exact number of acres each state can irrigate. It also set aside two separate water seasons. The period from October 1 through April 30 is considered the storage season, while the time from May 1 through September 30 is the irrigation season. Different rules about water use apply to each season.

The North Platte management had a slow, steady course for nearly forty years, but in the 1980s Wyoming proposed projects to develop some of its unused water allocation. The primary project—Deer Creek dam and reservoir in central Wyoming—would provide municipal water for Casper, the state's largest city at that time.

Nebraska, concerned that a proposed Wyoming dam would lessen the water supply for irrigators in the panhandle and for wildlife on the Platte, protested and in 1986 filed a lawsuit against its neighbor. Nebraska wanted a guarantee of water in the river for waterfowl, particularly sandhill cranes, piping plover, and other threatened or endangered species. It also wanted a guaranteed water right for supplies held in Lake Alice and Lake Minitare, which are known as the Inland Lakes and are located near Alliance. In 1995 the U.S. Supreme Court affirmed that water right, but other issues in the lawsuit remain unresolved.

Scottsbluff–Wyoming Border
22 miles

The fertile North Platte River valley provides the backdrop for US 26 as it crosses from Scottsbluff to Wyoming. The life-giving waters of the North Platte turn this country green every spring, and huge old trees (and young supple ones) protect fields from wind and snow.

MITCHELL
Gen. Robert B. Mitchell ordered the construction of military stations in 1864 to protect overland communications between Julesburg, Colorado, and South Pass, Wyoming, and his name is now associated with Mitchell Pass and Mitchell, Nebraska. Fort Mitchell started as an outpost of Fort Laramie in 1864. Its original site is located along Nebraska 92. Camp Shuman had already been established in the area.

Drawing of Camp Mitchell, east of the Wyoming and Nebraska state line, built in 1864 and named for Brig. Gen. Robert B. Mitchell. –Wyoming State Museum

It later became Camp Mitchell, and correspondence from 1865 refers to the place as Fort Mitchell.

Robert Mitchell was born in Ohio in 1823 and served during the Civil War with a Kansas regiment, distinguishing himself in battles at Wilson Creek and Perryville. Early in 1864 he met with Sioux on the South Platte River but couldn't negotiate a peace agreement. He proceeded up the Oregon Trail with 160 members of the 7th Ohio Cavalry, reaching Fort Laramie July 27. There leaders reached the decision to develop additional military posts, including one near Scotts Bluff, some fifty miles east of Fort Laramie. Others would be at Ficklin Springs (near present-day Melbeta), at Mud Springs (near Bridgeport), and at Julesburg, Colorado.

Company H of the 11th Ohio Volunteer Cavalry under Capt. J. S. Shuman built Fort Mitchell in 1864. The structure was some 180 feet long and 100 feet wide, with exterior and interior adobe walls about three and a half feet thick. As the fort walls went up, a meeting took place in Denver between Col. John M. Chivington of the 1st Colorado Cavalry, Colorado Territorial Governor John Evans, and Cheyenne chief Black Kettle. The chief agreed to a peaceful settlement in Colorado and took his people along with some Arapahos to eastern Colorado, where they camped on Sand Creek. While under protection of the military—or so they thought—Black Kettle's band prepared for winter. Their peaceful camp erupted into confusion and carnage the morning of November 29, 1864, when Chivington and a regiment of 100-day volunteers attacked. Although Black Kettle furiously waved both an American flag and a white truce pennant, the soldiers fired upon the Cheyenne and Arapaho families, killing hundreds of individuals.

Almost immediately the plains tribes retaliated. By December hundreds of warriors, including Oglala and Brulé Sioux, Cheyenne, and Arapaho, gathered near Julesburg to start a series of avenging maneuvers. They declared war, and 1865 became the "Bloody Year on the Plains."

Fort Mitchell immediately became a strategic location. In February 1865 troops from Fort Laramie marched to Fort Mitchell, from which place they proceeded to Mud Springs, where the Sioux attacked on February 5. The U.S. Army won that encounter. Fort Mitchell troops also participated in a skirmish known as the Battle of Horse Creek, which occurred in June 1865. Prior to that engagement, the army decided to remove about 1,500 Brulés, who had been friendly to the whites, from Fort Laramie to Fort Kearny. As they left the encampment at Horse Creek on June 14, the Sioux broke from the north side of the river, killing Capt. William D. Fouts and three soldiers. The Brulés, who had been thought to be peaceful, headed north across the river, where they joined other Sioux known to be hostile. Although speculation runs that the "friendly" Sioux had been encouraged to revolt by the "hostiles," it is more likely that the Sioux did not want to go to Fort Kearny because they knew their enemies, the Pawnees, were nearby.

The well-situated post had a stockade with sally port, firing loopholes, and sentinel tower, as seen in an 1866 drawing by William Henry Jackson. That same year Margaret Carrington passed Fort Mitchell with her husband, Col. H. B. Carrington, who would command the notorious Fort Phil Kearny along the Bozeman Trail in Wyoming. She gave this description:

> Almost immediately after leaving the Bluffs, and at the foot of this descent, after the gorge is passed, we find Fort Mitchell. This is a subpost of Fort Laramie of peculiar style and compactness. The walls of the quarters are also the outlines of the fort itself, and the four sides of the rectangle are respectively the quarters of officers, soldiers, and horses, and the warehouse of supplies. Windows open into the little court or parade ground; the bedrooms, as well as all other apartments, are loop-holed for defense.

Fort Mitchell remained in place at least until 1867, but there is no documentation about when it was finally abandoned. Presumably it saw little use after the 1868 treaty with the Sioux, negotiated at Fort Laramie.

MORRILL

A Treaty at Horse Creek

The federal government recognized the Plains Indians' right to the western lands in 1851 when one of the largest gatherings of tribes to ever occur took place along a grassy creek in Nebraska. Ten thousand or more Sioux, Cheyenne, Arapaho, Crow, and Shoshone tribal members first met at Fort Laramie, located in present-day Wyoming, for the "great smoke."

They had with them between 20,000 and 30,000 horses, which quickly ate the forage available at and near Fort Laramie, so the entire gathering moved downstream to Horse Creek, at a site along the Nebraska-Wyoming border. Certainly the participants camped on both sides of what is now the state border and on both Sand and Horse Creeks. The Horse Creek site was well known to the tribes. The Kiowa, Arapaho, Apache, Cheyenne, Crow, and Sioux tribes had used it as a rendezvous location.

An early story of the Sioux Nation is that periodic gatherings took place on the banks of the western stream. Each year the young men of the tribe took the goods made by the women to trade with other

U.S. commissioners and Indian chiefs participating in treaty talks at Fort Laramie, Wyoming, 1868. From left: unidentified, Packs His Drums (sitting), John Finn, Amos Bettelyon, W. H. Bullock (sitting), Old Man Afraid of His Horses, Benjamin Mills (sitting), Red Bear, and James Bordeaux. —Wyoming State Museum

tribes for different types of clothing and goods. Once the young men attended such a trading rendezvous and were astonished when some of the southern traders arrived riding "big dogs." The Sioux men were so enamored with the large animals (horses) that they traded for some of them. When they returned to their village to the northeast, in the land now called Minnesota and eastern South Dakota, the women scorned their trade. The men rode the "big dogs," and the area of their thighs was rubbed and burned by the friction of bare legs against rough hair. The women called them the Burnt Thigh Men, or Brulés, and the tribe soon became the Brulé Sioux. Another version of their naming, however, is that in 1762 a big prairie fire caused many of them to burn their legs.

The council sessions on Horse Creek started September 8, 1851. In the discussions that followed, the tribes agreed upon lands for themselves, and they recognized the right of the government to build roads and forts on those same lands.

The Indian people of the 1800s didn't believe they owned the land. For them it was a place to live on and to live from. They killed the animals of the region for food, clothing, and shelter; they burned the grasses to revitalize them for spring. When the government offered the tribes $50,000 worth of goods annually for fifty years in exchange for an agreement that white people could travel over the land to Oregon and California, the Indians saw no reason to refuse.

On September 17, 1851, the representatives of the various tribes signed the treaty, and the formal agreement became the first of many misunderstandings between the whites, particularly the military, and the tribes. The government almost immediately changed the terms of the treaty, and then it failed to provide the annuities promised under the Horse Creek covenant. For their part, the Indians may not have understood the treaty. Further, while the military leaders recognized certain Indian leaders, calling them chiefs, the Indian people didn't necessarily agree that those "chiefs" had a right to bargain on their behalf. Each Indian as an individual had the right to take his or her own actions. Leaders could only try to persuade them to abide by treaty terms; they couldn't force compliance.

In May 1993 four governors—Ben Nelson of Nebraska, Mike Sullivan of Wyoming, George Mikelson of South Dakota, and Roy Romer of Colorado—planned a new set of historic roadside markers near Horse Creek to recognize the 1851 treaty. The markers were cast and ready for a dedication, with Hollywood star Kevin Costner (of *Dances with Wolves* fame) invited to attend, when South Dakota's Governor Mikelson died in a plane crash. In spite of Governor Mikelson's death, the dedication took place as planned.

HENRY

The federal government established Red Cloud Agency near present-day Henry in 1871 as a distribution center for annuities for the Sioux. However, the army and people traveling the Oregon Trail route to the west felt uncomfortable having the agency so close to the great migration route, so the military relocated it to a site on the White River near Camp Robinson and present-day Crawford. Camp Robinson became a permanent site in December 1878, changing its name to Fort Robinson.

Hyannis—Crawford
117 miles

Nebraska 2 runs through the heart of the Sandhills from Grand Island to Broken Bow and Hyannis, then continues into the extreme northwestern corner of Nebraska. From Hyannis the route passes through Ashby, Bingham, Ellsworth, Lakeside, and Antioch. It is a marvelous drive through rolling hill country in the spring, summer, or fall, but it can be a difficult journey if a winter storm blows over the hills. Buffalo have long roamed this country and still do. Cattle ranchers and Kinkaid homesteaders claimed the land; most of the homesteaders departed, unable to forge an adequate living. Some of the cattlemen remain, and a few have even started raising buffalo, recognizing the economic potential of that species.

ELLSWORTH

Spade Ranch

Cowboys started moving cattle into Montana after 1870, and by 1879 they had pushed the first herds into the Sandhills, which they quickly recognized as a prime area. That same year Bartlett Richards came west from Massachusetts, taking a job on a Wyoming ranch, where he eventually became a ranch manager. In 1885 Richards and his brother DeForest founded the First National Bank of Chadron, bought interest in the Harrison bank, and soon started dealing in ranch land.

Bartlett Richards purchased the Spade Ranch in August 1888 from Bennett Irwin, who had started the ranch near Bean Soup Lake. Richards, his brother Jarvis, a partner named John J. Cairnes (vice

A cowboy moving Hereford cattle. —Nebraska State Historical Society

president of South Dakota's large Anglo-American Cattle Company), and Cairnes's wife filed homestead claims in the hay meadows near the Spade Ranch, giving them control of upland range.

Richards assisted in formation of the Nebraska Stock Growers Association. By 1899 Cairnes and his wife had sold their holdings, and Richards, his two brothers, and partners Will Comstock (a Montana rancher) and E. C. Harris of Chadron formed the Nebraska Land and Feeding Company. The new company had about 500,000 acres enclosed by 292 miles of fence; it ran some 25,000 to 40,000 head of cattle, and the Spade served as the "home ranch."

The fence is what got Richards and his partners into trouble. Not all of the land fenced by Richards belonged to him; a goodly portion remained in the public domain. In 1901 the cattlemen looked toward Congress for a land-lease law that would allow them to continue operations much has they had done in the past. However, President Theodore Roosevelt instructed the secretary of the interior to have the illegal fences removed. When Richards and Comstock didn't remove their fences as ordered, they faced misdemeanor charges and in 1905 pleaded guilty to fencing 212,000 acres of public land. Each man was fined $300 and sentenced to six hours in the custody of a U.S. marshal (which was actually served in the custody of their attorney).

The lightness of the sentence aroused the press and President Roosevelt. In 1906 Richards and Comstock answered to new felony charges. They didn't testify and were convicted, sentenced to a year in federal prison, and ordered to pay a $1,500 fine. They lost an appeal and went to jail in Hastings in 1910. Richards died there following emergency surgery for an intestinal ailment in September 1911, just a few weeks prior to the completion of his sentence. After his release from jail Comstock returned to the Spade, but its heyday had passed, and bankers foreclosed on the ranch. Other ranchers throughout the West faced charges of illegal fencing during what is called "Roosevelt's Roundup."

Local residents know the region along Nebraska 27 between Ellsworth and Gordon as "Old Jules country" because Swiss immigrant Jules Sandoz lived here, forging a life that involved four wives and six children. Sandoz homesteaded along the Niobrara River country, known early as the Running Water. He ran a freight trail, worked for agricultural development, and had a fruit tree orchard. Midway between Ellsworth and Gordon is a marker to his daughter, author Mari Sandoz, and a highway rest area is dedicated to her (see page 353).

Nebraska 250 between Lakeside and Rushville crosses through the extreme western edge of the Sandhills, with their rolling hills and native meadows. The naturally high underground water table leads to good grass growth, and ranchers harvest the native grass in alternating pastures each year by rolling it in big round bales, which they store for use in feeding cattle during the winter months. In certain areas blowholes appear in the Sandhills, looking like sand traps on a golf course.

Twenty-four men in the 24th Infantry (buffalo soldiers) tried to make their way from Montana to St. Louis on bicycles in June 1897 to prove that the two-wheeled conveyances would bring the army into the twentieth century. Each man carried at least forty pounds of supplies. They followed the Burlington Railroad tracks, traveling some 2,000 miles in forty-one days, but once they reached the sandy soils of central Nebraska's Sandhills, they bogged down and had a difficult time proceeding.

ANTIOCH

As early as 1900 people started investigating the possibility of developing potash from the alkaline lakes of western Nebraska. In 1911 John Show and Carl Modisett conducted their own investigation into the potential of potash development, and the following year they opened a plant on the shore of Jesse Lake, some three miles north of Hoffland. They sold their product to Cudahy's in Omaha, the Swift Packing

Potash production area near Antioch. —Nebraska State Historical Society

Company in Chicago, and the General Chemical Company in New York, but the operation didn't do well, and by 1913 it had closed. The following year Show, Modisett, and other investors reopened the plant as the Potash Reduction Company, better known as the Hoffland Company. In 1915 the company decided to build a new plant along the railroad and a pipeline to bring in water from Jesse Lake.

World War I broke out, causing a shortage of potash from Germany, and the Nebraska potash industry boomed. Hoffland expanded, and plants at Antioch and Lakeside went into production. Eventually five factories worked twenty-four hours a day producing potash from the dry beds of Sandhill lakes. The potash was needed not for use in gunpowder production but for a more mundane, albeit important, product: fertilizer for cotton fields.

Antioch became the nation's potash capital and had an estimated population of 5,000 by 1918. Antioch passed a $100,000 school bond for a new school, and the district hired a superintendent for a three-year contract. But then the war ended and with it the need for potash, so the superintendent found himself with barely enough students to hold classes. The Alliance Potash Plant, constructed in Antioch in 1917 at a cost of $600,000, had little time to recover building costs. It sold at a sheriff's auction in 1921, bringing only $32,000. During the boom a large number of houses and quite a few tar-paper shacks went up for the workers, but when the factories closed people moved the smaller houses to Alliance and ranchers bought the shacks, which they dismantled for the materials.

In the mid-1980s Fred T. Hanson of McCook started an effort to preserve a portion of the wooden pipeline used in the potash industry at Antioch. With cooperation from area landowners, he excavated a section and donated it to the Knight Museum in Alliance. The Antioch plant remains, located on private ranch property, are visible from Nebraska 2.

ALLIANCE

The Burlington Railroad started Alliance with a land sale in 1888 as the line moved through the area, and the town remains as a major rail division point. Initially the community went by the name Broncho Lake, but postal officials rejected that title. Railroad officials then proposed Grand Lake, which postal officials also nixed, saying it was too similar to Grand Island. Eventually Burlington officials selected Alliance.

It took three elections in 1890 to determine the governmental seat of Box Butte County, with Hemingford winning over Nonpareil and

Cutting alfalfa in western Nebraska. —Nebraska State Historical Society

Alliance. County seat supporters in Alliance protested and schemed to physically seize the county records on the theory that possession is nine-tenths of the law. However, the railroad thwarted those plans by providing a trainload of "detectives and special agents," according to a local history. The mere threat of the train stalled talk of an armed takeover, and the county seat moved quietly from Nonpareil to Hemingford. But Alliance continued to lobby and eventually claimed the county seat in an election in 1899. Because there was a perfectly good courthouse in Hemingford, it was placed on a rail car and moved to Alliance, with the moving commemorated in photographs, plates, spoons, and ashtrays. The population grew after approval of the 1904 Kinkaid Homestead Act, and in 1912 the county decided to build a new courthouse, which was dedicated in December 1914.

Alliance received national attention in 1987 when James Reinders arranged old automobiles to look like the ancient site of Stonehenge. He calls his version Carhenge. It is located just north of Alliance adjacent to US 385.

Located sixteen miles north of Alliance, along Nebraska 2, is a flat-topped hill known as Box Butte to early cowboys and travelers. The butte became a landmark for miners and freighters headed to the Black Hills during the 1870s gold rush. Box Butte City started to the east in the mid-1880s as a cluster of sod and frame buildings and included a post office, grocery store, drugstore, land locator's office, livery barn, hotel, restaurant, cream station, and two blacksmith's shops. There was a small sod church on the west side of the "city," but the town withered when postal officials discontinued the post office in 1910, and only pioneer graves remain.

HEMINGFORD

Newspaper editor Joseph Hare founded Hemingford in 1880, and by 1887 the town had two newspapers, the *Gleander* and the *Box Butte Rustler*. With the support of those publications the town became the official seat of Box Butte County in 1891, but it only retained that status until 1899, when Alliance claimed the designation.

A variety of crops, including wheat, oats, rye, and corn, grow in this region, but it has always been known for its potatoes. By the 1930s it had several large potato warehouses with sorters, graders, and conveyors. Many farmers still raise potatoes, with most of the crop used to make potato chips or for seed potatoes.

MARSLAND

The Running Water Stage Station on the Sidney-Deadwood Trail sat about three miles southwest of Marsland. Several stations provided services such as meals, relief horses, and blacksmithing. The trail itself ran parallel to Nebraska 2 in this area, twisting back and forth across the highway. Now the region has scattered ponderosa pine, but wood hasn't always been readily available here, and some fenceposts are made of an alternative material, limestone.

US 20
Gordon—Wyoming Border
104 miles
GORDON

Situated along the northwestern edge of the diamond-shaped Sandhills, Gordon is ranching and farming country. The community has museums and collections related to the region's most well-known writer, Mari Sandoz, and to the old-time cowboys.

The Story of Old Jules

By all accounts Jules Sandoz commanded respect. The eldest son of a comfortably well-off Swiss family, Jules studied medicine in Zurich

*Jules Sandoz and his wife,
Mary, at their home in 1926.*
—Nebraska State Historical Society

for four years. He asked for an increase in his allowance from his family and heard a bevy of reasons why it couldn't be done. So Jules, who had worked as a mail clerk and had fallen in love with a young girl named Rosalie, told his family he didn't need their money. He would go to America to make a new life for himself, and he would take his beloved Rosalie with him over the protests of his family that she wasn't good enough for him.

In spite of his arrogance, Jules Sandoz found that life wasn't that easy. First, to his great heartbreak, Rosalie refused to accompany him to America. He moved to Nebraska anyway, wrote glowing accounts of the region to his lovely Rosalie, and begged her to join him. She refused, so after three years of pleading with Rosalie, he gave up and married the first woman who crossed his path: Estelle. But when his new wife refused to harness his team and build the fire each morning, he slapped her across the face, dumped their supplies, and left both her and his home in Knox County, Nebraska.

Jules headed west to Valentine, site of the land office for homestead claims in the region to the south and west. It was 1884 and Jules determined he would get land, and then a new wife. He would make his way in America, without Rosalie and without Estelle. On April 19, 1884, the day before he turned twenty-five, Jules Sandoz reached the Niobrara River, near which he intended to stake his homestead claim. Despite warnings that the cattlemen then ruled the country, Jules marked a piece of land and dug a home out of the grass-covered hills, built out of what is known as Nebraska marble: sod.

Sandoz made friends with the Oglala Sioux, who hunted near his chosen land. He trapped, hauled freight, and put his medical knowledge to work, delivering babies or tending to wounds and illnesses. Three years later, in April 1887, he got married again, this time to a woman named Henriette, a friend of his sister, Elvina. A week later he filed a homestead claim. He kept to himself and, even more important, kept his neighbors from Henriette. She didn't know about much of his past, including Rosalie, Estelle, or the money he owed his father.

Henriette had money of her own and a determination to succeed in America. She obtained a cow so she could have milk and butter to sell in Hay Springs, and she hired two men to build a house for her. Eventually Jules told Henriette of Rosalie, and his former love even sent a gift to Henriette.

That winter of 1887–88 killed a lot of people and more livestock. November and December had crisp, cloudless days, but in January it started to snow, and the wind rose as the mercury plummeted. For days the storm raged all across the plains, from the Dakotas and Montana south to Texas. Two weeks after it started, Jules forced his saddle horse to Rushville, where the newspapers gave the grim tally: at least fourteen people dead in Nebraska, more than two hundred dead elsewhere in the region. Range cattle died, as did milk cows and pigs.

But spring finally arrived. Henriette saved enough money to satisfy the debt Jules owed to his father, and the Sandoz family settled into a life of routine.

In 1890 the Sioux on the Pine Ridge Reservation north of Gordon became involved in the Ghost Dance movement. The Ghost Dancers believed a new messiah would come, bring buffalo, and force the white people who lived on Sioux and other Indian lands to leave. They danced and they believed. Their actions alarmed the settlers in the region south of Pine Ridge, but the Sioux never really threatened anyone.

Even as the Ghost Dance craze swept the plains, a feud started brewing in the Sandhills to the south. Henry Freese moved in and claimed land across the river from Henriette's place (it was always hers, never Jules's). Trouble started almost immediately. Freese's dogs chased some of the neighbor's colts into a barbed-wire fence; Jules killed the dogs. Fires scorched the region; Jules went to court on a charge of shooting at Freese. He got off. Some of Freese's grain stacks burned; the sheriff arrested Jules, but he had an alibi and the charge didn't stick.

Eventually Jules went to court on other charges, but each time he proved his innocence. After a long, bitter, costly fight, the feud withered. Freese had patented his land and offered it as a settlement in the lawsuit Sandoz had filed against him involving other burned grain. The court deeded the land to Henriette, and the county ended up $5,000 in debt after three years of wrangling on the ground and in the courts. Henriette finished the deal when she pitched Jules's belongings, guns, and traps into the road, then rode to Rushville to file for a divorce. Freese eventually went to an asylum following a series of fires in Rushville.

Jules sent a note to Rosalie, asking her, again, to join him in Nebraska. She refused. He didn't pine but wrote to Emelia, a Swiss woman he met through an introduction by a mutual friend. She responded that she'd like to move to America, but she had no money for her passage. He sent it, she came, and they married. But two weeks after Emelia arrived in Nebraska she was gone from Jules's home, spirited away with assistance from Paul Wurthier, a young Swiss man, who gave her a ride to Rushville.

Even as he wrestled with the vexing problem of what to do with Emelia (who refused to return to the homestead), Jules had another fly in the ointment: Estelle showed up. That Jules Sandoz had a temper is no secret, and eventually his first three wives became a part of his past, no doubt relieved he wouldn't have another chance to knock them around.

But the man who pined for Rosalie didn't like living alone, so he married a fourth time, to Mary Fehr, a German Swiss girl, and she gave him everything she had: $100. Later she learned he'd been married before, three times. She wanted to leave but didn't, and when she again felt the need to do so it was too late. Jules sought to perpetuate his and Mary's names, and in order to accomplish that he named their first two children for themselves.

As he had beaten his wives, Jules also whipped his children. The father, who became Old Jules, lived a life that reads like a novel, or a soap opera. He had left his family and his beloved Rosalie in Switzerland to make his way in a new country. He had four wives and six children and spent much of his life in a dugout or a plain two-room cabin. He became a friend to many Sioux. He trapped, freighted, hunted, and beat his wives and kids. By all accounts he was a mean, cantankerous, ornery cuss. His life is chronicled in the classic, award-winning book *Old Jules*, written by his daughter, Mari Sandoz.

Mari Sandoz entered a story in the Harper Intercollegiate Short Story Contest using the name Marie Macumber (her married name). Her father forbade her to write, and when he learned of the work he sent her a cryptic, one-line message: "You know I consider writers and artists the maggots of society."

Fortunately for Nebraska and for western literature Mari Sandoz had developed the strength and character of the mean old SOB, and she let the criticism roll from her tall shoulders. Mari Sandoz went on to become a writer, certainly one of Nebraska's finest and, indeed, one of the greatest of all western writers.

Mari's Story

Old Jules's violent rages shaped his eldest daughter. He denied Mari the opportunity to attend much school; she had only four years of rural instruction. She didn't have her first pair of shoes until she was nine, even though by the time she turned seven Mari often cared for her younger siblings for days at a time when her parents went to town for supplies.

Old Jules beat her senseless when she was only three months old, and he once broke her hand by hitting it with a chokecherry tree club; Mari watched as he beat her mother with four-foot iron stays and knew her mother tried to commit suicide following that particular incident. But despite his treachery and brutal ways Old Jules gave Mari something else: a sense of story. He told tales of the early days out on the Niobrara River, which he called Running Water. He talked of vigilante justice and feuds, of freighting, trapping, and tending to wounds. Once, when a rattlesnake bit Jules on the hand, he shot himself in the same location to force the poison from his body. Mari inherited his toughness and tenacity, and she developed his stories into her own.

At age twelve, Mari published her first short story, "The Broken Promise," in the *Omaha Daily News*. Upon learning of this news, Jules pitched a fit. Despite being beaten and locked in the cellar, Mari continued writing. At age seventeen she got a teaching certificate and a teaching position. A year later she married Sandhills rancher Wray Macumber, and for a time she wrote as Marie Macumber. But the marriage lasted only five years.

Mari became determined to succeed. She saved money, attended the University of Nebraska in Lincoln, eventually worked for the Nebraska State Historical Society, and wrote. Her success came through dogged hard work. More than a dozen publishers rejected the biography of her father, *Old Jules*, before it eventually appeared in 1935. That book, which won Mari Sandoz a $5,000 publishing award (and another $5,000 when it became a Book-of-the-Month Club selection), had been rewritten numerous times from the first time she submitted it to a publisher.

The $10,000 Mari Sandoz earned from her father's life story represented quite a sum during the Depression. It gave her the independence and freedom to continue writing. Subsequently she wrote *Slogum House*, a novel about a woman who dominated the Niobrara country, which was banned in McCook and Omaha because of its language and violence. A later book, *Capital City*, brought her threats and harassment in Lincoln because some people viewed the story about seamy politics as somehow reflecting upon their city.

In 1940 Sandoz left Lincoln for Denver and just three years later moved to New York, where she remained for the rest of her life. Even though she left Nebraska, the state still provided her with inspiration and material for her books. She wrote volumes that traced the development of the Great Plains, particularly dealing with how changes affected the environment. The titles included *Crazy Horse* (1942), *Cheyenne Autumn* (1953), *The Buffalo Hunters* (1954), *The Cattlemen* (1958), and *The Beaver Men* (1964). During the course of her career, Mari Sandoz wrote many other books as well, including her poetic *Love Song to the Plains*.

In modern time children from abusive family situations sometimes become abusive themselves. They may opt for a life of crime and then blame their childhood for their actions. While Mari Sandoz certainly had a difficult childhood, she chose to draw upon it for strength, even inspiration. She rose above the abuse to become a powerful writer, and her legacy is a literary offering to the world.

Mari Sandoz died of cancer in 1966. She is buried in the Sandhills, south of Gordon along Nebraska 27.

Like Old Jules, David C. "Doc" Middleton raised havoc throughout the Sandhills during the 1870s, eventually serving prison time for horse theft in Nebraska. But upon his release from prison, Middleton mended his ways. He eventually settled in Gordon, where he operated a saloon and gambling parlor. He traveled extensively, gambling at various locations. In a strange twist, the former convict became the Sheridan County deputy sheriff in Gordon. He filed on a homestead but sold it before proving up and eventually died in a Wyoming jail, where he had been incarcerated for drunkenness (see page 288).

RUSHVILLE

By fall 1890 government officials thought it necessary to put an end to the Ghost Dance movement sweeping through some Indian tribes, including the Sioux, whose reservations lay in South Dakota just north of the Nebraska border. Talk of impending problems escalated during the harvest season. In the Rushville area residents barred their doors. Some of them joined together and built a two-story sod fortress, cutting gun slits in the upper floor as pictured in an old history book.

By November 1890, correspondents from various publications had arrived in Rushville, which had the train station closest to Pine Ridge. Frederic Remington arrived in January 1891, reporting for *Harper's*. Business in the small town boomed (one miller contracted to supply 68,000 pounds of flour for government troops), and freighting activities picked up. Within a month the furor quieted, and settlers returned to their homes, no longer feeling the need for security at a sod fortress. They had barely returned to their farms when the people heard of the senseless killing of Big Foot's Sioux band at Wounded Knee just over the border in South Dakota.

WHITECLAY

North of Rushville on Nebraska 87, Whiteclay is now little more than a spot in the road, but in 1881 an important Sioux Sun Dance took place nearby. The community rests at the edge of the Pine Ridge Reservation in South Dakota. The grave of Red Cloud, one of the great Sioux leaders, is at Pine Ridge, just inside South Dakota, and the Wounded Knee mass grave is to the east, also in South Dakota. Lakota who live on the Pine Ridge Reservation regularly cross the state border to buy beer in Whiteclay, a small community that features a few

An Indian camp at Pine Ridge, 1891. —Nebraska State Historical Society, Solomon D. Butcher Collection

businesses and several abandoned houses and stores. In the late summer, Nebraska farmers take corn to Whiteclay, where they find a ready market among Pine Ridge residents, who dry the corn along with squash and wild turnips for use in winter cooking.

From Whiteclay, a series of secondary and rural roads provide access to the Beaver Wall and the sites of Camp Sheridan and Spotted Tail Agency. Crazy Horse liked this region and often gathered here with his people. Rural roads to the west and south provide access to Hay Springs.

Camp Sheridan

The Indian treaty of 1868 established locations at which the various Indian tribes were to receive their government annuities. After 1874 Brulé Sioux chief Spotted Tail and his followers had an agency located about ten miles north of Hay Springs. The military established Camp Sheridan to protect Spotted Tail Agency. Red Cloud and Spotted Tail each had various agencies for their people.

Spotted Tail's band of Brulés had been at the Whetstone Agency near Fort Randall in eastern South Dakota from 1868 to 1871. They moved to a second Whetstone Agency (called Spotted Tail Agency) near Camp Sheridan, where they remained in two different locations from 1871 to 1877, then moved to a site east of Fort Randall at Spotted

Sin-Tig-A-Las-Ka, or Spotted Tail, who had his own agency in northwest Nebraska.
—Wyoming State Museum

Tail Agency No. 2. They remained here for a year before once again relocating, this time farther west to Spotted Tail Agency No. 3, better known as the Rosebud Reservation, located north of Valentine in South Dakota.

Red Cloud had his first agency along the North Platte River just inside the Wyoming border from 1871 to 1873, then moved north to the second Red Cloud Agency near Camp Robinson, (now Fort Robinson) west of Crawford. In 1877 Red Cloud's people moved north to the Missouri River in present-day South Dakota, where they remained for a year. Meanwhile, in 1872 the government had also established the Pine Ridge Agency (known as Red Cloud No. 4) at a site north of Whiteclay, also in South Dakota.

All those agencies are somewhat confusing to keep track of, so we will deal primarily with only two of them: Spotted Tail Agency, near Camp Sheridan north of Hay Springs, which the Brulés used from 1871 to 1877, and Red Cloud Agency No. 2, near Camp Robinson, which served Lakota from 1873 to 1877.

The two agencies are named for two of the finest Sioux leaders ever, and the fate of perhaps the greatest of the Sioux war chiefs, Crazy Horse, ties to both agencies. Crazy Horse distinguished himself on the battlefields of Wyoming's Powder River Basin. He fought at the Fetterman Battle on December 21, 1866, in which the Sioux killed Lt. William J. Fetterman and eighty of his men. Crazy Horse had a role in the Wagon Box Fight at the base of the Bighorn Mountains the following August, and he and Hunkpapa holy man Sitting Bull led the Sioux nation in its greatest battle ever: the fight on the Greasy Grass of Montana (Battle of the Little Bighorn), where Lt. Col. George A. Custer and his men died under a blazing sun on June 26, 1876.

After years of conflict Crazy Horse gave up his weapons. In the company of Red Cloud, Crazy Horse and his people met with Lt. W. P. Clark near Hat Creek Station in Wyoming Territory. It was spring 1877. The soldiers accompanied Crazy Horse to Red Cloud Agency on the White River, where the great war chief surrendered his horses and mules (2,000 head), guns and pistols (117 in all), and his people (899 men, women, and children). The summer passed with few problems, but by late August Crazy Horse started showing discontent. When the army started to recruit Indian scouts to help capture Chief Joseph and the Nez Perces, who were then racing toward Canada in a desperate bid for freedom, Crazy Horse believed they really intended to bring back Sitting Bull, who had gone to Canada. Crazy Horse told the military he would fight the Nez Perces, but an error in interpretation had him saying he would fight the military.

An artist's drawing depicting the killing of Crazy Horse at Camp Robinson, September 1877. —Wyoming State Museum

The military leaders and some agency Indians, including Red Cloud, knew Crazy Horse had not been entirely cowed; they believed he posed a real threat to peace on the plains. Gen. George Crook on September 1, 1877, ordered Crazy Horse arrested, but the war chief slipped from the grasp of the military and struck out with some of his people, moving down the White River. Crazy Horse headed for the Spotted Tail Agency, where military leaders found him on September 5, 1877. Other soldiers rounded up those who had fled along with Crazy Horse. The party with Crazy Horse went to Camp Robinson. When authorities attempted to place Crazy Horse in the guardhouse, he resisted. There, in front of the guardhouse, a scuffle ensued, and a sentry stabbed Crazy Horse. He died later that night; his burial scaffold was placed near Spotted Tail Agency.

Soon after, on October 29, 1877, Spotted Tail's Brulés moved to South Dakota, where the government established the Rosebud Agency, now the Rosebud Reservation, in 1878. The military abandoned Camp Sheridan on May 1, 1881.

HAY SPRINGS

Some years after the events at Camp Sheridan and Spotted Tail Agency, homesteaders started settling the Hay Springs area. In the ensuing years, residents reported seeing a water monster living in Alkali Lake (now Walgren Lake, named for a settler family). The lake is south of Hay Springs. Several people reported seeing a strange monster "of prehistoric kind." Although there may have been earlier reports, the majority of the tales surfaced in the 1920s. Among the descriptions of the monster, as reported in the Nebraska folklore pamphlet of the Federal Writers Project in July 1938, are these: "Its head was like an oil barrel shiny black in the moonlight," "It eats a dozen calves when it comes ashore," "It flattens the cornfields," and "Its flashing green eyes spit fire."

One man from Omaha reportedly spent the night at Walgren Lake in order to view the monster. When he returned to Omaha he had lost his voice and his hair was white. Three days later, upon recovering his voice, the man said the monster was three hundred feet long and could have opened its mouth wide enough to swallow the Woodmen of the World building.

It's true that at one time Alkali Lake may have been large enough for a 300-foot-long sea monster, but the creature itself never existed except in the mind of *New York Herald* correspondent John G. Maher. While Maher contributed greatly to his country (he served in both the Spanish-American War and during World War I) and wrote a fair number of honest stories about western Nebraska for the paper, the truth is he liked to tell stories—the taller the tale the better he liked it.

The sea monster of Walgren Lake is just one of Maher's fictitious accounts. It is also one of his finest achievements. At one point in the 1920s, locals formed the Hay Springs Investigating Association, apparently as a fund-raising scheme. They would drag the lake and charge spectators for the chance to see the sea monster as it was removed. But when area landowners around the lake said they needed $4,000 as a lease payment for three month's use of the land and it became clear that the dragging operation itself would cost another $1,000, promoters dropped that scheme.

Then the *Omaha World-Herald* on November 20, 1925, reported that Bruce Hewitt and J. Mayes of Rushville had solved the Walgren Lake mystery by finding a mermaid frozen in the ice at the lake.

Of course there was no sea monster in the lake, just as there was no petrified man located near Chadron. For that practical joke, Maher made a plaster cast of a large black soldier who was stationed at Fort Robinson. Once the cast was complete, Maher hauled it in a dray wagon to the region northwest Hay Springs, where John Bell Hatcher of Yale University had discovered fossils in 1887. Eventually a "discovery" of the specimen occurred, and it was quickly classified as an "ossified man" from a "prehistoric century," according to Louise Pound writing in *Nebraska Folklore.*

Maher's lawyer, D. W. Sperling of Chadron, took the "petrified man" on tour but eventually ceased the display. The "specimen" was put away in a vault in Champaign, Illinois. At one time the Nebraska State Historical Society considered obtaining the "petrified man" but gave up the idea because "the expenditure would have been too great for something of no historical or educational value," according to an account by Florence Tierney Maher, as reported in Pound's *Nebraska Folklore.*

CHADRON

The country between Hay Springs and Chadron is good land for ranching and the cultivation of wheat and other crops. The Sandhills to the east give way to the breaks of Pine Ridge in the west. This country served as an early gathering place for Indian tribes, from the ancient Gatakas or Kiowa Apaches to the Cheyennes and Sioux. It became an important fur trade region; the Bordeaux trading post operated at a site just on the eastern edge of present-day Chadron from 1841 to 1872, and Chartran's Trading Post sat on Chadron Creek, south of the city, from 1841 until about 1845.

Western Nebraska Fur Trade

Chartran's Trading Post on Chadron Creek opened to do business with the Brulés. By late November 1841 the post had a substantial log trading house, complete with a stone chimney and log storehouse. Although trading went well during the fall, by January the buffalo had migrated out of the region, and the Brulés followed. When the traders ran short on supplies in January, they retreated to Fort Platte, located near the site of Fort Laramie.

A major trade route developed between Laramie and Fort Pierre, South Dakota. One trail headed in a nearly straight diagonal line from Fort Laramie to the White River west of the site that eventually became Camp Robinson, then continued to Fort Pierre by following the White River. A secondary route ran to the south, crossing the Niobrara River at a point near present-day Agate Fossil Beds National Monument south of Harrison, then continuing along the Niobrara for several miles before turning due north to Camp Robinson, where it connected with the main Fort Laramie–Fort Pierre Trail. This is similar to the route known as the "Old Spanish Trail."

Because the fur trade in western Nebraska didn't begin in earnest until 1841—and since beaver prices had plummeted by then—it's fairly certain that most of the fur trade along the White River country involved buffalo hides.

James Bordeaux quickly became the main trader in the Chadron Creek area. He started operations as early as 1841 and remained in operation until 1872, when the first Indian agency opened in the region. His name is on Bordeaux Bend, near the site of the 1854 Grattan Massacre along the North Platte River, and along Bordeaux Creek, near Chadron.

Bordeaux had had a harrowing experience on October 15, 1849, when a party of Crow Indians under Chief White Bear looted his post and made off with eighty-two horses and mules. Bordeaux had good relations with the Brulés, and a party of Sioux warriors raced after their enemies, the Crows, catching up to them at a place now known as Crow Butte, midway between Chadron and Crawford. The Brulés cornered the Crows against the north face of the butte, causing the Crows to abandon their horses and climb the single trail to the top of the butte.

Knowing they had them surrounded and isolated in an area which had no water, the Sioux camped below and waited for their enemies to come down. Three days later a Sioux scout found a rope of rawhide and horse hair. The Crows eluded their pursuers by using the rope. While some stayed on the butte dancing and keeping the fires lit so the Sioux wouldn't become suspicious, the rest slipped through the Sioux barricade. The Butte subsequently became known as Place Where the Crows Danced or Dancer's Butte, although it is most commonly called Crow Butte, and became a pioneer landmark for Indians, soldiers, and cattlemen.

By the 1860s, as relations with the Native Americans deteriorated, the traders conducted more of their work by taking wagons to friendly Indian villages, hoping not to encounter hostiles on the way to and from the trading sites. The traders' main advantage was the trust of the tribes, and many of them married Indian women. When the Sioux agreed to the conditions of the 1868 treaty, the Brulés settled on the Whetstone Agency near Fort Randall and the Red Cloud Agency on the North Platte River. The Indian Peace Commission appointed Joseph Bissonette and Sefroy Iott interpreters and put Bordeaux in charge of distributing all rations and subsistence items. The work had to be done in a huge area, but the experienced fur traders did their job well.

The Bordeaux trading post is now a private, nonprofit museum in Chadron. The Bordeaux cabin has been reconstructed and an interpretive center added to chronicle the fur trade operations of the region and the West.

Negotiations for the Black Hills

Between Chadron and Crawford, the Red Cloud Buttes rise toward the sky. From them it is possible to see Crawford, Fort Robinson, and the site of the Red Cloud Agency. In this region the Allison Commission met with Sioux leaders in an attempt to buy the Black Hills. An official state marker describes the Treaty Tree, which stood about half a mile away, where in September 1875 the Allison Commission failed in its negotiations to buy the hills. The government offered $400,000 per year to lease the mining rights, $6 million to purchase the land outright. The Sioux asked for more.

Red Dog wanted enough money to provide for seven generations of Sioux. Red Cloud wanted that and much more: Texas steers for seven generations of Sioux, plus flour, coffee, sugar, tea, bacon, rice, tobacco, soap, salt, a wagon with a span of horses, six yoke of working cattle, a sow and a boar, a cow and a bull, a sheep and a ram, and a hen and a cock for each family. He asked for furniture, a sawmill, a mower, and a scythe.

"Maybe you white people think that I ask too much from the Government," Red Cloud said, "but I think those hills extend clear to the sky—maybe they go above the sky, and that is the reason I ask for so much."

Some sources say the Sioux asked for $700 million in exchange for the Black Hills. Others believe the price was misinterpreted and the Sioux really wanted only $7 million. In any event, the negotiations broke off without a deal. Eventually the government got the land, and the Sioux received $4 million.

The Winter of 1949

Winter storms sometimes sweep out of the northern plains, gathering speed and power as they cross into Nebraska. The worst ones seem to come unexpectedly. Those include the snow covering of December 1, 1856; the Schoolchildren's Blizzard of January 12, 1888; and the raging twentieth-century storms of 1949 and 1975.

Of them all, the winter of '49 was perhaps the worst, though not necessarily the most deadly. In 1888 more than two hundred people throughout the plains died, including many schoolchildren. The blizzards of 1949 claimed seventy-six people throughout the Great Plains. No doubt the death toll would have been higher, much higher, had not the U.S. Army, the Nebraska National Guard, and hundreds of volunteers pitched in to provide relief.

It's impossible to compare the effects of the blizzard of 1888 with those of the winter of 1949. The intervening time had changed life on the Great Plains too much. In 1888 Nebraska farmers and ranchers, even those who lived in the state's towns and cities, expected isolation during the winter months. They hauled wood, buffalo chips, or corncobs to burn for winter heat; they killed wild game and harvested gardens to fill the cellar with food for the winter; and before the storms of winter started sweeping over the country they stockpiled staples such as flour, sugar, coffee, and beans. A few had rigged telephone lines by stringing wires from home to home over barbed-wire fences. For the most part, however, if someone wanted to talk to his neighbor he got on his horse and rode over to do so. When storms blew in, people took shelter and waited until the winds died down, then went outside, surveyed the damage, and checked on neighbors and livestock.

Americans had come into the modern age by 1949. They had automobiles, tractors, and heavy equipment such as graders and tractor-crawlers. Each morning and evening they could tune in to the radio to get news and weather reports. Telephones connected most homes and communities to one another, and people used kerosene or even propane for heating fuel. City dwellers didn't lay in food stocks as in years gone by; they didn't see the need, with grocery stores providing fresh necessities just down the road. In rural areas, farmers and ranchers now put up hay each summer so they had feed for their livestock during the winter (the horrible losses of 1888 had taught men all across the region the necessity of doing that).

As with the Schoolchildren's Blizzard of 1888, the great storms of 1949 came without warning. A storm buried Nebraska in mid-November 1948, but then the weather cleared until nearly Christmas, when another snowstorm dumped on the region. By New Year's Day the roads were open, and the sun shone brightly. Weather forecasters predicted snow flurries. They had no inkling of the fury about to be set loose.

January 2, 1949, it started snowing, and winds blew sixty to seventy miles per hour, piling the flakes into drifts ranging from twelve to twenty feet deep. The temperature dropped well below zero. The storm hit so quickly and so hard that people had no time to prepare. By January 4 snowdrifts blocked every road and every rail line across Nebraska and much of the Dakotas, Wyoming, Montana, Colorado, Utah, Idaho, even Nevada and northern Arizona.

City dwellers holed up, but they had limited food supplies, and stores and restaurants used to routine deliveries quickly ran short. Rural residents had fewer concerns about food; they had larders full of canned homegrown fruits and vegetables, and they had chickens and cows to provide eggs and milk. While the city folk worried about how to feed themselves, the country people agonized over their livestock. It took hours and became a life-threatening proposition every time ranchers left their homes and their fires to venture forth to feed cattle, horses, sheep, and hogs.

As one storm after another hammered the region, ranchers did the best they could to get hay and feed to their animals, but the brutal temperatures and wind-driven snow bested them. Hundreds of thousands of cattle and sheep died. Horses huddled in ravines seeking protection and were buried by drifts. Hogs suffocated in barns completely covered by snow.

By late January relief efforts were under way. The counties and states first tried to help themselves, but as storm after storm bombarded the region the burden became too heavy. On January 24, President Harry Truman took action. He obtained $500,000 from Congress and launched "Operation Snowbound" in an effort to save millions of head of sheep and cattle from starvation. Troops under the direction of Maj. Gen. Lewis A. Pick mobilized. They launched an armada of C-82 "Flying Boxcars" and started airlifting hay to stranded animals. On the ground, military snowmobiles, known as weasels, took food, medicine, and other supplies to stranded people, picking up individuals who needed medical attention and transporting them to hospitals. Road graders and plows led trucks loaded with hay to stranded livestock. Within eleven days the Fifth Army under General Pick opened 32,900 miles of road, providing access to some 69,000 people and 1.5 million head of livestock.

The initial work by the army eased the situation, but the overall picture was so bad that some ranchers didn't get relief until late February. Even while relief efforts were under way, storms pounded the region. On March 1 General Pick determined that his soldiers had done their job. By his estimate seventy-six people died, and overall losses totaled at least $190 million. More than 2.7 million head of cattle and more than 2.8 million head of sheep died or were severely harmed by the storms.

Through it all, however, most Nebraskans could remain in touch with each other. They listened to their radios for news and weather reports and called each other on telephone lines that somehow managed to remain in operation through the worst of the blizzards. They got food for themselves and their stock from mercy pilots, and the army came to help dig out from perhaps the whitest winter in Nebraska's history.

As it turned out, most residents had relief by late February. Without the powerful equipment then available, it might have been May before some neighbors saw each other.

CRAWFORD

Crawford sits in the scenic White River valley at the edge of Pine Ridge country. It is on the Fort Laramie–to–Fort Pierre traders' trail of the 1840s and 1850s and on the Sidney–Black Hills road that saw heavy use in the latter 1870s.

Much of Crawford's early history is associated with the development of Red Cloud Agency and Camp Robinson to the west. On October 22, 1876, eight companies of cavalry under the command of Col. Raynald Mackenzie left Camp Robinson for the Sioux camps on Chadron Creek. En route, Colonel Mackenzie's soldiers were joined by Maj. Frank North and forty-two Pawnee Scouts. The troops divided forces early the morning of October 23 as they neared the two camps of Red Cloud and Red Leaf, surrounding the Native Americans, who surrendered without a fight not far from present-day Crawford.

The Pawnee Scouts and Major North collected the Sioux horses, leaving only enough to haul the Indians' household items and carry the elderly. Then the military leaders forced the tribal members to march to Camp Robinson. Although women, children, and the elderly were allowed to camp one night on the way, the Sioux men made the entire trip on foot in one day. Upon their arrival at Camp Robinson, the military confiscated all the Sioux horses, giving one to each of the Pawnee Scouts and turning the rest over to Colonel North, who sold them in Cheyenne.

At one time sculptor Gutzon Borglum had a popular plan to carve an entire tribe of Indians into the natural rock buttes west of Crawford. Borglum, the creator of Mount Rushmore, died in 1941 without finishing the tribal project.

Crawford started as a tent city on land owned by homesteader and newspaper correspondent William E. Annin in 1886 when the Fremont, Elkhorn & Missouri Valley Railroad pushed through. To incorporate the town, newspaper editor William Edgar supplemented civilian signatures with those of soldiers at Fort Robinson. After the Burlington line pushed north in 1887, Crawford became a supply depot and entertainment center for the fort. The town takes its name from Capt. Emmet Crawford, a former Fort Robinson soldier.

Red Cloud Agency and Fort Robinson

On February 9, 1874, Lt. Levi Herbert Robinson of the 14th Infantry and Cpl. James Coleman, Company K, 2nd Cavalry, rode west out of Fort Laramie as an escort for a wood train. Sioux from Red Cloud Agency attacked, and when the conflict ended Robinson and Coleman lay dead upon the prairie.

Trading post of J. W. Dear, Red Cloud Agency, January 10, 1876.
—Wyoming State Museum

Sgt. George S. Howard, a scout with the U.S. 2nd Cavalry, Company E, joined a search party for the missing men, whom they found in a ravine where the battle had taken place. A diary kept by Howard recalled the scene: "The Lieut. had 13 wounds but all were in front or face; the Corporal had 11 and all in back. It showed the Indian way of discriminating Bravery and Cowardice, for the Corporal had not pulled off his gloves, but the Lieut. had apparently used his revolver."

The treaty of 1868 signed by the Sioux and Cheyenne at Fort Laramie called for the U.S. government to open Indian agencies and provide goods to the Indians annually in exchange for land. The goods included food, clothing, tools, and cattle. The first agency for the followers of Oglala chief Red Cloud—called Red Cloud Agency—stood east of Fort Laramie in what is now Wyoming. The Indians preferred that location near the North Platte River, but military leaders thought it could create conflicts with travelers on the Oregon-California Trail, and in 1873 the military established a new agency along the White River. Some 13,000 Cheyenne, Arapaho, and Oglala Sioux lived at the agency from 1873 to 1877. The military then established an adjacent military post to serve as a security area for the new Red Cloud Agency.

The military post on Soldier Creek took its name from Lt. Levi Robinson. Originally, the soldiers stationed at Camp Robinson guarded the Sidney-Deadwood Trail. The camp was strategically located so troops stationed there could quickly be transferred to other areas whenever trouble arose. In 1877 a sentry killed Crazy Horse at Camp Robinson in front of the guardhouse. In December 1878 Camp Robinson became permanent, and was renamed Fort Robinson. In 1885 Fort Robinson replaced Fort Laramie in importance, and the 9th and 10th Cavalry, two all-black units known as buffalo soldiers, headquartered there. The 9th Cavalry served during the 1880s and 1890s, while the 10th Cavalry occupied the fort after 1900. During the 1880s the Fremont, Elkhorn & Missouri Valley Railroad laid tracks through the White River valley, leading the army to expand Fort Robinson.

The officer's houses were built of sun-dried adobe bricks. They had wide, overhanging porches to keep off rain, which would soften the bricks and make the houses collapse. Although its earliest mission involved various dealings with the Sioux, the threat of Native American revolt seemed unlikely after Wounded Knee in 1890. By 1919 Fort Robinson had became a quartermaster remount depot where the U.S. Army prepared horses and mules for the cavalry and artillery, with the most extensive horse herds held at the fort during World War II. By 1943 Fort Robinson had some 12,000 horses and served as a training center for pack mules.

Fort Robinson, on the north bank of the White River, 1878–79.
—Wyoming State Museum

The previous year a K-9 reception and training center opened, so personnel trained some 14,000 dogs for the U.S. Army, Army Air Force, Coast Guard, Navy, and civilian agencies. The "Dogs for Defense" program included 2,000 kennels and an obstacle course called "Crazy Horse Run." The first dogs arrived at Fort Robinson in October 1942. Training and taking care of 14,000 dogs is no small chore. As one soldier wrote: "There's thousands of ways of fighting a war, but don't ever let them talk you into the K-9 corps." Just feeding and cleaning up after the dogs presented quite a challenge. However, with a polo field, regular fox hunts, tennis courts, and a swimming pool, Fort Robinson gained a reputation as the country club of the army. The U.S. Olympic equestrian team even trained at Fort Robinson for the 1936 Olympic Games, although they didn't compete because the games weren't held that year.

Besides housing and training horses and dogs, Fort Robinson served as a German prisoner-of-war camp after November 1943. That camp sat north of the fort, just a few hundred yards south of the site of the former Red Cloud Agency. Located on rolling grassland with a view of the cliffs to the northwest, the POW camp provided manpower—inmates earned 80 cents per day—for area farms and ranches. Originally designed for 1,000 prisoners and a guard detachment, the camp soon expanded to house 3,000 prisoners in 160 temporary frame buildings. The earliest prisoners were members of the German Afrika Korps. Much of the time about 500 to 1,500 prisoners lived at the camp, but it was at full capacity in 1944–45. The last prisoners left the camp in 1946, and the government sold the buildings for surplus. Foundations of the POW garrison and administration area remain in the tall grass of western Nebraska, but there is no sign of the buildings nor of the six-foot-high barbed-wire fence that enclosed the camp.

Cheyenne Outbreak

Two miles west of Fort Robinson gently rolling grassland gives way to high bluffs on the north. In this area one more scene in the epic flight of the Cheyenne Indians occurred.

On September 9, 1878, after a year of suffering on reservations in Indian Country (now Oklahoma), about 300 Northern Cheyenne headed north. In Nebraska the military captured Dull Knife and 149 of his people and took them to Camp Robinson. For months they refused to return to the Indian Country reservation and remained under guard at the camp, held in log barracks by order of Capt. Henry W. Wessels, Camp Robinson's commanding officer, who attempted to starve them into submission. When they could handle the conditions no longer, some of the younger warriors broke away from the camp on January 9, 1879. In a desperate running battle, the Cheyennes followed the banks of the White River, scaled the buttes, and escaped. Although the Native Americans couldn't find horses, they eluded pursuing troops for a dozen days as they raced through the Pine Ridge country. Soldiers discovered their hiding place on January 22, 1879, but the Indians wouldn't surrender. Before the situation was resolved, sixty-four Cheyennes and eleven soldiers had died; the military recaptured more than seventy Cheyenne at various locations.

In an epilogue, in October 1993 the remains of eighteen Cheyennes who had been killed in Nebraska during the 1879 outbreak were buried in Montana; they had been held in museums in the intervening period.

HARRISON

Between Fort Robinson and Harrison lies the southern Pine Ridge, an area with big rolling hills and pine trees. A forest fire burned 48,000 acres in the Soldier Creek Wilderness west of Fort Robinson July 8–14, 1989, but new growth has already started, and the wilderness area will be allowed to regenerate naturally. The Soldier Creek Wilderness was set aside by Congress in 1986 and is a part of the Pine Ridge Ranger District of the Nebraska National Forest.

A loop route linking Harrison with Crawford takes visitors to the Oglala National Grasslands, Toadstool Geological Park, and the site of the Warbonnet skirmish, where Buffalo Bill Cody killed Cheyenne warrior Yellow Hair (sometimes referred to as Yellow Hand). From Crawford take Nebraska 2 and Nebraska 71; from Harrison follow Nebraska 29, known as Sowbelly Canyon Road because according to local legend a group of soldiers stranded here lived for several days on the sowbelly they had with them at the time. The route traverses a variety of landscapes, including the rough country of the Pine Ridge, mountain streams, and a section of badlands, which are dry and sparsely vegetated.

At a site just south of the Nebraska–South Dakota line on Hat Creek, which in this region is also known as Warbonnet Creek, William F. Cody took the "first scalp for Custer." Lt. Col. Eugene A. Carr and troops of the 5th U.S. Cavalry left Fort Laramie in early June 1876 for northwest Nebraska. They blocked the Indian trail leading from the Red Cloud and Spotted Tail Agencies toward Wyoming and Montana, where Sioux and Cheyenne were engaged in battles with troops commanded by Lt. Col. George A. Custer and Col. George Crook. Among those scouting for the 5th Cavalry were Baptiste "Little Bat" Garnier and William F. Cody. On July 1, Lt. Col. Wesley Merritt of the 9th Cavalry was appointed to fill the vacancy created by the retirement of the 5th Cavalry's colonel, William H. Emory. Merritt replaced Carr as commanding officer of the troops; Carr remained with the unit, however. On July 7, Merritt received news of the Custer defeat in Montana Territory. He decided to return to Fort Laramie by way of Camp Robinson.

On July 16, the 5th camped on Warbonnet Creek. Just after dawn the following day, Lt. Charles King surveyed the terrain near the cavalry's camp with a Corporal Wilkinson. As they viewed the area, Wilkinson spotted a small group of Cheyenne warriors headed up a ravine toward the west. The Cheyennes were watching a quartermaster's party headed to the area to provide supplies for the nearby military, and they didn't realize Merritt's men were so close. The soldiers kept their eyes on the Indians as the supply wagons approached.

Merritt ordered Carr to have the troops mount and prepare for a battle. Suddenly the Cheyennes started down a ravine toward two troopers who had broken away from the oncoming supply train. Cody and several companions rushed to get into position to attack the Indians when they came within range. Lieutenant King remained at a sentry position on top of a hill, watching through his binoculars until the Cheyennes drew closer to the waiting Cody and his associates. Then King gave the order: "*Now,* lads, in with you!"

Cody and company responded immediately, and when a bullet from Cody's gun crashed into Yellow Hair, the Cheyenne's companions turned and fled. In the ensuing years much has been made of Cody's killing of Yellow Hair and the fact that the army scout scalped the Cheyenne warrior. Although others later claimed they had killed Yellow Hair, Don Russell examined the various stories in *The Lives and Legends of Buffalo Bill* and found adequate reason to dispel all the other's claims.

Little blood spilled on the Warbonnet battlefield, and for decades the site's exact location wasn't even known. A town, Montrose, developed nearby, boasting a general store, church, post office, law office, and sixty-five residents by the mid-1880s. During the general threat of the 1890 Ghost Dance period, settlers at Montrose excavated a fortress, called Fort Montrose, on top of the very hill from which Lt. Charles King had given the order to attack the Cheyennes. No difficulties arose in 1890, and Montrose eventually became a ghost town.

In the late 1920s and early 1930s survivors of the Battle of Warbonnet Creek, accompanied by men interested in locating and marking the battle site, returned to the region and eventually identified the fight ground. In September 1934 two native rock markers were laid to commemorate Cody's and the 5th Cavalry's role in the battle.

Stacking alfalfa, 1905. —Nebraska State Historical Society

Toadstool Geological Park

To the east of the Warbonnet Battle site is Toadstool Geological Park, where a series of formations called "toadstools" attract visitors. The formations are made where hard sandstone sits atop Brulé clay. The clay erodes more quickly than the sandstone, so the resulting formations resemble toadstools. The deposits are from the Tertiary period of the Cenozoic era. The area is also filled with a wealth of vertebrate fossils, including tiny fragments of bones, teeth, and shell.

The region around Harrison is good cattle country with plenty of summer pasture, and winters are usually mild enough that animals can graze in the open. West of Harrison is Coffee Siding, which served the large border country ranch of James Coffee. The ranch had headquarters on Hat Creek in Nebraska and on Rawhide Creek in Wyoming, and it received a great piece of news in June 1886 when the Fremont, Elkhorn & Missouri Valley Railroad (later the Chicago & Northwestern) reached Harrison. On August 15, 1886, Coffee shipped the first load of cattle to Chicago.

Coffee Siding, located just east of the Wyoming-Nebraska border, was built by ranchers in order to avoid higher freight rates in Wyoming. Wyoming ranchers trailed herds to the area for shipment to eastern markets. The cattle pastured along the Niobrara River until trains arrived, then were worked into the seven cattle pens at the siding before being loaded onto railroad cars for shipment to markets farther east. The siding and pens were used through the 1940s and removed in 1958.

BIBLIOGRAPHY

Ahlgren, Carol, and David Anthone. "The Lincoln Highway in Nebraska: The Pioneer Trail of the Automotive Age," *Nebraska History* 73, 4 (Winter 1992).

Alfers, Kenneth G. "Triumph of the West: The Trans-Mississippi Exposition," *Nebraska History* 53, 3 (Fall 1972).

Alleman, Roy V. *Blizzard 1949.* St. Louis: Patrice Press, 1991.

Andreas, A. T. *History of the State of Nebraska.* Evansville, IN: Unigraphic, 1975.

Athearn, Robert G. *Union Pacific Country.* Lincoln: University of Nebraska, Bison Books, 1976.

Bennett, Mildred. *The World of Willa Cather.* New York: Dodd, Mead, 1951.

Blake, Gordon J. "Government and Banking in Territorial Nebraska," *Nebraska History* 51, 4 (Winter 1970).

Bleed, Ann, and Charles Flowerday, eds. *An Atlas of the Sand Hills.* Lincoln: Conservation and Survey Division, Institute of Agriculture and Natural Resources, University of Nebraska-Lincoln, 1990.

Blevins, Winfred. *Give Your Heart to the Hawks: A Tribute to the Mountain Man.* New York: Avon, 1973.

Bourn, Donna, and Don Bourn. "Ponca State Park," unpublished manuscript, March 1982, Ponca State Park, Ponca, NE.

Boye, Alan. *The Complete Roadside Guide to Nebraska.* St. Johnsbury, VT: Saltillo, 1993.

Bozell, John R. "The Cellars of Time: Chapter 11, Late Precontact Village Farmers and Agricultural Revolution," *Nebraska History* 75, 1 (Spring 1994).

Bradley, Glenn Danford. *The Story of the Pony Express,* ed. Waddell F. Smith. San Francisco: Hesperia House, 1960.

Bratt, John. *Trails of Yesterday.* Lincoln: University Publishing, 1921.

Breckenridge, Adam C. "Innovation in State Government: Origin and Development of the Nebraska Nonpartisan Unicameral Legislature," *Nebraska History* 59, 1 (Spring 1978).

A Bridge from the Past. Papillion Nebraska: 1970.

Brown, Joseph E. *The Mormon Trek West.* Garden City, NY: Doubleday & Company, 1980.

Brown, Marion Marsh. "The Brownville Story: Portrait of a Phoenix, 1854–1974," *Nebraska History* 55, 1 (Spring 1974).

Bruce, Robert. *The Fighting Norths and Pawnee Scouts.* Lincoln: Nebraska State Historical Society, 1932.

Buecker, Thomas R. "Fort Niobrara: Its Role on the Upper Plains," unpublished, n.d., American Heritage Center, University of Wyoming, Laramie.

Butcher, Solomon D. *Pioneer History of Custer County Nebraska*, 2nd Edition, Denver: Sage Books, 1965.

Butruille, Susan G. *Women's Voices from the Oregon Trail*. Boise: Tamarack Books, 1993.

Carrington, Margaret. *Ab-sa-ra-ka, Home of the Crows*. Philadelphia: J. B. Lippincott, 1868.

Carter, John E. "Niobrara, Nebraska: The Town Too Tough to Stay Put!" *Nebraska History* 72, 3 (Fall 1991).

Cather, Willa. *Later Novels*. New York: Library of America, 1990.

———. *My Antonia*. New York: Houghton Mifflin, 1918.

———. *O Pioneers!* New York: Houghton Mifflin, 1913.

———. *The Song of the Lark*. New York: Houghton Mifflin, 1915.

Clay, John. *My Life on the Range*. Chicago: privately printed, 1924.

Clow, Richmond L. "Mad Bear: William S. Harney and the Sioux Expedition of 1855–1856," *Nebraska History* 61, 2 (Summer 1980).

Coletta, Paolo E. "William Jennings Bryan's Second Congressional Campaign," *Nebraska History* 40, 4 (December 1959).

Crabb, Richard. *Empire on the Platte*. Cleveland: World Publishing, 1967.

Creigh, Dorothy W. *Nebraska, A Bicentennial History*. New York: W. W. Norton, 1977.

Creigh, James C. "Constructing the Interstate Highway in Nebraska: Route and Funding Controversies," *Nebraska History* 72, 1 (Spring 1991).

Danker, Donald F., ed. "The Journal of an Indian Fighter—The 1869 Diary of Major Frank J. North," *Nebraska History* 39, 2 (June 1958).

Dillon, Richard. *Meriwether Lewis*. Santa Cruz, CA: Western Tanager Press, 1988.

Drago, Harry Sinclair. *The Great Range Wars: Violence on the Grasslands*. Lincoln: University of Nebraska Press, Bison Books, 1985.

Dundas, J. H. *Granger History of Nemaha County*. Auburn, NE: n.p., 1902.

Dyer, Earl. *Headline: Starkweather*. Lincoln: Journal-Star Printing, 1993.

Everett, Dick. *Conquering the Great American Desert*. Lincoln: Nebraska State Historical Society, 1975.

———. *The Sod-House Frontier*. Lincoln: Johnson Publishing, 1954.

Farnham, Wallace D. "The Pacific Railroad Act of 1862," *Nebraska History* 43, 3 (September 1962).

Farrar, Jon. "The Impact of Crane Watching," *Nebraskaland Magazine* (March 1991).

Faulkner, Virginia, ed. *Roundup: A Nebraska Reader*. Lincoln: University of Nebraska Press, 1957.

Federal Writers Project, Works Progress Administration, State of Nebraska. *Nebraska, A Guide to the Cornhusker State*. New York: Viking Press, 1939.

Fite, Gilbert C. "William Jennings Bryan and the Campaign of 1896: Some Views and Problems," *Nebraska History* 47, 3 (September 1966).

Fitzpatrick, Lillian L. *Nebraska Place-Names, Including Selections from Link, J. T. Origin of the Place-Names of Nebraska*. Lincoln: University of Nebraska Press, Bison Books, 1960.

Franzwa, Gregory M. *The Oregon Trail Revisited*. St. Louis: Patrice Press, 1972.

Frison, George C. *Prehistoric Hunters of the High Plains*. New York: Academic Press, 1978.

Garey, Merlin R. *The Land Where the Meadowlark Sings*. Edison, NE: n.p., 1967.

Graebner, Norman A. "Nebraska's Missouri River Frontier, 1854–1860," *Nebraska History* 42, 4 (December 1961).

Green, Thomas L., ed. *Scottsbluff and the North Platte Valley*. Scottsbluff, NE: Golden Jubilee Centennial Committee, 1949.

Gregory, Annadora Foss. *History of Crete Nebraska 1870–1888.* Lincoln: State Journal Printing, 1937.

Grinnell, George Bird. *The Cheyenne Indians: History and Society.* Vol. 1. Reprint. Lincoln: University of Nebraska Press, Bison Books, 1972.

——. *The Cheyenne Indians: War, Ceremonies, and Religion.* Vol. 2. Reprint. Lincoln: University of Nebraska Press, Bison Books, 1972.

Griswold, Wesley. *A Work of Giants.* New York: McGraw-Hill, 1962.

Hafen, Leroy R., and Ann. *Handcarts to Zion: The Story of a Unique Western Migration 1856–1860.* Glendale, CA: Arthur H. Clark, 1960.

Haines, Aubrey L. *Historic Sites Along the Oregon Trail.* St. Louis: Patrice Press, 1981.

Hamil, Harold. *Nebraska: No Place Like It.* Kansas City, MO: Lowell Press, 1985.

Hanson, James. A. *Northwest Nebraska's Indian People.* Chadron, NE: Centennial Committee Historical Series, No. 2, 1983.

——. "Spain on the Plains," *Nebraska History* 74, 1 (Spring 1993).

Hasselstrom, Linda. *Roadside History of South Dakota.* Missoula, MT: Mountain Press, 1994.

Hedron, Paul L. *First Scalp for Custer: The Skirmish at Warbonnet Creek, Nebraska, July 17, 1876 with a Short History of the Warbonnet Battlefield.* Lincoln: University of Nebraska Press, Bison Books, 1980.

Herrington, George Squires, ed. "Levancia Bent's Diary of a Sheep Drive, Evanston, Wyoming, to Kearney, Nebraska, 1882," *Annals of Wyoming* 24, 1 (January 1952).

Hickey, Donald R. *Nebraska Moments: Glimpses of Nebraska's Past.* Lincoln: University of Nebraska Press, 1992.

Himmelberg, Robert F. and Raymond J. Cunningham, eds., "William Jennings Bryan, Orlando Jay Smith, and the Founding of The Commoner: Some New Bryan Letters," *Nebraska History* 48, 1 (Spring 1968).

Horan, Judy. "Omaha's Newest Attraction," *Omaha Magazine* (May/June 1995).

Hunt, N. Jane, ed. *Brevet's Nebraska Historical Markers and Sites.* Sioux Falls, SD: Brevet Press, 1974.

Hutton, Harold. *Doc Middleton: Life and Legends of the Notorious Plains Outlaw.* Chicago: Swallow Press, 1974.

——. *Vigilante Days: Frontier Justice Along the Niobrara.* Chicago: Swallow Press, 1978.

Hyde, George. *The Pawnee Indians.* 1951; reprint, Norman: University of Oklahoma Press, 1974; first paperback ed., 1988.

Hytrek, Anthony J. *The History of Fort Robinson, Nebraska from 1900 to the Present.* Chadron, NE: Chadron State College, 1971.

Irving, John R. Treat, Jr. *Indian Sketches Taken during an Expedition to the Pawnee Tribes,* ed. John McDermott. Norman: University of Oklahoma Press, 1955.

Irving, Washington. *The Adventures of Captain Bonneville.* New York: Co-Operative Publication Society, n.d.

Jenkins, Charles. "The Kearney Cotton Mill: The Bubble that Burst," *Nebraska History* 38, 3 (September 1957).

Jensen, Richard E. "Bellevue: The First Twenty Years, 1822–1842," *Nebraska History* 56, 3 (Fall 1975).

——. "Nebraska's World War I Potash Industry," *Nebraska History* 68, 1 (Spring 1987).

Johansen, Gregory J. "To Make Some Provisions for their Half-Breeds: The Nemaha Half-Breed Reserve, 1830–66," *Nebraska History* 67, 1 (Spring 1986).

Johnson, Dirk. *Biting the Dust.* New York: Simon and Schuster, 1994.

Kepfield, Sam S. "El Dorado on the Platte: The Development of Agricultural Irrigation and Water Law in Nebraska, 1860–1895," *Nebraska History* 75, 3 (Fall 1994).

Laurie, Clayton D. "The U.S. Army and the Omaha Race Riot of 1919," *Nebraska History* 72, 3 (Fall 1991).

Lee, Wayne. *Bad Men and Bad Towns.* Caldwell, ID: Caxton, 1993.

——. *Wild Towns of Nebraska.* Caldwell, ID: Caxton, 1988.

Luebke, Frederick C. "Ethnic Group Settlement on the Great Plains," *Western Historical Quarterly* (1977).

Mahnken, Norbert R. "The Sidney-Black Hills Trail," *Nebraska History* 30, 3 (September 1949).

Mattes, Merrill. *The Great Platte River Road.* Lincoln: Nebraska State Historical Society, 1969.

——. *Scotts Bluff.* Washington, D.C.: National Park Service, Historical Handbook No. 28, 1992.

McIntosh, C. Barron. "The Route of a Sandhills Bone Hunt: The Yale College Expedition of 1870," *Nebraska History* 69, 2 (Summer 1988).

McKinley, John Lawrence. *The Influence of the Platte River Upon the History of the Valley.* Minneapolis: Burgess Publishing, 1938.

Mears, Louise Wilhelmina. *The Hills of Peru.* Omaha: Klopp & Bartlett, 1911.

Mellberg, Russell J. "The Public Career of Moses P. Kinkaid," master's thesis, University of Nebraska, 1933.

Menard, Orville D. "Tom Dennison, the *Omaha Bee*, and the 1919 Omaha Race Riot," *Nebraska History* 68, 4 (Winter 1987).

Moll, Timothy L. "The Dreshler Broom Factory," *Nebraska History* 62, 1 (Spring 1981).

Mothershead, Harmon. "The Stockyards, A Hotel for Stock or a Holding Company," *Nebraska History* 64, 4 (Winter 1983).

Moulton, Candy. *Legacy of the Tetons: Homesteading in Jackson Hole.* Boise: Tamarack Books, 1994

——. *Roadside History of Wyoming.* Missoula, MT: Mountain Press, 1995.

Moulton, Candy, and Ben Kern. *Wagon Wheels: Journey on the Western Trails.* Glendo, WY: High Plains Press, 1996.

Mullin, Mrs. Charles H., et al. *Founders and Patriots of Nebraska.* Omaha: Members of the Nebraska Chapter of the National Society of Daughters of Founders and Patriots of America, 1935.

Nash, Gary B., et al. *The American People,* vol. 1, *Creating a Nation and a Society,* 2nd ed. New York: HarperCollins, 1990.

Nichols, Roger L. "Stephen Long and Scientific Exploration on the Plains," *Nebraska History* 52, 1 (Spring 1971).

Nicoll, Bruce H. *Nebraska: A Pictorial History.* Lincoln: University of Nebraska Press, 1975.

Niehardt, John. *Black Elk Speaks.* Lincoln: University of Nebraska Press, 1961.

——. *The River and I.* Lincoln: University of Nebraska Press, 1974.

Ney, Col. Virgil. *Fort On the Prairie: Fort Atkinson, on the Council Bluff, 1819–1827.* Washington, D.C.: Command Publications, 1978.

O'Gara, William H. *In All its Fury–The Great Blizzard of 1888.* Lincoln: J&L Lee, 1988.

Oglesby, Richard Edward. *Manuel Lisa and the Opening of the Missouri Fur Trade.* Norman: University of Oklahoma Press, 1963.

Olson, James C. *History of Nebraska.* Lincoln: University of Nebraska Press, 1966.

——. *J. Sterling Morton, Pioneer Statesman, Founder of Arbor Day.* Lincoln: Nebraska State Historical Society Foundation, 2nd ed., 1972.

——. *Red Cloud and the Sioux Problem.* Lincoln: University of Nebraska Press, 1965.

Osnes, Larry G. "Charles W. Bryan: 'His Brother's Keeper,'" *Nebraska History* 48, 1 (Spring 1967).

Paden, Irene D. *The Wake of the Prairie Schooner.* New York: MacMillan, 1943.

Parker, Jerry A. "Frank Jackson: Texas Bandit Cavalier," *True West* (May 1994).

Paul, R. Eli. "Battle of Ash Hollow: The 1909-1910 recollections of General N. A. M. Dudley," *Nebraska History* 62, 3 (Fall 1981).

Peterson, Nancy M. *People of the Moonshell, A Western River Journal.* Frederick, CO: Renaissance House, 1984.

Peterson, Paul V. "William Jennings Bryan *World-Herald* Editor," *Nebraska History* 49, 4 (Winter 1968).

Petsche, Jerome E. *The Steamboat Bertrand: History, Excavation and Architecture.* Washington, D.C.: National Park Service, 1974.

Phipps, Robert G. *The Swanson Story: When the Chicken Flew the Coop.* Omaha: Carl and Caroline Swanson Foundation, Inc., 1976.

Potts, James B. "North of 'Bleeding Kansas': The 1850s Political Crisis in Nebraska Territory," *Nebraska History* 73, 3 (Fall 1992).

Pound, Louise. *Nebraska Folklore.* Lincoln: University of Nebraska Press, Bison Books, 1989.

Price, David H. "Sectionalism in Nebraska: When Kansas Considered Annexing Southern Nebraska, 1856-1860," *Nebraska History* 53, 4 (Winter 1972).

Purcell, E. R. *Pioneer Stories of Custer County Nebraska.* Broken Bow, NE: Custer County Chief, 1936.

Reece, Charles S. *An Early History of Cherry County, Nebraska.* Simeon, NE: self-published, 1945.

Reneau, Susan C. *The Adventures of Moccasin Joe: The True Life Story of Sgt. George S. Howard.* Missoula, MT: Blue Mountain Publishing, 1994.

Riley, Paul D. "The Battle of Massacre Canyon," *Nebraska History* 54, 2 (Summer 1973).

Roberts, R. Jay. "The History of Agate Springs," *Nebraska History* 47, 3 (September 1966).

Rowley, William D. "The Loup City Riot of 1934: Main Street vs. The 'Far-Out' Left," *Nebraska History* 47, 3 (September 1966).

Russell, Don. *The Lives and Legends of Buffalo Bill.* Norman: University of Oklahoma Press, 1960.

Sandoz, Mari. *The Beaver Men: Spearheads of Empire.* New York: Hastings House, 1964.

———. *Love Song to the Plains.* Lincoln: University of Nebraska Press, Bison Books, 1966.

———. *Old Jules.* Lincoln: University of Nebraska Press, Bison Books, 1962.

———. *Old Jules Country.* Lincoln: University of Nebraska Press, Bison Books, 1982.

Schlissel, Lillian. *Women's Diaries of the Westward Migration.* New York: Schocken Books, 1982.

Sellers, James L. "These Centennial Years." *Nebraska History* 40, 4 (December 1959).

Settle, Raymond, and Mary. *Saddles and Spurs, The Pony Express Saga.* Harrison, PA: Stackpole, 1955.

Sheldon, Addison Erwin. *History and Stories of Nebraska.* Lincoln: University Publishing, 1919.

———. *Nebraska Old and New History, Stories, Folklore.* Lincoln: University Publishing, 1937.

Simmons, Jerold L. *"La Belle Vue": Studies in the History of Bellevue, Nebraska.* Bellevue, NE: Mayor's Advisory Committee on the Bicentennial, 1976.

Socolofsky, Homer. "Land Disposal in Nebraska, 1854-1906; The Homestead Story," *Nebraska History* 48, 3 (Autumn 1967).

Spring, Agnes Wright. *The Cheyenne and Black Hills Stage and Express Routes.* Lincoln: University of Nebraska Press, 1948.

Stevens, Betty. *Shifting Winds, Nebraska's Weather Story.* Lincoln: Journal-Star Printing, 1994.

Thrapp, Dan. L. *Encyclopedia of Frontier Biography.* Lincoln: University of Nebraska Press, CD-Rom, 1994.

Tibbles, Thomas Henry. *The Ponca Chiefs: An Account of the Trial of Standing Bear.* Edited with an introduction by Kay Graber. Lincoln: University of Nebraska Press. 1972.

Van Bruggen, Theodore. *Wildflowers, Grasses and other Plants of the Northern Plains and Black Hills.* Interior, SD: Badlands Natural History Association, 1992.

Warp, Harold. *A History of Man's Progress from 1830 to the Present.* Minden, NE: Harold Warp Pioneer Village, 1978.

Watkins, Albert. "The Evolution of Nebraska," reprinted from the proceedings of the Mississippi Valley Historical Association, vol. 3, n.d.

Webber, Bert. *Indians Along the Oregon Trail.* Webb Research Group, 1989.

Welsch, Roger. *It's Not the End of the Earth, But You Can See It from Here: Tales of the Great Plains.* New York: Fawcett, 1900.

——. *Shingling the Fog and Other Plains Lies.* Lincoln: University of Nebraska Press, 1972.

Wesser, Robert F. "George W. Norris: The Unicameral Legislature and the Progressive Ideal," *Nebraska History* 45, 4 (December 1964).

Wilhelm, Paul, Duke of Wurttemberg. *Travels in North America, 1822–1824. The American Exploration and Travel Series,* ed. Savoie Lottinville, trans. W. Robert Nitske. Norman: University of Oklahoma Press, 1973.

Wilson, D. Ray. *Nebraska Historical Tour Guide.* Carpentersville, IL: Crossroads Communications, 1988.

Works Progress Administration (Writers' Program, State of Nebraska). *Nebraska Folklore: Book Two.* Lincoln: Woodruff Printing, 1940.

Works Progress Administration (Writers' Program, State of Nebraska). *Nebraska Folklore: Book Three.* Lincoln: Woodruff Printing, 1940.

NEWSPAPERS

Beatrice Daily Express and Beatrice Express

Callaway Standard

Casper (Wyoming) *Star-Tribune*

Chicago Tribune

Daily Missouri Democrat

Fremont Daily Herald

Grand Island Independent

Hastings Independent

Hastings Tribune

Holdrege Nugget

Lincoln Star

Missouri Democrat

Missouri Intelligencer

Nebraska City Newspress

Nebraska Farmer

Nebraska Herald

New Callaway Courier

New York Times

Omaha Bee

Omaha Evening Dispatch

Omaha Weekly Bee

Omaha World-Herald

Osceola Homesteader

Portland Oregonian

Voices of the Sandhills

INDEX

Hone, Washington, 293
Hook's Ranch, 191
Hooper, 97
Hooper, Samuel, 96
Hoover, Herbert, 226
Horn, Jake, 280
Hornby, Richard, 117
Horse Creek treaty. *See* Indian treaties.
Horse racing, 291
Howard, Edgar, 220
Howard, George S., 366
Hupp, Robert P., 63
Huskers, 23
Hutzel, 2nd Lt. Kenneth L., 230
Hyannis, 267

Idaho Bill, 220
Immanuel Medical Center, 51
Indian Cave State Park, 155–156
Indian treaties, 6; at Council Bluffs (1825),
    31; of 1868, 366; at Horse Creek
    (1851), 341–343; at Portage des Sioux
    (1815), 31; with Omahas, 1854, 32; with
    Pawnees,1833, 79; with Pawnees and
    Mexico, 1824, 84; with Poncas, 1858,
    38; at Prairie du Chien (1830), 31, 156,
    157; with Santee Sioux, 107; at Table
    Creek (1857), 81, 140; with
    Winnebagos, 89–90. *See also* Black Hills,
    government purchase from Sioux of
Indianola, 223
Ingham, 221
Interstate Chautauqua Assembly, 159–60
Ionia "volcano", 105
Iott, Sefroy, 316
Iowa Beef Packers, 92
Iowa Indians, 22, 31
Irrigation, 14–18, 218–219, 268, 273,
    287–288, 337–339

Jackson, A. H., 44
Jackson, Frank, 31–15
Jackson, William Henry, 334, 336, 341
Jail Rock, 25, 330
James, Felix, 296
Jannsen, Cornilius, 177
Jannsen, David, 178
Jannsen, Peter, 177
Jansen, 177–78
Janus, Antoine, 243
Jayhawking, 112, 151
Jefferson County Historical Society, 177
Jelinek, Frank, 145
Jelinek, Joe, 145
Jenks, Stephen A., 194
Jensen, Robert, 131
Jerpe Commission Company, 48

Jewett, George, 302
Johannesen, Helga (Warp), 215
Johnson, Andrew, 161
Johnson, Charles A., 293
Johnson, Walter L., 230
Johnston, Albert Sidney, 84
Jones, Ben, 181
Jones, O. A., 230
Jones, Thomas, 178, 180
Joslyn Art Museum, 52–53

Kagey, Abraham N., 139
Kagi, John Henri, 138–39
Kamp Kaleo, 271
Kanesville, Iowa, 28
Kansas Indians, 5–6
Kansas Territory, 10–12
Kansas-Nebraska Act, 10
Kaufmann, Charles, 47
Kearney, 7, 69, 189, **193**, 223;
    industrialization at, 192, 194
Kearney Canal, 192
Kearney Electric Company, 192
Kearny, Stephen Watts, 84, 189
Keefe, James, 289
Kelsey, T. D., 320
Kenesaw, 181
Kern, John J., 177
Ketcham, Ami, 24, 275–277, 279
Key, Johnny, 300
Keystone, 325
Kilgore, 304
King, Carol, 131
King, Charles, 370
Kingsley Dam, 208, **338**
Kinkaid, Moses P., 164
Kiowa Apache Indians, 311, 324, 325
Kiowa Indians, 6, 325
Kirkpatrick, E. H., 337
Kleven, J. E., 237
Kool-Aid, 212
Kristofferson, Kris, 262
Kuhns, Henry W., 91
Kurz, Rudolph F., 54

La Balla (The Bullet), 68
La Flesche, Joseph, 93
La Flesche, Rosalie, 93
La Flesche, Susan (Picotte), 96
Lake McConaughy, 208
Lake Minnechaduza, 299
Lakota Indians, 325
Lame Duck Amendment, 225
Laramie Irrigation Canal, 337–338
Lashley, Pluma (Norris), 224
Latta, John A., 7
Lawrie, Lee, 122

Middleton, David C. "Doc", 288–291, **288,** 318, 354
MidState Irrigation Project, 186
Midway Stage Station, 199–200
Mikelson, George, 343
Miller, Alfred Jacob, 334
Miller, Andrew J., 202
Miller, Mrs. Charles Jr., 229
Miller, Charlotte, 229
Miller, Dale, 229
Miller, Joseph, 181
Miller, Malcolm Ansley, 257
Mills, Benjamin, 342
Minden, 215
Miner, Carrie, 234
Missouri Compromise, 10
Missouri Fur Company, 56–57
Missouri River, 9
Missouria Indians, 5–6, 31
Mitchell, 223, 339–341
Mitchell, James C., 66
Mitchell, Luther, 24, 275–76, **276,** 277, 279
Mitchell, Gen. Robert B., 339–40
Mix, Tom, 61
Modisett, Carl, 346
Monahan Ranch fire, 267
Monowi, 309
Montrose, 370
Moore, Jim, 198
Morgan, N. M., 280
Mormon Church, 9, 28
Mormon emigration, 9, 114, 145, 185, 190, 200, 308–09
Mormon Trail, 69
Mormons, 64–66
Morrill, 223
Morris, Sam, 290
Morton, Carl, 142
Morton, Carolyn, 140
Morton, J. Sterling, 139–142, 152; **home, 141**
Morton, Joy, 141
Morton, Mark, 141
Morton, Nancy, 194
Morton, Paul, 141
Morton, Thomas, 140
Morton, Tom, 194
Moulton, Charles, 185
Moulton, Charlotte, 185
Moulton, Sarah, 185
Moulton, Sophia Elizabeth, 185
Moulton, Thomas, 185
Mount Vernon College, 154
Mullen, 266–267
Murday, Rob, 274
Murphey, Michael Martin, 334
My Antonia, 184

Nance, Albinus, 279
National Arbor Day Foundation, 142
National Cattle Trail, 211
National Grange of the Patrons of Husbandry. *See* Grange
Neal, Louis, 157
Neapolis, 70, 71
Nebraska Advertiser, 148
Nebraska City, 8, 22, 111, 134–144, **135**
Nebraska City News, 140
Nebraska City–Fort Kearny Cutoff, 111, 116, 136–137
Nebraska Cooper Nuclear Power Plant, 154
Nebraska Environmental Trust Fund, 255
Nebraska Farmer, 151
Nebraska Farmer's Holiday Association, 261
Nebraska Game and Parks Division, 84
Nebraska Good Roads Association, 306
Nebraska Hall of Agricultural Achievement, 158
Nebraska Land and Feeding Company, 345
Nebraska National Forest, 263–264, **264, 265,** 305
Nebraska National Guard, 205
Nebraska State Capitol, 122
Nebraska State Grange. *See* Grange
Nebraska State Historical Society, 177
Nebraska State Prison, 123
Nebraska Stock Growers Association, 345
Nebraska Territory, 10–12, 28, 59
Nebraska, Wyoming & Western Railroad, 331
Neihardt, John, 84, 93–95, **93**
Neligh, 99
Neligh, John D., 97, 99
Neligh Mill Company, **98,** 99–101
Nelson, Ben, 343
Nelson, John Y., 222
Nelson, Willie, 262
Nemaha River, 9
Nemaha Valley Seminary and Normal Institute, 154
Nenzel, 304–305
Nenzel, George, 304
New Callaway, 280–81
New Callaway Courier, 280–81
Newcastle, 105
Newport, 287
Nickerson, 93
Nickerson, Reynolds K., 93
Nicolett, J. N., 105
Nielson, Nels, 229
Niobrara, 108–109
Niobrara River, 9, 10
Niobrara State Park, 108
Nixon, Tom, 314

Victoria Springs State Recreation Area, 272
Villasur, Don Pedro de, 2, 54
Virtel, Max E., 304
Vogel, Joe, 208

Waddell, William B., 13637, 175
Wade, Albert "Kid", 291–293
Wahoo, 117–118, **117, 118**
Walgren Lake, 359
Wall, Aaron, 277
Walthill, 96
Warbonnet Battle, 369
Ward, C. Lauer, 131
Ward, Clara, 131
Warp, Harold, 215–217
Warp, John Neilsen, 215
Water development projects, 185–187, 218–219, 337–339
Waterfowl, 9–10, 85, 220; migration, 186–189,
Waterloo, 68
Wayne, 103
Weather: balloon testing, 215; blizzard of 1888, 16; blizzards, 15–17, 248, 296; drought, 119, 214, 248, 316; drought of 1873, 16; drought of 1893, 16; drought of 1934, 296, 298; Omaha flooded, 41; Omaha tornado hits, 41; School Children's Blizzard, 254; winter of 1949, 362–364
Weaver, James B., 260
Webb, Walter Prescott, 16
Weber, Amalia, 67
Weber, Jacob Jr, 67
Weber, Jacob Sr., 67
Weber, Lyman, 67
Webster, John L., 39
Weeping Water, 120–121, 223
Wegner, Nicholas H., 63
Well digging, 116–117
Wellman, Horace, 176
Welsch, Roger, 252
Wes Stevens archaeological site, 323–324
Wessels, Henry W., 368
West Point, 97
Westermark, Victor, 227
Western Bohemian Fraternal Association (Zapadni Cesko Bratrske Jednota [ZCBJ]), 169

Western Engineer, 30
Western Heritage Museum, 36
Westervelt, James H., 281
Westerville, 282
Wheeler, Judge C. W., 150
Whetstone Agency, 356
Whig Party, 10–11
Whistler, 222, 240
White Bear, 361
Whiteclay, 355
Whitman, 267
Wilbur, 165
Wilhelm, Paul, 56
Williams 96 Ranch, 199
Williamson, James, 296
Williamson, John, 243
Willie, James Grey, handcart company, 185
Wilson, Anna, 52
Wilson, Woodrow, 129
Winnebago, 89
Winnebago Indians, 22, 27, 32, 89–90. *See also* Indian treaties
Winter Quarters, 28, 64, 66
Winters, Rebecca, 332
Wisner, 97
Wisner, Samuel P., 97
Wood Lake, 293–294
Woodbury, Daniel P, 135, 198
Woods, James, 176
Woods, Joseph A., 282
World War II: airfields, 18–19; ammunition depots, 18; balloon bombs, 40; prisoner-of-war camps, 19, 220, 223, 231, 368. *See also* North Platte Canteen
World-Herald Theater, 116
Wounded Knee Massacre, 302, 355
Wright, Ed, 268
Wright site, 78
Wurthier, Paul, 352
Wynot, 107
Wyoming (ghost town), 144–45

Yates, Halsey, 263
Yellow Hair, 205, 368–69
Yellowstone Expedition, 82
York, 133
Young, Brigham, 9, 28, 308
Young, Neil, 262
Yutan, 68

ABOUT THE AUTHOR

In 1897 Candy Moulton's great-grandparents emigrated from Ponca, Nebraska, to Encampment, Wyoming, where they helped settle the new town. Moulton still lives in the Encampment area with her rancher husband, Steve, and their two children, Shawn and Erin Marie.

After receiving degrees in journalism from Northwest Community College in Powell, Wyoming, and the University of Wyoming in Laramie, Moulton worked five years as editor of the *Saratoga Sun*. During her twenty-odd years as a journalist, she has written extensively on Nebraska water issues. Currently, she is editor of *Roundup* magazine for Western Writers of America; staff writer for *Persimmon Hill*, publication of the National Cowboy Hall of Fame; and a regular contributor to *American Cowboy*, the *Casper Star-Tribune*, and the *Rawlins Daily Times*. She provided exclusive coverage of the Mormon Trail sesquicentennial festivities for the *Star-Tribune* in 1997. Her historical, travel, agricultural, and public-land management articles have appeared in many regional and national publications.

In 1996 her *Roadside History of Wyoming*, published by Mountain Press, earned awards as best nonfiction book from the Wyoming Media Professionals and from the National Association of Press Women.

Moulton is the author of six previous books, including *Legacy of the Tetons: Homesteading in Jackson Hole* (1994) and *Wagon Wheels: Journey on the Western Trails* (1996).